THE UNITED STATES
CAVALRY

TIME OF TRANSITION
1938 • 1944
Horses to Mechanization

by
GARY W. PALMER

Voyak Publications
San Diego, California

The U.S. Cavalry: Time of Transition, 1938-1944 — Horses to Mechanization
Copyright © 2013 Gary W. Palmer. All Rights Reserved.

No part of this book may be reproduced in any form or by any means, electronic, mechanical, digital, photocopying or recording, except for the inclusion in a review, without permission in writing from the the publisher.

Except where noted, all photographs, materials, and graphics reproduced in this volume are the property of the individual copyright holders, including those photographs reproduced from personal and archival collections.

Published in the USA by
Voyak Publications
P.O. Box 420065
San Diego, CA 92142
www.voyakpublications.com

ISBN-10: 0615785832
ISBN-13: 978-0615785837

First Edition

Design and layout by Allan T. Duffin

Printed in the United States of America

TABLE OF CONTENTS

Preface ix

Introduction xv

I. Louisiana Maneuvers of 1938 thru 1941   1

II. The Battle of the Bayous   51

III. The Argument for Mechanization   81

IV. National Guard Participation in August 1940 Maneuvers   109

V. Development of the Bantam   177

VI. 1941 Louisiana Maneuvers (The Big One)   213

VII. The Argument to Mechanize grows louder   265

VIII. Pearl Harbor, Panama, and Beyond   307

IX. Life Stateside during 1942   351

X. Camp Coxcomb, Camp Hood, Camp Maxey   387

XI. Departure from the U.S.A. en route to Jolly Old England   421

XII. 2d Cavalry arrives in England and Meets General Patton   457

Glossary   477

DEDICATION

In Memory of those who served - - -

PREFACE

My father, Leroy Louis Palmer, served with the U.S. Army's 106th Cavalry Group during World War II, but in the ensuing years he spoke little of his combat experiences. I grew up knowing very little about what he'd done during the war. Years later, my mother, Ila Mae Palmer, showed me a copy of a book entitled *The 106th Cavalry Group in Europe, 1944-1945*. Six members of my father's military unit wrote the book immediately after the end of the war, and each trooper in the group received a copy before he left Europe to return home. Curious, I sat down and flipped through the volume. Colonel Vennard Wilson, commanding officer of the group, wrote in his introduction:

> I want this book to contain the name of every man who rode with us, of every one who reached the final goal, their flights, their wounds, their victories. Some years from now these cavalrymen will have sons

and daughters who will ask, "Father, what did you do in the big war?" This book is to help father's answer that question.

I read the book from cover to cover. When I was done, I wanted to know more. I spent the next 12 years hunting for information about the 106th Cavalry—an adventure that resulted in the book you now hold in your hands. During that period of research and revelation, I realized that my father's near silence about his war experiences was not unusual amongst the veterans of World War II.

To learn about the 106th and the men who served with my father, I initially turned to the Internet for information. To my surprise I found a Web site, written by a member of the 106th Cavalry Group, which included information about their annual reunion in Urbana, Illinois. I decided to attend one of the reunions and meet the members.

In 1996 I traveled to my first reunion in Urbana. I was met by Lorraine Gerhart, the group's secretary and wife of one of the original officers. I was made to feel at home and welcomed into the group's membership. I was introduced at a dinner as the son of one of the group's troopers, but I soon realized that I was not invited to attend some of the group's smaller, more personal gatherings. When I returned the following year I noticed that the members began to include me in more of their private get-togethers. By the 1998 reunion the group openly welcomed me into many of the smaller gatherings where they often chatted about their World War II experiences.

By the time I attended my fourth reunion in 1999 I had read the *The 106th Cavalry Group in Europe* at least five times. The book packed a lot of information into its 250 pages, but I realized that there was a lot more to the history of the 106th Cavalry Group and units like it.

Preface

One day it hit me: *I could write a book.*

During the 1999 reunion, as the veterans reminisced about their wartime experiences, I listened as I usually did—but this time I took notes. When I returned for the next year's gathering, I felt as if I were traveling to a family reunion of which I was a part. During that reunion I addressed the 106th Cavalry Group Association's board of officers and asked their permission to write a newer version of their book. I wanted to expand and improve upon its contents. The board of officers unanimously agreed. Little did I realize that my task would be a monumental one.

Over the next several reunions I met with many members of the 106th and took copious notes. I also sat down with Robert Moore, one of the original authors of *The 106th Cavalry Group in Europe*, who showed me the diary he'd kept throughout the war. Unfortunately I had only a brief opportunity to discuss my book and his diary. Old age took its toll on Robert, and with it his incredible memory of those times.

Providentially, several years later I was contacted by Robert's son, Michael Moore, who had come across a letter I had written to his father. Michael asked me if I was still interested in reviewing his father's notes and informed me that his father had passed his diary to him. Happily, Michael and I became close friends, and he collaborated with me on the contents of this new book. I cannot thank him enough.

In the meantime, I headed to Europe to investigate leads and observe areas where the 106th Cavalry had fought during the war. During one of those trips I traveled with members of the 28th Infantry Division, whose soldiers the 106th Cavalry helped rescue from a prisoner-of-war camp in Bad Orb, Germany, in April 1945. I was subsequently invited by William "Gus" Hickok to attend the 28th Infantry's reunions at Fort Indiantown Gap National Guard

Training Center in Pennsylvania. In doing so I discovered they maintained a battalion museum on the grounds of the installation. The museum was a valuable source of information, and I visited many times.

Through the 28th Infantry Division I met Elizabeth Bailey, who had traveled with the division members on their World War II tour of Europe in order to research her father's wartime experiences. Bailey worked as a librarian at the Cleveland Library in Ohio, and she took the time to school me in basic principles of writing. For this I owe her my gratitude and thanks.

During subsequent reunions of the 106th Cavalry Association I met several members with whom I became closely associated and who also became good friends. I appreciate them all and want to express my gratitude to each of them for their help and encouragement. To name them all would take up as much space as one of the chapters in this book. Nevertheless, I want to take a moment to thank Glen Kappelman. He had completed a reprint of the original book *The 106th Cavalry Group in Europe*, adding several pictures from his own personal collection. Later, when he learned of my project, he presented me with copies of his collection and gave me his written permission to use them as I saw fit in the new book. For his generosity I must express my gratitude.

Then there is Raymond Teske, Jr., who became a close friend and associate. Raymond was incredibly supportive as I struggled to write this new version of the 106th Cavalry Group's history. Like Michael's father and mine, Raymond's father served in Europe with the 106th.

As I dug into the 106th Cavalry's history I was surprised to learn that things took an immediate and unexpected turn following the bombing of Pearl Harbor. It appears that D Troop, 106th Cavalry Regiment (Horse-Mechanized), was detached and sent to Panama. There they were met by the 32d Cavalry Regiment and inducted into what would become the "new" 27th Cavalry Regiment. The stories relating to their adventures in Panama, and their reassignment to different cavalry groups following their return to the U.S., introduced me to a long list of other resources that added to the information in this book.

While following these leads I was contacted by two men who contributed immeasurably to this book: Ervin Aden, a former 106th Cavalry trooper and member of the 4th Cavalry Group, and Clinton Alexander, who is associated with the 4th Cavalry Group and whose father, uncle, and grandfather were members of the 4th Cavalry Regiment. The stories, manuscripts, and personal photographs they provided me, which related to the 106th Cavalry's experiences during the Louisiana Maneuvers and subsequent adventures in Panama (as well as those of the 4th Cavalry in Europe) enriched the stories within this book.

I know there are many more people whom I could name and need to thank for their contributions and support over the years, but I can only hope they realize that I do remember them. I could tell stories about each and every one of them; however, to do that would take another book by itself.

Gary W. Palmer

INTRODUCTION

This book was written to complement the original *The 106th Cavalry Group in Europe, 1944-1945,* which was created by members of the 106th Cavalry Group at the end of World War II. The stories found herein not only tell the history of the 106th Cavalry Group—one of only five National Guard units deployed to Europe during World War II—but also encompasses the history of several Regular Army cavalry units who shared their wartime history with that of the 106th Cavalry.

To examine the events leading up to the mechanization of the U.S. Cavalry, the pre-war history (1938-1944) covers arguments presented for mechanization, in addition to the struggles and training as they evolved during the Louisiana Maneuvers. With the outbreak of World War II the book attempts to enlighten the reader with little-known facts pertaining to the deployment of troops in Panama and the construction of the Desert Training Center located near Indio, California. The book includes several personal interviews and stories as told by the men that experienced the nation's transition from a peacetime Army to that of a nation at war.

Furthermore, the book attempts to clarify some of the interim years that preceded the deployment to England, and the reorganization and training as experienced by the troops in preparation for D-Day. Included are a number of personal stories that highlight the reorganization of the cavalry regiments (if not accomplished prior to deployment) to cavalry groups once they arrived in England. The book also touches upon the memories of individual troopers who experienced this transition.

A series of books to follow this one covers the deployment to Normandy and the debarkation as well as first-time battle experiences. This is done so the reader may get an overview and appreciation of the tactics used by the cavalry during those first months of battle leading up to the Liberation of Paris. In doing so the author acknowledges that the books are not complete in every aspect of the military history for the period, but that they attempt to present the reader with enough details to gain a firm grasp of the goals and missions as viewed by the Army groups, corps, divisions, and cavalry units involved.

In short, the author has used *The 106th Cavalry Group in Europe, 1944-1945,* to lay a foundation upon which to illustrate the trials and tribulations of the men preparing for war, and to record their history during the Allies' military advance across Europe during World War II.

CHAPTER I

LOUISIANA MANEUVERS OF 1938 THROUGH 1941

For the first time I have seen "History" at close quarters, and I know that its actual process is very different from what is presented to Posterity.
—*WWI General Max Hoffman*

As the sun rose over the Silesian village of Leuthen on the misty morning of 5 December 1757, Frederick II of Prussia faced an enormous challenge. His opponent, Prince Charles of Lorraine, had posted 65,000 Austrians on well-chosen terrain to thwart Frederick's intended route toward Breslau. Although he brought only 35,000 troops onto the frozen battlefield, Frederick immediately attacked his enemy. In broad daylight the superbly trained Prussians marched across the front of the Austrians, shattered their line with a flank attack, and sent them reeling from the battlefield.[1]

Despite his army's numerical inferiority, Frederick enjoyed an enormous advantage at the battle of Leuthen. In times of peace, Frederick conducted his autumn maneuvers at the close of each summer's training season. These maneuvers were full-sized simulated battles in which Frederick perfected his tactics and tested the skills of his generals. Such exercises helped make the Prussian Army the finest in Europe. Leuthen was one of the battlegrounds on which those exercises took place, meaning that Frederick was intimately familiar with every fold of the ground. Little wonder that he sought a battle there so readily.[2]

Maneuvers such as those conducted by the Prussian Army departed significantly from the eighteenth-century norm. In that era, most training took the form of drill, in which the individual soldier acquired an automatic, mechanical obedience to orders. The objective of this training was to weld the regiment into a single responsive weapon. The maneuvers of the Prussian Army, on the other hand, involved large units locked in simulated battle, replete with the fog and friction of real war. The objective was to test for weakness and to accustom all ranks to the sights and sounds of battle. It was the free maneuver—in which two forces competed for victory, free from the restrictions of script or scenario—which represented the ultimate form of such an exercise.[3]

Although Frederick apparently (according to histories of the period) originated the practice of ending each training season with autumn maneuvers, the use of simulated battle in military training is probably as old as organized warfare itself. In more recent times, Peter the Great of Russia, who as a boy enjoyed playing war with living soldiers, modernized his army through the use of professionally run maneuvers involving tens of thousands of

---

1 Christopher R. Gabel; *The U.S. Army Ghq Maneuvers of 1941:* Published the Center of Military History United States Army, Washington, D. C., 1991 (Page 3)
2 ibid (Page 3)
3 ibid (Page 3-4)

troops. Napoleon's Grande Armée of 1805, one of history's most celebrated fighting forces, prepared itself for Ulm and Austerlitz through a comprehensive training program that included corps-level maneuvers. In the last half of the nineteenth century, annual autumn maneuvers became a fixture on the European military scene. Armies composed of conscripts and reservists, headed by general staffs, capped their summer training with simulated battles that tested doctrine, training, and leadership. In some instances, the routine of maneuvers hardened into ritual. Under Wilhelm II, the German autumn maneuvers always concluded with the annihilation of one army by the other. Predictably, the Kaiser was always to be found in command of the winning side.[4]

By contrast, the U.S. Army conducted no autumn maneuvers during the late nineteenth century and, in fact, sponsored little unit training of any sort. Scattered across a continent in constabulary garrisons and seacoast fortifications, the Army languished in obscurity until the Spanish-American War of 1898 highlighted the inadequacies and anachronisms of the American military establishment. Subsequent reforms implemented by Secretary of War Elihu Root included provisions for bringing together regular and National Guard units in summer encampments that usually included maneuvers. However, the emphasis of these exercises was on instruction rather than the realistic simulation of large-scale engagements. Reforms such as these set important precedents for the future, but for the present their impact was limited.[5]

AN ARMY IN TRANSITION

World War I revealed that the U.S. military was still quite unprepared for modern war. Doctrine was out of date, experience in the command of large forces was nonexistent, and the

---

4 Christopher R. Gabel; *The U.S. Army Ghq Maneuvers of 1941:* Published the Center of Military History United States Army, Washington, D. C., 1991 (Page 4)
5 ibid (Page 4-5)

coordination of arms and services was largely a matter of theoretical conjecture. Once the United States declared war, it took a year and a half to create an American field army capable of mounting an offensive on the Western Front. Even during the Meuse-Argonne offensive, the last major operation of the war, American amateurism remained painfully obvious. Overoptimistic planners set unrealistic objectives. Some division commanders proved inadequate and had to be replaced. Logistics and communications foundered. Tactical commanders, who had never mastered the employment of supporting weapons, resorted instead to ruinous frontal attacks by their brave but artless infantry. Colonel George C. Marshall of the American Expeditionary Forces (AEF) staff noted with dismay the "stumbling, blunderings, failures, appeals for help, and hopeless confusion" that characterized the initial phases of the Meuse-Argonne campaign.[6]

At the end of World War I, conflict arose over the U.S. Army's transition to a peacetime force. What were the required military policies and doctrine, and how would the United States prepare for a subsequent conflict if one occurred? After the armistice with Germany, the U.S. Army tried to move forward by incorporating the lessons of the Great War, especially in the creation of a Tank Corps and an Air Service arm—two organizations that had existed on a temporary basis under wartime legislation.

What were the visions for each of the Army's combatant arms, especially that of the cavalry? Wartime experience triggered doubts about the mobility of traditional horse cavalry executing missions on the fringe of battle. Were the days of hell-bent-for-leather cavalry charges, with the glint of sunlight on drawn pistols or sabers, over?

The cavalry's activity had diminished during the war due to the introduction of machine guns, a preponderance of rapid-firing field artillery, and the use of airplanes for deep reconnaissance.

---

6 ibid (Page 5)

Moreover, the cavalry lacked experience in static warfare and in combined operations with the infantry.

There was talk within the Army that tanks would take over the traditional mission of cavalry. What would be the value of cavalry in the future? The chief of the Tank Corps, Brigadier General Samuel D. Rockenbach, viewed tanks as weapons that restored to the battlefield the mobility previously provided by the cavalry. Weeks before the armistice he presented at an Allied Expeditionary Force conference a lecture entitled "The Role of Tanks in Modern Warfare." In his presentation Rockenbach stated that tanks were not mechanized cavalry, artillery, or armored infantry; rather, tanks were separate weapons to aid the infantry. Rockenbach rejected the concept of a pure tank attack. However, he did support the use of high-speed infantry raider tanks to carry out the traditional cavalry role of creating havoc behind the enemy's front lines. Heavy tanks, he argued, facilitated the breakthrough, while medium and light tanks exploited the success.[7]

BOARDS OF INQUIRY

During its postwar downsizing the U.S. Army studied the experience of the Allied Expeditionary Force in World War I and controversial issues such as the future of the cavalry. Serious debate flared over a postwar doctrine adaptable to the new weapons of war.

The most controversial board that the Army convened was called the Westervelt or Caliber Board. It was convened in December 1918 by the chief of staff, General Peyton C. March, whom one young officer called "a grim and cold-blooded driver" who was detested by everyone around him. Yet, continued the officer, March "built a fire under foot draggers." Brigadier General William I. Westervelt headed the board. Westervelt's prior service

---

7 George F. Hofmann; *Through mobility we conquer: the mechanization of U.S. Cavalry:* Published by the University Press of Kentucky-2006 (Page 76-77)

at the various manufacturing arsenals and proving grounds had given him well-rounded experience in the design, testing, and manufacturing of ordnance materiel.

The Westervelt Board made a comprehensive study of the artillery caliber sizes, types of ammunition, and transport best suited for the United States Army. The board's conclusions, which declared that mechanical transport was the prime mover of the future, had a major impact on artillery as well as the cavalry and infantry. An example of the board's foresight was its recommendation of a 75 mm weapon for use as an anti-tank gun. In making this proposal the board correctly foresaw the future of tank development.

The Westervelt Board also recommended the development of the 105 mm Howitzer M2, a field gun that would see wide use during the Second World War. General Westervelt noted that the board's reports frequently produced a look of amazement on the faces of ranking officers, especially those among the artillery who relied upon the future use of horses.[8]

Meanwhile, in April 1919, General Headquarters (GHQ) AEF, France, convened the influential Superior Board. The Superior Board's mission was to consider the lessons of the war as they affected the organization and tactics of all combat arms, especially the infantry. Major General Joseph T. Dickman, whom Pershing had just relieved as commander of Third Army in Germany, chaired the review board, which was composed of senior AEF officers. The Superior Board examined the combat results of heavy infantry divisions during the war and considered their future organization. The board recommended that the Army sanction the use of heavy square divisions of 29,000 officers and men. Motorized artillery, along with tractor-drawn artillery, was considered appropriate, providing there were suitable roads. For flexibility, the board suggested one regiment of horse-drawn 75

---

8 ibid (Page 78)

mm guns for each infantry regiment. Another recommendation: that another new weapon, the airplane, be employed in a squadron by the division for distant reconnaissance, photography, and observation and registration of artillery.[9]

The Superior Board endorsed the Civil War doctrine of cavalry based on the mobility of the horse, with the breech-loading rifle as the principal weapon. Though World War I had no influence on cavalry operations because virtually no U.S. cavalry units were employed in combat, traditional attitudes among the Army brass persisted. The war, the board noted, furnished few reasons to change cavalry doctrine. However, it was decided that deep reconnaissance was now more obtainable by using aircraft in that role. Thus the strategic employment of cavalry was directed again to defeat the enemy's cavalry, break up his communications, provide flank and rear guard security, employ shock action, carry out pursuit and harassment, and engage in tactical reconnaissance.

The Superior Board concluded that the conditions of northern France probably could not be reproduced in America. As a result, the U.S. Cavalry was expected to find useful employment as it had in the past. No consideration was given to wheel-or track-mounted vehicles to supplement the horse.[10]

In April 1919, another board convened in France by special order of the GHQ, AEF. The Lewis Board, or infantry board, considered infantry tactics and organizational lessons by formulating a series of questions, to be discussed with key officers, regarding their experiences during the war. Due to the number of machine guns on the battlefield, the Lewis Board's questions displayed a general indifference toward the employment of cavalry alongside the infantry. Only two questions dealt with the use of tanks: should tanks be assigned to division control or to the chief of the tank corps for particular missions, and should there be a cargo-carrying tank?

---

9 ibid (Page 78)
10 ibid (Page 79)

Most officers interviewed by the Lewis Board had no experience with the tactical deployment of tanks. One general officer who did was Lieutenant General Hunter Liggett, I Corps commander, who was First Army commander during the Meuse-Argonne offensive. (Pershing had considered Liggett one of his best and most effective corps commanders.) Liggett stated that infantry and tank cooperation was poor. He emphasized that tanks served in an auxiliary role to the infantry, and the idea that tanks could be used for independent operation was "sheer folly." Liggett believed that the main value of tanks was as artillery accompanying the main guns on the battlefield.

When the Lewis Board interviewed Major General Frank Parker, the commander of the 1st Infantry Division, he stated that tanks and airplanes should retain their own tactical control and direction, and suggested that there be more cooperation between the infantry and its supporting arm. Apparently Parker was not convinced that the infantry's solution—allowing tactical control of tanks to remain independent of the division—was supportive of Pershing's doctrine of open warfare.[11]

General Charles P. Summerall, Parker's corps commander during the last part of the war, took a different view. Summerall felt that tanks and airplanes should constitute organic parts of the division, along with substantial supporting artillery. When Colonel Adna R. Chaffee, Jr., was interviewed, he supported the cooperation of tanks and airplanes as troops within the corps, and viewed cargo-carrying tanks as useful. Chaffee also supported the concept of having a horse cavalry regiment for each infantry division.

Like Parker, Chaffee was a graduate of West Point, was commissioned in the cavalry, and attended the Ecole d'application de cavalerie (cavalry school) at Saumur, France, prior to the war. When the United States joined the fighting in Europe, Parker

---

11 ibid (Page 80)

served primarily as a general staff operations officer. Later he became one of the most influential officers in changing the meaning of mechanized cavalry while serving under Parker, who was then assistant chief of staff, G-3 (operations).

Most of the officers interviewed by the Lewis Board supported the doctrine of open warfare advanced by General Pershing in France. Pershing believed that infantry soldiers trained in rifle practice and maneuver were always ready for the conditions of trench warfare. Pershing also emphasized that the infantry have close cooperation with the artillery. Furthermore, the infantry now had the Browning Automatic Rifle (BAR), a squad support weapon first developed in 1917 that would be more flexible in its field use and therefore able to outperform a less maneuverable machine gun. Pershing's opinion was that men, rather than armament, were the most important factor in war. The Lewis Board's report contained no suggestions on the role of cavalry operating with infantry divisions.[12]

When the AEF formed its Cavalry Board, its view was that the recent conflict had changed little regarding wars of movement. The Cavalry Board did admit, however, that the concept of mounted combat using large bodies of cavalry was outdated. Regarding future organization, the board objected to cavalry being assigned as organic elements with the infantry, arguing that cavalry should be attached only for operations as needed.

Pershing appeared before a joint session of the Committee on Military Affairs in 1920. His recommendations were put into motion, and the Tank Corps ceased to exist as an independent arm. The National Defense Act placed all tank units under the control of the chief of infantry. Pershing's influential endorsement of the Superior Board's 1919 report on organization and tactics indicated he felt that in the future the U.S. Army would probably operate on the North American continent. He expected mobility

---

12 ibid (Page 80)

to be more of a necessity in America than in Western Europe, where warfare was more static.

Infantry and cavalry were expected to develop greater mobility. The infantry would train for open warfare, fostering the offensive spirit of the cavalry with rifle firepower and successful bayonet charges with supporting tank and artillery. The cavalry, in turn, was to maintain the cardinal principles of mobility and firepower by developing good horse mounts and training its personnel thoroughly. The Army anticipated that the cavalry would find useful employment in other locations and under different conditions than in France—in particular, the U.S. southern border area with Mexico.[13]

HORSES OR TANKS?

Many traditional cavalrymen believed that tanks would have no effect on their future whatsoever—that tanks were valuable weapons for the infantry only in trench and siege warfare.

By contrast, a small minority of officers thought otherwise. Siding with Parker were such young leaders as Colonel George S. Patton, Jr., of the AEF Tank Corps; and Captain Dwight D. Eisenhower, who trained tank troops at Camp Colt, Pennsylvania, and at Camp Meade, Maryland. Both Patton and Eisenhower wrote articles in the *Infantry Journal* in defense of tanks, forecasting their value in future wars. Both men supported an independent tank corps and addressed the doubts of officers who questioned its value. Patton's war experience and his cavalry background emphasized light tanks for mobility and maneuver.

Eisenhower later wrote that he and Patton were given an order to cease and desist. According to Eisenhower, he was called before General Farnsworth, the first chief of infantry, and ordered to

---

13 ibid (Page 80)

conform to infantry doctrine or face a court-martial. The young officer conformed. [14]

Beginning in 1930, the Army's cavalry branch created its own experimental mechanized force. In order to circumvent the National Defense Act of 1920, which assigned all tanks to the infantry, the cavalry called its tanks "combat cars." The cavalry's attitude toward mechanization was somewhat more innovative than the infantry's, although hardcore horse troopers deeply resented the intrusion of motor vehicles in their ranks.

Figure 1-1. A Combat Car M1 of the 1st Cavalry Regiment (Mechanized) at Fort Knox, 1939. *NATIONAL ARCHIVES*

Nevertheless, in May 1931 the new chief of staff, General Douglas MacArthur, changed the Army's approach to mechanization. He observed that recent experimental units had been based on equipment rather than on mission, and that an item of equipment was not limited to one arm or service. MacArthur instructed *all* arms or services to develop fully their mechanization and motorization potential. Under MacArthur's concept, the cavalry continued working with combat vehicles to enhance its

---
14 ibid (Page 88-89)

role in such areas as reconnaissance, flank action (security), and pursuit, while the infantry explored ways to use tanks to increase its striking power.

MacArthur's decision spelled the end of the separate Mechanized Force, and five months later it was disbanded. As expected, Colonel Van Voorhis was unhappy over the breakup of the Mechanized Force and the loss of tanks. Years later he commented that he had explained in person to MacArthur and his deputy, George Moseley, "that to assign the mechanized mission of the Army to one particular branch would be a great mistake; that mechanization was a problem which concerned all branches of the service and that they should not be deprived of the opportunity to develop mechanization as applied to their respective branches in a coordinated all-out mechanized effort; that I could not conceive of branches developing mechanization within their own respective spheres." Van Voorhis believed that cavalry influence provided the strength of the Mechanized Force. Nevertheless he understood it was not the cavalry but a composite of combined arms and services that would provide the most effective battlefield tools for future wars.[15]

The War Department decided that a new combat branch such as a mechanized force was not in the best interests of the Army, especially when the country was experiencing its worst depression in history. To resolve this issue, a new cavalry unit was established: Detachment for the Mechanized Cavalry Regiment. Because of this move, combat arms theory became compartmentalized and, while still intact, it was driven by separate doctrine and missions. Units and men assigned to the tank force returned to their former assignments, except for about 175 officers and enlisted men (including Colonel Van Voorhis) who remained with mechanized cavalry. On 2 November 1931, the new unit of about four hundred

---

15 ibid (Page 157)

officers and men left Fort Eustis and began a four-day march to Camp Knox, 35 miles southwest of Louisville, Kentucky.[16]

Van Voorhis and his post executive officer, Adna Chaffee (then a lieutenant colonel), liked Camp Knox's large acreage and varied terrain, and found the camp both scenic and primitive. However, Major General Guy V. Henry, Jr., the chief of cavalry, had some reservations. He considered Camp Knox far removed from the cavalry school at Fort Riley, where doctrine was taught. Van Voorhis found Camp Knox more suitable than Fort Eustis for organizing and training the mechanized cavalry regiments, and wanted his unit's new home free of influence by any of the line branch chiefs.

From the beginning, the mission of the mechanized cavalry at Camp Knox was to provide cavalry with a significant role in war fighting, using new mounts in deep mobile-oriented operations. Colonel Van Voorhis was tasked with developing tactical and training doctrine for all units there. Van Voorhis worked with a new breed of young cavalryman, who began to develop a more aggressive method of war fighting than the horse cavalry or the infantry used.

Accordingly, Camp Knox began the great experiment of combining cavalry tactics with modern armor. This new station would later become the home of the U.S. Army Armor Center and School of Mounted Warfare, and the Patton Museum of Cavalry and Armor.[17]

Unfortunately the cavalry's new missions proved too ambitious due to its lack of manpower, obsolete equipment, and fiscal restrictions. It was a case of establishing a doctrine before developing suitable equipment for it. In the meantime, Major Robert W. Grow, Van Voorhis' S-3, drew up a table of organization and equipment for the anticipated 7th Cavalry Brigade (Mech).

---

16 ibid (Page 158)
17 ibid (Page 158)

Grow was far from optimistic, expecting little to happen under current economic conditions. Cavalry regiments that were to be converted to mechanized units were slow in coming. Years of debate and congressional budget restrictions occurred before the 7th Cavalry Brigade finally formed up with two regiments. In the meantime, the newly arrived 1st Cavalry detachment for the mechanized cavalry regiment was composed of headquarters and an armored car unit (A Troop, 2d Armored Car Squadron, commanded by Captain Charles H. Unger), which was in the cavalry tradition of pairing a reconnaissance element with each major unit or command. The detachment also consisted of C Company, 13th Engineers, 19th Ordnance Company, and the 28th Motor Repair Section from the Quartermaster Corps.

When the 1st Cavalry detachment arrived at Camp Knox, it found dilapidated troop barracks left over from World War I, a few shops, a warehouse, and a run-down clubhouse referred to as the Central Mess. The cavalrymen and support troops had their hands full that wet autumn as they set up the camp for the anticipated arrival of the 1st and 4th Cavalry Regiments. However, at the end of November 1931 Camp Knox received word that only the 1st Cavalry Regiment was coming, but not until May or June of 1932.[18]

On 1 January 1932, Congress designated Camp Knox as a permanent garrison, and its name was changed to Fort Knox. A new post commander, Brigadier General Julian R. Lindsey—an old horseman—arrived on 6 February 1932. Now Colonel Van Voorhis could devote more time to mechanizing the cavalry. Subsequently, on 1 March 1932, Van Voorhis organized the 7th Cavalry Brigade to experiment further with mechanization.

Although General Lindsey devoted most of his time to improving living conditions, he was nevertheless vocal in other

---

18 ibid (Page 159)

Figure 1-2. 13th Cavalry Regiment of Chaffee's 7th Mechanized Cavalry Brigade. *NATIONAL ARCHIVES*

artillery. He met with Van Voorhis, Chaffee, and Grow about adding an artillery unit to the mechanized cavalry. Much to the disappointment of Van Voorhis and Chaffee, Lindsey preferred motorized (towed) rather than self-propelled artillery for force balance. This debate continued until the Army entered World War II.[19]

At one point Van Voorhis received a memorandum from the Cavalry School at Fort Riley that upset him greatly. The memo outlined the Cavalry School's expectation that future mechanized units would assist the horse cavalry. Van Voorhis could not fathom why the people at Fort Riley were writing regulations for the purposed redeployment of cavalry regiments to Fort Knox. He believed the elites at Fort Riley knew nothing about mechanization and the importance of employing mechanized regiments as a whole. What about the possibility of employing mechanized regiments as an effective force *without* horses? The attitude of Fort Riley and of the chief of cavalry, Grow recorded, was not to carry out full substitution of "iron horses for flesh and blood horses in an existing cavalry unit."

The detachment at Fort Knox still consisted only of a headquarters, but things were about to change. In January 1933

---

19 ibid (Page 160-161)

the 1st Cavalry moved from Fort D. A. Russell in Marfa, Texas, to Fort Knox, where it became part of the brigade.[20]

Shortly thereafter the regiment adopted tentative tables of organization that provided for a covering squadron, a combat car squadron, a machine gun troop, and a headquarters troop. Each squadron had two troops, and the regiment had a total of 78 combat cars. This structure lasted until 1 January 1936, when the War Department outlined a new organization that consisted of a headquarters and band, two combat car squadrons of two troops each, a headquarters and service troop, machine gun troop, and armored car troop. The new table also authorized the regiment to have 77 combat vehicles—all developmental items.

Eventually the War Department assigned to the brigade a second cavalry regiment, a field artillery battalion equipped with 75 mm guns (mounted on self-propelled half-tracks), ordnance and quartermaster companies, and an observation squadron. The brigade was the Army's first armored unit of combined arms, contributing much to the development of mechanized theory in the interwar years. However, bureaucratic infighting, lack of support, and lack of financial backing often stifled the unit's development.[21]

Although many European theorists urged the development of independent armored forces, their armies made little progress toward the formation of such units. The British abandoned their experiments in 1927 and did not organize their first armored divisions until 1939. The French organized light armored divisions in the 1930s but put most of their tanks in various infantry support roles. In the United States the Regular Army fielded two partially organized tank regiments as part of the infantry arm between 1929 and 1940.

---

20 ibid (Page 161-162)
21 John B. Wilson; *Maneuver and Firepower-The Evolution of Divisions and Separate Brigades (Army Lineage Series):* Published by the Center of Military History –United States Army-Washington, D. C. 1998 (Page 125)

The German and Russian armies took a different approach. Neither had employed tanks in World War I, but both saw their potential. Only after Adolf Hitler abrogated the military provisions of the Versailles Treaty in 1935 did the German Army develop offensive-oriented armored Panzer tank divisions. Nevertheless, their interest in mechanization—especially with tanks—was evident throughout the period, as witnessed by the several visits by German officers to the 7th Cavalry Brigade at Fort Knox in the mid-1930s. At the same time the Russians experimented with tanks from all industrial nations and favored the use of mass armor. On the eve of World War II, however, the Russians had shifted emphasis to small tank units in support of an infantry role.[22]

Modernizing American Combat Forces

In the United States the military establishment saw modest changes in the mid-1930s. Military funding increased slowly from 1932 on, Army Chief of Staff Douglas MacArthur and his successor, General Malin Craig, tried to make mobilization planning more realistic. MacArthur and Craig insisted that staff planners base their initial mobilization schemes on existing Army and National Guard forces rather than assume the existence of forces not likely to be formed for years. The General Staff sought a modest increase in National Guard numbers so that units originally authorized on paper in 1921 could finally be organized. Congress responded in 1935 by approving an expansion of the Guard from 190,000 to 210,000 in 5,000-man increments over the next four years.

To improve training for the Guard, MacArthur initiated combined field maneuvers at the corps and army levels in 1935—

---

22 ibid (Page 125)

the first such exercises in 20 years. These maneuvers and war games continued through the summer of 1940.[23]

The question of the infantry division's organization lay dormant until October 1935, when Major General John B. Hughes, assistant chief of staff, G-3, revived it. In a memorandum for General Malin Craig, MacArthur's successor as chief of staff, Hughes suggested that the General Staff consider modernizing the Army's combat organizations. Although great strides had been made in the development of weapons, equipment, transportation, and communications, Army organizations were still based on the World War I model.

Hughes also noted that such organizational initiatives were the purview of the General Staff—an obvious reference to the resistance of the chief of infantry in 1929 to reexamine divisional organizations. After conducting a thorough examination of the prevailing attitudes of senior commanders, Craig discovered that the infantry division in particular had foot, animal, and motor units, all with varying rates of speed, that did not meet the demands of modern warfare. In addition, he found that there was no consensus of opinion among the three champions of infantry: the Infantry School, the Infantry Board, and the chief of infantry. All of their approaches differed, especially regarding the continued existence of infantry and field artillery brigades as intermediate headquarters between the regiment and the division.[24]

The brigade had remained the largest type of cavalry unit in the National Guard, but in 1936 the National Guard Bureau, formerly the Militia Bureau, returned to federally recognizing cavalry division headquarters. By mid-1940 the bureau had headquarters for the 22d, 23d, and 24th Cavalry Divisions, but not for the 21st. At that time the 21st consisted of the 51st and 59th Cavalry Brigades, the 22d was composed of the 52d and 54th

---

23 Jerry Cooper, The Rise of the National Guard (The Evolution of the American Militia, 1865-1920); Published by the University of Nebraska Press (Page 177)
24 ibid (Page 126)

Brigades, the 23d Division had the 53d and 55th Brigades, and the 24th Division was composed of the 57th and 58th Brigades. (The 56th Cavalry Brigade served as a non-divisional unit.)[25]

On 16 January 1936, Craig created a new body, the Modernization Board, to examine the organization of the Army. Under the supervision of Hughes, the board explored such areas as firepower, supply, motorization, mechanization, housing, personnel authorization, and mobilization. The board's report, submitted on 30 July 1936, rejected the square infantry division and endorsed a smaller triangular division, which could easily be organized into three "combat teams." The proposal cut the infantry division from 22,000 officers and enlisted men to 13,500 and simplified the command structure. The brigade echelon for infantry and field artillery was eliminated, enabling the division commander to deal directly with the regiments.

The enduring problem of where to locate the machine gun was dealt with again. The solution? One machine gun battalion was included in the infantry regiment, which also had three rifle battalions. The field artillery regiment consisted of one 105 mm howitzer battalion and three mixed battalions of 75 mm howitzers and 81 mm mortars. The mixed battalions were attached to the infantry regiments during combat operations.

To assist in moving, searching, and operating quickly on a broad front, cavalry returned to the division level—its home prior to World War I—in the form of a reconnaissance squadron equipped with inexpensive unarmored or lightly armored cross-country vehicles. The anticipated rapid movement of the division minimized the need for extensive engineering work except when the vehicles traveled on roads. Therefore, an engineer battalion replaced the existing regiment. Because the engineers would

---

25 John B. Wilson; *Maneuver and Firepower-The Evolution of Divisions and Separate Brigades (Army Lineage Series):* Published by the Center of Military History –United States Army-Washington, D. C. 1998 (Page 116)

be primarily concerned with road conditions, they would also provide traffic control in the divisional area. A signal company maintained communications between the division and regimental headquarters, and attached signal detachments performed these services within regiments.[26]

To comply with General Craig's directive that the division employ the latest weapons, the board recommended that infantrymen be armed with the new semi-automatic Garand rifle, which the War Department had approved in January 1936. For field artillery, the board wanted the even newer 105 mm howitzer, which was not yet in the Army's inventory.

In a separate letter to Craig, Hughes summarized the advantages and disadvantages of the new infantry division. While drawbacks appeared to be minor, there was still concern over how the states would view such a change in organization. As a federal force the National Guard divisions served only in national emergency or war, but as a state force they frequently responded to local emergencies and disasters. Hughes questioned the splitting of communications functions between the arms and the signal company and the pooling of transportation for baggage and other noncombat equipment into the service echelon. Both arrangements might generate friction because the functions were outside the control of the user. Hughes was also concerned about the stacks of training literature that would need revision and dissemination to the field.[27]

After reviewing the report, Craig decided to test the proposal by creating a provisional infantry division (PID) with three attached components: an anti-mechanized (anti-tank) battalion, an anti-aircraft artillery battalion, and an observation squadron. He selected the 2d Division, commanded by Major General James K. Parson, to conduct the test between September and November 1937. The PID included 6,000 men from the 2d Division and a

---

26 ibid (Page 127)
27 ibid (Page 129)

similar number from other commands, which also furnished much of the equipment. The examination—the first in the history of the Army—was held in Texas, where space and terrain permitted a thorough analysis of the temporary unit.

Even before the test ended, Major General George A. Lynch, the chief of infantry, vetoed the proposed organization in a report to the War Department staff in Washington. After witnessing part of the exercise, Lynch highlighted two mistakes: the separation of the machine gun from the rifle battalion, and the attachment of the signal detachment and mortar battery to the infantry regiment. He suggested that the Army return to the fixed army corps, in which divisions did the fighting and the corps provided the logistical support.[28]

The final report on the PID test—mostly the work of General McNair—noted many of the divisional weaknesses as identified by Lynch. Nevertheless, instead of assigning the division to a fixed army corps, McNair proposed a smaller and more powerful company with three battalions, each with one machine gun and three rifle companies. The machine gun company was to be armed with both machine guns and mortars. By including the anti-tank company within the regiment, there was no need to attach such a battalion to the division. Like Lynch, McNair suggested eliminating signal detachments in favor of infantry, artillery, and cavalry troops. To increase firepower and range, McNair wanted to replace 75 mm howitzers with 105 mm guns and to replace a battalion of 105 mm howitzers with 155 mm howitzers. Because the reconnaissance squadron operated in front of the division and on its flanks, McNair proposed that it be moved to corps level. The quartermaster service company and motor battalion were to be combined into a single quartermaster battalion which would supply the division with everything except ammunition. Each combat element would remain responsible for its own ammunition

---

28 ibid (Page 130)

supply. These changes produced a division of 10,275 officers and men.[29]

After analyzing all reports and comments, the Modernization Board redesigned the division structure, retaining three combat teams built around the infantry regiments. Each regiment consisted of a headquarters and band, a service company, and three battalions. Each battalion had one heavy weapons company (armed with 81 mm mortars and .30 and .50 caliber machine guns) and three rifle companies, but no anti-tank unit. The .50 caliber machine guns in the heavy weapons companies and the 37 mm guns in the regimental headquarters companies were to serve primarily as anti-tank weapons.

The large four-battalion artillery regiment was broken up into two smaller regiments, one with three 75 mm gun battalions and the other with a battalion of 105 mm howitzers and a battalion of 155 mm howitzers. Within the combat arms regiments, signal functions fell under the regimental commanders, while the divisional signal company operated the communications system to the regiments. The engineer battalion was retained but was reduced in size, consisting of three line companies in addition to the battalion headquarters and headquarters company. Traffic control duties moved to a new military police company that combined those activities with the provost marshal's office.[30]

With no change expected in total Army strength, the new division had two authorized strengths: a wartime total of 11,485 officers and enlisted men, and a peacetime one of 7,970 personnel. During peacetime all elements of the division were to be filled except for the division headquarters and military police companies, which were combined. Other divisional elements required only enlisted personnel to bring them up to wartime manning levels.

After the Modernization Board redesigned the division structure, General Craig decided to spend a year evaluating it

---

29 ibid (Page 131)
30 ibid (Page 131)

before determining its fate. The 2d Division, selected once more for the task, again borrowed personnel and equipment from other units to fill its ranks.[31]

Two decades later, General George C. Marshall, who replaced General Craig as chief of staff on 1 September 1939, faced the task of readying the U.S. Army for another world war. Although Marshall wanted to avoid the heartbreaking amateurism he had witnessed in 1918, the Army was wholly unprepared for another war and showed little hope of improving. Twenty years of inadequate funding and skeletonized units left the Army a token establishment. Periodic maneuvers with the Regular Army and National Guard during the interwar years were little more than playacting between imaginary forces.

Prior to Marshall's arrival, General Craig had ordered further testing of the newly proposed provisional infantry division (PID), under Major General Walter Krueger.[32] Between February 1939 and Germany's invasion of Poland on 1 September 1939, the "Provisional 2d Division" commanded by Krueger completed its new set of tests. Krueger found the organization sound except for problems in the quartermaster battalion and minor adjustments required in a few other elements. Major General Herbert J. Brees, the Eighth Corps Area commander and the test director, concurred with most of Krueger's findings except for the issues with the engineer and quartermaster battalions. Brees opposed the motorizing of the engineer unit because the engineers were limited to the divisional area instead of operating across a broad front. Instead, Brees favored an increase in the number of trucks assigned to the quartermaster battalion, but not to the extent suggested by Krueger. Brees also saw no need for infantry and artillery sections led by their own general officers, because the

---

31 ibid (Page 132)
32 Christopher R. Gabel; *The U.S. Army Ghq Maneuvers of 1941:* Published the Center of Military History United States Army, Washington, D. C., 1991 (Page 5)

division commander could easily deal with all elements. Brees recommended that a staff officer—not necessarily a general officer—coordinate field artillery fire.[33]

On 14 September 1939, Lieutenant Colonel Harry Ingles of the Modernization Board summarized the evolution of the division's organization, focusing on the Krueger's report and Brees' comments. Two days later General Marshall approved a new peacetime division structure which included the following: infantry and artillery sections headed by general officers in the division headquarters, a motorized engineer battalion, a divisional band within the headquarters company, and an increase in the number of trucks in the quartermaster battalion.

Marshall's division was completely motorized. Still, the new organization did not totally satisfy him. Having followed its development closely as chief of the War Plans Division and later as deputy chief of staff, Marshall believed that the division should be even stronger to cope with sustained combat. In Marshall's view, the new organization's overwhelming advantage was that the National Guard divisions could easily adopt it. Furthermore, the onset of war in Europe added urgency because the Army could no longer delay modernizing its forces.

A few days after Marshall approved the new structure he authorized the reorganization of the 1st, 2d, and 3d Divisions and the activation of the 5th and 6th Divisions, each with a strength of 7,800 officers and enlisted men. No division had all of its units located in the same place because the Army did not have a post large enough to house one.[34]

In 1936 the Modernization Board focused on the structure of the cavalry division. Most cavalry officers still envisioned a role for the horse because the animal could travel to places that were inaccessible to motorized and mechanized equipment.

---

33 ibid (Page 132)
34 ibid (Page 133)

Using recommendations from the Eight Corps Area, the Army War College, and the Command and General Staff School, the Modernization Board developed a smaller, triangular cavalry division. The 1st Cavalry Division evaluated this structure during maneuvers at Toyahvale, Texas, in 1938. Like the infantry division test held the year before, the maneuvers concentrated on the divisional cavalry regiments around which all other units were to be organized.

Following the test, a board of 1st Cavalry Division officers headed by Brigadier General Kenyon A. Joyce rejected the three-regiment division and recommended retention of the two-brigade (four regiments) organization. The latter configuration allowed the division to deploy easily in two columns, which was the standard cavalry tactic. However, the 1st Cavalry board did support the reorganization of the cavalry regiment along triangular lines, which would give it a headquarters and headquarters troop, a machine gun squadron with special weapons and machine gun troops, and three rifle squadrons, each with one machine gun and three rifle troops.

Although the Modernization Board study did not lead to a general reorganization of the cavalry division, the wartime cavalry regiment was restructured effective 1 December 1938 to consist of a headquarters and headquarters troop, machine gun and special weapons troops, and three squadrons of three rifle troops each. The special troops remained in their original 1928 structure, and no observation squadron or chemical detachment (smoke generating/concealment ammunition) found a place in the division.

With these paper changes to the cavalry division, along with other minor adjustments, the strength of a wartime division rose to 10,680 personnel.[35]

---

35 ibid (Page 137)

Such paper changes characterized much of the Army's work during the interwar years. Although planners lacked the resources to man, equip, and test functional divisions, they gave considerable thought to their organization. The planners developed a new concept for the infantry division, experimented with a larger cavalry division, and explored the organization of a mechanized unit. Designing the new infantry division with a projected battlefield in North America, officers took into account the span of control, the number of required command echelons, the staff, the balance between infantry and field artillery, the location of the reconnaissance element, the role of the engineers, and how to organize the services and supply system. According to the planners, the triangular infantry division offered the best solution to these requirements. Such a recommendation led Marshall to believe that the concepts arrived at by the planners were among the best in the Army.[36]

During the period between the two world wars, officers of the U.S. Cavalry debated whether the future of their branch lay with the horse or the tank. In 1938, Major General John K. Herr—a graduate of West Point (Class of 1902), the Mounted Service School (1910), the Cavalry School Advanced Class of 1925, the Command and General Staff School (1926), and the Army War College (1927)—became the last chief of cavalry.

Herr was a fine horseman and one of the army's best polo players. He was commanding the 7th Cavalry when he was appointed as chief of cavalry—an appointment that was warmly welcomed. It was generally believed that Herr's honesty, forthrightness and dedication to the cavalry were desperately needed in Washington. Herr believed that the General Staff was determined to destroy the cavalry because they did not like cavalrymen, considered the cavalry obsolete, and wished to profit at the expense of the cavalry. While somewhat paranoid in

---

36 ibid (Page 137)

Figure 1-3. Major General John K. Herr. *NATIONAL ARCHIVES*

retrospect, Herr fully believed the Army was moving toward the liquidation of the cavalry branch with intentions of forming an all-mechanized army to face future wars.

General Herr was ranked among the most prominent of the horse cavalry adherents, and he consistently opposed mechanization. He was sad that so many cavalry officers sought experience in the mechanized units and in the burgeoning armored force at Fort Knox. Herr was especially distressed that among these officers were many of the best horsemen and polo players in the cavalry.[37]

Although Herr tried to offer military reasons for his traditionalist position, his devotion to the horse rested primarily on personal and emotional attachments. As the U.S. Army implemented its mechanization plan, Herr's obstructionism hampered the efforts of other officers to modernize both cavalry technology and doctrine. Herr fought every form of

---

37 Lucian K. Truscott, Jr.; *The Twilight of the U.S. Cavalry (Life in the Old Army, 1917-1942):* Published by the University Press of Kansas-1989 (Page 157)

mechanization at the expense of the horse cavalry at a time when all trends in military thought in all modern armies were toward mechanization and armor. He preached the doctrine that "cavalry (meaning horse cavalry) should be employed in large masses," but few military men and no military students agreed with him. Herr attempted to appease his critics through the continued testing and deployment of portee units that were designed to use trucks to move fresh horses to the battle, where troopers would mount up and operate as traditional horse cavalry.

Even when they proved successful during maneuvers, such efforts were a last gasp for the horse cavalry. By 1940 more cavalry officers were seeking experience in the new field of armor, and cavalry stalwarts such as Chaffee, Patton, and Scott supported them. But the resistance of other cavalry officers, particularly General Herr, to full mechanization and its corresponding doctrinal changes left the cavalry weaker than necessary for combat—a fact that was demonstrated on battlefields in North Africa and Sicily.[38]

Having observed the French during World War I, many American officers thought that the French Army was the best in the world. American officers patterned certain aspects of their doctrine on the French model. However, Germany's defeat of the French Army in September 1939 forced a revision of strategic contingency plans involving any American expedition to Europe. France's political capitulation to Hitler raised the specter of German troops occupying French colonies around the world, even in the western hemisphere. Worse, the German occupation of France's western coastline gave the dreaded U-boats open access to the Atlantic, negating Britain's blockade of the North Sea.

With the defeat of France, the war could reach America's doorstep. The German invasion of Poland in September 1939

---

38 John B. Wilson; *Maneuver and Firepower-The Evolution of Divisions and Separate Brigades (Army Lineage Series):* Published by the Center of Military History –United States Army-Washington, D. C. 1998 (Page 155)

not only marked the beginning of World War II in Europe but also signaled the end of American isolationism. During this period General Marshall announced that the U.S. Army, with only 190,000 regulars, ranked 17th in the world—just behind the Rumanian Army and one slot ahead of Argentina. One reporter was overheard saying that compared to the German Army, the U.S. Army was just "a bunch of nice boys playing with BB guns." Of nine Regular Army infantry divisions, all of which existed mainly on paper, only the 2d Division was in any sense a complete unit. There was no full-time corps or army headquarters. The National Guard, with its 18 infantry divisions, officially stood at "maintenance strength." As the Axis threat grew even larger, the "paper units" would no longer suffice for the nation's defense.[39]

One week after the Polish invasion, President Roosevelt declared a "limited state of emergency" and directed the Army to boost its troop strength to 227,000 men. The outbreak of war in Europe allowed for modest increases in funding and manpower, enabling the Army to initiate some long overdue modernization measures. One such attempt at modernization occurred in the autumn of 1939 when the Regular Army adopted a new structure called the "triangular division." Nearly every echelon within the triangular division possessed three maneuver elements and a means of fire support. Each echelon—the rifle company or the division itself—could establish a base of fire using both direct and indirect fire support. Then that echelon could use one maneuver element to fix the enemy, task a second element to find the enemy's flank, and maintain a third element in reserve. Thus doctrine and organization meshed elegantly.[40]

Another innovation within the triangular division was the replacement of all animals with motorized transportation. (The infantry, however, still traveled on foot.)

---

39 Terry Isbell; *The Battle of the Bayous, The Louisiana Maneuvers;* The Old Natchitoches Parish Magazine, Volume II-1997 (Page 2)
40 Christopher R. Gabel; *The U.S. Army Ghq Maneuvers of 1941:* Published the Center of Military History United States Army, Washington, D. C., 1991 (Page 10)

Finally, to keep the triangular division lean at around 15,000 men, the War Department streamlined all support and service elements not essential to the division. These units were pooled in reserve at higher echelons until they were needed. The smaller division structure enabled Marshall to create five embryonic triangular divisions out of three skeletonized square divisions when he realigned the Regular Army in September 1939. After he received Congressional approval for a partial mobilization, Marshall approved the new triangular division structure and authorized the reorganization of the 1st, 2d, and 3d Divisions and the activation of the 5th and 6th Divisions, each with strength of 7,800 officers and enlisted men. Marshall also ordered the Army to purchase a wide array of armored fighting vehicles, transports and tanks, along with new semi-automatic rifles for the soldiers.[41]

Meanwhile, President Roosevelt ordered that the National Guard increase its manning to 235,000 personnel. During the coming year Roosevelt wanted Guardsmen to conduct 60 armory drills rather than the traditional 48, plus seven days of field training during their summer camp.

Impressed by the success of German armor in Poland and France during 1939 and 1940, the War Department General Staff conducted a study to determine future requirements for horse cavalry and the extent to which it should be mechanized. The study concluded there was little need for horse cavalry, but there was an urgent requirement for mechanized reconnaissance units. As a result, the four National Guard cavalry divisions were broken up on 1 November 1940 and their 16 cavalry regiments reorganized or converted into seven horse-mechanized cavalry regiments (corps), seven field artillery regiments, seven coast

---

41 John B. Wilson; *Maneuver and Firepower-The Evolution of Divisions and Separate Brigades (Army Lineage Series):* Published by the Center of Military History –United States Army-Washington, D. C. 1998 (Page 143-144)

artillery regiments forming a separate battalion, and one separate anti-tank battalion.[42]

After the demobilization that followed the end of World War I, many trained officers and enlisted men returned to civilian life. Thus the nation had a natural reservoir of manpower for the Army for a decade or more. Only a few men joined the Enlisted Reserve Corps, but many officers maintained their commissions in the Officers' Reserve Corps, where they received further training during brief tours of active duty.

The composition of the Officers' Reserve Corps, which averaged about 100,000 men between the wars, increased as its ranks were refilled by men newly commissioned after training in the Reserve Officers' Training Corps (ROTC) or Citizens' Military Training Camp (CMTC) programs. Many of these officers were assigned to the 24 reserve cavalry regiments within the six reserve cavalry divisions scattered throughout the United States. One of these reserve officers was Lieutenant Ronald Reagan, one-time member of the 322d Cavalry and later President of the United States. None of these divisions were called into active military service during World War II; however, they were broken up in 1942 and the cavalry regiments assigned to them were either disbanded or converted to Signal Aircraft Warning Regiments and Tank Destroyer Battalions.[43]

The circumstances of America's entry into World War II afforded General Marshall one enormous advantage that no other Army Chief of Staff had enjoyed: a period of partial mobilization that preceded the declaration of war. The Protective Mobilization Plan was a product of the Army's lean interwar years. During the 1930s, Chief of Staff Douglas MacArthur and his successor, Malin

---

42 James A. Sawicki; *Cavalry Regiments of the U.S. Army:* Published by Wyvern Publications, Dumfries, Virginia 1985 (Page-106)
43 ibid (Page 106-108)

C. Craig, recognized that the skeletal Army they commanded was incapable of providing even the most basic protection to the country. Under Craig's direction, the War Department drafted the first Protective Mobilization Plan in 1937-1938. The objective of this plan was to raise a small but combat-effective Army as quickly as possible in time of emergency. This would be accomplished by fleshing out existing Regular and National Guard units, starting with the units that were closest to being combat-ready. After a battle-worthy PMP Army of 1,224,357 officers and men was trained and equipped within eight months of mobilization, additional units would be activated. This ambitious plan was predicated on the assumption that all the equipment for the PMP Army would be produced and stockpiled in advance—something that Congress did not consider feasible.[44]

Although stockpiles of modern equipment did not exist and the sequence of events did not go exactly as planned—for example, there was no "mobilization day" that triggered the plan—Army mobilization from 1939 to 1942 followed the general outlines of the Protective Mobilization Plan. While few new ground combat units were activated in that period, manpower and resources were dedicated to existing Regular and National Guard forces.[45]

Despite the trend of foreign armies replacing horse cavalry with mechanized units, Major General Frank M. Andrews, assistant chief of staff, G-3, decided to table any organizational decisions affecting the American cavalry until necessary. Andrews contended that until a definite theater of operation could be ascertained, the Army needed to prepare general-purpose forces. The horse was capable of going where a machine could not, and therefore the traditional cavalry appeared to have a place in the force. Andrews wanted to determine whether the division should be based on a triangular or square configuration. He also wanted

---

44 Christopher R. Gabel; *The U.S. Army Ghq Maneuvers of 1941:* Published the Center of Military History United States Army, Washington, D. C., 1991 (Page 9)
45 ibid (Page 9)

to explore if and how horse and mechanized units could operate together within a cavalry corps.[46]

FORT KNOX GROWS UP

By 1940 Fort Knox had been the home of the 7th Cavalry Brigade (Mechanized) for nearly 10 years. The permanent brigade post was composed of brick buildings for headquarters, troop barracks, and officers' and noncommissioned officers' quarters.

Despite the permanent construction that had taken place, there was still a lack of facilities for the Headquarters Armored Force and the First Armored Division, both of which were organized at Fort Knox during the spring and summer of 1940. In the meantime, a collection of temporary buildings left over from the World War I cantonment was still in use, and a vast amount of construction was underway. The barracks for the 13th Armored Regiment and the 68th Field Artillery faced south on Third Avenue, looking across the parade ground. Officers' quarters lined Fourth and Fifth Avenues, and just to the south there was another parade ground, where the barracks of the 1st Armored Regiment faced north on Sixth Avenue. Centrally located between the parade ground and the highway were more officers' quarters, the officers' club, the officers' mess, and headquarters for the Post and Armored Headquarters post and the Regiment.[47]

The 13th Armored Regiment was born not from legislation but by War Department directive, in a manner reminiscent of the procedure by which General Sherman had established the school at Fort Leavenworth, and possibly for similar reasons. Quite appropriately, the first chief of the armored force was Major General Adna R. Chaffee, Jr., a well-known cavalryman from a

---

46 John B. Wilson; *Maneuver and Firepower-The Evolution of Divisions and Separate Brigades (Army Lineage Series):* Published by the Center of Military History –United States Army-Washington, D. C. 1998 (Page 145)

47 Lucian K. Truscott, Jr.; *The Twilight of the U.S. Cavalry (Life in the Old Army, 1917-1942):* Published by the University Press of Kansas-1989 (Page 158)

Figure 1-4. In June 1940, Brigadier General Adna R. Chaffee was appointed as the commander of the Armored Force Command.

U.S. ARMY

distinguished Army family who was widely known and greatly admired throughout the Army. Unfortunately Chaffee died from cancer in August 1941. It was a great loss to the armored force that he had been so instrumental in creating.

Chaffee was replaced by Major General Charles L. Scott, who had been organizing the 2d Armored Division. Scott had been chief of the remount service immediately after the First World War. He was assigned as director of instruction at the Cavalry School when Colonel Bruce Palmer was assistant commander, and had done yeoman service in assisting Palmer in making all cavalrymen aware of the capabilities of mechanization and armor in the further development of the cavalry.[48]

---

48 ibid (Page 159)

(Above) A tank park of Light Tank M2A2s. The nearest vehicle is missing its .50 caliber main armament in the port turret which has been removed for cleaning. These vehicles were popularly called "Mae Wests" by tank troops for their twin turret design. The playing card markings on the turret sides designated companies while the number signified the individual vehicle. (National Archives) (Below) A company of M2A3s and M2A2 (second vehicle) on the march during 1939 maneuvers. The M2A3 and late production M2A2s had slab-sided welded turrets while those on the earlier M2A2 were round. (National Archives)

Figure 1-5. *NATIONAL ARCHIVES*

The 7th Cavalry Brigade (Mechanized) formed the backbone of the armored force. The two regiments of this brigade, originally the 1st and 13th Cavalry Regiments, had also added the term "Mechanized" to their designations. In the Armored Force, however, the designations were again changed, and they became the 1st and 13th Armored Regiments. As such, the two regiments formed the basis for the two combat commands "A" and "B" which constituted the 1st Armored Division. The division was stationed at Fort Knox with the Headquarters Armored Force.

Brigadier General George S. Patton, Jr., assumed command of the 2d Armored Division when Major General Scott was assigned command of the 1st Armored Force in November 1940. The 2d Armored Division was organized as a heavy armored division, with two armored regiments consisting of four medium tank battalions and two light tank battalions of three companies each. Along with the 3rd Armored Division, the 2d Division retained this organization throughout World War II.[49]

Preparing for War

In the early spring of 1940, the U.S. military faced a seemingly insurmountable task. With Poland overrun by German armored columns that were now poised to strike at France, and with China under assault by Japan, America's commanders had to prepare the U.S. military for war. Fortunately the problem was not a dearth of troops: after Adolf Hitler's blitzkrieg rolled through Poland in September 1939, Congress mobilized the National Guard and Reserve and approved an increase in the size of the Army.

The problem was that existing troops were poorly trained or not trained at all. No one was more acutely aware of this than Army Chief of Staff General George C. Marshall. A student of history, Marshall was certain that American boys were as courageous as any German or Japanese soldiers but lacked sufficient training and

---

49 ibid (Page 159)

combat experience—and time was short. Marshall concluded that what America's burgeoning ranks needed was a complex training exercise, an exacting test in an environment that would closely approximate the realities of the battlefield.

Marshall believed strongly in the 4-H Club motto of "learn by doing." He planned a series of training maneuvers, splitting his army into two opposing forces in order to let them experience both attacking and defending against a larger or equal force. Marshall decided that the troops—and, more importantly, their commanders—must be trained in the new concepts of mechanized warfare.

To advance this goal, on 2 March 1940 the War Department published a training directive for 1940-41 that marked a turning point in American military history. The document said, in part: "The primary objective [of training] is to prepare units to take the field on short notice, at existing strength, ready to function effectively in combat." While this statement may seem unremarkable, the idea of preparing for combat while the nation was at peace was something of a novelty. However, the early 1940s was a period of unprecedented danger for Western democracy. Although the United States was not at war, the world was far from peaceful.[50]

The War Department called for combat-ready units in its training directive, but the reality was quite different. Nevertheless, the infantry branch had begun to acquire machine guns and mortars for its battalions and companies. These weapons would revolutionize infantry warfare and make the foot soldier a combined-arms force in his own right.

The artillery branch adopted an experimental system of forward observers and fire direction centers that would make American gunners the best in the world. Deliveries had begun

---

50 Christopher R. Gabel, PhD; *The 1940 Maneuvers: Prelude to Mobilization;* Published by Louisiana College as thesis for doctorial-1945

on a new 105 mm howitzer that the artillery branch had asked for 20 years earlier. Armor did not yet have its own branch; its resources were still divided between infantry and cavalry. Even so, for the first time, tank advocates such as General Chaffee were encouraged to explore the potential of massed armor formations.

And so, during the months of 1940-1941, Fort Knox was became a beehive of activity. As troops trained or traveled to their training areas, the roads and streets were filled with the incessant clanking of tanks and combat cars, the clatter of armored cars and half tracks, the deep-throated roar of motorcycles, and the accompanying clouds of dust and the pungent fumes of burning gasoline.[51]

After the May 1940 maneuvers Major General Kenyon A. Joyce, commanding the 1st Cavalry Division, recommended that the Army retain the square cavalry division. A division with two brigades, each with two cavalry regiments, was easily split into strike and reserve forces. By contrast, if the division were organized along triangular lines, the regiments would have to be enlarged to maintain their firepower, but it would make them too large for effective command and control. Joyce suggested that the cavalry regiment comprise a headquarters, a headquarters and service troop, a machine gun troop, a special weapons troop, and two rifle squadrons of three troops each. He wanted to strengthen the two-battalion field artillery regiments by creating batteries of six rather than four 75 mm howitzers and adding a truck-drawn 105 mm howitzer battalion. To improve mobility, the division needed enough trucks to move horses and equipment to the battlefield. Joyce suggested the elimination of only one organization (headquarters, headquarters service troop, or special troops) that

---

5151 ibid (Page 3)

facilitated administration in garrison but could be eliminated in the interest of mobility in the field.[52]

As the National Guard's forces did not fit into any current war plans, the General Staff initiated a study in August 1940 to determine the Guard's requirements for horse and mechanized units. The report concluded that the Guard needed both types of units but not four horse cavalry divisions. It was rumored that the personnel from two cavalry divisions would form the nuclei of two armored divisions. The states, however, objected to the loss of cavalry regiments, and Armored Force leaders believed that armored divisions were too big and complicated for the Guard. On 1 November 1940 the National Guard Bureau withdrew the allotment of the 21st through 24th Cavalry Divisions, in effect disbanding them. Some of their elements were used to organize mechanized cavalry regiments. After November the 56th Cavalry Brigade, a Texas unit, remained the only large unit in the Guard that was authorized to have horses. The 23d Cavalry Division, which consisted of the below listed units, would enter federal service before the end of the year:[53]

23RD CAVALRY DIVISION–NATIONAL GUARD–1940
- 105th Cavalry Regiment
- 106th Cavalry Regiment
- 108th Cavalry Regiment
- 109th Cavalry Regiment
- 141st Field Artillery Regiment
- 23d Tank Company
- 23d Signal Troop
- 127th Ordnance Company
- 123d Quartermaster Squadron
- 23d Reconnaissance Squadron

---

52 John B. Wilson; *Maneuver and Firepower-The Evolution of Divisions and Separate Brigades (Army Lineage Series):* Published by the Center of Military History –United States Army-Washington, D. C. 1998 (Page 147)
53 ibid (Page 153)

127th Engineer Squadron
123d Medical Squadron

The modernization of the Army was still in its infant stages in 1939, while the National Guard was largely unaffected by either the expansion or modernization—such as it was—being enjoyed by the Regular Army. The President and Congress wanted the 242,000 men serving in the Guard available to expand the existing 190,000 men of the Regular Army into a force that could

Figure 1-6. Cavalry troops near Dowden Creek in northern Vernon Parish, Louisiana. CAMP BEAUREGARD COLLECTION

prepare for an enemy attack. Prompted by worsening conditions in Europe, and after much debate within the General Staff and the White House, the Roosevelt administration asked for and received congressional approval in late August 1940 to order the National Guard to active duty for one year's extended training. With this activation came an acute need to test new doctrine and force structures, particularly as they applied to the transition from horse to motor transport. The addition of Guard personnel to the Regular Army allowed the Army to field division-sized forces for maneuvers and testing for the first time in two decades. At Fort Benning, Georgia, the War Department created IV Corps, consisting of the 6th Cavalry Regiment and the newly triangulated 1st, 5th and 6th Infantry Divisions.[54]

Due to German victories in Western Europe during the summer of 1940, Chief of Staff George C. Marshall wanted the Guard mobilized in order to leave part of the Army free to act as an expeditionary force in the event of an emergency. More important, with a peacetime Selective Service bill pending in Congress, Marshall argued that the Army would need the Guardsmen to train selectees (draftees).

The first of 18 increments of National Guard troops reported for duty on 16 September 1940, just as Congress approved Selective Service. With conscription in the offing, the Guard was permitted to accept volunteers only until the draft actually began. Guardsmen reported to forts located across the country. The last Guard units were called to active duty in the spring of 1941.

All told, some 300,000 state volunteers served in World War II—100,000 fewer than in the Great War. From September 1940 through the Japanese attack on Pearl Harbor on 7 December 1941, state soldiers discovered, as they had in the 1916 border call-up and the World War I mobilization, that once in federal service the National Guard was wholly under the command of the War Department. Despite promises to respect the integrity of individual Guard units, the Army totally reorganized the state forces, breaking up the World War I-style divisions the states had maintained through the interwar years.

Many Guardsmen did not understand or appreciate the geopolitical necessity that had mandated their peacetime

---

54 James A. Sawicki; *Cavalry Regiments of the U.S. Army:* Published by Wyvern Publications, Dumfries, Virginia 1985 (Page 116)

mobilization. When Congress extended their length of active duty in September 1941, grumbling similar to that heard along the Mexican border in 1916 swept through the Guard training camps.[55]

FINDING THE RIGHT SPOT

The announcement to Congress that the Army planned to conduct major field training exercises was followed by growing political concern from all over the country as to where those exercises would be held. Politicians correctly saw the maneuvers as a way to help the Depression-ravaged economies in their states and districts.

Despite the pressure, General Marshall knew exactly what he wanted: an economically feasible, underpopulated site that could sustain the damage the maneuvers would produce. Scouts traveled the country, searching for just the right area. After sifting through the resulting data, Marshall settled on the Sabine River area in Louisiana. Sparsely populated, thick with undergrowth and uncharted swamps, and scarred by rural tracts that turned to muck at the slightest hint of rain, central Louisiana was an ideal place to prepare an army.

To help implement his idea, Marshall called on Lieutenant General Stanley D. Embick, a veteran soldier and commander of Third Army, headquartered in Atlanta, Georgia. Marshall directed Embick to find a suitable location where thousands of U.S. troops could be deployed in a series of maneuvers to test their readiness. Accompanied by his aide, Major Mark Clark, Embick traveled to central Louisiana, where the Army had trained many of its soldiers during the First World War. Using a tattered road map as a guide, Embick and Clark tramped through Louisiana's

---

55 Jerry Cooper, The Rise of the National Guard (The Evolution of the American Militia, 1865-1920); Published by the University of Nebraska Press (Page 178)

backcountry, noting the roads, trails, swamps and forests around them.

The north-central part of Louisiana was home to the Kisatchie National Forest, a 604,000-acre wilderness of pinewood hills. Just south of the national forest was Camp Evangeline, a 23,000-acre tract established by the Army in 1930. By linking the two tracts, the military had a ready-made training ground. However, Embick determined the training area needed to be larger still. So the Army secured Louisiana's permission to conduct maneuvers in rural areas south of the national forest.[56]

Figure 1-7. Lieutenant General Stanley D. Embick, chief of the Joint Strategic Survey Committee. *U.S. ARMY CENTER OF MILITARY HISTORY*

---

[56] Christopher R. Gabel, PhD; *The 1940 Maneuvers: Prelude to Mobilization;* Published by Louisiana College as thesis for doctorial-1945

Once the site was selected, events moved quickly. With the help of state organizers, in particular Louisiana Adjutant General Raymond Fleming, a location was chosen and secured from 6,500 landowners. When the landowners were approached regarding the sale of their property, they were told it was their patriotic duty to do so.

Embick and state officials worked quickly to iron out the details, and by early June 1940 the Army had secured the right to deploy across thousands of square miles in Grant, Natchitoches, Winn, Rapides, Vernon, Claiborne and Webster parishes. Embick went even further, securing the rights to use land in East Texas that bordered the primary Louisiana deployment grounds. Like central Louisiana, East Texas was then sparsely populated, with a network of unfinished roads that would challenge military topographers and unit commanders. The 3,400 square miles of combined maneuver area was also laced with rivers: the Sabine and Calcasieu to the west and the Red to the north. These were natural barriers that would present valuable training obstacles for the engineer units obliged to bridge them.

The training area was located in a 40-by-90 mile stretch of rugged pitch pine forest and bayou country that was heavily infested with ticks and chiggers. The maneuvers would occur between the Sabine River, the Calcasieu River to the east, and the Red River to the north.[57]

The process of securing permission to lease the land, or buy it outright, led to one of the tallest of the tall tales associated with the maneuvers. Supposedly, after a backwoods woman refused to sign, a Lieutenant asked her, "Didn't you know that Louisiana is at war with Texas? Don't you want Louisiana to win?" The woman thought for a second and said, "Of course I do! Give me that paper."

---

57 Terry Isbell; *The Battle of the Bayous, The Louisiana Maneuvers;* The Old Natchitoches Parish Magazine, Volume II-1940 (Pages 3)

Despite such patriotism, when the national media covered the start of the maneuvers, it focused on the few signs posted by locals that said, "ARMY—STAY OUT."[58]

Camp Beauregard, named after the famous Confederate general from Louisiana, Pierre G. T. Beauregard, had been activated for World War I and was currently the home for the 39th Infantry Division. The camp was reactivated as a federal training facility early in 1940 and would become the headquarters for first of the Louisiana maneuvers.

During the 1940 maneuvers two corps operated out of Camp Beauregard. As a consequence the camp became the focal point where governmental dignitaries would visit and review the results of the field maneuvers. However, since Camp Beauregard lacked an airfield of its own, the special visitors were driven from a remote airfield located miles away from the main post. The airfield was located near the artillery range and was called the Artillery Range Airport Camp, a.k.a. "Artillery Field." Stationed at this primitive airfield was the 107th Observation Squadron, which was used for artillery spotting and observation of troop movements. The airfield was later renamed Eisler Field in honor of Lieutenant Wilmer Esler, the pilot of an O-47 observation aircraft who died in a crash on the airfield on 11 April 1941.[59]

Lieutenant General Walter E. Kruger (under the command of Lieutenant General Stanley D. Embick of Third Army) commanded IX Corps, composed of part of the 2d Infantry Division and the 7th Cavalry Brigade—reputedly two of the most combat-ready forces in the U.S. Army.

Third Army's home station was Fort Sam Houston, and their shoulder patch derived from World War I. The white "A" on a

---

58 Rickey Robertson; *Do you remember Camp Beauregard:* Published Manuscript in Army Motors-Journal of the Military Vehicle Preservation Association (Page 3)
59 ibid (Page 3)

blue background, circled by a red "O," reflected Third Army's service as an army of occupation after the Armistice was signed on 11 November 1918 in the U.S. Occupation Zone of Germany. When Third Army was reactivated in 1932, the shoulder patch was also revived and worn by the troops and the personnel of Headquarters Third Army. While under the command of Lieutenant General Krueger (soon to be Major General Krueger), Third Army became the premier training and maneuvering army in the country. This role was neither easy nor glamorous. Third Army was composed of hundreds of units ranging from corps to small detachments located in camps, posts, maneuver areas, and other military installations that extended from Mississippi to Arizona and from Arkansas to the Mexican border.[60]

Burr's Ferry, a small community on the Sabine River 15 miles west of Leesville, Louisiana, was selected to be the scene of countless river-crossing exercises during the maneuvers. During the early 1800s "Old Burr's Ferry" (Highway Bridge) was an important communications point between Texas and the United States. The bridge was named for Dr. Timothy Burr (1790–1852), second cousin of U.S. Vice President Aaron Burr.

The crossing, previously called Hickman's Ferry, allowed pioneers to enter Texas with their stock, household goods, and other property. Burr's Ferry was one of four main points of entry on the Texas-Louisiana border. Besides the famous El Camino Real (King's Highway) from the city of Natchitoches, the other entry roads were the Upper Route from present-day Shreveport, the Lower Route from Opelousas, and The Old Beef Trail, which was used as early as the 1820s and 1830s to drive thousands of cattle from Texas to Alexandria for shipment to such cities as New Orleans.

---

60 Colonel Robert S. Allen; *Lucky Forward:* Published by MacFadden-Bartell Corp, 205 East 42d St., New York, NY, 10017 -1947 (Page 12-13)

During the Civil War, Burr's Ferry served as a Confederate camp and as a location for the internment of Union prisoners of war. In preparation for a possible Federal invasion the Confederacy constructed extensive breastworks in the area. (Today the breastworks can be seen north of Louisiana Highway 8, a short distance from the bridge. The location is now noted for a handsome concrete bridge spanning the Sabine River and connecting Louisiana with Texas.)

Nearby, the terrain features of Peason Ridge made it another prime area for the Army's training maneuvers. A stump-knobbed sector, Peason Ridge was once part of the vast virgin pitch-pine forests that covered this section of Louisiana. Hundreds of thousands of Army troops sweated, froze and choked on the dust of Peason's sandy trails and denuded slopes.

The Army fought more simulated battles and river crossings at Burr's Ferry and Peason Ridge than in all the campaigns of World War II. Most of the crack divisions became skilled at the art of war during maneuvers in these two Louisiana locations. The troops learned the hard way because the Sabine River is treacherous: an inoffensive flowing body of water one day, and a raging, ruthless killer the next. Many troops drowned in the river during training maneuvers.[61]

CORPS VS. CORPS

The corps vs. corps maneuver, which began on 9 May 1940, was intended to be a series of experiments rather than competitions. The maneuver director, Lieutenant General Stanley D. Embick, commanding general of Third Army, wanted to collect data on the movement and maneuvers of large units under combat conditions.

---

61 Terry Isbell; *The Battle of the Bayous, The Louisiana Maneuvers;* The Old Natchitoches Parish Magazine, Volume II-1940 (Page 13)

During this particular exercise Embick explored the techniques needed to coordinate traditional combat arms with air and armored forces. A provisional tank brigade under Brigadier General Bruce Magruder incorporated most of the infantry's armor; and the 7th Mechanized Cavalry Brigade, under General Chaffee, included most of the cavalry's tank establishment.

National Guard units were not involved in these early maneuvers, but the commanders and staffs of certain Guard divisions were on hand to observe their Regular counterparts in action. In some cases the Guard officers took the reins and directed operations for a day.

Since training maneuvers had never been attempted on such a large scale within the continental United States, it was decided that every three days there would be a two-day break to resupply the units in the field and point out any weaknesses that had been observed.[62]

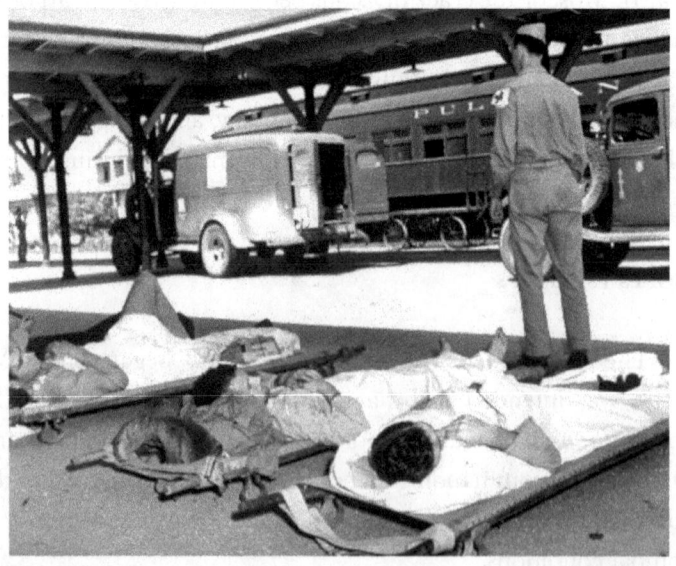

Figure 1-8. Designated "wounded" troops being transported to a railhead, en route to rear-area hospitals. *Camp Beauregard collection*

---

62 Mark Perry; *Louisiana Maneuvers (1940-41):* Published by Historynet.com

Embick sought logistics assistance from senior armored and infantry corps commanders, who insisted that the maneuvers be as realistic as possible. Loudspeakers thundered the recorded sounds of battle, canister smoke shrouded the battlefield, and bags of white sand were dropped from aircraft to simulate the impact of both bombs and artillery shells. U.S. Army Air Corps spotter and reconnaissance planes gathered intelligence, while transports delivered troops to newly constructed airfields.

Planners stockpiled millions of rounds of blank ammunition, and Embick established rules to govern when units would join the line of fire and what kinds of (simulated) casualties they would suffer. Embick's goal was not only to determine who could "kill" whom, but also to test the time it took medical units to transfer the wounded to rear-area combat hospitals. Finally, Embick appointed and trained hundreds of maneuver "umpires" who, armed with clipboards and armbands, monitored and assessed units and leaders according to a complex grading system. While the umpires' conclusions were important, even more important was feedback given by individual commanders, who were to assess their own performance and that of their troops. Embick's goal was not to determine winners and losers of the exercises, but to create an effective training regiment for the coming war.[63]

General Short's IV Corps was, at the time, the U.S. Army's only fully constituted corps, consisting of the 1st, 5th and 6th Infantry Divisions plus the 1st Cavalry Division. Meanwhile, the 7th Cavalry Brigade (Mechanized), under the leadership of General Adna R. Chaffee, had compiled an enviable record of accomplishments during field tests and maneuvers. As a result, the 7th Cavalry was quite popular among competing commanders during the Louisiana maneuvers.

---

63 Mark Perry; *Louisiana Maneuvers (1940-41):* Published by Historynet.com Terry Isbell; *The Battle of the Bayous, The Louisiana Maneuvers;* The Old Natchitoches Parish Magazine, Volume II-1940 (Page 13)
 Mark Perry; *Louisiana Maneuvers (1940-41):* Published by Historynet.com

In addition to gaining the 7th Cavalry Brigade for the Louisiana maneuvers, General Embick also added Brigadier General Bruce Magruder, who commanded the Provisional Tank Brigade, which consisted of light and medium tanks. This was to be the force to oppose IV Corps in what would soon be known as the Great Louisiana Maneuvers.[64]

---

[64] Rickey Robertson; *Do you remember Camp Beauregard:* Published Manuscript in Army Motors-Journal of the Military Vehicle Preservation Association (Page 23)

CHAPTER II

THE BATTLE OF THE BAYOUS

The Army had planned its exercises and selected the units that would engage each other in simulated warfare. The Louisiana area would soon become host to nearly half a million men and 19 divisions. These soldiers would battle rain, mud, mosquitoes, chiggers, ticks and each other in Natchitoches and surrounding parishes in Louisiana. The mobilization was called the Louisiana Maneuvers and would be larger than any war games ever attempted by the U.S. Army.[65]

However, the manuevers weren't simply a mix of men and machines: Although the Army was starting to use tanks in its operations, some of the cavalry units were still using horses.

One of the more significant portions of the maneuvers involved some 70,000 soldiers who trained and "fought" in four

---

65 Terry Isbell; *The Battle of the Bayous, The Louisiana Maneuvers;* The Old Natchitoches Parish Magazine, Volume II-1997 (Pages 2)

separate exercises that lasted over a period of three days each. These exercises began on 9 May 1940 and were the first large-scale Regular Army field exercises since the end of the First World War. These first maneuvers, said General Embick, were "experiments," not contests.

The first exercise was a test to see whether armored units could mobilize and travel long distances. The War Department ordered Major General Walter C. Short's IV Corps to move from its headquarters at Fort Benning, Georgia, to Louisiana. It was an unprecedented operation: the corps would travel 550 miles in six days, the longest motor march ever undertaken by the U.S. Army. Shortly after arriving in Louisiana, the 41,000 men of IV Corps were thrown into a series of corps-on-corps exercises that pitted Short's armored columns (designated as the "Blue Army") against Krueger's IX Corps (the "Red Army").[66]

As previously mentioned, the U.S. Army was in bad shape at the time. Neither its structure nor its armament had changed since the end of WWI. Its ranks were undermanned. Soldiers were still armed with bolt-action Springfield rifles, and the Army had only a handful of light tanks, none of them a match for the Nazi Panzers. American officers were still being trained in warfare strategies. The only division close to full strength was the cavalry, which, like the Polish Army, still relied on horses.[67]

The troops were split into two groups, with one group massing itself along the Texas side of the Sabine River while the other group dug in at positions stretching south from Mansfield to Leesville. The largest concentrations of troops were in Natchitoches and Alexandria.

---

66 Christopher R. Gabel; *The U.S. Army Ghq Maneuvers of 1941:* Published the Center of Military History United States Army, Washington, D. C., 1991 (Page 23)
67 Terry Isbell; *The Battle of the Bayous, The Louisiana Maneuvers;* The Old Natchitoches Parish Magazine, Volume II-1997 (Page 3-4)

The Battle of the Bayous

Figure 2-1. Lieutenant General Walter C. Short. *National Archives*

General Marshall set the stage for the upcoming simulated hostilities by supplying his commanders with the following scenario:

> Blue (East) is a small nation with a common boundary at the Sabine River with another small nation, Red (West). Blue has a small army, normally scattered throughout the country. Red has an even smaller army. These troops, however, are highly trained and are concentrated along the border.
>
> Boundary disputes, local border incidents and alien minorities have resulted in increasing tension between the two nations. On April 20, the Red government provocatively announced it would hold its spring maneuvers just west of the Sabine River. The Blue

government became alarmed, increased its garrison at its border town of Alexandria and announced that it would move its Army to the vicinity of Alexandria for large-scale maneuvers.[68]

STREAMLINED UNITS TO BE TESTED

ATLANTA, Ga., April 6 — (By A. P.)—The United States army is shelving simulation for duration of blitzkrieg maneuvers which will test its newly streamlined units May 5-25, a departure in such war games.

No mythical division will be presented by a sheet of paper for the action which will occupy 67,000 or more regular troops in the Sabine river valley of Louisiana and Texas.

No rifle squad will be sent out with orders to become, for purposes of the problem, a cavalry brigade or a battalion of tanks. Likewise, the red flags which traditionally represent "superior force" will be left in storage.

For once in its life, the general staff expects to have enough men, vehicles and weapons to see what will happen when two of its army corps meet without undue recourse to the imagination.

Only the effect of projectiles will be missing in this million-dollar-a-day check of national defense. Camera guns and the observations of a hundred referees will take care of that.

Motorized infantry, mechanized cavalry, aviation, coast and field artillery and modernized engineering, supply and medical units are in corps training for the test, the largest peacetime maneuvers in the history of the army. Quartermasters are assigned the task of providing 177 freight carloads of food for the men; 190 carloads of gasoline for the vehicles.

Basically, the problem pits the army's Fourth (Southeastern) corps against the Ninth (Southwestern) corps. Together they make up the regional "Third army." But the forces of each are swelled now by thousands of troops moved in from Northern and Western posts for mass training. Chief observer of the war games will be Lieut. Gen. Stanley D. Embick, commander of the Third army.

He will have headquarters at Camp Beauregard, Louisiana, near the city of Alexandria. Fourth corps Blues, ordered to take the offensive, will "jump off" from Fort Benning, Ga., by diverse routes early in May. The Ninth corps Reds will base at Nacogdoches, Tex.

The "combat zone" between Camp Beauregard and Nacogdoches is in an area over which federal and Confederate forces fought intermittently for months in the War Between the States. Down the river occurred one of the oddest clashes in military history, officially set down as "the Engagement at Sabine Pass."

Federal Engineer W. B. Franklin was ordered from New Orleans in 1863 to hoist the United States flag at some point in Confederate Texas to avoid European complications in the war. With 5,000 men, transports and four light gunboats, he was assigned to take Sabine City, a gateway to Houston.

A Confederate fort of eight guns, manned by forty-four officers and men, held the town. Ordered to land his men ten or

Figure 2-2. Article by the Associated Press from the Rapides Public Library.

---

68 ibid (Page 3-4)

With the stage set, the air war started on 6 May and the ground war on the 9th. All of central Louisiana seemed to be engulfed in war; for almost a week the region swarmed with soldiers. The Red Army poured across the Sabine River at Burr's Ferry, Merryville, and Pendleton. The troops constructed a 367-foot-long pontoon bridge at Toledo Ferry. The northern forces of the Red Army advanced quickly towards their objective: to capture Alexandra, the "capital" of the Blue country.

At first the Red Army appeared to make a clean sweep, but they were stopped cold at Natchitoches, where they ran into a large force of Blue Army soldiers dug in at the Normal School (now known as Northwestern State University). For the next few days of the maneuver, there were attacks and counterattacks throughout the area. In the end, the Blue forces successfully pushed the Reds back to the River.[69]

Figure 2-3. Mechanized troops on the move during the Louisiana Maneuvers of 1940. *Camp Beauregard collection*

---

69 ibid (Page 4)

Figure 2-4. Troop movement during maneuvers.
CAMP BEAUREGARD COLLECTION

LOCAL LEGENDS

While participating in the war games, military leaders addressed the question of how an armored unit would perform when combined with an infantry division under a single command. Combining tanks and motorized infantry proved to be a strategic breakthrough. The poorly equipped United States Army had few armored vehicles, so the sight of 54 tanks rolling through the countryside caught everyone's attention.

The new tank unit advanced some 75 miles in one day and won various simulated battles including a surprise dawn attack on Leesville on Tuesday, 15 May 1940. The residents of central Louisiana were awakened by the roar of military tanks speeding down the quiet country roads. Few people had seen a tank, much less the thundering fleet advancing on Leesville.[70]

The maneuvers were a huge event for the local population. It was great fun to watch the troops, tanks and airplanes, as all were novelties. Many of the schools let students out—and students in the other schools let themselves out—to watch the show. Young people reclined on the banks of the Cane River to watch formations of fighter planes and bombers zoom overhead.

At the end of each scheduled phase of the games, troops were allowed to stand down and relax in the communities closest to their bivouac areas. For the Red Army that meant a choice of either alcohol-dry East Texas, with its hot dogs and ice cream socials; or Leesville, Louisiana, with its open bars such as the Red Hound and the Silver Dollar.[71]

Blue Army troops in the Natchitoches area were entertained with community-sponsored dances at the Natchitoches Country Club. These were lively affairs with a lot of laughing and jitterbug music, but with enough slow music to make romance possible. More than one Natchitoches Parish belle lost her heart to a dashing soldier, and the maneuvers did result in a few marriages.

However, not every resident of Natchitoches Parish appreciated the presence of the soldiers as much as the Natchitoches belles did. Some people saw the exercises as an occupation by an invading army.[72]

The media covered the common soldier in addition to reporting on the commanders of the war games. National magazines and local newspapers did their best to spotlight the "typical" soldier. The composite soldier was 20 years old and probably came from Texas, as did some 12,000 of the 66,000 enlisted men. Their monthly pay was $21 for buck privates, $30 for privates first class, $42 for corporals, and $54 for sergeants. Most of the soldiers had

---

70 ibid (Page 4)
71 ibid (Page 4)
72 ibid (page 4)

either attended or graduated high school. The average soldier weighed 145 pounds; stood five feet, eight inches tall; had blue eyes and brown hair; and retained at least 12 of his original teeth. Newspaper readers could assume that the soldier was fairly good-looking, as "just plain facial ugliness" was cause for rejection of would-be Army recruits.

During the maneuvers, the soldiers had few comforts in the field. They were given one mosquito bar (a mosquito net on a frame) to be shared between two soldiers. Sleeping bags were not issued, although the troops could buy them from the quartermaster for five dollars each.[73]

In Robeline, Louisiana, Don Stoker remembers soldiers "borrowing" his father's prize possession, a mechanical hay mower, and hooking it to a jeep to clear a landing field for observation planes. While driving the mower, the troops hit a survey marker and cracked the casing of the mower, spilling all the oil and destroying the machine. Don's father, Dewitt Stoker, put in a claim for the damage and a "smart aleck" Army captain visited to discuss the claim. Mr. Stoker and the captain argued over the cost of the mower. The captain started to leave, but came back and told Mr. Stoker that the whole parish was trying to steal from the Army, and that Mr. Stoker was "a ragged, deadbeat farmer, just like the rest." Mr. Stoker, a WWI veteran, hit the captain so hard that the captain's feet flew off the ground and he was knocked cold. Later that evening, the Natchitoches sheriff and an Army officer came out and told Mr. Stoker he'd have to go to a hearing for breaking the captain's jaw.

At the hearing, both the captain's driver and his assistant testified as to how the captain provoked Mr. Stoker, who didn't go to jail and was compensated for his mower.[74]

---

73 ibid (Page 6)
74 ibid (Page 5)

The Battle of the Bayous

Another interesting tale that originated from the 1940 Louisiana Maneuvers took place near Peason Ridge and involved one of the participating cavalrymen and his horse. According to Ricky Robertson,

> One thing that my family always talked about since they were farmers was the magnificent cavalry horses. Both the 1st and 2nd Cavalry Divisions were involved in the maneuvers, and they were everywhere and they performed great feats such as fording the Sabine River at midnight to attack George Patton's Red Army tanks at Zwolle, Louisiana.
>
> My Dad told of a magnificent cavalry horse coming past their house up the lane, lickety-split, with full cavalry gear on him. Then a while later a small, tired and dusty cavalryman came trudging up to my grandpa's farm. When he started talking my folks immediately knew he was a Yankee from his accent. He told them that he had tied his horse in some bushes. All of a sudden it was covered by "little yellow flies" that started stinging both him and his horse, and then his horse tore loose and ran away.
>
> Little did he know, not knowing the insects of Louisiana, but he had tied his horse in a yellow jacket nest! My dad pointed the direction his horse had run, and several hours later here came the little cavalryman, leading his horse back to his camp.[75]

There were other incidents of soldiers turning out livestock to sleep in dry barns, tearing down fences to get their convoys through, draining farmers' wells dry, and burning all the wood farmers had cut and stacked for syrup making. Armored vehicles

---

[75] Ricky Robertson: Information regarding the Louisiana Maneuvers: Published from an email received on 05-16-2010 addressed to G. Palmer.

destroyed a number of country bridges that were simply not built for that kind of weight and use. However, such incidents were rare, and Natchitoches and the surrounding area enjoyed a much-needed economic boom from the two million dollars spent on the maneuvers.[76]

It's not surprising that an event with the scale and impact of the Louisiana Maneuvers produced some tall tales. One of the most endearing and enduring legends among the residents of Natchitoches Parish involved then-Colonel George S. Patton.

> One morning, troops under Patton were approaching Bermuda Bridge with orders to secure it. Patton was famous for "never losing a battle." This is true only if you don't count the skirmish known locally as the Battle of Bermuda Bridge.
>
> As Patton's troop approached the bridge, the sound of light artillery rang out from the woods. Troops scurried for cover and their commanders halted the advance while they tried to locate the enemy. Reconnaissance had shown no opposing forces in the area. The column was halted for over half an hour while new air reconnaissance was ordered and scouts were sent out.
>
> Imagine the look on George Patton's face when scouts came back with two local boys—the Prudhomme brothers, aged 9 and 11—and their brand new toy carbide cannon!
>
> After the boys were discovered, Colonel Patton reportedly asked their father to have his sons cease-fire so the other war could proceed.

---

76 Terry Isbell; *The Battle of the Bayous, The Louisiana Maneuvers;* The Old Natchitoches Parish Magazine, Volume II-1997 (Page 5)

Years later, radio commentator Paul Harvey would hear the story of the Battle of Bermuda Bridge—or, as it was originally called, "The Pop Gun War"—and use it in his *Rest of the Story* radio broadcast.[77]

The last phase of the maneuvers was marked by heavy rains, which turned roads and fields into mud. The rain left the soldiers in the field wet and miserable. Conditions were so rigorous that one of the officers in charge, Colonel Gruber, stated that "in addition to the enemy, there are two redoubtable antagonists lurking to . . . break up the best laid plans of a commander: Old Man Fog and his twin brother, Bog."[78]

The mud and bad weather weren't soon forgotten. In a scene from the 1945 war movie *A Walk in the Sun*, soldiers are asked to

Figure 2-5. Troops of the 106th Cavalry fighting in the Louisiana mud. *Camp Beauregard collection*

---

77 ibid (Page 5-6)
78 ibid (Page 6)

take a farmhouse held by the enemy. One soldier comments that as bad as the fighting might get, "It can't be worse than the Louisiana maneuvers."

While the Army used the maneuvers to test its new mobile field kitchens, a number of soldiers were denied access to hot chow and instead told to try out a new invention, the C-ration. Each soldier was issued a 12-ounce can of meat and beans, one can of beef stew, a can of meat and vegetable hash, and three companion cans: crackers, sugar, and pulverized coffee. These rations would be a source of soldier's jokes and complaints for generations to come.[79]

RESULTS AND FINDINGS

To check on progress during the maneuvers, General Embick followed up constantly, crisscrossing the "battlefield" to question commanders and soldiers on both sides. What he learned was not encouraging: the Army evidently had a lot to learn about mobile warfare. Vehicle breakdowns, repair team shortages, repeated traffic jams and poorly worded orders were all commonplace. More important, senior commanders' failure to lead from the front resulted in uncoordinated attacks and jumbled defenses. "Commanders and staffs mistakenly believed that they could run the war from headquarters," Gabel noted, "relying on maps and telephones, much as they had in the static warfare of 1918."[80]

The maneuvers were designed to train commanders in coordinating air/ground operations, deploying troops across open terrain (as opposed to trench warfare) and effective deployment of mechanized forces. That they fell somewhat short of success in these goals was illustrated by Major General Herbert Brees' harsh comments during the debriefing of officers. General Brees

---

79 ibid (Page 6)
80 Christopher R. Gabel, PhD; *The 1940 Maneuvers: Prelude to Mobilization;* Published by Louisiana College as thesis for doctorial-1945

squarely blamed the officers, saying that they had "failed to play the game" and that their attitude had infected the troops in the field. He cited the lack of artillery support and noted that attacks were so weak they would have failed against an actual defense. In addition, Brees said that commanders ignored air defense to the point that if the air attacks had been real, there would have been "sure murder" of "helpless infantry." Brees' criticisms were so harsh (and public) that the Army soon issued new guidelines for softer—and private—debriefings.[81]

Other senior officers shared Brees' views. Omar Bradley commented on "the undistinguished and unimaginative leadership by the generals." Bradley also referred to the close air support as "a joke," stating that "of 34 air missions requested by the ground commanders, only two were carried out." In addition, there was a human cost: at least 13 soldiers died during the maneuvers. (It is worth noting that a number of senior commanders retired from the Army in the year following the maneuvers.)[82]

Despite their shortcomings, the Louisiana maneuvers had two very important results for the Army. First, the exercises proved that such large-scale training exercises were both possible and desirable. Over the next two years, corps vs. corps training exercises would take place in New York State and again in Louisiana.

The second result of the Louisiana maneuvers was to prove that the Army was woefully short of men and matériel. Bradley observed that the training exercises showed the urgent need for "infantry divisions, more tank and anti-tank units, armored vehicles, artillery and a dozen other major items." Several powerful senators, including Henry Cabot Lodge, Jr., observed the maneuvers firsthand, resulting in immediate funding for much needed equipment.

---

81 Terry Isbell; *The Battle of the Bayous, The Louisiana Maneuvers;* The Old Natchitoches Parish Magazine, Volume II-1997 (Page 7)
82 ibid (Page 7)

As a result of this 1940 "Battle of the Bayous," the U.S. Army was in a better position to respond, 19 months later, to the Japanese attack on Pearl Harbor. History would show that in those few short months, the Army evolved from a military organization ranked just behind Rumania's to one that could defeat the best-trained and equipped soldiers the world had ever seen. Years after the war, General George Marshall commented, "The maneuvers were not only valuable; they were invaluable. We never could have made our way in Europe without these."[83]

Recommendations from the Basement

The data gathered during the 1940 maneuvers would provide invaluable in modernizing the Regular Army. One lesson that the Army learned was that, despite continued opposition from high-ranking traditionalists, it needed to upgrade its armored forces. A case in point: On 25 May 1940, the day the maneuvers ended, an important meeting took place in the basement of Alexandria High School. Armored brigade commanders Adna R. Chaffee and Bruce Magruder and other officers, including Colonel George S. Patton, Jr., met with Brigadier General Frank Andrews, the War Department's chief of staff, G-3, to discuss the creation of an armored branch. The gathering was kept secret from some of the Army's most powerful officers including the chief of cavalry, Major General John K. Herr, and the chief of infantry, Major General George A. Lynch—both of whom were nearby observing the maneuvers.

The topic of tanks was so highly charged that attendees to the basement meeting risked their careers by participating. Nonetheless, these men had just witnessed how effective tanks could be on the battlefield. The experience convinced them that the Army had to change quickly to be effective against potential

---

83 ibid (Pages 7-25)

enemies. At the meeting, the group—later called the "Basement Conspirators"—agreed that an independent branch was necessary for the new armored force because the cavalry and infantry arms had procrastinated too long. The group recommended that two armored divisions be activated, using the 7th Cavalry Brigade (Mechanized) and the Infantry Provisional Tank Brigade as a basis.[84]

General Chaffee subsequently met with Major General Herr and presented the plans and recommendations suggested by the basement group. Herr procrastinated; he was not willing to sacrifice horses for tanks. Major General Robert W. Grow noted that Herr "lost mechanization for the cavalry, and . . . cavalry . . . lost a prestige that it can never regain."[85]

Figure 2-6. Infantry getting a close-up look at an M2A1 medium tank during the 1940 Louisiana maneuvers. NATIONAL ARCHIVES

One of the "Basement Conspirators," Major General Frank M. Andrews, assistant chief of staff, relayed the participants' recommendations to the Pentagon and his boss, General George

---

84 Christopher R. Gabel; *The U.S. Army Ghq Maneuvers of 1941:* Published the Center of Military History United States Army, Washington, D. C., 1991 (Page 23-24)
85 Donald E. Houston; *Hell on Wheels (The 2d Armored Division):* Published by Presidio Press – 1977 (Page 33-34)

C. Marshall. Not only did Andrews present Marshall with written plans for the organization but he also included suggestions for the tactical use of the two proposed armored divisions.

The ideas were presented to other staff sections and to the service chiefs for their comments. Lieutenant Colonel Jonathan W. Anderson of the War Plans Division agreed with the armored concept and suggested that one division be immediately organized from the 7th Cavalry Brigade.

Predictably, major objections to the proposed force came from the chief of infantry and the chief of cavalry. On 6 June 1940 Major General Gilbert X. Cheves of the adjutant general's office sent a telegram to Colonel Grow, advising that Grow would be reassigned to mechanization headquarters at Fort Knox or Fort Benning. Cheves added: "Very confidential, [it] looks like the Mechanization Force boys have won the day." When he arrived at Fort Knox, Grow discovered that he would be assigned as the G-3 (operations) officer for the division stationed at Fort Benning, Georgia.[86]

THE ARMY CONTINUES ITS GROWTH

Toward the end of May 1940, France appeared ready to fall to the Germans. During a 10-day period a German army group spearheaded by nine Panzer divisions punched a hole through the French defenses along the Meuse River and raced to the English Channel. The once proud French Army was a shattered and discredited force; many of its finest elements were destroyed or penned up ignominiously along the coast.[87]

Modernization efforts had proven difficult if not elusive. In the past the Army had the time but lacked the money it needed. Now it had the money but not enough time. In accordance with

---

86 ibid (Page 34-35)
87 John B. Wilson; *Maneuver and Firepower-The Evolution of Divisions and Separate Brigades (Army Lineage Series):* Published by the Center of Military History –United States Army-Washington, D. C. 1998 (page 144)

the Protective Mobilization Plan, General Marshall intended to continue the modernization and re-equipping process while pursuing only a limited expansion program. Both he and his naval counterpart, Admiral Harold R. Stark, the chief of naval operations, believed that a drastic increase in munitions production should precede any large-scale augmentation of military manpower.[88]

However, Germany's stunning conquest of France and its subsequent aerial assault on Britain during the summer of 1940 compelled preparedness-minded legislators to act. In particular, Senator Edward Burke and Congressman James Wadsworth proposed expanding the Army at once—not by inducting the reserve components, as called for in the Protective Mobilization Plan, but through the first peacetime conscription in the nation's history. Burke and Wadsworth introduced the Selective Service bill on 20 June 1940. Although a protracted debate ensued, as the summer progressed passage of the bill seemed increasingly likely.

The debate over the selective service bill concerned the National Guard for two reasons. First, many Americans in and out of Congress opposed selective service on the grounds that the National Guard alone already provided ample security for the United States. Second, passage of the bill would make federalization of the National Guard units an imperative. The Guardsmen demanded it, the Protective Mobilization Plan required it, and the War Department needed the 18 undermanned Guard divisions to absorb thousands of selectees who would otherwise swamp the nine regular infantry divisions and undo the modernization process entirely.[89]

To counter operations such as the German blitzkrieg, which had proven so successful in Poland and France, the Army centralized anti-tank resources within the infantry regiments to

---

88 Terry Isbell; *The Battle of the Bayous, The Louisiana Maneuvers;* The Old Natchitoches Parish Magazine, Volume II-1940 (Page 12)
89 ibid (Page 12)

form regimental anti-tank companies outfitted with 37 mm anti-tank guns. In infantry battalions the number of anti-tank guns (the .50 caliber machine guns) was doubled. To attack targets of opportunity, more 81 mm mortars were added to the heavy weapons company, and three 60 mm mortars were authorized for each rifle company. A reconnaissance troop appeared in the division, reflecting the growth in its operational area on the battlefield. The number of collecting companies in the medical battalion was increased from one to three. Finally, new tables of organization eliminated the infantry section, with its general officer in the division headquarters, but provided an assistant division commander with the rank of brigadier general. These changes brought the strength of the division to 15,245 officers and enlisted men, with its combat power still focused in the three regimental combat teams.[90]

From late June through mid-July 1940, the War Department set a rapid pace. On 30 June 1940 it selected Brigadier General Charles L. Scott, a cavalryman, to command the 2d Armored Division at Fort Benning. In addition, Brigadier General Bruce Magruder, an infantryman, was to command the 1st Armored Division at Fort Knox, and Brigadier General Adna R. Chaffee was selected on 10 July 1940 to assume command of the I Armored Corps. Chaffee was double-hatted as chief of the Armored Force, headquartered at Fort Knox, Kentucky. The Armored Force was responsible for establishing armored formations, doctrine, and training in the use of armored vehicles.

Soon Congress implemented the selective service system, and thousands of citizen soldiers were ordered to Fort Knox, where they were introduced to the tank. To support these new troops Fort Knox underwent a massive building boom and acquisition of

---

90 John B. Wilson; *Maneuver and Firepower-The Evolution of Divisions and Separate Brigades (Army Lineage Series):* Published by the Center of Military History –United States Army-Washington, D. C. 1998 (Page 144-145)

land. Within a year, a third armored division was added and soon moved to its new headquarters at Camp Polk, Louisiana.[91]

Figure 2-7. D Company, 192d Tank Battalion, on a parade ground at Fort Knox during their training, winter of 1940. *PATTON MUSEUM*

Between June and August 1940, in compliance with the War Department's newly authorized troop increase, the Army activated the 4th, 7th, 8th, and 9th Infantry Divisions. Unfortunately neither the new nor existing divisions had sufficient personnel to meet the new manning levels. The 1st Cavalry Division did not adopt the revised division configuration until early 1941, when it concentrated at Fort Bliss for training.

Until then American officers remained sharply divided on the issue of mechanization. This time no one could claim that special circumstances alone made the mechanized triumph possible. France had been well armed, alerted, and mobilized and had opened the battle on ground of her own choosing. This campaign

---

91 ibid (Page 35)

made it clear to all that mechanization had established a new era in warfare.[92]

Despite the trend in foreign armies to replace horse cavalry with mechanized units, the assistant chief of staff, G-3, Major General Frank M. Andrews, decided to table any organizational decisions affecting the cavalry. Until a definite theater of operations could be ascertained, the Army needed to prepare general-purpose forces. The horse was capable of going where a machine could not, and the cavalry division appeared to have a place in the force. Among the questions Andrews wanted answered was, again, whether the division should be built on a triangular or square configuration. He also wanted to explore if and how horse and mechanized units could operate together within a cavalry corps.[93]

During the May 1940 maneuvers, the 1st Cavalry Division and the 7th Cavalry Brigade (Mechanized) had successfully conducted joint operations. Impressed, Major General Kenyon A. Joyce, commanding the 1st Cavalry Division, decided that horse and mechanized units were compatible within a cavalry corps. He urged the Army to maintain a corps that included both types of units. The proportion of horse to mechanized units could vary to meet different tactical situations. In addition, Joyce thought the corps should be strong in artillery and engineers and contain sufficient support troops to enable it to operate with maximum speed, flexibility, and striking power. The U.S. Army had made a good start towards modernizing its Regular forces by June 1940, after 20 years of neglect. The War Department had authorized an increase in the number of active Regular Army infantry divisions. The triangular division had been adopted and tested, and commanders had gained valuable experience in employing

---

92 Christopher R. Gabel; *The U.S. Army Ghq Maneuvers of 1941:* Published the Center of Military History United States Army, Washington, D. C., 1991 (Page 23)
93 John B. Wilson; *Maneuver and Firepower-The Evolution of Divisions and Separate Brigades (Army Lineage Series):* Published by the Center of Military History –United States Army-Washington, D. C. 1998 (Page 145)

it under field conditions. Although modern equipment was still critically scarce, Major General Walker C. Short, IV Corps commander, commented at the conclusion of the spring exercises that "the Regular Army's equipment problem is on its way to being solved in another year if Congress continues its liberal appropriations."

The revised cavalry division remained in a square configuration with 11,676 officers and enlisted men. Divisional cavalry regiments conformed to Joyce's recommendations, but instead of increasing the size of the field artillery regiment, one truck-drawn 105 mm howitzer battalion and two 75 mm pack howitzer battalions replaced it. As in the infantry division, the cavalry division received anti-tank weapons. The new wartime division tables authorized a divisional anti-tank troop. Each brigade fielded twelve 37 mm anti-tank guns and a weapons troop with anti-tank guns and 81 mm mortars. Draft, pack and riding horses were limited to the cavalry brigades and the division artillery, while other elements of the division were motorized. Headquarters, special troops, was eliminated.[94]

Figure 2-8. Cavalry portees were in use during the 1940 General Headquarters Maneuvers in Louisiana. The specially built tractor-trailers were capable of rapidly transporting eight fully equipped troopers and their horses to any staging point.
THE CAVALRY JOURNAL, SEPTEMBER-OCTOBER 1940

---

94 ibid(Page 147)

The U.S. Cavalry: Time of Transition

The Creation of Camp Polk

After the maneuvers of 1940 the Army realized it needed to establish a base to provide logistical support to units operating in the Sabine River area. When the officials in Vernon Parish got wind of the plan, they formed the Vernon Parish Committee for Co-operation with Defense and Military Training. Members of the committee met with Major C. E. Morrison and Lieutenant A. G. Sage about the possibility of placing the support base within the parish.[95]

On 28 September 1940, Lieutenant Colonel Dwight D. Eisenhower, a member of General Joyce's staff, was contacted by Marvin A. Beaver of Leesville. Would Colonel Eisenhower like to reconnoiter the Vernon/Beauregard Parish region as a possible location for the new Army camp? Eisenhower agreed.

Beaver happened to be an employee of the Kansas City Southern Railroad, so he requested the use of the special *Kay See* car, the most luxurious railcar in the United States, to transport Colonel Eisenhower to Louisiana. The railroad cooperated with Beaver, and Eisenhower was brought to Leesville in grand style.[96]

When Eisenhower arrived in Leesville he rested aboard the train overnight. The next day J. A. Porter provided horses for seven men to ride as they surveyed the barren cut-over hills of the surrounding countryside. Members of the exploratory group included Colonel Eisenhower, Porter, Mr. Beaver, Mr. Jean M. King (mayor of Leesville), and three other military officers.

About seven miles east of Leesville, in the timberland atop a mile-long humpback ridge, Eisenhower dismounted and looked over the area. He used a walking stick for support—the result of a

---

95 Rickey Robertson, *Do you remember Camp Polk and the Louisiana Maneuvers;* Published by the Military Vehicle Preservation Association; Army Motors-Number 122 (Page 26)
96 ibid (Page 27)

football injury dating back to his days at West Point. Eisenhower jammed his walking stick into the sandy soil and declared that this was where the new camp would be built.[97]

After receiving the go-ahead, Major Morrison advised the Vernon Parish Committee of the decision. He gave the committee the names of the landowners, a description of the land, and the acreage of each tract that the Army desired. Morrison also explained that the Army needed the land by the end of the week!

The parish committee began the momentous task of securing leases and purchase agreements. The members worked an entire Sunday. With help from the clerk of the court for Vernon Parish, Jack Hadnot, and his office staff, the committee completed its work in record time. On Monday afternoon, the Army received title to the lands for its new installation. It would be the first Army camp in Vernon Parish's history. The main post would consist of about 100,000 acres, mostly in the Kisatchie National Forest. Obviously the committee members had been encouraged by the fact that another new Army installation, Camp Claiborne in nearby Rapides Parish, had begun construction on 3 September 1940, and troops had been arriving since December.[98]

The Army issued its General Orders for the creation of Camp Polk, Louisiana, on 10 January 1941. Camp Polk was named for West Point-educated Reverend Leonidas Polk. He had the notoriety of being the first Episcopal Bishop in Louisiana. In addition, Polk served as a general in the Confederate Army, where he was known as the "Fighting Bishop of the Confederacy." He was killed in a skirmish at Marietta, Georgia, in June 1864.

Fort Polk is located in west-central Louisiana, about 45 miles from Alexandria, 70 miles from Lake Charles, 120 miles from Shreveport, 150 miles from Baton Rouge, 250 from New Orleans, and 180 from Houston. Close to the front gate are the towns of Leesville, located in Vernon Parish, and DeRidder, located in

---

97 ibid (Page 27)
98 ibid (Page 27)

Beauregard Parish. (Louisiana has parishes rather than counties, as other states do.) Camp Polk quickly surpassed the timber industry as the dominant force in the parish economy. The population of the parish seat of Leesville jumped from 3,500 to 18,000 after the camp opened.[99]

Construction of Camp Polk began on 28 January 1941 on the broad, rolling plains that at the time contained little but cut-over pine forests, a few dilapidated shacks and some range-wire fencing. In March 1941 the camp's first commander, Colonel Otto Wagner, arrived at the post with a few soldiers. Thousands of wooden barracks sprang up virtually overnight to support an army preparing to battle Axis forces on the North African, European and Pacific fronts. Camp Polk was officially completed on 1 August 1941.[100]

The Town of Leesville

Leesville was a small, dying lumber town in 1940 until thousands of troops arrived in the area. Almost overnight the town became one of opulence and sloth. While other communities in the area conducted themselves with some semblance of restraint and decency, the officials and merchants of Leesville operated by one rule: get it fast, and get it big. The officer staff at Camp Polk came to view Leesville, the "metropolis" of the maneuver area, as notorious for its filth, greed and vice.

As Camp Polk grew into one of the largest armed camps in the country, its medical inspectors repeatedly placed Leesville's restaurants "out of bounds" for Army personnel. It wasn't uncommon to find heaps of putrefying garbage piled behind these establishments, or to come upon a broken, uncovered sewer pipe that had been in need of repair for several years. Landlords

---

99 ibid (Page 27-28)
100 Jessica Yahn; Fort Polk, LA: Military Wife Confessions; Published by Fort Polk Community Housing Press (Page 1)

got into the act as well, renting miserable, leaky shacks and sheds that lacked electricity, water, or toilet facilities for the price of comfortable modern apartments.[101]

Figure 2-9. Military convoy passing through Leesville, Louisiana, during the 1940 maneuvers. *CAMP BEAUREGARD COLLECTION*

On the outskirts of town was a black community almost as large, and as decrepit, as Leesville itself. This pestilential hole lacked streets, lights, water or sewers. After dark the area was a fantastic nightmare of horrors and violence. To the general staff at Camp Polk, nothing the troops later saw in Europe equaled the squalor and degradation of this place, with the except of the unspeakable horror of the Nazi death camps.

To protect the hundreds of thousands of American youth who trained in the area, Leesville should have been cleaned up—forcibly, if required. However, state and federal agencies lacked the courage and decency to act.[102]

---

101 Colonel Robert S. Allen; *Lucky Forward:* Published by MacFadden-Bartell Corp, 205 East 42d St., New York, NY, 10017 -1947 (Page 13-14)
102 ibid (Page14)

> **VERNON PARISH PREPARES FOR MANEUVERS**
>
> LEESVILLE, La., April 8.—(Special)—With increasing activities in the Vernon parish area in preparation for the United States army maneuvers to be staged during May, all local health and law enforcement officials have joined with state and national officials in sounding a warning to all undesirables who may seek to carry on any kind of racket during the maneuvers. Thousands of visitors are expected to come into the maneuver area to witness the first "war" carried on in this section of the country.
>
> Visitors attracted to the area because of an interest in the maneuvers will be welcomed, but undesirables are warned to stay away. Special officers will watch all hotels, rooming houses, clubhouses and other places where undesirables may seek to carry on any unlawful practices, officials state.
>
> Undesirables coming into the area from another state will be subject to federal prosecution, and state laws provide for penalties for natives, according to authorities.
>
> Cooperating here with state and federal authorities are: Dr. F. P. Jones, parish health officer; Dr. M. W. Talbot, city health officer; J. M. King, mayor of Leesville, and Dr. W. E. Reid, sheriff.

Figure 2-10. Warning to undesirables during Louisiana Maneuvers, April 1940. (AP News Article)

Not all of the soldiers at Camp Polk thought Leesville was a total mess. According to Cecil R. (Mick) Maguire, a 19-year-old enlisted man,

At that time I was politically naïve and still trying to learn about the world, people, the Army, myself, and ethics. My early post-high school brain was downloading information, sights, and sounds at an accelerated rate. I did, however, form a lot of vivid opinions.

We (the 106th Cavalry Regiment) were stationed in Camp Livingston and stayed in camp there when not actually in the field. I only remember being in downtown Leesville about seven or eight times, total. Some of those times were only about four hours at a time. Some of those times were in connection with Army business in Camp Polk. A few other sergeants and I attended tank driving school at Polk for three days. At night we went into Leesville on passes. Most of the other times, maneuvers made it possible to pass through Leesville or from camp, which was close by.

My view of Leesville was the same as Alexandria— only about one-third as big. It was *saturated* with G.I.s: four hanging on every lamppost or street sign, six leaning on every building on the corners, squads walking in both directions on either side of the streets.

I should clarify by saying that condition existed only on weekends. During the weekdays and evenings, the crowd thinned out about 50 percent, from unbearable to only terrible. The people of Leesville were the same as the people of any small U.S. town that happened to be close to an army base. They were almost smothered by soldiers, their property was damaged and their daughters and wives were pursued, accosted, and seduced.

The civilians were crowded out of the movie theaters, saloons, drug stores, restaurants, parks, and almost out of their churches. It's no wonder that many of the "Leesvillians" were cold to the soldiers, and many more tried to wring every penny out of their pockets.

Many of the longtime Leesville residents were businessmen of long standing. They made a tidy profit off all the G.I.s present, and rightfully so. But there was [also] a large group of hustlers and would-be entrepreneurs from New Orleans, Saint Louis, and other large cities who gravitated to army towns to set up shop. These businesses employed gamblers, bar girls, bartenders, pimps and whores. So no wonder the soldiers considered the "Leesvillites" to be a bunch of cold-hearted money-grubbers.

I believe, on the other hand, that most of the soldiers—especially the newer ones—were really good, average American young guys from good families. Something strange happens to a clean-cut youngster who suddenly finds himself in the Army (Navy, Coast Guard, Marines, Air Force) and 800 miles away from home. He is now a man and tough and eager to prove it to himself, so given a little free time, he's going to raise a little hell!

Add to that group the Regular Army—the professionals—and the ones that had two or three hitches in the service before 1940, plus those who had joined up during the Great Depression because they couldn't find jobs elsewhere to support themselves. All these regulars had for years been living a slow, boring life and now were beginning to have a more interesting time of it with the rebuilding of the modern army. They raised a lot of hell. So the Army and Leesville lived out a touchy, distrustful existence during those years.

These are my thoughts today. In those days I was infected with the soldiers' viewpoint and felt exploited by civilian businesses. My prejudices were somewhat modulated by an old guy I became acquainted with who was a WWI veteran and ran a gasoline station in Colfax, Louisiana. One time he explained his take on the whole problem of wars, soldiers, army camps, camp followers and exploitation. [He said that it had] existed since ancient Roman times.[103]

---

[103] Cecil R. (Mick) Maguire; Excerpts from personal emails shared between the author and Mr. Maguire -2008

CHAPTER III

THE ARGUMENT FOR MECHANIZATION

The publication of FM 100-5, *Tentative Field Service Regulations, Operations*, on 1 October 1939 marked the first revision of Army operations doctrine in nearly two decades. The new manual contained almost twice as much material as its predecessor, even though all discussion of administration was moved to a separate volume. The manual added General Headquarters Aviation as a tactical organization and addressed the modern use of temporary task forces in its discussion of the "tactical grouping" of combined arms.

The new 1939 Field Service Regulations added sections on anti-aircraft, anti-mechanized, and chemical defense. Whereas the 1923 Field Service Regulation manual had addressed combat operations in a single chapter, the new manual devoted a chapter each to offensive, defensive, and special operations. The special operations chapter now addressed urban combat, combat in mountainous terrain, and guerrilla warfare. Nearly every chapter reflected progress in motorization, mechanization, aeronautics, and radio communications, though not to the degree one might expect after 16 years of important technological advances. While the new material acknowledged the developments it did not prescribe fresh doctrine that incorporated new capabilities. Most of the changes emphasized the increased capabilities of the separate arms but did not significantly revise the combined arms doctrine. Despite some forward-looking features, the doctrine was remarkably similar to that contained in the 1923 Field Service Regulations manual.[104]

The U.S. Army's doctrine was sound, but the methods of application had long since changed. Technological advances had neither invalidated the principles of objective and offense nor eliminated the human element from war. However, significant changes had occurred that altered application of the principles. The individual's role had also changed. The idea that "man is least vulnerable when merely clothed against the weather and armored by his own agilities and a steel helmet" was no longer valid.

The modern soldier's challenge was mastery of new weapons and equipment and, most important, the combination of the two. The 1939 Field Service Regulation Manual revealed that the Army was unprepared to meet that challenge. In fact, the new manual reflected the Army's incomplete understanding of the innovative operational and tactical mobility advances brought about by motorization and mechanization.

The discussion of maneuver illustrated the manual's limited prescriptions. Envelopment remained the preferred form of maneuver. Despite great strides in mobility technology that had significantly improved opportunities for passing around enemy

---

[104] William O. Odom; *After the Trenches (The transformation of U.S. army Doctrine, 1918-1939):* Published by Texas A&M University Press-College Station 1999 (Page 132-133)

THE ARGUMENT FOR MECHANIZATION

flanks, the manual limited itself to noting briefly that "superior mobility increases the prospect of success." This conservative assessment underlined both the Army's lack of experience with mechanized forces and its unreceptive attitude toward a major change in its approach to combat. [105]

HORSE VS. MACHINE

As late as 1937, the infantry was not far removed from its post-World War I state of readiness. It still moved by foot, animal-drawn transport, or two-wheel drive motor vehicle; lacked a high-angle weapon; and had no light machine gun. Messengers and wire were the only reliable means of communication. The infantry still lacked an anti-tank gun capable of defeating anything but a lightly armored vehicle, even though all other major armies had one. The .50 caliber machine gun was the main anti-aircraft weapon, but lack of a fire control system or vehicular mount severely hindered its effectiveness. The infantry had yet to field a medium tank even though the Spanish Civil War demonstrated the inadequacy of light tanks for assault missions, which was the principal role for an infantry tank. The Army had standardized the M1 Garand—a clip-fed, gas-operated, semiautomatic rifle that doubled the infantryman's rate of fire without loss of accuracy—but only a few production models were in the hands of troops. Although the Army still considered the firepower of heavier weapons secondary to that of the individual rifleman's capability, it sought to develop a lighter automatic weapon to that carried in World War I. In the interim, the highly inaccurate, 1918 Browning Automatic Rifle (BAR), with its .30-06 caliber, was utilized.[106]

The "walkie-talkie" portable radio—though it represented a notable advance in tactical communications—was ineffective in broken terrain and could function only within a limited

---
105 ibid (Page 134-135)
106 ibid (Page 139)

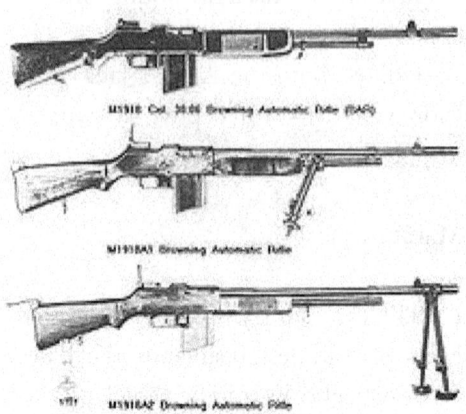

Figure 3-1. M1918 Variants. *U.S. Army*

radio network. Tank and vehicular radios still exhibited serious deficiencies, and the Army had not yet tested light-wire telephone sets.

For the vast majority of infantrymen, experience with new weapons amounted to reading about them in the pages of the *Infantry Journal*. The M1 rifle did not replace the 1903 Springfield model until after World War II had begun, and a true light machine gun did not receive widespread distribution until the end of the war.

Modern heavy infantry weapons—mortars, anti-tank guns, and heavy machine guns—were even scarcer. Experiments with 60 mm and 81 mm mortars, improved 37 mm anti-tank guns, and .50 caliber machine guns failed to result in the mass procurement of new weapons. As late as 1941, stovepipes and broomsticks continued to serve as surrogate mortars and machine guns during training. In short, the infantry's ability to shoot, move, and communicate was not far removed from that of two decades earlier.[107]

---

107 ibid (Page 140)

The Argument for Mechanization

Mobility is the quintessential characteristic of the cavalry, so advances in mobility technology foreshadowed more changes in the cavalry than in any other branch. The successful execution of traditional cavalry missions—reconnaissance, security, reserve, exploitation, and pursuit—hinges on the possession of an advantage in mobility.

Since the dawn of warfare, the horse had provided that advantage, but early developments in aviation and ground mobility technology challenged that tradition. By the end of the interwar period, motor-driven ground and air vehicles could accomplish all cavalry missions. However, Army leaders in general and cavalry officers in particular were slow to accept this fundamental change. This impeded the progress of cavalry doctrine.

On the other hand, the horse was reliable, highly mobile, and economical. The horse cavalry had been selected to spearhead operations along the Mexican border, the Army's most important security mission of the period. Simply put, the horse was superior to mechanized and motorized vehicles for the execution of cavalry missions because mobility technology had not eclipsed the horse in all situations.

Other arguments in support of the horse were less practical but no less important. Advocates drew successfully from fact and fantasy in their defense of horse cavalry but fought an increasingly desperate battle as both motorized and mechanized capabilities improved.[108]

Horse advocates within the Army remained alive and well even as the mechanized cavalry regiment gained strength. Even the most die-hard horse lover conceded operational and tactical reconnaissance to the motorized and mechanized forces. However, tactical reconnaissance still offered the horse a viable role.

---

108 ibid (Page 145-146)

The appointment of Major General John K. Herr as chief of cavalry in 1938 marked the horse cavalry's last great push to retain its niche in the Army's modern combat organization. Herr believed that mechanized forces succeeded in Europe only due to improved road networks and because the horse was still a vital asset in unimproved areas.

Under Herr's efforts, the strongest formation the cavalry adopted was a combined horse-mechanized corps reconnaissance unit. While Herr's predecessors, Major Generals Guy V. Henry and Leon B. Kromer, had advocated the balanced development of cavalry forces, the new chief of cavalry personally spearheaded a crusade to reestablish the horse-based unit as the principal type of cavalry organization. Herr saw the mechanized cavalry as a drain on manpower that could be assigned to horse units. Herr also believed that the mechanized cavalry had reached its fullest state of development and that any further effort on its behalf would occur at the expense of horse units. Herr wanted a cavalry corps of three horse divisions and one mechanized cavalry division. He would not permit any increase in mechanized cavalry strength without a similar increase in horse cavalry. As a result, the 7th Cavalry remained the army's only mechanized brigade until 1940.[109]

The 1939 Field Service Regulation Manual reflected the transitional state of the cavalry. The manual acknowledged the cavalry's progress by expanding its discussion of mechanized units, dropping the previous manual's warning about the cavalry's lack of firepower, and noting a reliance on radio as the primary means of communication.

However, much of the discussion in the 1939 manual treated both types of cavalry forces as one. The manual stressed that "cavalry is characterized by a high degree of mobility; its special

---

109 ibid (Page 147)

The Argument for Mechanization

value is derived from the rapidity and ease with which its power can be displaced from one position or locality to another." All cavalry forces, regardless of type, executed "missions of reconnaissance, counter-reconnaissance, and security for large units." However, when the manual addressed the capabilities of horse and mechanized units, the incompatibility of the two forces became obvious. Horse cavalry continued to provide a highly mobile force for traditional reconnaissance and security missions and was capable of operating on most types of terrain. By contrast, the mission of mechanized cavalry was to exploit and pursue in the offense and to counter-attack in the defense. The mechanized cavalry's ability "to intervene rapidly at a decisive point in battle, exploit a success," and "seize an objective" stressed its firepower and armored protection as much as its mobility.[110]

It is just as important to note that an Army-wide training program did not exist until 1941. When it did, the glaring differences between mounted and mechanized units finally came under close scrutiny. Field army commanders (and corps area commanders before them) were responsible for training their commands. For a time, the maneuvers heralded in annual reports amounted to little more than assembly exercises. Large-scale maneuvers conducted in the late 1930s consisted of individual units, many at half strength or less, training without critically important supporting units. As late as 1939, the First Army could muster only 23 percent of its wartime strength, and its weaponry amounted to a few anti-tank weapons, only 6 percent of its mortars, about 33 percent of its machine guns, and 17 percent of its trucks. Moreover, First Army had no 155 mm howitzers at these maneuvers. Therefore the exercises offered little to support development of doctrine, whether new or included in the newly published 1939 Field Service Regulations manual. Worse, the

---

110 ibid (Page 148)

Army's inability to train with modern weapons and equipment led some participants to conclude that horse cavalry and World War I organizations were still useful.[111]

THE NATIONAL GUARD'S IMPROVING FORTUNES

In conjunction with the growing pains of the Regular Army, the 1920 amendment to the National Defense Act had designated the National Guard as the first Federal Reserve force and set Guard strength at a maximum of 435,000 soldiers. At the same time, the law defined the "National Guard of the several States" as consisting of the voluntary members of the state militias that served under the governors of those individual states. In concurrence with the new National Defense Act, and in an effort to enhance the Guard's influence in the War Department, it was decided the chief of the Militia Bureau would be a National Guard officer. The first Guardsman to serve in this capacity was Major General George C. Rickards of Pennsylvania. [112]

An important amendment to the 1920 National Guard legislation came in 1933. Since the passage of the Dick Act some 30 years prior, the Guard's dual nature—its role as both a state and federal force—had confused and confounded soldiers and legislators alike. Under the leadership of Major General Milton A. Reckord, adjutant general of Maryland, officers of the National Guard and its supporters drafted and passed into law legislation that defined and institutionalized the Guard's unique status.[113]

Presented as an amendment to the National Defense Act of 1920, the 1933 legislation established the "National Guard of the United States" as a permanent "reserve component" of the Army,

---

111 ibid (Page 204)
112 Jerry Cooper, *The Rise of the National Guard (The Evolution of the American Militia 1865-1920);* Published by the University of Nebraska Press, Lincoln-1997 (Page 174)
113 Lieutenant Colonel Michael D. Doubler; *Not So Calm Before the Storm: 1920 to 1940;* Published by the National Guard Association, One Massachusetts Avenue, N.W., Washington, D.C. 20001

consisting of federally recognized National Guard units. The organized Reserves would provide a pool of officers in wartime, and it would also man nine Reserve divisions to absorb and train conscripts during national emergencies. In simplest terms, the "National Guard of the United States" referred to the Guard's federal role as a deployable asset of the Army, while the "National Guard of the several States" recognized the role of Guardsmen on state active duty. Henceforth, officers would take a dual oath to both the nation and their state. In addition, the President had the power to order these units to active duty during a national emergency or once a war began. The legislation also changed the name of the Militia Bureau to the National Guard Bureau.[114]

The War Department established requirements for officers' commissions, assigned specific plans, and set efficiency standards for training. Yet during the interwar years, Washington seldom intruded in state military affairs, and then only when states failed to meet minimum federal requirements. With basic military policy firmly established, the General Staff made no effort to alter Reserve policy or change the Guard's organization. Lack of funds prevented the War Department from supporting joint Army-Guard maneuvers until 1936, leaving the states to conduct their annual summer training camps according to their own dictates.[115]

Federal dollars in the interwar years, however, provided the National Guard with a prosperity it had never known. States did not benefit from the expanded funding authorized by the 1916 National Defense Act until after 1920, but from 1921 through 1940 federal aid averaged $32 million annually—more than five times the amount allotted just before the war. Washington paid for all state military costs except administrative expenses, maintenance and construction of camps, and armories. After 1935 the Works

---

114 Jerry Cooper, *The Rise of the National Guard (The Evolution of the American Militia 1865-1920);* Published by the University of Nebraska Press, Lincoln-1997 (Page 174)
115 ibid (Page 174)

Progress Administration, a New Deal relief agency, built armories and summer camp facilities in many states.

Moreover, the Guard's permanent place in military policy compelled states to spend more money than they had before 1917, if for no other reason than to qualify for their federal allotments. Texas, for example, rarely spent $40,000 on its Guard soldiers prior to World War I but appropriated nearly $120,000 in 1921, before the state had fully reorganized its Guard organization. Texas' annual federal allotment through the 1930s ranged between $250,000 and $300,000. Remarkably, few states cut their military budget substantially during the Depression, and the Guard fared well during those years.[116]

Federal support also ensured stability in the Guard unlike anything it had ever experienced. The steady flow of money from Washington ensured unit continuity and allowed most companies, troops, and batteries to establish permanent places in their communities. Most importantly, the improved armory and camp pay solved the Guard's recruiting problem. Although privates only earned a dollar per drill, the 12 dollars paid quarterly proved attractive to new recruits—mostly teenage boys—who filled the ranks. Depending on their rank and years in service, officers and NCOs could garner 200 to 500 dollars a year simply for armory service.

The onset of the Depression in the early 1930s made recruiting goals even easier to accomplish, and many units had waiting lists for men eager to earn even a dollar a week. In the 1920s the lure of drill pay, social and athletic activities at the armory, and life in nearby towns proved attractive to Guard recruits from rural areas. World War I veterans and young second lieutenants produced by the Reserve Officer Training Corps (a provision of the 1916 National Defense Act) provided the Guard with more seasoned leaders than had been available before 1917.

---

116 ibid (Page 175)

The Argument for Mechanization

Although the interwar National Guard had its drawbacks, the state soldiery was more stable, better equipped, more fully manned, and better commanded during these years than at any time since its revival in the 1870s. Although national defense laws constrained their activities in significant ways, Guardsmen would never again experience a two-decade period during which they were permitted so much leeway in governing themselves while receiving substantial federal funding.[117]

However, money was only one of several key topics that affected the Guard during those years. The Secretary of War conducted a series of meetings and initiated studies concerning another issue, the continuity of command. Perhaps the best example of this problem was illustrated by the questions raised over the organizing of the 23d Cavalry Division. The following passage is from a letter written by Brigadier General Lewis B. Ballantyne, Chairman, Mounted Service Section, Headquarters 59th Cavalry Brigade, New Jersey National Guard. The letter is dated 26 January 1939 and addressed to General Carlos E. Black, Adjutant General of Illinois.

> On 29 December 1938 I learned that Texas had filed an objection with the Secretary of War against authorization for the organization of the 23d Cavalry Division, as agreed to on 12 December 1938; and that due to this action on the part of Texas, General Lawton, representing the 6th Corps Area states, had thereupon filed an objection to the organization of the 22d Cavalry Division. As chairman of the Mounted Service Section I immediately communicated with all of the Cavalry concerned, excluding Texas, New Mexico and the states comprising the 6th Corps Area, recommending that they take appropriate action through their

---
117 ibid (Page 176)

Congressional Representatives, with the result that authorization for organization of the 21st and 22d Cavalry Divisions has been granted.

Every effort has been made to get Texas to withdraw its objection and abide by the agreement reached in Washington at the meeting of the Executive Council of the National Guard Association, at which session it was agreed that providing the proper authorization approved, Texas would be allotted two additional rifle squadrons necessary to bring Texas Brigade to full strength, and a separate armored car squadron in addition thereto...

It was not until last week that Texas agreed to withdraw its objection to the formation of the 23d Cavalry Division. Such agreement, however, is definitely predicated on the proposition that the War Department and National Guard Bureau will allocate out of the third increment sufficient officer and enlisted personnel, horses, equipment and materiél to form the 3d Squadron of two troops each in the 112th and 124th Cavalry Regiments, said squadrons to be activated immediately upon release of the third increment. It further provided that the armored car squadron applied for by Texas be authorized and activated to the 56th Cavalry Brigade... and further that the 56th Cavalry Brigade be classed as a reinforced brigade and be given proper statue in mobilization plans.

At the time that this matter was under discussion at the Executive Council meeting in December 1938, the question was raised as to whether the War Department could legally authorize the formation of these four horse units without violating the "Collins Clause" in the Annual Appropriation Bill, which prohibits the use of any funds for the organization of mounted or horse-drawn units in excess of those in existence in the year 1932. This objection has been disposed of by both a statement made by Congressman Collins to Major General Milton Reckord and an opinion of the Judge Advocate General of the Army. It is therefore free of legal hindrance.

The question of authorizing the organization of an independent armored car squadron, consisting of a small headquarters and two small troops, has not yet been submitted to the General Staff, as far as I know, but inasmuch as there appears no opposition at this time to the organization of any type of motorized or mechanized unit, and the general usefulness and flexibility of a unit such as this is apparent to all, there should be no difficulty in obtaining such approval.

In reply to your specific inquiry I recommend that all of the states concerned in the organization of the 23d Cavalry Division and the State of Texas convey to the Secretary of War, through their respective Congressional Representatives, their desire that approval be granted to organize the two horse squadrons and one armored car squadron in Texas, as outlined above. When this has been accomplished there should be no further delay in submitting the plan for the organization of the 23d Cavalry Division to the General Staff for approval. For the purpose of comity and propriety, request for immediate authorization of the 23d Cavalry Division should be included therewith.

Inasmuch as you state in your letter you have conferred with General Raymond H. Keehn of Illinois, General Ralph M. Immel of Wisconsin, General Fleming of Louisiana and Colonel John S. Bersey of Michigan, and have indicated that they desire to be advised as to the present status of the subject, I am forwarding to each a carbon copy of this communication for such action as may appear appropriate and desirable for each to take.[118]

As late as 14 March 1939, General Black was surprised to learn that there was continued opposition to the formation of the 23d Cavalry Division. However, a letter from General Fleming, The Adjutant General of Louisiana, stating the following:

> I had a long talk with General Pyron, commanding the 56th Cavalry Brigade, Texas National Guard, a few days ago. I really believe that if they could be allocated two squadrons of two troops each, which would bring them to the strength of other National Guard cavalry brigades, they would withdraw their objections to the formation of the 23d Cavalry Division. The question is where we can dig up the 240 men necessary to bring it up to this strength. They have a start of 92 men, which has been allocated to the Infantry Division in Texas and which they are willing to contribute to this brigade if the War Department will permit it. We have no troops in Louisiana whatsoever from the 3d increment and therefore have nothing that we can share ourselves.
>
> Think it over, talk to the other fellows and let me know if you have any ideas in the matter. I understand that the 393 men allocated to the 23d Cavalry Division are still being held up and will not be distributed until such time as the various Cavalry States come to an agreement as to the allocation of these personnel. I do think Texas should have the right to organize its Cavalry along the same lines as the other Cavalry of

---

118 Letter from Brigadier General Lewis B. Ballantyne, Chairman, Mounted Services Section-Headquarters 59th Cavalry Brigade, New Jersey National Guard-dated 26 January 1939; addressed to Brigadier General Charles E. Black, Adjutant General of Illinois.

the National Guard, but I cannot see the necessity of holding up the organization of our Division because of this situation.[119]

Finally, on 1 April 1939, a letter to General Raymond H. Keehn of Illinois, from Colonel Kenneth Buchanan (Regular Army), War Department General Staff, indicated the formation of the 23d Cavalry Division was near:

> I believe that the 23d Cavalry Division, comprising the 53d and 55th Cavalry Brigades, is now well on its way to approval. I am enclosing Illinois' copy of an agreement to aid in accomplishing the purpose. While the important step, that of final approval by the War Department, still remains, I feel confident at this time that the final approval will be granted. I have delayed writing to you on the matter for the reason that I wanted assurance of such approval before giving you "final" information.
>
> Illinois suffers most by the delay, as that delay applies to the units allotted to our state. The delay is not serious, as I previously said, as equipment is not available at this time, but will be some time after this summer. This equipment will be purchased from funds provided by the $110,000,000 augmentation bill, which seems to be in the final stages of being passed by Congress.
>
> Illinois is allotted the following divisional units:
>
> Armored Car Squadron (Now designated Reconnaissance Squadron) consisting of two troops

---

[119] Letter from Raymond H. Fleming, The Adjutant General, Louisiana – dated 14 March 1939; addressed to Brigadier General C. E. Black, The Adjutant General of Illinois

and a small squadron headquarters: Troop strength—8 officers, 88 enlisted men.

Division Headquarters Troop: Strength—3 officers, 50 enlisted men.

Division Light Tank Troop: Strength—3 officers, 66 enlisted men.

These are all very desirable units and I believe that the fourth increment will provide personnel for activating all three. Other states wanted each one of these units. However, I prevented the matter becoming a subject for debate amongst the states. I persuaded the Bureau to make the assignment to Illinois without making it a matter for general agreement by the states. The assignment of units to states is a Bureau function. I believe the assignment will stand without question. Had we gone into debate on the matter, we may have lost the Reconnaissance Squadron, which we particularly want. By taking a direct assignment of all three units, we have protected our "rights."

If this distribution is accepted as to Corps Area, the several states in each Corps Area can then decided as to distribution among states. The Bureau is sending letters to General Immel and General Fleming suggesting the acceptance of the above. While I would without question prefer to remain with the 106th Cavalry, even in my present grade, I shall cheerfully occupy any position in which you may think I can be of service. I do want to be useful, however, and rank is decidedly secondary to my desire to be of service. I am happy to leave the matter to your decision.

Figure 3-2.

Figure 3-3.

I am much more concerned with the new units we will have for the state. I would like to be back on the "job" in Illinois in time to help organize them. While my detail here is officially not up until a year from today, I will actually return about the first of the year. I have over three months leave coming to me which I intend to take on the end of my tour. It is possible that I may return earlier—and can, of course, be relieved from this detail at any time I desire.

The possibility of an earlier return is in view of the necessity for lining up something that will bring me some income. In other words, I am looking for a "job." I sold my interest in the *Urbana Courier* about a year before I came here and have nothing definite at this time to return to—unfortunately, I haven't reached the stage in prosperity where I can sit down for the rest of time and not work. Please pardon the diversion of thought—I merely wanted to point out that I expect to be back in Illinois in time to help organize the units allotted to us.

In a letter in December I suggested locations for the Reconnaissance Squadron and Division Headquarters Troop. The Light Tank Troop is a unit that I didn't anticipate. I believe it should be organized in Chicago and the entire Reconnaissance Squadron in Springfield. This will give a good distribution of the mechanized units and will keep the squadron in one place. It will correspond to putting all of the 2d Squadron, 106th Cavalry in Chicago in order that it may be combined under the direct control of the Squadron Commander. The Division Headquarters Troop can be organized in

Urbana unless some town like Jacksonville particularly wants it.[120]

Final organization of the 23d Cavalry Division did not occur until 15 January 1940. On that date, the Division (along with the the 23d Reconnaissance Squadron, under the command of Captain Mark Plaisted in Springfield, Illinois) was recognized by the federal government. In an article in the March 1940 issue of *Illinois National Guardsman Magazine*, the (newly promoted) Major Plaisted examined changes in the cavalry and Washington's support of the Guard. Plaisted reported that the cavalry was quick to embrace mechanization as an additional reconnaissance element that helped save horses and strengthened the reconnaissance and security power of the arm. Previously, on 1 April 1939, the War Department had authorized the organization of four divisional mechanized squadrons. The state of Illinois was allotted the 23d Reconnaissance Squadron, composed of Headquarters and Headquarters Detachment, with A and B Troop organized from units of the 106th Cavalry Regiment. The two new Troops were composed from the former F Troop and Machine Gun Troop of the 106th Cavalry. F Troop became A Troop. The Machine Gun Troop became B Troop and was stationed at Springfield, Illinois. This change became effective on 1 January 1940 with Major Plaisted commanding.[121]

The new squadron was allocated 19 scout cars, model M3A1, with ¾-inch armor. Each scout car had a cruising radius of 300 miles without refilling the gas tank and could reach speeds of up to 75 miles per hour. The vehicle weighed approximately 11,660 pounds and was equipped with four-wheel drive and a transmission and transfer case that provided eight speeds forward. The tires were pneumatic and puncture-proof. Each scout car was

---

120 Letter from Colonel Kenneth Buchanan – dated 1 April 1939: to General Raymond (Roy) D. Keehn, Chicago, Illinois.
121 Major Mark Plaisted, *The Mechanized Reconnaissance Squadron:* Published in the March 1940 Illinois National Guardsman Magazine (Page 4)

armed with one .50 cal heavy machine gun, two .30 cal machine guns and one .45 cal. submachine gun for aerial, anti-tank and ground defense. Also included on the scout car was equipment for

Figure 3-4. Model M3A1 Scout Car, with ¾-inch armor, sporting one .50 cal machine gun and two .30 cal machine guns.
Camp Beauregard Collection

combat engineers (also known as "pioneers"), plus demolition gear to impede the enemy's progress by destroying bridges and the like.

The typical crew of a scout car consisted of a commander, driver, radio operator, gunner, and four assistant gunners. In addition to basic military subjects, the crew received training in the care and use of assigned automatic weapons, car and ground marksmanship, care and operation of motor vehicles, cavalry signal communications, scouting and patrolling (mounted and dismounted), demolitions, roadblocks, and bridges. The old warning "Keep your heels down" was soon replaced by "Keep your hands on the wheel and your eyes on the road."[122]

---

122 ibid (Page 4)

All command and scout cars were equipped with one SCR-193-A radio for two-way communication in the air and on the ground. This was a powerful 75-watt set that communicated using a carrier wave (CW), an electromagnetic signal. The radio operator could transmit by voice or electronic tones over tactical radio nets employed within each troop and squadron to the division commander. Other means of communication included panels, pyrotechnics and visual signals.[123]

Figure 3-5. Command car from Camp Beauregard.
CAMP BEAUREGARD COLLECTION.

In addition to the scout cars, squadrons were allocated armed motorcycles for scouts and messengers, command cars, maintenance trucks, portable kitchens and cargo trucks. Both car and ground mounts were provided for mounted and dismounted action. In addition to the above inventory, each troop would receive three motorcycles, a sedan and several trucks.[124]

123
124 ibid (Page 4)

The Argument for Mechanization

Per existing doctrine the normal mission of a cavalry troop was distant reconnaissance of the principal routes within a given zone to locate and report on the main body of enemy troops. As detailed reconnaissance of a large area was generally impossible,

Figure 3-6. Typical motorcycle scout as depicted during the August 1940 maneuvers. JOHN BECK

initial reconnaissance was confined to the main roads on which movements of large hostile forces would of necessity be confined.

The best reconnaissance was performed by stealth. Combat was avoided unless necessary to accomplish the mission. Dismounted reconnaissance often resulted in securing vital information without the risk of sacrificing vehicles. Great initiative must be displayed by the scout car crew, requiring a thorough understanding of the situation, mission and orders. Early and accurate information of the enemy strength, composition and movements was imperative, and for this reason radio communication was vital to successful and efficient reconnaissance. However, other means of communication could be utilized.[125]

---

125 ibid (Page 4)

Major Plaisted, commanding officer of the 23d Reconnaissance Squadron, maintained that mechanized cavalry did not supplant horse cavalry reconnaissance. Instead, mechanized cavalry relieved horse cavalry, before close contact, of the tremendous burden of locating enemy forces over a relatively wide and distant front. Plaisted also said that mechanized cavalry should be expected to perform the duties of normal close-in security detachments, as the mounted trooper was still the most efficient means of seeking out the small hostile patrol and of reconnoitering. When the main body of the force was committed to combat, the reconnaissance troop, in the absence of other instructions, maintained continuous battle reconnaissance but avoided combat except when necessary to protect the flanks of the main body. In performing this mission, the reconnaissance troop would be careful to avoid losing freedom of maneuver due to the cross-country limitations of the armored vehicle.

When performing advance flank or acting as rear guards, the reconnaissance troop was most valuable in performing distant patrolling missions, thereby saving horseflesh and assisting greatly in committing the close-in detachment to action. With an advance guard, the reconnaissance troop proceeded by sections, with motorcycle scouts attached, one or two hours ahead of the close-in security elements.

The scout cars operated at speeds of 15 to 45 miles per hour, depending on road conditions and visibility, between terrain features where the enemy might be located. A motorcycle scout preceded the section as the point. The commander was responsible for deciding the actual need for long-distance reconnaissance beyond the scope of the normal security detachment.[126]

All personnel in the reconnaissance troop had to learn the international code for telegraphic radio communications in the

---

[126] Major Mark Plaisted, *The Mechanized Reconnaissance Squadron:* Published in the March 1940 Illinois National Guardsman Magazine (Page 5)

THE ARGUMENT FOR MECHANIZATION

field. They spent many hours, outside of drill each week, practicing sending and receiving messages. Personnel spent extra hours learning new skills such as driver training, motor maintenance, radio operation and mechanized tactics as well as gunnery.

Toward the end of January 1940, Major Plaisted and Lieutenant Joseph McCarthy were temporarily attached to the 13th Cavalry, A Troop, to spend a week at Fort Knox learning about the tactical use and maintenance of the new scout cars.[127]

By 15 July 1940 the arguments against mechanization came to an end with the formation of the First Armored Corps. The struggle to define a role for mechanization inside the Cavalry Branch was largely over, and the roles were about to be reversed. The horsemen had never been interested in using mechanization to do more than assist them in performing their missions. Had they not equipped themselves with heavier machine guns to counter the mechanized threat posed by other nations? They paid a considerable amount of lip service to the proper employment of mechanized ground reconnaissance, but their actions during numerous exercises spoke to a genuine disinterest and misuse of the assets that were available to them. Horse cavalry soldiers viewed themselves as full-fledged warriors and a valuable commodity.[128]

Advocates of mechanized cavalry, on the other hand, had always aspired to more than the limited role they were given. They advanced the use of mechanized reconnaissance because they had no alternative. Their aspirations for a combat role eclipsed their interest in the narrow field of reconnaissance, but along the way they helped define the best ways to equip such forces. After 15 July 1940, the mechanized men assumed the role they had always wanted: as equal actors on the modern battlefield, no longer constrained to those missions allowed them by the horsemen.

---
127 ibid (Page 30)
128 Matthew Darlington Morton; *Men on Iron Ponies(The Death and Rebirth of the Modern U.S. Cavalry):* Published by North Illinois University Press- 2009 (Page 70-71)

The mechanized men were free to develop even their ground reconnaissance forces in accordance with what they had already learned and what they thought might work in the future.[129]

The old cavalry had always admitted there was a place for mechanization in reconnaissance operations. But as world events focused new attention on its own 7th Cavalry Brigade (Mechanized) in the latter half of the 1930s, Cavalry Branch staunchly resisted being forced into the role of reconnaissance agency. Its interest in mechanized reconnaissance had grown, but its professional contribution lagged behind that of its mechanized peers.

The blows Germany struck against Poland and France fell with some impact on the men of the old Cavalry Branch, but it was the Army chief of staff who struck the hardest. By taking away the most advanced elements and thinkers on mechanization, he crippled the Cavalry Branch when it needed assistance the most. Even Patton, who sat on the proverbial fence throughout the interwar years, could not be lured away from taking command of an armored brigade in Major General Charles L. Scott's 2d Armored Division. When Colonel Patton was offered command of the 1st Cavalry Division—the premier cavalry assignment in the United States Army—he wrote to General Herr:

> I have kept this letter for a long time trying to make up my mind about your generous and flattering thoughts about me and the Cavalry Division. Of course it is the dream of every cavalry man who is worth a damn to command that out fit [sic] and I think I could do a job of it. However, I have decided that as I was selected to come here to help make this Brigade I should in loyalty finish the job.[130]

---

129 Matthew Darlington Morton; *Men on Iron Ponies(The Death and Rebirth of the Modern U.S. Cavalry):* Published by North Illinois University Press- 2009 (Page 70-71)
130 ibid (Page 71)

The Argument for Mechanization

Although it seems highly doubtful today, Patton believed that Herr was the "only person" who could understand how hard it was to decline command of the horse cavalry division. Patton postulated that under the same circumstances Herr "would have done the same thing."

Patton tried to ease the branch chief's ego by saying that Herr was "dead right to push the Reconnaissance Cavalry Regiments," and that more would be better. Patton predicted in 1940 that the United States would fight by corps and that single mechanized cavalry troops would be insufficient for infantry divisions. He proposed one regiment per corps, so that in theory, each maneuver division could be allotted its own cavalry squadron. In this way each division would have "more men," and it would afford "more rank" to the men who would command these yet-to-be-formed mechanized cavalry squadrons.

In addition, Patton wrote that the armored divisions "are pure cavalry in their functions and tactics and all the foreign writers so state." How ironic that Patton, having gone with the upstart armored force in the divorce of the cavalry family, clearly recognized that his adopted branch had usurped the fighting characteristics of cavalry that Herr, the letter's recipient, was so eager to preserve. Patton foresaw that cavalry would ultimately be viewed as an agency of mechanized reconnaissance.[131]

---

131 ibid (Page 71-72)

CHAPTER IV

NATIONAL GUARD PARTICIPATION IN AUGUST 1940 MANEUVERS

As the Congressional debate continued over the Selective Service Act, the War Department recognized that the National Guard should be brought to peak readiness as quickly as possible. The opportunity to do so came in August 1940 when the Guard was scheduled to report for its annual summer camp. Whereas the May maneuvers had tested the Regular Army's new doctrine, the August maneuvers would focus on training that the National Guard urgently needed.

Lieutenant General Stanley H. Ford, commanding the Second Army, announced that plans had been completed for maneuvers to be held in central Wisconsin from 11 August 1940 to 31 August 1940. Guardsmen from Illinois, Michigan, Wisconsin, Ohio,

Indiana, Kentucky, and West Virginia would participate. The 1940 encampment would last three weeks instead of the traditional two.

The Guard maneuvers would begin with two weeks of physical conditioning. This was followed by five days of platoon, company, and battalion training; two days of regimental

Figure 4-1. Lieutenant General Stanley H. Ford.
U.S. Army File Photo

and brigade training; and two days of division training. The maneuvers culminated with a week of corps-vs.-corps exercises conducted with the Regular Army. Both sides would be presented with a great four-day challenge: the corps were opposed, over a large area, while making full use of 65,000 troops, the largest gathering of soldiers in the Midwest since 1918.

Operating under the optimistic assumption that 60 evenings a year spent in armory drills had provided the Guardsmen with adequate basic, technical, and theoretical training, the War Department ordered the commanders of the four field armies (which existed primarily on paper) to bring together all of the Guard units in their geographic areas for massed unit training. Accordingly, in August 1940, some 200,000 Guardsmen reported to five separate encampments in New York, Wisconsin, Minnesota, Washington, and Louisiana, where they joined some 100,000 Regular Army troops for these maneuvers.[132]

According to General Ford,

> The Guardsmen who undergo this training will make an important and patriotic personal contribution to National Defense. They will devote their summer vacations to the sole purpose of rigorous military training and will forego tempting opportunities for complete rest and relaxation. Year after year, they have responded to the call upon their patriotism for a period of two weeks. It is recognized that their indicated readiness to go for an additional week will constitute a personal sacrifice in more ways than one. The most pressing question facing these men is the effect that

---

132 Lieutenant General Stanley H. Ford, *Second Army Maneuvers:* Published in the May 1940 Illinois Guardsman (Page 6)

their absence will have upon their employment and personal finances.[133]

Camp Beauregard was the center of activity for the Louisiana encampment, which was supervised by Third Army with Lieutenant General Embick commanding. Army Chief of Staff George Marshall visited Camp Beauregard on 13 August to observe some of the Guard units. Marshall's escort was Colonel John S. Wood, who later commanded the 4th Armored Division in Europe under General George S. Patton.

As mentioned, each encampment was to conclude with a corps-vs.-corps maneuver between supposedly field-worthy Guard divisions. Unfortunately, as the initial two-week training period drew to a close it was obvious to all that the Guard units were woefully unprepared for any such large-scale maneuvers.[134]

During the 1940 Louisiana maneuvers, General Embick had recognized the limitations of the forces under his command. Accordingly, he devised a detailed script for the soldiers to follow. Embick's Third Army headquarters closely supervised the movement of all forces through a group of "control officers" who directed units to advance or retreat. As Embick explained, "The maneuvers are not intended as a competitive test of troops or individual commanders, but rather were intended to provide National Guard Divisions with experience in field operations as part of a larger force."

For the Second Army maneuvers, Embick created two corps. One of these was IV Corps, with 28,000 personnel commanded by Major General Albert H. Blanding. Also known as the Blue Army, IV Corps assembled in the Simpson-Flatwoods area of Louisiana and consisted of several different units: the Regular Army's 6th Cavalry Regiment (horse-mechanized), the 23rd Cavalry Division

---

133 ibid (Page 6)
134 Christopher R. Gabel; *The U.S. Army GHQ Maneuvers of 1941:* Published by the Center of Military History-United States Army-Washington, D. C. 1991 (Page13)

(an improvised National Guard unit that employed rented horses), the 30th and 31st National Guard Infantry Divisions (drawn from the southwest United States), and a provisional tank battalion consisting of two companies. The provisional tank battalion had the only tanks in the maneuvers. Most of the Armored Force was concentrated at Forts Knox and Benning, where two armored divisions were being activated.[135]

Opposing IV Corps was the Red Army, which consisted of an improvised VIII Corps under Major General Krueger. (During the May 1940 maneuvers Krueger had commanded the provisional IX Corps.) Krueger's 37,000 troops included two Regular formations, the 1st Cavalry and the 2nd Infantry Divisions, which had participated in the May maneuvers. Krueger's two National Guard divisions were the 36th and 45th Infantry from the southwest United States. In accordance with Embick's script for the maneuvers, Krueger's VIII Corps gathered in the vicinity of Cravens and Pitkins, Louisiana.[136]

Ready or not, the great maneuvers began in the pre-dawn hours of 17 August 1940 with IV Corps' cavalry crossing the Calcasieu River in Louisiana. There, around daylight, they encountered the 1st Cavalry Division. This kicked off a daylong cavalry battle, pitting horse cavalry against horse cavalry—the last such battle in Army history. When the action subsided, the 23d Cavalry Division's rented horses were so exhausted they had to be left behind; the troopers redeployed by truck.

On the next day, 18 August 1940, both corps moved up the infantry to relieve the cavalry. The Red VIII Corps assumed the offensive, driving in IV Corps' covering force and placing the 2d Division in position to envelop the Blue Army's right flank. The envelopment proceeded as planned on 19 August when 2d

---

135 Rickey Robertson; *Do you remember Camp Beauregard;* Published by Published by the Old Natchitoches Parish Magizine-1997

136 Christopher R. Gabel; *The 1940 Maneuvers: Prelude to Mobilization:* Published by the Center of Military History-United States Army-Washington, D. C. 1991 (Page10)

Figure 4-2. B Troop, 252d Quartermaster Regiment Squadron, unloading horses at Camp Polk, Louisiana. *NATIONAL ARCHIVES*

Division found it was opposed only by the 23d Cavalry Division (whether with or without rented horses is not clear). The maneuver ended on 20 August 1940, with a IV Corps counterattack that was built around the Blue Army's 30th Division.[137]

Although the corps-vs.-corps maneuvers in each of the encampments varied, they all revealed that the National Guard's state of training was wholly inadequate. Individual soldiers, physically unprepared for marching and living in the field, collapsed

---

137 ibid (Page 11)

from exhaustion with alarming frequency. Observers noted that the enlisted men were poorly trained in basic discipline as well. Platoons, companies, and battalions wandered aimlessly through the exercises, demonstrating clearly that the few days devoted to small-unit training had been grossly insufficient. At the higher levels of command, officers frequently failed to issue coherent orders and often disobeyed the orders they received. Brigade and division commanders proved generally inept at coordinating the weapons and units under their control. Communications were usually in a state of collapse, and in some cases even the administration of supply broke down, leaving the Guardsmen without food. The reports that emanated from National Guard training camps in August 1940 supported General Marshall's determination to bring the Guard under federal control. [138]

Figure 4-3. 23rd Cavalry Division (an improvised National Guard unit that employed rented horses) participating in the 1940 Louisiana maneuvers. CAMP BEAUREGARD COLLECTION

---

138 Christopher R. Gabel; *The U.S. Army GHQ Maneuvers of 1941:* Published by the Center of Military History-United States Army-Washington, D. C. 1991 (Page 13)

Guard units. At a post-maneuver critique General Krueger, VIII Corps Commander, stated point-blank that the National Guard needed extensive training, from the individual level on up, before large-scale operations should be attempted. Despite his bluntness, Krueger was not anti-Guard. In fact, he was one of the Guard's best friends among high-ranking Regular Army officers.

Other observers of the Third Army during these exercises noted a widespread lack of discipline and inadequate physical conditioning, as evidenced by many Guardsmen incapacitated by heat exhaustion, sunburn, and gastric distress (triggered by the guzzling of soda pop purchased at roadside stands). War Department observers were not pleased with the scripted nature of the Third Army exercise and recommended that they be referred to as "tactical drills" rather than "maneuvers."[139]

ALL THE GUARD'S HORSES AND ALL THE GUARD'S MEN

Another issue that General Embick noted during the 1940 Louisiana maneuvers was the size of the mechanized units. Embick recommended that the mechanized brigades be expanded into divisions, which they were; but he also supported the retention of the horse for reconnaissance operations as the Army's horse units continued their motorization and mechanization. So the Cavalry Branch still had its horses and continued to advance the horse-mechanized concept, thus retaining a role for the horse, even if the role concentrated on reconnaissance. Meanwhile the Army chief of staff required Cavalry Branch to develop an entirely new concept—organic divisional cavalry troops—to support each of the new triangular infantry divisions. This presented a further problem for the cavalry regiments, as they were also tasked with

---

139 Christopher R. Gabel; *The 1940 Maneuvers: Prelude to Mobilization:* Published by the Center of Military History-United States Army-Washington, D. C. 1991 (Page 10)

coordinating with the smaller reconnaissance units operating to their rear.[140]

The horse-mechanized regiment consisted of a headquarters and headquarters troop, a horse squadron portee of three rifle troops (each troop consisted of three rifle platoons and a light-machine gun platoon), and a mechanized squadron consisting of two scout car troops and a motorcycle troop. The regiment totaled 61 officers and 1,088 men.

Figure 4-4. Typical horse portee. *ERVIN ADEN*

In the spring of 1941, the 115th Cavalry Regiment (Horse-Mechanized) of the Wyoming National Guard was called into active service and joined the 9th Army Corps. The 115th Cavalry was split into three separate units on 1 January 1944, and only the headquarters and headquarters troop saw combat in the European Theater. The other two units never deployed overseas, but many

---

140 Matthew Darlington Morton, "Men on Iron Ponies" (The death and rebirth of the modern U.S. Cavalry); Published by Northern University Press-2009 (Page 72)

of the officers and men were shipped to every theater of the war as replacements.

The newly "triangular" infantry divisions with increased motor mobility made it almost impossible for the horse to keep up, even with compromise combinations. Worse, Cavalry Branch lost control of its own future. The chief of cavalry, General John Kerr, wanted full divisions and corps of horse-mounted warriors; the chief of staff wanted nothing more than bodies for his army, and mechanized bodies at that. The cavalry had missed its chance to do something important in World War I . . . and it looked as if it would miss again in the next.[141]

Following the 1940 maneuvers, certain officers' concern for the preservation of precious mechanized assets continued to persist. The commander of the 6th Cavalry Regiment (Horse-Mechanized) summed up the dilemma succinctly when he asked the rhetorical question: "Is it important enough to use this asset today in combat, knowing it may prevent me from doing reconnaissance in the future?" An observer of the Army's other regular horse-mechanized regiment, the 4th Cavalry, concluded with the same thought, remarking, "Corps reconnaissance regiments as now organized should be used primarily for reconnaissance and should be employed in combat when such employment is unavoidable."

Observers and participants in the horse-mechanized experiments suggested changes in equipment and organization, but their offerings were inconsistent with the doctrinal definition of how they saw the corps reconnaissance agency acting. The suggestions made it obvious that horses were not at the forefront of the commanders' minds as their staffs assembled "wish lists" for future organization and equipment.[142]

Horse-mechanized regiments still lacked organic vehicles to escort them safely while they moved behind the mechanized squadron with all of their horses and soldiers loaded on trucks.

---

141 ibid (Page 72)
142 ibid (Page 74)

One solution was to attach scout cars from the mechanized squadron, but this reduced the number of reconnaissance assets the regiment could use to cover the corps' advance. Another option was to increase the number of scout cars in the regiment so that the horse squadron could receive its own. Additional cars would improve the deficient communication assets in the horse squadron. More horse trailers—another solution offered—were large and heavy when loaded and thus also posed a problem. The 113th Cavalry Regiment (Horse-Mechanized), an Iowa National Guard unit, detailed its pioneer and demolitions platoon to the horse squadron to inspect and repair bridges along the routes the trailers had to cross.

There was also a call for increased firepower, because commanders wanted more 37 mm anti-tank guns mounted directly on the scout cars.[143] An article written in August 1940 by Colonel Guy W. Chipman, senior instructor at the Illinois National Guard, supported this view. Chipman suggested that all National Guard cavalry units be equipped with a scout car similar to the latest models then being furnished to the 23d Reconnaissance Squadron. Those cars had six wheels with six-wheel drive and could go practically anywhere that tanks or tracked vehicles could go. In some cases the scout cars were more suitable, faster, and much more noiseless than tanks.

Chipman suggested that the scout cars have more powerful engines in order to carry thicker armor to protect personnel and equipment from recently developed anti-tank weapons. He further stated that the scout cars corresponded closely to the horse in performing the fundamental missions of cavalry. Like the horse, the scout cars had great mobility, transported cavalrymen, carried a great volume of firepower, and were capable of shock action if suitably armed and equipped. When required, the scout cars could be supported by tanks and other weapons from higher

---

143 ibid (Page 74)

headquarters, especially when engaged in offensive action in close cooperation with the main forces.[144]

While tanks or combat cars would normally be part of the armored forces of the Regular Army, Chipman concluded that due to the great amount of time and care necessary for the maintenance of the tanks and the time required for training, the bulk of the National Guard cavalry should be composed of scout cars. He suggested that the scout car be equipped with weapons suitable for firing from the cars or capable of being quickly dismounted for firing from the ground. In addition to the normal number of .30 caliber machine guns, the scout cars' anti-mechanized and anti-aircraft weapons should be of larger caliber than what was currently available. Chipman said that there should be considerable artillery mounted on self-propelled mounts and that those guns should be capable—in addition to performing normal artillery missions—of firing against aircraft or mechanized units. Chipman estimated that the annual cost of maintenance of a mechanized regiment would be approximately $26,000 less than that of a horse regiment.[145]

Other officers echoed Chipman's recommendations for higher-powered weaponry. Lieutenant Colonel Charles R. Johnson, Jr., commander of the 106th Cavalry Regiment (Horse-Mechanized) of the Illinois National Guard, even suggested that anti-tank platoons adopt the 75 mm pack howitzer. Commanders of other units called for the inclusion of mortars to strike against enemy anti-tank gun positions and machine gun nests.

With this clamor for additional firepower, only one commander requested fewer scout cars in the reconnaissance platoons. Lieutenant Colonel Johnson, Jr., commander of the 106th Cavalry Regiment (Horse-Mechanized), requested more jeeps, which could "peak and sneak" with greater ability. In an act of sacrilege

---

[144] Colonel Guy W. Chipman, Senior Instructor, Illinois National Guard; *Mechanization of National Guard Cavalry:* Published by Illinois Guardsman, State of Illinois-Governor Henry Horner-Volume 7 (Page 21)
[145] ibid (Page 30-31)

at the end of the 1941 maneuvers, Johnson did *not* recommend the retention of the horse squadron. After acknowledging the special attributes horses brought to reconnaissance, all Johnson wanted was another mechanized squadron. He was not alone in this view.[146]

COMMAND AND CONTROL

Throughout the history of the horse-mechanized regiments, a lack of radios hampered the units' performance. As with the lack of escorts for trailer trucks, the horse squadrons continued to borrow scout cars from the mechanized squadron, just as the horse regiments had done in the past. This improved command and control among the horse troops and allowed them to provide the corps with timely information.

Figure 4-5. Horse-Mounted radio set, 1940 Louisiana maneuvers.
CAMP BEAUREGARD COLLECTION

---

146 Matthew Darlington Morton, "Men on Iron Ponies" (The death and rebirth of the modern U.S. Cavalry); Published by Northern University Press-2009 (Page 74)

The 106th Cavalry Regiment filed their reports directly with the corps headquarters regimental liaison officer using field telephones tapped into the existing phone system. This was a creative improvisation, but not one that held real promise in the undeveloped corners of the world in which the horse cavalry was staking its future. Horse-mechanized units' after-action reviews considered motorcycle dispatch as a temporary solution to the existing communication weaknesses inherent in the units' design. But what the units really needed was more and better radios and a corresponding increase in the number of radio mechanics.[147]

Another command and control issue arose out of the conversion of the 6th Cavalry Regiment from an all-horse unit to a horse-mechanized unit. As the regiment added new troops (many of the citizen-soldier variety), the commander, Colonel John Millikin, redistributed his personnel evenly throughout the regiment, which allowed for some degree of experience at every level. With this reorganization in place, Millikin took his regiment through the 1940 maneuvers. Afterward he believed that the mechanized half of his regiment had performed better. According to Millikin, this showed that, given the composition of the nation's youth, "we (the Army) may expect to develop soldiers for mechanized and motorized elements much quicker."

Millikin also commented that the noncommissioned officer (NCO) leadership in the horse units had been good, but that those NCOs were not performing as well as their counterparts in the mechanized units. Millikin hoped to rectify the problem by increasing the number of officers assigned to the mechanized portion of his squadron.

Despite the shortcomings of the horse-mechanized unit, the troopers—whose increased numbers were forced to embrace the concept of mechanized ground reconnaissance—proved more

---

147 ibid (Page 75)

than capable of developing their own techniques, tactics, and equipment.[148]

POOR RESOURCES, WORSE RESULTS

News reports emanating from Camp Beauregard and other encampments during the National Guard's August 1940 maneuvers clearly demonstrated an overall lack of military preparedness. Since the poorly executed maneuvers occurred just three months after the German blitzkrieg overran France, any American who believed his nation to be militarily secure got a rude awakening.

However, few of the deficiencies exhibited in the August maneuvers were truly the fault of the National Guard. However inadequate the maneuvers may have been from a military perspective, it is clear that these exercises were of enormous political significance.

On 15 August 1940, Third Army's forces began moving to assembly areas for the corps-vs.-corps maneuvers. The news media descended on the Guard encampments—147 reporters at First Army's encampment alone!—to provide extensive coverage to the public. Any American who picked up a newspaper, read a magazine, or watched a newsreel at the movies could see the nation's low level of military readiness. Virtually every type of military equipment used in the maneuvers was obsolete or scarce or both. Guardsmen reported to their encampments with World War I tents, webbing, shoes, and blankets in various stages of decay. Images of soldiers dressed in World War I uniforms, which looked tattered and torn even before the maneuvers began, did not add to the public's level of confidence in its Reserve units or that of the standing Army.

The public lost even more confidence when the media released pictures of infantrymen carrying 1903 Springfield rifles, which

---

148 ibid (Page 75)

had but 10 rounds of blank ammunition per rifle per day, and artillerymen pushing and dragging antiquated 37 mm and 75 mm field pieces in the absence of adequate motor transport. The most striking image of all was a photograph that appeared in *Newsweek* showing a civilian delivery truck with the word TANK painted on the side, Springfield rifles labeled .50 CALIBER MACHINE GUN, and simulated anti-tank guns constructed of drainpipe. Civilian vehicles of all types substituted for military motorized transport.[149]

FINALLY, SELECTIVE SERVICE

Political repercussions came swiftly. President Roosevelt's support for the Selective Service had been rather lukewarm, but he returned from a visit to the New York maneuvers prepared to argue forcefully for a strong conscription bill. On 27 August 1940, he signed a resolution of Congress that authorized the federalization of some 300,000 Guardsmen and Reservists for 12 months of intensive training. Finally, on 16 September 1940, Congress passed a Selective Service bill providing for the conscription of 900,000 men for a one-year term.

Thus the sunburned, chigger-ridden Guardsmen who stumbled through the forests of Louisiana clicking empty rifles at each other during the August maneuvers helped win one of the most important battles of World War II: the struggle for pre-war mobilization of the U.S. Army. Roosevelt's signing of the Selective Training and Service Act began the first peacetime draft in the United States. It also established the Selective Service System as an independent agency responsible for identifying and inducting young men into military service.[150]

On 31 July 1940, Brigadier General L. V. Regan, the adjutant

---

149 Christopher R Gabel; *The U.S. Army GHQ Maneuvers of 1941:* Published by U.S. Government Printing Office, Washington, D.C., 1991 (Page 13-14)
150 ibid (Page 14)

general of Illinois, wrote a letter to the chief of the National Guard Bureau. Regan requested permission to convert the Illinois units of the 106th Cavalry and the 23d Reconnaissance Squadron into a reconnaissance cavalry regiment. At the time of the request the units were stationed as follows:

> Headquarters Troop and Machine Gun Troop, Urbana
> Troops E and F (Second Squadron), Chicago
> 23d Reconnaissance Squadron, Springfield

Regan further suggested that if such a conversion were authorized, the troops should be stationed as follows:

> Convert Machine Gun Troop into Rifle Troop thereby completing Horsed Squadron with station at Urbana—
> Motorcycle Troop (new) with station at Urbana—
> Service Troop (new) with station at Chicago—
> Headquarters Troop to remain at Urbana and Mechanized Squadron at Springfield—

Regan also requested that the conversion be made effective 1 September 1940, upon return of the units from Second Army maneuvers. Regan made his recommendations in the belief that they were in the best interest of the national defense, since approval would give Illinois an entire regiment. He noted that the experience with units split between states had not been satisfactory from a training and administrative standpoint. In closing, Regan mentioned that Colonel Kenneth Buchanan was presently on duty with the National Guard Bureau and was the colonel of the 106th Cavalry, which was currently divided between Illinois and Michigan.[151]

---

[151] Brigadier General L. V. Regan, The Adjutant General of Illinois; Letter dated 31 July 194 to Chief of the National Guard Bureau regarding conversion of 106th Cavalry with 23d Reconnaissance Squadron

Figure 4-6. August-September 1940 issue of *Illinois Guardsman*, about the maneuvers.

NATIONAL GUARD PARTICIPATION IN AUGUST 1940 MANEUVERS

Several letters of correspondence followed between Major L.S. Smith, Headquarters 6th Corps Area, Chicago; Brigadier General L. V. Regan, the adjutant general of Illinois; and Major A. V. Winton, representing the chief of the National Guard Bureau. The discussion ended with a letter from the chief of the National Guard Bureau, directing the conversion of cavalry units with an effective date of 10 September 1940. The final letter also authorized the adjutant general of Illinois to effect the following changes in the Illinois National Guard:

Organize:

Troop C, 106th Cavalry (H-Mecz), under Table of Organization 2-17 NG, approved 31 May 1940—

Troop F, 106th Cavalry (H-Mecz), under Table of Organization 2-47 NG.

Re-designate:As:

Machine Gun Troop, 106th Cavalry Service Troop, 106th Cavalry (H-Mecz)

Troop E, 106th Cavalry Troop A, 106th Cavalry (H-Mecz)

Troop F, 106th Cavalry Troop B, 106th Cavalry (H-Mecz)

Troop A, 23d Recon Squadron Troop D, 106th Cavalry (H-Mecz)

Troop B, 23d Recon Squadron Troop E, 106th Cavalry (H-Mecz)

On the next page is a copy of the official letter from Illinois National Guard files that documents the above reorganization of the 106th Cavalry and the 23d Reconnaissance Squadron into a regiment with the designation of the 106th Cavalry (Horse-Mech) Regiment, effective 1 September 1940.

On 1 September 1940, the 106th Cavalry was reorganized with Colonel Kenneth Buchanan assuming command after being relieved from assignment to the 23d Cavalry Division. The 1st Squadron in Michigan became the 1st Battalion, 177th Field Artillery; and the 3d Squadron, also in Michigan, became the 2d Battalion, 210th Coast Artillery (Anti-Aircraft). The 2d Squadron in Illinois was redesignated as 1st Squadron (Horse), and the 23d Reconnaissance Squadron became the 2d Squadron (Mechanized).

Figure 4-7. Colonel Kenneth Buchanan, commanding officer of the 106th Cavalry. Photo from the 23d Cavalry Album.

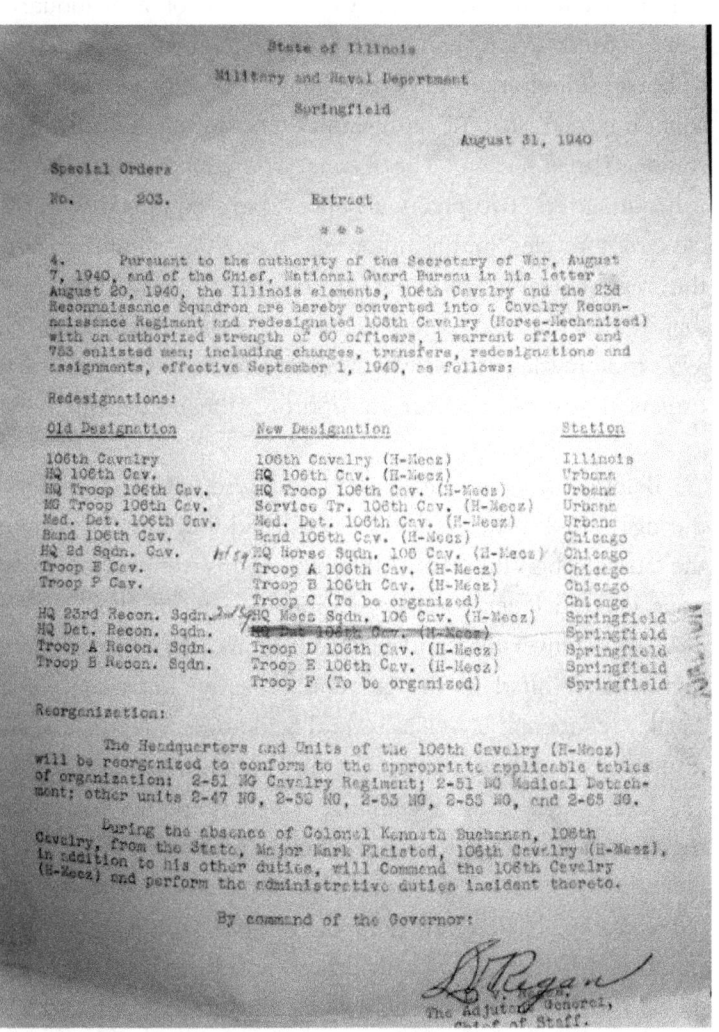

Figure 4-8. Letter redesignating 1st Sqd & 23d Sqd into the 106th Cavalry (Horse Mech), 1 September 1940. *NATIONAL ARCHIVES*

Pursuant to the above correspondence, the newly organized regiment was redesignated as the 106th Cavalry (H-Mecz). The newly formed regiment was composed of a headquarters, headquarters troop, band, medical detachment, service troop, a horse squadron, and a mechanized squadron. The horse squadron consisted of a headquarters and three rifle troops stationed in Chicago. The mechanized squadron consisted of a headquarters, two reconnaissance troops equipped with scout cars, motorcycles, and a motorcycle troop. At full authorization, the regiment was allocated 70 officers, one warrant officer (band leader), 1,520 enlisted men, 574 horses, 8 scout cars, 177 motorcycles, forty-five 2½-ton trucks, and 77 tractor-trailers (horse portees) for transporting the horses on roads.[152]

Before any of its units were inducted into federal service during 1940-41, the National Guard had four cavalry divisions, the 21st through the 24th. All four divisions were disbanded and none entered federal service, although many of their elements did. Also, conversions and reorganizations of 17 Guard cavalry regiments resulted in the creation of seven horse-mechanized cavalry regiments, as well as several field artillery regiments, coast artillery regiments and battalions, and an anti-tank battalion.

Thus, after the reshuffling, seven partially mechanized regiments and a brigade with two horse cavalry regiments entered federal service. The horse-mechanized regiments were the 101st (New York), 102d (New Jersey), 104th (Pennsylvania), 106th (Illinois), 107th (Ohio), 113th (Iowa), and the 115th (Wyoming). The horse brigade was the 56th, consisting of the 112th and 124th Cavalry (both from Texas).

While in federal service, all of the horse-mechanized regiments were completely mechanized and split into groups. Each group consisted of two separate but identical squadrons, similar on

---

[152] William H. Collier, *The 106th Cavalry's Story:* Published by Trafford Publishing - 2012 (Page 13)

structure to those of the Regular Army. The horse regiments (the 112th and 124th) were dismounted, withdrawn from the 56th Cavalry Brigade, and reorganized as infantry with much the same composition as regiments of the 1st Cavalry Division.[153]

The National Guard Mobilization Act of 1940 authorized the President to activate Guard units and incorporate them into the regular U.S. Army. The Illinois 106th Cavalry Regiment was inducted into federal service during 25 and 26 November 1940, with headquarters and service troops located in Urbana, 1st Squadron (Horse) in Chicago, and 2d Squadron (Mechanized) in Springfield. While housed at the Illinois state fairgrounds in Springfield, the 431 men and officers of the 2d Squadron received medical examinations, were administered the federal oath, and signed enlistment papers.[154]

Figure 4-9. The Chicago Black Horse Troop and Mounted Band of the 106th Cavalry on parade in Chicago.
ILLINOIS NATIONAL GUARD MUSEUM

---

153 John B. Wilson; Army Lineage Series-Maneuver and Firepower (The Evolution of Divisions and Separate Brigades): Published by the United States Army Center of Military History, Washington, D. C., 1998 (Page 153)

154 Mark S. Plaisted, *Document 50; Letter Concerning the Mobilization of the Illinois National Guard* (ca. November 13, 1940)

Among the various units mustered into service during November 1940 was the 106th Cavalry Regimental Band. Recognized by the War Department with the support of General Summerall and unofficially designated the Chicago Black Horse Troop and Mounted Band, the unit was one of few mounted bands in military service. Headquarters Troop, 106th Cavalry, had received federal recognition on 27 April 1929 and the Mounted Band as early as 12 June 1929. Units were "to be given a character

Figure 4-10. Chicago Black Horse Troop 1929-1940. *Wikipedia*

as distinctive as to constitute one of the outstanding attractions of the city and be representative of the civic achievements of Chicago."

To fully equip a troop and band of this character, approximately 100 matched black horses were required. Unfortunately the federal government was authorized to support a peacetime strength of only 42 horses. To secure the additional mounts, special uniforms, and overhead for care and maintenance, prominent citizens of Chicago underwrote the units in the amount of $100,000.

Maintaining these organizations required an additional $9,000 annually. This support was achieved by soliciting prominent businessmen who were interested in fine horsemanship. Leonard A. Busby, Britton I. Budd, Frederick H. Rawson, Frank O. Wetmore, and other well-to-do Chicagoans undertook the task of raising the funds by private subscription. A corporation, the Chicago Black Horse Troop Association, was organized, with the authority "to assist and promote the organization, maintenance and welfare of the Chicago Black Horse Troop and Mounted Band, including the raising of funds to aid such purpose." Black Horse Troop members turned over their drill pay to the Association, and military exhibitions and polo matches also provided extra funds. The Chicago City Council designated the Black Horse Troop as the official military escort for distinguished visitors to Chicago.[155]

The distinctive uniform worn by the troopers was selected by a committee composed of Mrs. John Alden Carpenter, Mrs. Leonard A. Busby, Mrs. Chauncey Keehn, Britton I. Budd, John T. Knight, Jr., Robert M. Lee, Albert Cook and Eames MacVeagh. The committee arrived at a final decision following a series of compromises. Company member Mr. Hugh Charles Mcbarron, Jr., presented several designs to the committee before it settled on a uniform patterned after that of the United States Dragoons of

---

[155] Jess Krueger; (Origin-Troops E and F and Band, 106th Cavalry Regiment, Chicago Black Horse Squadron and Mounted Band): Published by The Chicago Black Horse Troop Association-1945 (Page 7)

the War of 1812. The dragoons were stationed at Fort Dearborn, Illinois, before and at the time of the Fort Dearborn massacre. The tall plume on the captain's shako seems to have been an addition to the original uniform design, as were the officer's epaulettes as the sole designation of rank. The change made for an impressive appearance in a 1932 photograph taken of the unit. The troop was redesignated as Troop E in 1935, and Troop A in 1940.[156]

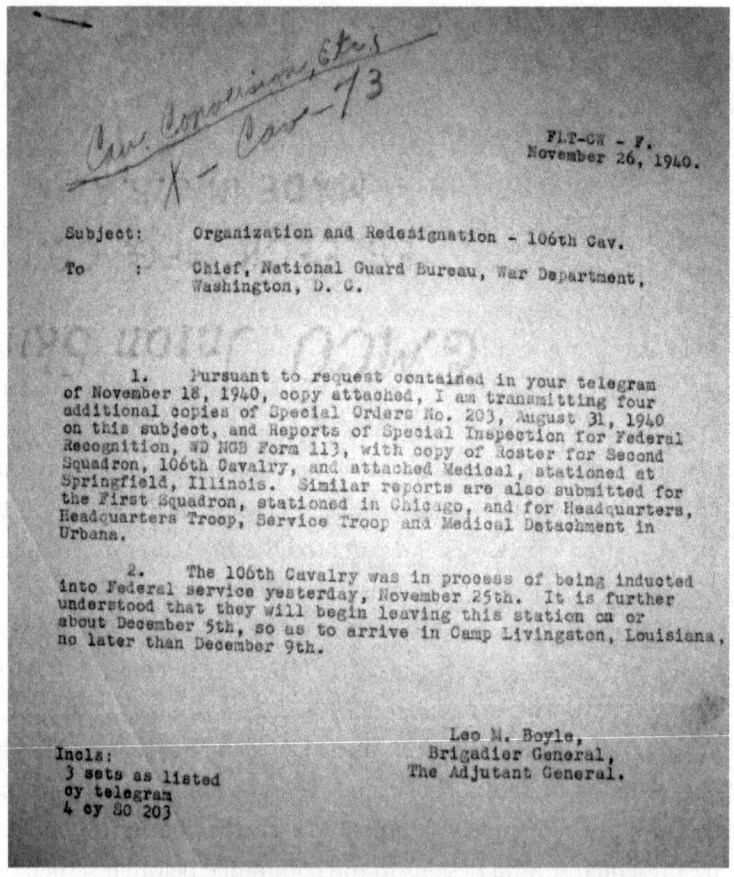

Figure 4-11. Letter of redesignation and organiaation, 106th Cavalry. *National Archives*

---

156 ibid (Page 7)

The balance of the 106th Cavalry Regiment's 1,200 men was headquartered at Chicago and Urbana, where they were inducted in November 1940. At this time Colonel Buchanan left the regiment for an assignment with the War Department in Washington, D.C. Lieutenant Colonel Charles Radcliffe Johnson, Jr., the regiment's Regular Army instructor, became the unit's new commanding officer. He remained with the regiment until 1 February 1942, when he was promoted to colonel and assigned as military attaché to Morocco and Algeria.

The 106th was a horse-mechanized cavalry regiment equipped with armored scout cars, motorcycles, and transport trucks. Once formed up, they proceeded in convoy fashion to Camp Beauregard in central Louisiana, where they were to receive a year of intensive training.[157]

The 106th Cavalry Regiment received its movement orders in the following format:

Field Order Number 1
9 December 1940

Pursuant to directions contained in letters, Headquarters 6th Corps Area dated 14 & 22 November 1940, this regiment moves by rail and marching, starting 13 December 1940, to Camp Beauregard, Louisiana for permanent station.

MASTER MOVEMENT TABLES

Units   *Travel Departure*

Hq; Hq Tr (less det)
Tr D (less det); Tr E (less det)   Road 17 Dec 1940

---

[157] Mark S. Plaisted, *Document 50; Letter Concerning the Mobilization of the Illinois National Guard* (ca. November 13, 1940)

Attached drivers of private cars
And attached riders of private mtcls (Motorcycles)

Service Tr, with attached
Surplus from HQ TR   Rail 16 Dec 1940

Tr F with attached
Surplus from 2d Sq   Rail 16 Dec 1940

1st Squadron   Rail 16 Dec 1940

The Commanding Officer, 1st Squadron, will cause furloughs to be applied for in the case of enlisted men of his command desiring to drive privately owned automobiles to Louisiana. These men need not be held with the unit pending regimental approval of the furloughs, but will be permitted to leave at the proper time. In no case will they arrive at Camp Beauregard prior to noon, 16 December 1940, and departure from Chicago, based on three days travel, will be timed accordingly. Men may be furloughed two men per car.

The Commanding Officer, 1st Squadron, will permit such men as may desire to ride their private motorcycles to leave Chicago at their own expense at such time as to place them at Urbana, Illinois, prior to 9:00 p.m., 11 December 1940. These men will bring with them on their machines all field equipment needed for the trip south. They will be prepared to perform full duty with the column as cyclists.

Such enlisted men in the Urbana and Springfield commands as may desire to drive their private vehicles to Louisiana, will, provided the vehicles are approved by the organization commanders concerned, be formed in convoy to follow their columns.

Each owner of any vehicle accompanying the column will sign an appropriate release to the United States and to the column commanders, and will state there-on that he realizes that the United States will bear no expense whatsoever incident to the transportation of his vehicle.

All officers will travel with their commands. They may detail enlisted men who volunteer for the duty to drive their cars for them.

For organizations travelling by road, organizational equipment will be limited to the necessary kitchen and maintenance material. Vehicle weapons mounted.

Headquarters Troop and the 2d Squadron (less its motorcycle troop) left their home stations on 12 December 1940 and road-marched to Camp Livingston (originally called Camp Tioga), Louisiana, stopping en route at armories in Illinois, Arkansas, and Mississippi. The weather failed to cooperate. It rained almost continuously during the trip, but there were neither accidents nor incidents to mar the journey.

Cecil R. (Mick) Maguire recalled the long days of the march:

> When we left Urbana, we had all our old National Guard equipment: Dodge 4x4, 1½-ton trucks, T-13 scout cars, a couple of Indian Chief motorcycles with sidecars, and a few Chevy "paddy wagons." The C.O. had a Dodge 4x4 command car, which we called a "Jeep." The "Jeeps" we know now were still being sorted out then.
>
> Anyone who wanted to could bring his own transportation, and did. Fred Gourley brought his 1940

Harley 61 OHV motorcycle on which he rode herd on the convoy. I bet he covered 1,500 miles going from Urbana to Camp Livingston.

We had old-style steel helmets (like Limeys and U.S. 1918), blue denim "fatigue" uniforms. The government was really hustling to expand and modernize the whole army.

We had with us an old portable field kitchen that the mess sergeant had installed in the bed of a 1½-ton 4x4 Dodge truck. We had fresh food for several days packed in ice in another 4x4. The plan was to prepare breakfast with the troop stationary before each daily move, wash pots and pans upon departure, and cook lunch on the move. We were to stop and have lunch. In the afternoon leg, we were to again clean up and start the evening meal.

In actual practice, however, on day one we had a successful breakfast and a so-so lunch (cold sandwiches and hot coffee). When we arrived at the supper stop, the First Cook had a bad burn on his arm. One of the KPs ["kitchen police," part of the kitchen staff] was telling all hands that, having gone through a rain squall earlier in the day, the steel floor in the truck had become quite slippery. Everyone aboard had to work with one hand and hang on to the top bows with the other. When we went through a detour somewhere in Arkansas, the truck went through a series of bumps, causing the First Cook to lose his footing, burn his arm, and drop a huge pan of potatoes. With admirable composure the cook scooped up the 'taters and dumped them back in the pan. This was bravely done before having his burn treated.

Our first overnight stop and snooze was in the Blytheville, Arkansas, National Guard Armory. In Blytheville, HQ Troop descended on the locals like a pack of wolves, swarming up and down the main street, trying to pick up all the girls and women, captivated by southern accents. And such a short distance from Illinois!

We had a 12:00 midnight curfew, and two of our HQ troop sergeants got into a fistfight in a honky-tonk when each was trying to pick up the same girl. Captain Flewelling (a WWI veteran with two sons in HQ troop) had to go to the *po' leece* (southern accent) department to talk the local cops out of detaining the sergeants. There was some damage to the bar, and the rumor was that our troop fund was considerably smaller thereafter.

The next day was an attempt to repeat the operations of the first, but without using the field stoves or other heat sources while in motion.

The second day we continued south in more rain. When we arrived in Vicksburg, Mississippi, we went into bivouac in a city park and pitched pup tents. We pulled our vehicles into the park over soggy ground and a recently grown expanse of grass. We spent a soggy night in the pup tents and, after chow in the morning, struck camp and prepared to move out.

One of our many debacles ensued. One of the loaded supply trucks got stuck in the mud up to the axles. No problem! We hooked another 4x4 onto the first with a tow chain and promptly had *two* buried trucks. Then we put the tire chains on two scout cars (T-13s with Ford V8 engines and Marmon-Harrington front axles) and added these by tow cable to the train. We tested this combination gingerly.

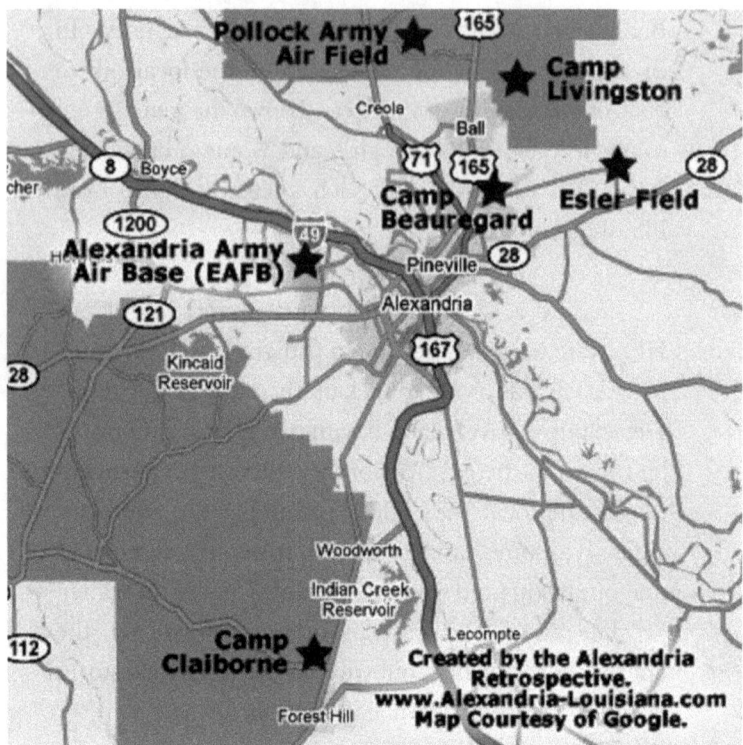

Figure 4-12. Military camps in central Louisiana.
GOOGLE MAP CREATED BY THE ALEXANDRIA RETROSPECTIVE

This trial moved the whole outfit about two truck lengths, slowly, and deepened all the ruts about six inches quickly. We stopped again and all the officers and sergeants had a powwow. Finally a workable plan was hatched. The paved part of the park road was not too far away and almost aligned with the stuck vehicles. We hooked another scout car to the group with a double length of cable, and hitched another T-13 and two trucks on by means of a really, really long group of chains and cables. This meant that one scout car and two trucks were on dry pavement.

We wound up all the engines and engaged clutches on signal. This ugly caravan slowly crept up onto the asphalt, throwing mud and grass everywhere. What a mess we made! I've been told that, in those days, officers running convoys and other military operations always had papers with them that would enable civilians to file claims against the Army. I assume that something

Figure 4-13. Photograph of Camp Livingston, Louisiana, 1940.
JOHN BECK

like this must have taken place, because our troop fund couldn't handle damage of that magnitude.

That morning we got back on the road again and, with mud-caked wheels and a motley assortment of civilian cars following, continued on. We went south of Vicksburg, turned west, and crossed the Mississippi at Natchez. We worked our way southwesterly past Lake Catahoula and into camp. What would soon become known as Camp Livingston was still unfinished at that time!¹⁵⁸

Half a century later, in 1995, reporter Paul Wood of the Chicago *News-Gazette* attended the 50th Reunion of the 106th Cavalry Regiment. The reporter talked to the veterans about their induction into federal service, early training, and participation in the Louisiana Maneuvers.

By PAUL WOOD
News-Gazette Staff Writer

The Cavalry—It called up images of proud horses, bright spurs, flashing sabres and flocks of Betty Grable babes in 1940, when Urbana National Guard enlistees were called up as well to join in a one-year "emergency" force. The emergency was Adolf Hitler, though it would be a Japanese force that would bring the United States into World War II a year later and would extend the one-year call-up into five years, including combat in Europe.

After boot camp, Champaign's Jim Mitsdarffer didn't see much of the horses he had been promised. "I probably did eat horse meat, though," he says, in cafeterias and in K-rations. At least one base announced that's where its horses were headed.

This Weekend—About 90 veterans and 60 family members are in Champaign for the 50th reunion of the 106th. Both the romantic early days, and the hard-fought ending of the war, are distant memories. "This was supposed to be a romantic war; now it's a rheumatic one," says Urbana's George Floyd.

---

158 Cecil R. (Mick) Maguire; Orange Socks and Saddle Shoes: Unfinished manuscript as of 06-10-2010

NATIONAL GUARD PARTICIPATION IN AUGUST 1940 MANEUVERS

It wasn't even supposed to be a war. In 1940, many of the men were members of the state's National Guard. As Hitler moved into Czechoslovakia, Poland and Austria, American politicians worried that the United States would be unprepared if it had to enter battle.

The 106th became the first officially designated Cavalry unit for war in Europe, though its men were not told that at the time. "They said we were inducted for a year," says Fred Gourley of Champaign, who also remembers an Andrews Sisters hit of the day: "Goodbye Dear, I'll be Back in a Year."

Friends chatted casually and swapped cigarettes as they were inducted at the Urbana Armory, as Floyd remembers the November day. On Dec. 16, they joined a convoy for Louisiana's Camp Livingston and Cavalry training. It was still a casual, if long trip. Gourley even drove his own motorcycle on the four-day trip, stopping at Cairo—then sin city—en route to the Clarkdale, La., mud where they'd build the camp they trained in. "There was a camp there, but it was mostly mud," Champaign's Chuck Flewelling recalls. "We had our work cut out for us." Gourley remembers stepping carefully on planks to keep out of the mud. It didn't work.

Weapons were hard to come by. Recruits were supposed to learn to use anti-tank guns, but the parts weren't in, so with makeshift adapters they fired small .22 rifles mounted inside the guns. "They popped off like a popcorn fart," Floyd recalls. "It wasn't like the real thing."

Death was real enough. A quiet Sadorus 17-year old named Ralph Fogel signed up for the 106th to build his confidence and become a man. He never grew any older, though; in training at the camp, a half-track flipped over top of him. Mitsdarffer remembers helping to pull it off him with a winch. Mr. Fogel's tombstone in Craw Cemetery just north of Sadorus bears the cavalry's crossed sabres. "Most of us had gone to high school together," Flewelling says. "I'd known Ralph, he was a solitary youth, and it made the emergency a lot more real when he died."

Before the war was over many in the 106th had gone beyond theory in finding war was hell. Mitsdarffer, a University of Illinois sophomore in 1940, had signed up for the National Guard to avoid being drafted into the Regular Army. After his Guard unit was absorbed into the 106th he would end the war In a German POW camp. A friend of Floyd's, a minor league baseball player, enlisted to get his military service out of the way before he hit the big leagues. His legs were shattered in the war.

As for service on horseback, the dream had an abrupt, early ending. "The British had decided battle on horseback was (obsolete) after World War I," recalls Flewelling, whose father was a career military officer. "We had to catch up with the British. We still thought horses could do it as the war was about to begin."

"Some of us were pretty good horsemen and you bet we were disappointed that we didn't get to use them."

Floyd had a hard time in Panama, where units were transferred before shipping out to the Pacific or Europe. Though it would be years before most of the 106th would see any combat, they had support and building work to do. "I would have given anything for a horse, or a mule in the Pacific, as the men dropped in the heat. There is a lot to be said for horsepower in getting physical labor done."

Figure 4-14. (Left to right) Ervin Aden, John J. Cour, Fred A. Twyman, Fred E. Fitch. Camp Livingston, 1940. *ERVIN ADEN*

Ervin Aden joined the 106th Cavalry Regiment, D Troop, in September 1940. He told the following story about his early days with the 106th Cavalry and their arrival at Camp Livingston, Louisiana:

> Jack Rosseter, a scout for the Cincinnati Reds professional baseball organization, picked me up in Springfield, Illinois, where I was playing sandlot ball for a goodwill tour throughout Central America. There were minor and major league all-stars chosen to play from February until mid-April 1940. Rosseter offered me a contract with the Reds after their tour.
> The men in Central America were playing nine months out of the year and were in excellent shape—

Figure 4-15. General Marshall with officers of the Illinois National Guard at Camp Beauregard, Louisiana, 1940.
CAMP BEAUREGARD COLLECTION

so much so that our players were losing and no one was hitting. In the third game in Mexico City I pinched hit and got a triple. Jack Rosseter was so excited, I became leadoff hitter from then on.

Plans were made then that we would be going to Argentina in November 1940 for another all-star group to which I was assigned. However, Argentina was leaning toward the Germans during the early part of the war, and it was too risky to take us down there. Jack advised me to join the Illinois National Guard to get my one-year service time over with (per the new Conscription Bill), and return to play with the Reds, as he said I had a great career ahead of me.

National Guard Participation in August 1940 Maneuvers

I joined up in September 1940 in Springfield, Illinois, and was assigned to D Troop, 106th Cavalry Regiment, with Captain Greenup in command. Grigsby was the 1st Sergeant.

Shortly thereafter we left for Camp Livingston, Louisiana. We were the first troops to be assigned to this new camp, which did not even have its roads in yet. While workmen were putting down pine trees, four inches in diameter, as a base for the streets, others were building perennial tents in which the troops were to live. They were definitely not ready for our arrival. Uniforms were issued then: World War I vintage, with leggings, along with an issued bolt-action 1903 Springfield rifle.

I rose from private to staff sergeant in a very short period of time. We had to buy our own footlockers and personal items from our enlisted pay, which left me with only a few pennies. Needless to say, I spent my first Christmas in camp, as I had no money.

Alexandria, Louisiana, was the nearest city located near Camp Livingston, and as such was overrun with military personnel from Camp Claiborne, Camp Polk, as well as Camp Livingston and Camp Beauregard on the weekends. Meant as an insult to all of us were signs posted on lawns that read Soldiers and Dogs Keep Off.

D Troop, 106th Cavalry Regiment, was tasked with the duty of providing transportation to the engineers from Camp Claiborne so they could check all bridges' capacity in preparation for the upcoming maneuvers.

We trained in various areas of simulated combat and were graded by our performance. We used scout cars, but there were other groups who had trucks with

Figure 4-16. Sergeant Grigsby. *ERVIN ADEN*

Figure 4-17. 106th Cavalry postcard at Camp Livingston.
CAMP BEAUREGARD COLLECTION

canvas over them, and printed on the canvas was TANK as we had no (or very few) tanks there as yet.

Maneuvering in the humid Louisiana weather was awful. Red bugs, coral snakes, as well as other snakes and abundant rain made life miserable, but we were being trained for any unpleasant situation in war. I was a three-striper during and after this training.[159]

Individual units of the regiment began arriving at Camp Livingston on 16 December 1940. They were soon followed by the service troop and the unequipped motorcycle troop, which had travelled by rail and arrived on 4 January 1941. First Squadron arrived the next day.

Although the regiment's camp was still under construction, the men were comfortable in their gas-heated tents. It was not until the end of April 1941 that the regiment received some of their motorcycles and portees (without tractors), as well as 300 horses from the remount station at Front Royal, Virginia.[160] (The remount stations procured and trained horses for military service.)

Cecil R. (Mick) Maguire recalled the regiment's living conditions and daily routine during the early days at Camp Livingston:

> After the tents were installed and the main streets were asphalted, the horse troops and their mounts came to camp. Some time before the horse troops arrived, I had two jobs. No. 1 was as the HQ Troop armorer under the troop supply sergeant, Bill Lorch. No. 2 was driving the mail wagon (a '38 Chevy station

---

[159] Ervin Aden; e-mail sent to Gary Palmer regarding World War II service; 26 September 2006
[160] William H. Collier, *The 106th Cavalry's Story:* Published by Trafford Publishing-March 2012 (Page 15-16)

Figure 4-18. Troopers from the 106th Cavalry (Horse-Mecz) Regiment put two of their horses through their paces in Louisiana. *EUGENE JOHNSON*

wagon) for Fred Gurley who, I think, was sergeant at that time. There was no post office in Camp Livingston then, so Fred and I drove into Alexandria, Louisiana, every morning and got back to camp about lunchtime with the mail. I felt important—a little kid like me, just out of high school, handling the mail and going in public places and public buildings carrying a loaded .45 on my hip!

We really had a small and ill-equipped army at that time. The small "Regular Army" was getting all the new equipment, and the National Guard was getting all the old stuff.

After the horse troops came in and got settled, and after the entire Springfield contingent joined us, we started functioning as a complete regiment. Then three-and-a-half to four years of growing pains began.[161]

Even though these maneuvers highlighted many shortcomings that occurred at the division, corps, and field army level, the Mechanized Cavalry Brigade and its regiments performed superbly. They demonstrated that mechanized cavalry was a decisive force when confronted on the battlefield.

No Control

To an extent the maneuvers were an exercise in the development of organizations, equipment and doctrine to further the deployment of mechanized cavalry and other mechanized units. Nevertheless, the mobilization of 1940 destroyed the illusion of the interwar years that the National Guard had partial control over its own affairs.[162]

From September 1940 until the Japanese attack on Pearl Harbor on 7 December 1941, state soldiers discovered—as they had during the 1916 border call-up and the mobilization for World War I—that once in federal service, the National Guard was wholly under the sway of the War Department. Despite promises to respect Guard unit integrity, the Army totally reorganized the state forces, breaking up the World War I-style divisions the states had maintained through the interwar years.[163]

Many Guardsmen did not understand or appreciate the geopolitical necessities that mandated a peacetime mobilization. Although Guardsmen and selectees entered federal service for one-year terms, a shortage of training facilities forced the Army

---

161 Cecil R. (Mick) Maguire; Orange Socks and Saddle Shoes: Unpublished manuscript as of 06-10-2010
162 Jerry Cooper, *The Rise of the National Guard (The Evolution of the American Militia 1865-1920);* Published by the University of Nebraska Press, Lincoln-1997 (Page 178)
163 ibid (Page 178)

to stagger the induction of National Guard divisions over a six-month period. The last Guard division reported for duty in April 1941, at which time the first divisions to report had only six months of federal duty remaining.

The day that the National Guard would begin to demobilize—15 September 1941—was General Headquarters' target date for attaining the training objective of the Protective Mobilization Plan. In September 1941, as the year of active duty rolled toward an end, Guard soldiers began to grumble. Such phrases as **OHIO** ("over the hill in October") were heard whispered amongst the troops. Fortunately, Congress acted at the last minute to extend the period of service for another six months, thereby avoiding a potential disaster.[164]

When the war scare started and a draft appeared to be imminent, Frank "Lindy" Fancher weighed his choices. If he was drafted, he was obligated to a four-year term. However, he could enlist for only one year. Fancher decided to enlist in the Army and get his military service out of the way. On 6 October 1940 he joined the Illinois National Guard, 106th Cavalry Regiment. Since Pearl Harbor was attacked on 7 December 1941, it turned out that he went to the party early but stayed late.

> As an outsider, I didn't have much chance of picking my job or of advancement. Looking at the jobs that were available, I found one with the Pioneer and Demolition Team, which for some reason no one seemed to want. It was a job in which one had to work with explosives. I found out later there had been an accident with dynamite.

---

[164] Christopher R Gabel; *The U.S. Army GHQ Maneuvers of 1941:* Published by U.S. government Printing Office, Washington, D.C. 1991 (Page 17)

National Guard Participation in August 1940 Maneuvers

The Table of Organization for this job called for a non-commissioned officer (NCO) to head the team, so there was a great chance for advancement. The job description called for the building of bridges, blowing bridges, laying and clearing mine fields, building roadblocks, installing booby traps and working with chemical warfare. To me it sounded like a good deal, although with my limited education it would require me to do a lot of studying.

As NCO I had to use and operate a lot of equipment including armored cars, Bantams (later called Jeeps), motorcycles, tanks, 6x6 trucks, rifles, machine guns, mines, and booby traps as well as radios. I also had to be proficient in radio codes, demolition, and hand-to-hand combat.

Along with all the military regulations, this was a pretty heavy load. I had to do a lot of homework while the other guys played. Failing to qualify in any of the above meant you lost your rank, so it was an incentive to work hard. Besides, with explosives, you don't get many second chances.

D Troop of the 106th Cavalry was known at that time as Second or "Down State" Squadron of the 106th Cavalry Regiment (Horse-Mechanized) of the Illinois National Guard. The 2d Squadron was mechanized in the latter part of 1939. The unit was inducted in the federal service as a horse-mechanized regiment and moved to Camp Livingston, Louisiana, in late 1940.

During the unit's stay at Camp Livingston, the regiment participated in the First Army's maneuvers in the state of Louisiana. Prior to the First Army's maneuvers, the 2d Squadron made a reconnaissance of every bridge and culvert in Louisiana and the eastern part of Texas, mapping every road and cow path.[165]

NOT READY FOR WAR

From the outset, General Headquarters' efforts to create a combat-ready Protective Mobilization Plan (PMP) encountered numerous difficulties, including the creation of a uniform, Army-wide training program where none had existed before. Training had previously been the province of the field army commanders, even when the field armies were only paper organizations. Brigadier General Lesley J. McNair, as a staff officer, had only indirect authority over the lieutenant generals who commanded the field armies.[166]

At the lower levels, unit commanders found it increasingly difficult to provide meaningful instruction for their troops. The admixture of raw selectees, half-trained Guardsmen, and seasoned Regulars made it necessary for many units to conduct basic and advanced training at the same time.

Furthermore, training facilities were swamped and equipment was scarcer than ever. In a typical case, a National Guard division received only one-quarter of the M1 rifles it needed, forcing the division's four regiments to take turns training with them. Other Guard units were stripped of whatever equipment they possessed so that the government could fulfill its lend-lease obligations.[167]

The major obstacle to training in the winter of 1940-41 was a serious shortage of officers who were qualified to train troops and command field units. Two decades of peace had left many Regular officers mentally and physically unprepared for the demands of

---

[165] Frank 'Lindy' Fancher; *WWII: Through These Eyes:* Published by Author House, 1663 Liberty Drive, Suite 200, Bloomington, Indiana 47403 – 04-26-2005 (Page vi-vii)
[166] Christopher R Gabel; *The U.S. Army GHQ Maneuvers of 1941:* Published by U.S. government Printing Office, Washington, D.C. 1991 (Page 15)
[167] ibid (Page 15)

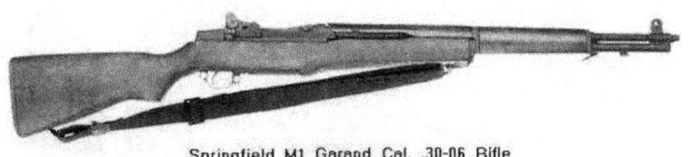

Springfield M1 Garand Cal. .30-06 Rifle

Figure 4-19. The M1 rifle was the first semiautomatic rifle to be the standard small arm of the U.S. military. "Semiautomatic" meant that the weapon required a trigger pull to fire a round but automatically chambered the next round. This not only greatly increased the rate of fire over bolt-action rifles but also made it easier to reacquire a target after each round.

The M1 Garand is gas operated, self-loading shoulder fired weapon weighing 8.94 pounds when unloaded, with an overall length of 43 inches. The barrel length is 22.30 inches. It is a full-blown combat rifle with a maximum range of 3,200 meters and maximum effective range of 400 meters (the greatest distance at which the weapon can be expected to fire accurately to inflict casualties or damage).

Fully loaded with an eight-round en bloc clip, cleaning kit in butt stock, sling, and with stock of dense G.I. issue wood, the M1 weighed in at 11-1/4 pounds. The M1 came into production in 1936 using the .30-06 rifle cartridge.

mobilization. Promotions in the Army officer corps operated on the seniority system. The promotion list was hopelessly clogged with some 4,200 World War I era officers, most of whom were still captains and majors. Inept officers had little trouble retaining their rank, and talented young men had no means of advancing.

In June 1940, Congress approved a War Department plan to automatically promote Regular officers according to a schedule based on their time in service. This measure shoved the Army's majors forward in rank, en masse, while they were still young enough to be useful as lieutenant colonels.

In October, Congress authorized the granting of temporary promotions to and within its group of general officers—a policy normally reserved for wartime. Finally, in 1941, the War Department inaugurated a removal procedure under which

Figure 4-20. 1st Lieutenant Kenneth M. Mountz of the 106th Cavalry Regiment at Camp Livingston, 1940. ERVIN ADEN

officers who had served honorably but who had outlived their usefulness could be retired quickly, regardless of age.[168]

National Guard officers, though partially trained in peacetime, as a group fell short of the Army's expectations. At the conclusion of the 1940 summer encampment, the National Guard Bureau estimated that 20 percent of staff and division officers were unqualified for their positions, in part because fewer than one-third of the National Guard officers inducted during 1940 and 1941 had completed an Army course in leadership.

However, National Guard officers who failed to meet the demands of active duty could be, and were, removed by the Guard's own review system. This necessitated the appointment of Regular officers to some of the vacancies in National Guard units,

---

168 ibid (Page 16)

causing friction and further reducing the Regular Army's officer pool.

That the officer shortage did not lead to the complete collapse of mobilization and training was due to the 106,000 Reserve officers who were eligible for call-up. By the end of 1940, these graduates of Reserve Officers' Training Corps (ROTC) courses and summer training camps constituted 90 percent of the Army's lieutenants and 60 percent of all officers on duty with field units. The chief of the Field Artillery reported that the Reservists "have in most cases taken hold with an enthusiasm and competence which more than justifies the time and money spent in developing and building up the Officers' Reserve Corps."[169]

Inevitably the attempt to merge officers from three sources into the same Army (and often into the same unit) led to friction and discontent. Regular officers who had labored for years to attain their ranks resented the ease with which Guardsmen and Reservists stepped from the comfort of civilian life into positions of authority. For their part, Guard officers suspected the Army of trying to supplant them completely with Regulars. Stories circulated about Regular officers who, being assigned to National Guard units, deliberately undercut their Guard associates to further their own careers. There is a grain of truth in the accusation that General McNair and his staff at General Headquarters failed to appreciate fully the National Guard's distinct character, and the GHQ observers were sometimes quicker to recommend the relief of a Guard officer than to offer him constructive aid.[170]

Although there was no shortage of enlisted men, troop morale declined as the crisis atmosphere of 1940 subsided. Shortages of equipment and training facilities resulted in makeshift work and poorly utilized training time, which the troops were quick to point out to their families and legislators. The officer shortage contributed to a generally low quality of instruction, which in

---

169 ibid (Page 16)
170 ibid (Page 16-17)

turn aggravated the morale problem. Some "old Army" officers and noncoms were decidedly unsympathetic toward their citizen-soldier subordinates. There were also too many cases of business-as-usual staff officers whose insistence on proper procedure resulted in inadequate provisioning of the troops.

General Marshall personally investigated some of the soldiers' complaints and issued pointed directives for their redress. He maintained, however, that overprotective families and scandal-hunting newsmen were partly responsible for depressing the morale of the troops.[171]

Steps to Training

In spite of these difficulties, General McNair was determined to produce the best-trained Army in American history. He formulated a training program that was carefully integrated and progressively structured, in spite of the need for haste. The policy that McNair prescribed, and that General Headquarters sought to implement in 1940 and 1941, started with training the individual soldier, progressed to integrating individuals into small units, and then turned to training successively larger units uniformly, step by step. McNair believed that ". . . these steps are the foundation of military efficiency. They can be hurried or slighted only at a price." Even though altogether too many steps would be hurried, slighted, or omitted because of the dictates of time and the scarcity of equipment, the McNair training program was, in theory, the best that the Army had ever pursued.[172]

The soldier who entered the Army in 1940-41 began his training with a mobilization training program (MTP) that lasted about 13 weeks. Prior to 1 March 1941, soldiers took such training in their permanent tactical units. After that time most recruits went to one of 12 replacement training centers established for that

---

171 ibid (Page 17)
172 ibid (Page 17)

express purpose, thus freeing the tactical units for more advanced training.

The maneuvers area was Third Army's "finishing school," where units came after completing their division training at their home stations. Combat training was divided into four phases, initially of 13 weeks each. As the demands of war intensified, the total was reduced to 37 weeks. The first phase was the ITP (Individual Training Period), in which the individual soldier learned how to use his weapons. The second phase of training was UTP (Unit Training Period), which stressed company training. The third step was the "D-problem" phase (division problems), in which major components of the division—battalions and regiments—operated together for the first time. The last phase involved field maneuvers in which divisions, with supporting functions such as anti-aircraft, tank destroyers, and airpower, were pitted against each other in a series of rigorous combat exercises. The exercises took place year-round, winter and summer, and the troops lived under battle conditions. In Louisiana, when it was hot, it was stifling; and when it was cold, it was bitterly cold.[173]

The corps and branch headquarters conducted the ITP, UTP, and "D-problem" tests for all units except Army troops. These were tested by Headquarters Third Army teams made up of officers of the various staff sections. Detailed reports were made to Headquarters, Third Army, on all personnel tested, including those who conducted the Louisiana maneuvers. For this purpose a large special staff was maintained in a field camp near Leesville. The field camp was known as Director Headquarters, Headquarters Third Army. Commander of the staff was the commanding general of Third Army, along with a deputy director who supervised the maneuvers. Once during each maneuver period, General McNair, commanding general, Army Ground

---

173 Colonel Robert S. Allen; *Lucky Forward (The History of General George Patton's Third Army):* Published by MacFadden-Bartell Corporation (1965), 205 East 42d Street, New York, New York, 10017 (Page 14-15)

Forces, flew in from Washington, D.C., for an inspection tour. He was accompanied by a large group of staff officers who inspected various aspects of the training. Their observations were combined into a report that was sent up the chain of command for corrective action.[174]

Figure 4-21. Selectees (draftees) undergoing machine gun training. *John Beck*

Figure 4-22. 106th Cavalry Regiment machine gun squad at Camp Livingston, 1940. *Eugene Johnson*

---

174 ibid (Page 15)

Figure 4-23. 106th Cavalry Regiment's machine gun troop at the 1940 Louisiana Maneuvers. *JOHN BECK*

Figure 4-24. Selectees (draftees) "take five" during a training break at Camp Livingston. *JOHN BECK*

Figure 4-25. The 4th Cavalry Regiment loads horses onto portees in preparation for a training exercise. *NATIONAL ARCHIVES*

Figure 4-26. It may not be fully mechanized, but General Herr would have approved of it for medical transport.
CAMP BEAUREGARD COLLECTION

Figure 4-27. Colonel George S. Patton studying map during the 1940 Louisiana Maneuvers.
Camp Beauregard collection

Figure 4-28. 4th Cavalry support truck driving through the beautiful Louisiana countryside during the 1941 maneuvers.
AMBROSE ZEN

Figure 4-29. The regimental baseball team served the dual purpose of maintaining high morale and physical fitness. ERVIN ADEN

Figure 4-30. Roadside country store where troopers often purchased soda pop and candy bars.
Eugene Johnson

Figure 4-31. Accident on a Louisiana road, 1941. One person in this U.S. Army Scout Car was killed. *Ervin Aden*

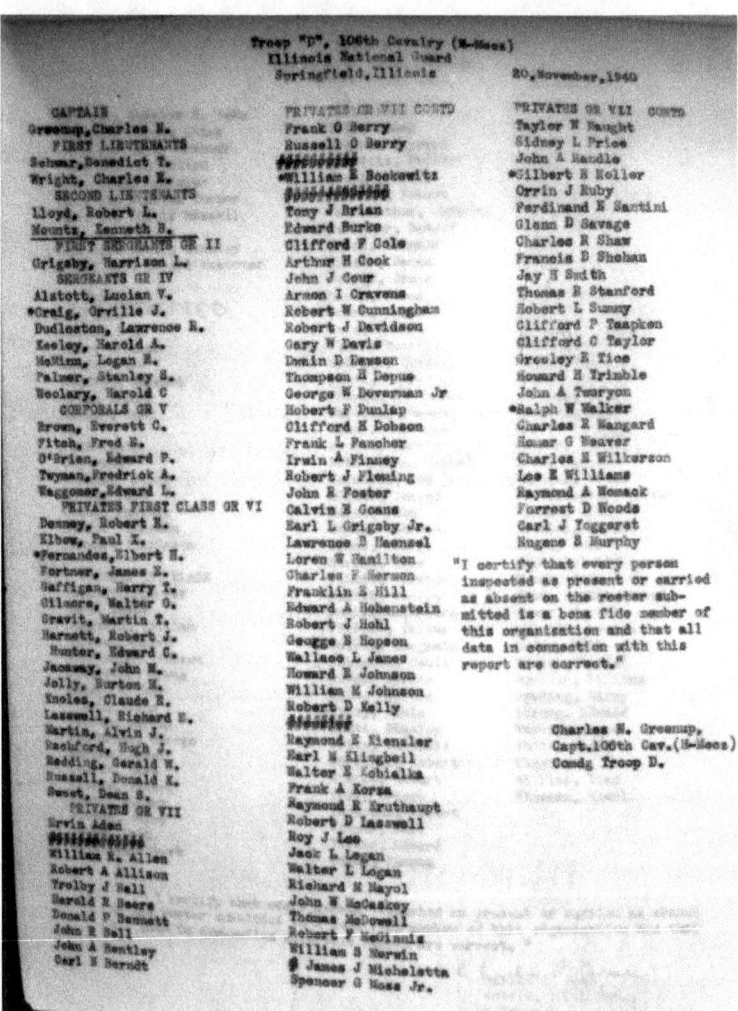

Figure 4-32. D Troop roster for November 1940. After the Pearl Harbor attack on 7 December 1941, many of the men listed in this roster were transferred to Panama.
SPRINGFIELD NATIONAL GUARD

National Guard Participation in August 1940 Maneuvers

In keeping with the ITP training schedule, the 106th Cavalry Regiment received some 350 inductees in the early spring of 1941. The new personnel were to be given their basic training via a special company within the regiment. Half the inductees were trained as horse troopers, and the rest were trained as mechanized troopers.[175] Frank Fancher went through boot camp with this group.

> Basic training was weekdays, Monday through Saturday, with reveille at 6:00 a.m., roll call at 6:25 a.m., calisthenics at 6:30 a.m., and lineup for breakfast at 7:00 a.m. Then, after breakfast, back to our tent to get into our uniform for the day, check and clean your tent, fall in for inspection.
>
> At 8:00 a.m., we started our day, usually with close-order drill, then to the motor pool to check and clean equipment. After that, depending on the schedule, it could be anything. Or it could be weapons training class where we had to field strip our weapon until we could do it with our eyes closed. Sometimes it would be a road march in armored cars, jeeps and motorcycles.
>
> At 11:30 a.m. we were marched back to the tent area where we had lunch, and then we were marched back to what was scheduled for 1 in the afternoon. This went on until 4:30 p.m., at which time we had dinner, dressed in our Class A uniform, and stood retreat. After this we were on our own unless we had special duty. This could be guard duty, KP (Kitchen Police), latrine duty, etc. The days were pretty busy.[176]

---

175 Christopher R Gabel; *The U.S. Army GHQ Maneuvers of 1941:* Published by U.S. government Printing Office, Washington, D.C. 1991 (Page 17-18)
176 Frank 'Lindy' Fancher; *WWII: Through These Eyes:* Published by Author House, 1663 Liberty Drive, Suite 200, Bloomington, Indiana 47403 – 04-26-2005 (Page 1)

After basic training came a promotion to Private First Class (PFC), which meant a little more pay than the private's $21 a month. They took out $8 for insurance and $3 for laundry. Paying for dry cleaning, toothpaste, shoe polish, metal polish and razor blades left very little for pleasure.

Then came advanced training courses. First there was the obstacle course. It was time-limited and began with a two-block run with full equipment. The first obstacle was an eight-foot-high solid wall. Believe it or not, with a little practice, you can run up the vertical wall one or two steps, grab the top and swing yourself over. We had to climb hand-over-hand up a rope to an eight-foot platform and jump off, then hand-over-hand above a mud pit, crawl through culverts, jump over foot-high logs, run through spaced tires, zigzag through trees, cross over a small stream on an eight-inch-wide log, then run four blocks to the finish line. I usually came in first. We had to do this course two or three times a week.[177]

The infiltration course was something that I was not used to. We started out running while shooting at some silhouette targets, then had to hit the ground and crawl under barbed wire strung only two and a half feet above the ground, while live machine guns fired over our heads. You also had to do this with all your guns and equipment.

This course was always muddy due to the fact that they set off quarter-pound blocks of TNT or nitro starch in mud pits several feet deep and only 12 to 15 feet from our position. This threw mud and water all over us. It was supposed to get us used to an attack on

---

177 ibid (Page 1-2)

a fortified position. Believe me, I don't think one could ever get used to this, but we did learn to move without freezing in position. If one quit moving, it was easy for the enemy to target mortar or artillery fire, which is much worse than machine gun fire.[178]

The infiltration course wasn't done too often, as there was a chance of someone getting hurt. In a few cases, someone would get frightened and attempt to stand up, but the people on the machine guns were on the ball and stopped firing. Some of these were at night. To look up and see live ammo with tracers just a few inches above your head can really shake you up.[179]

For the field problems, the Army was divided into two groups, the Blues and the Reds. The Blues were the Americans and the Reds were the enemy. The enemy would set up a defensive position and the Blues or Americans would try to capture it. The group that got the most points on these problems got extra passes or didn't have to pull KP or some such thing.[180]

The operation of the armored car or scout car was another of our fields of advance training. This was a 10,000-pound, four-wheel drive vehicle with a transfer case that gave it six speeds forward and two in reverse. This vehicle provided mobility and crew protection for reconnaissance under combat conditions. I learned to drive this vehicle when I first enlisted. Growing up in a rural community and working on farms when I was young, I had gained experience driving tractors, corn pickers, plows, dump trucks, etc., so I had no problem with it.

---

178 ibid (Page 2)
179 ibid (Page 2)
180 ibid (Page 3)

The scout car carried eight troopers, had a .50 caliber machine gun with 750 rounds of ammunition, two .30 caliber machine guns with 8,000 rounds of ammunition, as well as 540 rounds of .45 caliber ammunition for use with our sidearm and the Thompson submachine gun. We also had a long-range radio. Each trooper carried a .45 caliber revolver; and I, as car commander, carried a Thompson submachine gun.[181]

At this time the United States' preparedness for military conflict was almost nil. The regiment (the 106th Cavalry was known as Horse-Mechanized) participated in the First Army's maneuvers in 1941 in Louisiana and Texas. Prior to the maneuvers we made reconnaissance of every bridge and back road in Louisiana and Eastern Texas.

Figure 4-33. A typical road trip. *John Beck*

---

181 ibid (Page 3-4)

National Guard Participation in August 1940 Maneuvers

Since I was a Pioneer and Demolition corporal I was in charge of the group that was sent out to check bridges and roads. This was to make sure they would support our tanks, trucks and other vehicles before the First Army used them for maneuvers. We had to check out every back road and cow path. A lot of these areas were so remote that you wonder how people could live there. In some of the remote areas and bayous I don't think they knew that the Civil War was over. They were unfriendly and I don't think they trusted our government. This was a little upsetting. As a whole, the rest of the people were friendly and it was an interesting time.

We had to enter all this information on our maps and then turn them into headquarters. Some of these roads were under water part-time. One rainy night we slept in the armored car. The next morning, when we woke up, water was up to the bottom of the doors. We were finished, so we pulled out and went back to Camp Livingston, where we spent the rest of the day washing and cleaning our equipment.[182]

As a non-commissioned officer (NCO) you had to be able to operate all the equipment or you lost your rank. One more thing I had to learn was Morse code and radio operation. I also had to qualify as a motorcycle rider. This was accomplished by riding down the road at between 10 and 15 miles per hour as silhouette targets popped up along the road. When a target popped up you had to spill the cycle, pull a Thompson machine gun from its boot, and get at least three shots into the target. It's hard to do, but with practice, it can be done.

---

182 ibid (Page 4-5)

The little Indian Scout motorcycle we used was very easy to handle and a mighty fine machine.[183]

Another interesting phase of my training at Camp Livingston was that of bridge building. As demolition corporal, along with the demolition officer, I was responsible for getting men and equipment across small streams that could not be forded with vehicles. This was accomplished by building bridges. We were not equipped to build across rivers or bigger streams—that was left to the engineers. Our equipment consisted of two-man chainsaws, TNT or nitrostarch, safety fuses, instantaneous fuses and #8 tetra blasting caps, #8 galvanized wire, axes, shovels and so forth.

With my eight-man crew and as much extra help as we needed, we were supposed to build a bridge across a 20-foot stream that would carry our armored cars and tractor-trailer trucks.[184]

Figure 4-34. A trooper from the 106th Cavalry sitting astride a typical Harley-Davidson motorcycle of the 1940 era.
Eugene Johnson

---

183 ibid (Page 6)
184 ibid (Page 7)

Although by mid-1941 the regiment had not received horse portee trucks, drivers designated as part of the troop were trained by a local construction company. Due to ammunition shortages, initial marksmanship training emphasized familiarization with individual and crew-served weapons rather than completing prescribed marksmanship courses. For equitation (horsemanship) training, a steeplechase course and hippodrome were completed by mid-year as well. Each troop spent two to three days a week training and bivouacking in the field.

During the same period, Headquarters Troop made a road march to the Gulf of Mexico and back. It was the first time that many of the men saw such a large body of salt water. To further their knowledge of the many dangerous snakes in the area, the regiment built a snake house.

Simultaneously, several officers were sent to the Cavalry School at Fort Riley, the Command and General Staff school, and other short courses to further their education.[185]

Figure 4-35. Horse portee (trailer) assigned to the 4th Cavalry Regiment, with tractor attached. Ambrose Zen is on the right front fender. *Ambrose Zen*

---

185 William H. Collier, *The 106th Cavalry's Story:* Published by Trafford Publishing-March 2012 (Page 16)

By the summer of 1941, the regiment had completed its buildup to full strength, received most of its equipment, and trained its new personnel and integrated them into the regiment. Now it was time to show how the unit could operate tactically. The regiment participated in four division exercises, a corps command post exercise, and two corps field exercises.

Following these maneuvers, the regimental commander, Lieutenant Colonel Johnson, wrote a six-page article that was published in the November-December issue of the *Cavalry Journal*. The article described the regiment's operations in the field-army-

Figure 4-36. Training with the .50 caliber machine gun at Camp Livingston, fall 1940.

against-field-army exercise as an example of how to use and employ a horse-mechanized cavalry regiment in attack.

During the exercise, the 106th Cavalry covered a fan-shaped area 140 miles in depth, which fanned out to a width of another 140 miles, during a period of four days. As the exercise began the area of central Louisiana was hit by a hurricane, which dumped more than eight inches of rain on the troops. Most of the personnel were able to sleep dry because they had purchased hammocks over which they put their shelter halves.

Of particular interest were the employment of the motorcycle troop and the self-reliance of the individual troopers. The two scout-car equipped reconnaissance troops operated over long distances. The horse troops acted as mounted rifle units much like the dragoons of old. They secured areas by using their portees to ce over long distances, thus saving their horses' strength.[186]

Figure 4-37. Horse portees with mechanized units providing defense during the 1941 Louisiana Maneuvers.
CAMP BEAUREGARD COLLECTION

---

186 ibid (Page 16-17)

CHAPTER V

DEVELOPMENT OF THE BANTAM

The 1941 *Field Service Regulations: Operations* manual (FM 100-5), published after the creation of the proto-Armored Force and influenced by the success of German blitzkrieg, was more aggressive and attack-oriented than the 1939 *Field Service Regulations (Tentative)*. America's approach to the defense of the Western Hemisphere—influenced by the public's antiwar attitude and a government bent on isolationism and budget controls—produced an inadequate ground force. Since 1920 that ground force had never risen above 138,000 officers and enlisted men.

Even though the new regulation emphasized the American version of attrition warfare, where the infantry was the essential arm of close combat, the 1941 regulation triggered new debate over a maneuver-oriented doctrine. In the new regulation, more attention was directed to the enemy's rear to degrade his center of communication and other vital areas. Dislocation and demoralization were important elements for defeating the enemy. The revised doctrine emphasized a turning movement with the objective of envelopment rather than engaging the mass of the enemy's frontline defenses. This operation was suitable for the newly created Armored Force.

Surprisingly, the new manual also noted that cavalry was "capable of offensive combat exploitation and pursuit." Nevertheless, the manual prescribed the primary missions of the cavalry as reconnaissance and counter-reconnaissance. The manual also warned of diluting the strength of cavalry by deploying it in "indiscriminate detachments." This warning, as will be detailed later, was ignored during World War II, when cavalry elements were detached to support higher units on various missions.[187]

In addition, the manual emphasized a defense-offense tank destroyer doctrine that weakened the emphasis on an offensive tank maneuver-oriented doctrine. Frank Parker first developed the mechanized maneuver-oriented operational concept, which was fine-tuned by Daniel Van Voorhis and finally the trio of Adna R. Chaffee, Jr., Bruce Palmer, and Winfield Scott. Because the concept was now built around a defensive mindset, cavalrymen and infantrymen in the Armored Force argued for greater offensive mobility with a balanced combined arms team.[188]

The assistant chief of staff, G-2, Brigadier General Sherman Miles, generated another game plan for the War Department. In March 1941 he proposed supplanting the infantry-artillery team with a tank-air team and motorized infantry divisions. Chaffee, however, did not exactly agree with the War Department's

---

[187] George F. Hofmann; *Through Mobility We Conquer (The Mechanization of U.S. Cavalry):* Published by The University Press of Kentucky-2006 (Page 273)
[188] ibid (Page 273-274)

evaluation of the modern battlefield as being dominated primarily by the tank-air team.

McNair also disagreed with the War Department's thoughts on the future role of armor. He believed that "the tank is superior to all other ground weapons, as a corollary, that troops in general have no place on the battlefield of today unless behind armor." This response supported his conviction that tanks should be used as infantry-accompanying weapons.

Nonetheless, strong resistance by the chiefs of cavalry and infantry continued. This stalled any legislation to authorize a new branch organization for the Armored Force. General Marshall, for the time being, placed it on hold. On 24 March 1941, McNair wrote to Scott (who at the time was temporary chief of the Armored Force due to Chaffee's recurring illness) that "the unfavorable action on a separate arm was to be expected, since the proposal is a bit brusque." McNair advised Scott that despite the setback, this was not to be the last word on the subject.[189]

Although war clouds were rapidly beginning to shroud the dogmatic thinking of the chief of cavalry, General Herr continued preaching that horse cavalry could be used en masse. This attitude was illustrated in the April 1941 issue of *Life* magazine, which featured horse cavalry maneuvers and the re-organization of a partially horse-motorized division at Fort Bliss, Texas. The 1st Cavalry Division, the article noted, "could lick its weight in enemy tanks" and, unlike road-bound trucks and cars, was at its best in rough terrain such as hills, rocks, and deserts.

By 1941, the 1st Cavalry Division was expected to ride into action and the fight dismounted, as it did during the American Civil War. Hundreds of trucks, scout cars, armored cars, motorcycles and more than a dozen light tanks were anticipated to support the horse units. It was expected that cavalry with more than 8,000 riding horses and supporting elements could be deployed in

---

189 ibid (Page 275)

The U.S. Cavalry: Time of Transition

Figure 5-1. April 1941 issue of *Life* magazine.

western defensive operations, such as in Mexico and the Panama Canal, or possibly along the eastern South American coast, where enemy landings might occur. Large cavalry trailers called portees would deploy riding horses in long lines (eight men and eight horses per truck-trailer combination) to terrain that favored cavalry tactics. The division also had hundreds of pack and draft horses and mules. M3 scout cars augmented the horse team by extending reconnaissance and acting as troop carriers. The scout cars could also provide anti-tank and anti-aircraft support when necessary.

Halting at roadside, cavalry trailers disgorge troops to saddle in preparation for surprise attack across desert country. Trucks will retire from action, meet men again if needed.

Figure 5-2. Picture taken 21 April 1941 by *Life* photographer Robert Landry.

The Bantam car (jeep), a ¼-ton, 4x4, four-wheeled vehicle capable of carrying four riflemen, was introduced during the September 1941 Louisiana maneuvers. Designed for the cavalry, Bantams were considered more efficient than motorcycles, which General Herr had supported. In fact, the small but agile vehicle would soon replace the horse. The next year, the Ford Motor Company and Willys-Overland mass-produced vehicles similar to those originally known as Bantams but later referred to as jeeps. The jeep vehicles could travel almost anywhere, and they rapidly became the Army's workhorses.[190]

---

190 ibid (Page 275)

In September 1940, the year before the *Life* article appeared, the Bantam Car Company of Butler, Pennsylvania, won an invitation-only bid over the Willys-Overland Company from Toledo, Ohio, to deliver to the Army a prototype vehicle similar to the German military version of the Volkswagen. The German four-seat vehicles were used during the blitzkriegs as small personnel carriers.

The Army received the Bantam prototype for tests. As mentioned, the diminutive, all-purpose, four-wheel-drive scout car would be known to the world as the Bantam or, more universally, as the JEEP. An early pre-production model of the Bantam was introduced under the presumptuous name of "Blitz Buggy." That prototype went head-to-head against Ford's Pigmy and Willys' Quad and, in the end, played a very important role in the outcome of the war.

The key to the Bantam's success was its mobility and nimble handling regardless of terrain. It was economical to build, easy to produce in large quantities, and able to be shipped in a crate for assembly in the field.[191]

A brief history on the development of the Jeep and the Bantam Car Company:
History of the Bantam and Willys Jeeps and the BRC (Bantam Reconnaissance Vehicle) by Curtis Redgap: - The origins of what would become the Bantam; Copyright © 1998-2000, David Zatz; copyright © 2001-2011, Allpar LLC (except as noted, and press/publicity materials); all rights reserved.

The story of the Bantam begins in Great Britain with Herbert Austin, who was born in 1866. He was a self-made engineer and toolmaker who rose to become the manager of the Wolseley Tool and Motor Car Company. However, he felt he could build better motor vehicles on his own. With his own funds he founded the Austin Motor Company in 1905. He located the new plant in Longbridge, which became part of

---
191 ibid (Page 276)

Birmingham in 1911, and built conventional cars with a 5.0-liter, four-cylinder engine.

When World War I became inevitable, Great Britain gave Austin Motor Car profitable military contracts. Herbert Austin was knighted at the end of the war, and Sir Herbert resumed motorcar production in 1918. The initial postwar offerings were based upon one model, powered by a 20-horsepower, 3.6-liter engine. Faced with slow sales and rising costs, Sir Herbert switched the single model into a commercial version, and built good tractors with the same chassis. This was to no avail. In 1921, bankruptcy procedures began.

The company was viable, but the board of directors protested over the new car that Sir Herbert had proposed to turn the company around. Sir Herbert threatened to take his design to Wolseley Motor Cars, and the board came to an agreement that allowed Austin Motor Car to be restructured in the same year it declared bankruptcy.

The new car was aimed at penetration of the mass market: smaller, lighter, well built, and economical. Introduced in 1922, the Austin 7 was a hit. The "7" represented the engine's horsepower rating, putting it into the current micro-car class and thus avoiding a tax. The car was much smaller than a Ford Model T; the wheelbase was 75 inches, and the body was just 40 inches wide. The four-cylinder was cut to 747 cc (¾ liters); the four-speed transmission was an integral part of the drive train. Mastery of shifting required double-clutching. This was a challenge to drivers who failed to match engine and transmission gear speeds. The front suspension was a transverse leaf spring, while the rear suspension was two semi-elliptical leaves. Four-wheel brakes were operated by cables on a hand lever, and the rear brakes were cable-operated from a foot pedal. The braking system would not be integrated until 1930.

The Austin 7 was successful in its first year. Sir Herbert made running changes to the car to improve it mechanically.

Figure 5-3. In 1922, an Austin 7 cost £225 and could reach a speed of 50 miles per hour.

The design went under license to Germany as the "Dixi" (part of a new company called BMW) and was licensed to France in 1928 as the "Rosengart." In the United States the Austin 7 was licensed in 1929 as the "American Austin." Sir William Lyons used the Austin 7 chassis to build his own car, the "Swallow," which gave him the knowledge and profits to form a new company, Jaguar, in 1935.

In 1929, Austin set up a factory to produce the Americanized Austin 7 in Butler, Pennsylvania. Even in the face of the Depression, initially the

American Austin sold fairly well, but the deepening of the Depression and the public's resistance to tiny cars forced American Austin into bankruptcy in 1934.

Roy Evans, former salesman for the company, bought it out of bankruptcy and renamed it the American Bantam Car Company, with headquarters in Butler, Pennsylvania. The word *bantam* means "small offspring," like a bantam rooster. Evans retained the small-car concept but made significant improvements. After updating the body, he set about getting a new engine to avoid having to pay royalties to Austin. The first version of the new engine was a 46-cubic-inch, four-cylinder flathead that may have developed 15 horsepower with about 40 foot-pounds of torque. With all its accessories, the engine weighed 148 pounds. Compression was set at 5.0 to 1. Top speed may have been upwards of 50 miles an hour, but that would be punishing for the engine, which at the time had two main bearings (ball bearings) on the crankshaft. This would allow for a free-turning unit, but the nature of ball bearings encouraged crankshaft "whip" internally.

Evans made the Bantam look different from the older Austin, and made the Bantam appear bigger than it actually was. First-year production was 1,200 units; 30 percent of production was for export to Canada, Australia, Mexico, and Great Britain, where the car competed directly against its progenitor, the Austin. The Bantam was unable make a significant dent in the American market, even though, by 1938, the automobile was on a par with Chrysler, Buick, and Mercury as far as quality, reliability, and appointments were concerned.

By 1938, Evans spotted the potential for a light reconnaissance vehicle for the army. American

Figure 5-4. The 1938 American Bantam Model 60 Roadster.

Bantam Motors hired a lobbyist: retired Navy aviator Commander Harry Payne. At the time, there was none better, because Payne believed in his job, and he was honest to a fault. Payne worked tirelessly for Bantam to draw out what the Quartermaster Corps might want for forces in the field. Payne loaned the National Guard three of his roadsters to evaluate.

Payne was armed with the knowledge that in 1932, the British Army had purchased two Austin Sedans for evaluation as a General Purpose Scout Car. The scout cars were now used in place of motorcycles and side-cars. A British infantry captain used the Austin chassis and parts to build a small, light vehicle with four-wheel drive. The vehicle was about 70 inches long, 37 inches wide, and weighed around 1,000 pounds. Those "specials" had machine gun and small artillery mountings and were given tough jobs to fulfill. They were given exceptional ratings and rave reviews from the British infantry. The Austin cars were well liked; they could carry more passengers and serve in more assignments than the motorcycles, especially considering that they could carry mobile machine gun mounts. The Austin cars were tough, but they needed four-wheel-drive to be fully effective.

By 1939 the US military needed a new, universal vehicle to replace the motorcycle and its other vehicles (such as the modified Ford Model T), so they invited 135 different car companies to compete for a contract to build a new vehicle. Only five companies entered the competition: Bantam, Willys-Overland, Ford, General Motors and the Checker Car Company.

The vehicle had to meet certain specifications including a payload capacity of 600 pounds, a wheelbase of fewer than 75 inches, a fold-down windshield, a gross vehicle weight of less than 1,200 pounds, and four-wheel drive. The earlier vehicle loans to the National Guard in 1938 got Bantam into the loop with the military and led to a series of meetings with the Army and to a set of specifications for a 4x4 car/truck type vehicle.

Eventually the Army, Willys, and even Ford claimed credit for the introduction of the small utility vehicle. However, evidence shows that Evans and Payne were ahead of their competitors. Hoping that the Army would see things Bantam's way, in 1938, Roy Evans arranged through Harry Payne to loan two small 4x2 Bantam trucks to the QMC for evaluation, knowing what the British had accomplished a year earlier with the Austin. Later on, a couple of roadsters were also sent over. The QMC expressed solid interest in the design, but the lack of four-wheel-drive and the thin cross-section of the tires led the vehicles to getting stuck a lot. However, experience with these loaners did lead to the Army's insistence that any light recon vehicle have four-wheel-drive.

As a senator from Missouri, Harry Truman had been lambasting the military for their "sweetheart" deals. The Truman Congressional Committee castigated the military's cost overruns, outrageous specifications, prices that shot up for commonplace items, lack of purchasing comparable on-the-shelf items, as well as a deplorable lack of contractual oversight. In early 1940 Harry Payne brought the two-decade-long dithering about a light recon vehicle to Senator Truman's attention. Payne also mentioned the "loan" (he never got the vehicles back) of the trucks and roadsters to the QMC two years earlier. Committee investigators wrote inquiries to the QMC. Wanting to avoid an appearance before the Truman Committee, the QMC officers quickly arranged a trip to the Bantam plant so that Army representatives could see a small, light vehicle being assembled.

In another bit of clever salesmanship, Roy Evans arranged to "loan out" two more Roadsters. These were vehicles that the visiting Army officers had seen assembled in the plant while on their tour. The 1940 Roadsters were driven to the local Army National Guard unit that was engaged in field maneuvers that very week. The two Roadsters—less some equipment removed by Bantam technicians—performed flawlessly. Evans made it clear that he'd ordered no factory oversight or restrictions on any use of the vehicles. Impressed, the Army contingent, which was not connected to the Headquarters group of naysayers, extended its stay at the Bantam factory in Butler. While no notes or minutes were recorded, clearly discussions were underway about what the light recon vehicle should look like. Obviously the Army did not know what it wanted.

In June of 1940, a pencil drawing was found on the desk of the Bantam president. Though the crude, childlike drawing was the object of much speculation, the sketch was clearly an outline of the BRC (Bantam Reconnaissance Car) vehicle. Although the evidence is not conclusive, the drawing can be attributed to Harry Payne. Despite his aviation background, he was a field man. He knew what would work for troops in the field given his keen eye on what the maintenance types would want. He was especially aware of what the Bantam production facilities were capable of producing, given the chance. Certainly the drawing did not come from the Army.

Figure 5-5. Jack Keenan drawing of a Peep.

The QMC finally released the specifications for the light recon vehicle on 11 July 1940, three weeks after the Army's visit to the Bantam plant. The specs fell right in line with what Bantam had been touting all along, making the crude pencil drawing a portent of the future.

The blueprint drawings rendered by the Army in its recon vehicle specifications were largely based upon submissions by Bantam. The design was about 20 percent Army and 80 percent Bantam—taken almost directly from the Bantam Roadster blueprints that Bantam had submitted for comparison purposes only. Most of the items in the Army specs were off-the-shelf, including regular-sized, blackout-capable headlights and taillights. There was an allowance for an additional 4.5 inches in the wheelbase because the Army wanted four-wheel-drive. This necessitated a transfer case for a wheelbase of 80 inches. The engine had to deliver 85 foot-pounds of torque. The vehicle would weigh 1,300 pounds and had to carry a 660-pound payload.

Although the competition among contractors had just begun, Bantam immediately ran into trouble. The Army headquarters contingent that had rejected everything began circulating disinformation about Bantam's ability to engineer and produce the recon vehicle. There were whispers that Bantam was too small to produce the quantity of vehicles that the Army required. Supposedly Bantam also lacked the engineering and production staff to get machines and tools set up for a high-capacity production line, particularly for making transfer cases and axles. (The latter was true for the Butler facility.) On the other hand, the rumors said, Ford had more than enough production capability to build what the Army needed.

In reality, though, Bantam had two production facilities. In addition to Butler, Pennsylvania, Bantam had a factory in Detroit which built bodies and shipped them to Butler for attachment to chassis. The two factories were more than able to produce over 200,000 vehicles a year. This statistic was backed up by an independent audit that analyzed the two plants. Despite its production capability, Bantam never sold enough vehicles to use the full capability of its facilities.

The next problem that reared its head was the price Bantam paid Ford for transfer cases and axles for the four-wheel-drive system. Bantam was almost out of money and was unable to acquire the tooling to build its own transfer cases and axles. Bantam seemed trapped: if the company won the Army contract it would have money to buy the tooling, but since it didn't have the tooling it probably couldn't get the contract.

The rumors about a lack of engineering staff should have died quickly. The vice president of Bantam was none other than Harry Miller of Indianapolis racing fame. Miller had built the Miller and Gulf Oil Special racecars. He won Indianapolis with front-wheel-drive and four-wheel-drive racing machines, largely with four-cylinder engines of 122 cubic inches. By 1937 Miller had built, raced, and perfected cutting-edge technology such as twin cams, hemispherical heads, tuned exhaust engines and high-lift camshafts.

Miller rented a space at the Butler facility to assemble his Indy racers. He was visited by many people in the profession. The people around Miller were the cream of the engineering profession. One of them was Harold Christ, who had worked on the first Duesenberg automobile. Christ moved to the Stutz Motor Company, where he spent 18 years working on their racecars; and then to Bantam as its general factory manager. Using off-the-shelf Bantam parts, Christ built a V-8 engine that was used in midget car racing. He welded together two Bantam four-cylinder blocks, then fabricated a crankcase. He built the crankshaft by machining down a solid steel block.

Christ was also credited with building a test transfer case by cutting apart two Chevrolet transmissions. He changed the gears, realigned the shafts, drilled out the fittings, cut the halves in half, and welded the cases together. The equipment performed flawlessly. No doubt Miller and Christ, by themselves, could have figured out any potential engineering problems in the manufacture of a light reconnaissance vehicle.

It appeared that someone in the hierarchy of the QMC wanted the Ford Motor Company to win the contract bid. Of course, the Ford company was considerably larger than Bantam, but Ford was not prepared to build a small-wheelbase vehicle. Once Ford became aware of the potential size of the contract, Henry Ford used every bit of influence to rig the bid.

On 11 July 1940, the Army QMC released its specification to 135 manufacturers. Bids had to be returned in 22 days. As well, the specification demanded that a pilot vehicle be available in 49 days. Further complicating things, it demanded that 70 prototype vehicles be available for evaluation in 75 days.

The European war had started in 1939 and threatened the entire world. Despite protests against the U.S. entering a "foreign" war, President Roosevelt was a practical man. He understood that, sooner or later, America would have to get involved. He quietly ordered the military to procure items it needed to go to war. With the Truman Commission looking into everything that the military was doing, the rush was on. Since the German Blitzkrieg had been powered by motorized equipment, American military planners scrambled to correct a deplorable lack of prewar planning.

Development of the Bantam

Only three companies submitted bids for the recon vehicle: the American Bantam Car Company, Ford Motor Company, and Willys-Overland Motor Company. Of the three, only Bantam made a commitment to provide a pilot vehicle within the 49-day time frame, along with providing 70 vehicles in 75 days. Willys was the lowest bidder; however, they could not provide a pilot vehicle.

The Army decided that the $739 per-unit-cost bid by Willys was the best value compared to the $1,166 bid submitted by Bantam. The Ford bid was over $1,200 which pretty much ended their further consideration—for a time. In truth, neither Ford nor Willys had a clue on how to build the vehicle, given the bid specifications. Thanks to some questionable moves from the QMC, that situation would soon change.

Figure 5-6. The "Blitz Buggy," a 1940 Bantam prototype.

An interesting note: Roy Evans was one of the largest Willys dealers, even as he ran Bantam. To this day, few people know that, in 1935, Evans organized a syndicate to save the floundering Willys-Overland by purchasing 12,000 vehicles from Willys. This saved the company but gave controlling interest to Evans. In 1938, former Chrysler salesman and executive Joseph Frazer became president of Willys and ordered improvements to the 12-year-old four-cylinder Whippet engine. This would be important to Bantam's entry in the competition to build the new Army vehicle.

Bantam enlisted the help of engineer Karl Probst, and on 23 September 1940 was the first competitor to submit a working prototype to the military. Since their production cars were based on the British Austin 7, Bantam's BRC (Bantam Reconnaissance Car) used chassis components imported from the United Kingdom, along with other off-the-shelf parts. The BRC's four-wheel-drive train components were made by the Spicer Company, which also provided components for the Ford and Willys-Overland prototypes.

The Bantam Company hand-built its first pilot car. It was powered by a 20-horsepower engine and used a three-speed synchronized manual transmission, operated from the column. The vehicle, code named the "Blitz Buggy" by Bantam, was completed just one day before the deadline. Nicknamed "Old Number One," the pilot vehicle had to be delivered to Camp Holabird in Maryland (450 miles away) to meet the bid. Unfortunately no one at Bantam had figured out how to get it there. Frantic calls to local trucking companies were unsuccessful. In the end, two volunteer technicians put together a picnic basket full of food and drink and set out for Fort Holabird. In a time before reliable roads were commonplace, the technicians drove straight through, with stops only for gasoline. They used maps provided by gasoline companies and beat the delivery time by half an hour. Along the way, the car generated an extraordinary amount of interest, since nothing like it had ever been seen before.

Soon, however, Bantam would regret their haste to be the first entry in the vehicle competition. On hand at Camp Holabird were representatives from Ford and Willys. The Army handed over all the technical drawings, representing the patented construction of the Bantam Reconnaissance Car, to Willys and Ford. When questioned about this dubious activity, the Army claimed that the information was theirs to do with what they wanted. Bantam should have initiated a series of lawsuits, but Roy Evans felt that, if he rocked the boat, the QMC would kill his Bantam bid completely.

Subsequently, on 13 November 1940, the Willys-Overland Company submitted a prototype, called the "Quad," Under the hood was Willys' four-cylinder flathead engine, heavily re-worked by ex-Studebaker engineer Barney Roos. Engine modifications included closer tolerances, tougher alloys, aluminum pistons, and a lighter flywheel. Using a bore-and-stroke ratio of 3.125 to 4.375 inches, the L-Head engine produced 60 British horsepower and 105 pound-feet of torque, exceeding the Army's specifications.

As a further insult to Bantam, whenever the BRC was in the garage, Ford and Willys people were allowed to examine and take photographs of it. As a result, by the end of November 1940, both Ford and Willys had prototype vehicles at Camp Holabird for evaluation. Willy's "Quad" and Ford's "Pygmy" were in direct

Figure 5-7. The 1940 Willys-Overland prototype known as the "Quad."

competition with Bantam's "Blitz Buggy." Two of them were good vehicles; one was not.

The Willys-Overland vehicle outline almost perfectly matched the Bantam pencil drawing. Despite today's rave reviews from some aficionados, the Willys "Quad" was a piece of junk. Evaluation sheets from the trial period of November 1940 to the end of December 1940 were highly critical of the prototype vehicle. On the one hand, the "Go-Devil" Willys engine was the highest-rated at 60 horsepower, turning 105 foot-pounds of torque—nearly doubling the capacity of the Bantam's motor and Ford's tractor engine. However, despite the Go-Devil's impressive performance, the Willys vehicle went through three engines in fewer than 8,000 miles. Allegedly, someone at Willys quality had not paid attention to quality control. Almost all the other Willys components failed, including the transmission, the transfer case, the windshield braces, and the radiator along with its mounts, wheel bearings, lug bolts, battery, and generator. In addition, the Ford and Willys prototypes were overweight. Only the Bantam vehicle was in the proper weight range.

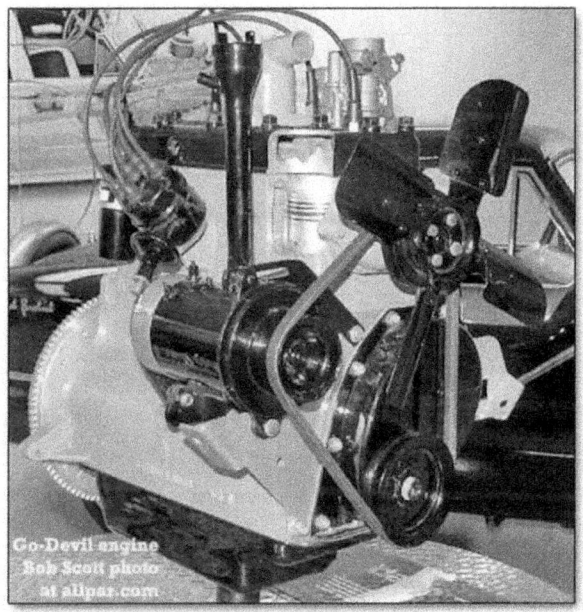

Figure 5-8. Go-Devil engine.

The U.S. Calvary was eager to get the equipment it needed. Colonel George S. Patton brought a lot of pressure to bear, attempting to obtain as many of the light vehicles as possible. He had excellent connections in Washington, D.C., through his society wife. Patton and his supporters put a lot of pressure on the QMC, and most of the country club officers in the organization were reassigned elsewhere.

However, the pace of the vehicle's development was still agonizingly slow, with requisitions for funding crawling through Congress. Even with the Democrats in the majority, Congress was torpedoing President Roosevelt's wishes. He causing some hostility by trying to push through major legislation in 1939 to "pack" the Supreme Court, adding more justices without consultation with the party leaders,.

With evaluations of the prototype vehicles completed by the end of December 1940, lobbying efforts began in earnest in early January 1941. Despite its low $739 bid, it appeared that Willys' Quad would be written off due to concerns about its quality. The QMC bid requirement for weight had been increased at least twice and maybe three times, allowing Ford to build its LRV (Light Reconnaissance Vehicle). Henry Ford had powerful political connections, despite the fact that his Belgium Ford plant was building trucks for the Nazi regime. Ford had also made several utterances that provoked accusations of anti-Semitism. (In *Mein Kampf*, Adolf Hitler credited his philosophy to Henry Ford, and Ford was the only American to receive highest honors from the Nazi party.)

The original weight restriction on the Army's new vehicle had increased from 1,275 pounds to 1,500 pounds, then increased again to just over 2,000 pounds. The Calvary labeled a vehicle of this weight "tubby" and voiced its disapproval. Only Bantam, who had built another model (the BRC60) in December 1940, had maintained the weight requirement. The BRC60 had many improvements, all of which had been recommended by the Army. The prototype met the

1,500-pound specification that the QMC had allowed for its additional suggested equipment.

Still, Roy Evans must have felt fairly secure during the bid competition. After all, he controlled two of the bidders, Bantam and Willys. The latter company was in better shape not only financially but also in its tooling and production capabilities. Its Toledo plant was huge.

Willys expended great effort to rebuild its Quad into a new model labeled the "MA," for "Military A" model. Rumors flew that the original Willys Quad vehicle had been a target of sabotage. These rumors were likely hushed up to display a good face to the public. Whatever the case, it did seem very odd that the Go-Devil engine, which had been around since 1926, would have suffered so greatly in its improved form.

One thing that Willys still needed to accomplsih was to bring the MA vehicle from a whopping 2,400 pounds down to the specified weight. When the MA was presented, it had lost 240 pounds compared to the Quad. The Quartermaster Corps could not disqualify the vehicle based on weight because they had accepted the Ford Pygmy, which weighed 2,125 pounds. The finalized weight was set at 2,160 pounds, and all three competing contractors qualified.

The Ford "Pygmy" was completed in November of 1940 and was ready for testing in December 1940. The slotted steel grille incorporating the headlights was an original design and would be adopted by Willys in its final design stages. Power came from a 120-cid tractor engine mated to a three-speed Model A gearbox. The paperwork called the vehicle a GP. The "G" stood for "Government," and "P" was Ford's designation for an 80-inch wheelbase. Later the "Pygmy" name would

Figure 5-9. The 1940 Ford "Pygmy" would become the Ford GP, better known as the famous WWII Jeep. *NATIONAL ARCHIVES*

be changed to GP (General Passenger). The Ford designation stuck—and GP was pronounced as "Jeep."

In March 1941, the Army awarded contracts to all three competitors to build 1,500 vehicles each. This occurred about three weeks after Willys held a press conference on the steps of the U.S. Capitol Building on 20 February 1941. One of the Willys vehicles nimbly drove up the steps to the veranda in front of the building. The vehicle also drove down the steps. After the vehicle transported some senators, congressmen, and reporters up and down, the conference ended. One of the reporters asked the Willys representative what the vehicle was called. "We call it a JEEP," said the Willys rep. The story appeared the next day in the Washington newspapers.

Development of the Bantam

LAWMAKERS TAKE A RIDE—With Senator Meade, of New York, at the wheel, and Representative Thomas, of New Jersey, sitting beside him, one of the Army's new scout cars, known as "jeeps" or "quads," climbs up the Capitol steps in a demonstration yesterday. Soldiers in the rear seat for gunners' were unperturbed

Figure 5-10. Senator Meade of New York driving Representative Thomas of New Jersey in the new "scout car" (Jeep) up the steps of the Capitol in Washington, D.C.

After all three companies got their production lines up and running, the Army wanted to insure that it had a reliable source for Jeeps. It also wanted to standardize the vehicle's parts and assembly methods. In July 1941 the Army issued a Request for Proposal (RFP) for 16,000 vehicles. Maintaining three different sets of parts and with three different assembly points was not practical. Willys won the bid, coming in at its already set price of $739 per unit. That amounted to nearly

$12 million in new assembly alone, but did not account for maintenance or replacement parts.

Over at Bantam, the production line slowed down after the company lost the contract. However, passage of the Lend-Lease Act in May 1941 gave some impetus to the Bantam vehicles. Most of what the company produced was sent to Great Britain and Russia.

Figure 5-11. "Hurricane" Four engine.

Bantam's hopes rose and were dashed again when the Army indicated in October 1941 that it needed a second source of Jeep assembly because Willys couldn't keep up with the demand. Ford easily won the bid in early November 1941 for 15,000 more Jeeps. Ford agreed to build the vehicles strictly to Willys factory specifications. Ford had lobbied heavily over the summer for a slice of the Jeep pie. They stated that they could build Jeeps to standards, making exact copies of the Willys version.

Development of the Bantam

In a bit of one-upsmanship, Ford agreed to use the Go-Devil engines that were built and supplied by Willys. The Go-Devil engine was subsequently replaced by the Willys "Hurricane" engine. Since Ford was supplying the transfer cases and axles to Bantam, the Army in essence allowed Ford to set the bid. Ford got $890 for each unit—a $14 million deal.

Ford also received credit for the seven slotted, stamped-steel grills that became the standard for the Jeep. Willys had been building a welded, flat iron, slat radiator grill. Ford developed methods to build their item more cheaply. The stamped-metal sheet steel grill was more effective, far less costly, solved the headlight mounting design, and gave the front end of the vehicle a distinctive look. Willys quickly adopted the design early in 1942.

Bantam's production of the BRC60 (MA) Jeep slowly wound down. Roy Evans was disappointed. Over $30 million had been spent since the first BRC was submitted for bid, and Bantam got only a tiny part of the contract. Evans set Harry Payne on a military contract hunt, as he was convinced that President Roosevelt wasn't being forthcoming with the public about America's possible entry into the war.

On 7 December 1941, war did come as the empire of Japan attacked the United States at Pearl Harbor, Hawaii. On 8 December, President Roosevelt asked Congress for a declaration of war against Japan. The money for war materiel immediately began to flow to various industries.

The Bantam Motor Car Company got enough contracts to keep working for the duration of World War II. However, Bantam built their last Jeep at the end of December 1941 after making 2,675 of them. They would never build another.

No one had really taken notice, but the Bantam production line for civilian cars had already ground to a halt in the summer of 1941. There was no money left, and not enough sales, to sustain production. The Detroit production facility shut down and the company quietly made arrangements to sell or move the equipment. Bantam made a tidy profit from selling the facility to the War Requisitions Board in February 1942. By then, all civilian car manufacturers had been ordered to cease making cars and turn their factories over to war production.

Bantam was given the task of designing and building a trailer suitable for towing items behind the Jeep. The trailer was to handle 500 pounds and be as rugged and reliable as the Jeep. Bantam built 73,689 trailers by the end of the war. They were also given contracts to build carburetors for Australia and a big engine to power landing craft.

Figure 5-12. Bantam Company military trailer.

Roy Evans departed Bantam at war's end and involved himself in Willys. Later, in the 1950s, he became the largest Willys dealer. He did this, mainly, by selling the CJ—the civilian version of the Jeep.[192]

USE IN THE FIELD

The end result of the Jeep's hectic design process was an incredible vehicle that had many uses and was adaptable to almost anything. Lieutenant Robert (Bob) Moore's platoon mounted a .30 caliber light machine gun to the dashboard of the vehicle; a trooper sitting in the front passenger seat operated the weapon. Alternatively, a heavier .50 caliber machine gun or even a mortar was mounted in the rear area of the Bantam and manned by two troopers. The famous military correspondent Ernie Pyle commented that the jeep was "faithful as a dog . . . strong as a mule . . . and agile as a goat." For years, many cavalrymen still referred to the jeep as the Bantam.[193]

An interesting variant of the Bantam was the GPA, an amphibious model. In 1942 Ford built a limited number of amphibious Jeeps, known as the "Seep." This little vehicle was basically an MB with a boat tub on the bottom (with cutouts for the wheels) and a power takeoff from the motor to the propeller.

Seeps were not the most seaworthy things in the world, but they were used in the invasion of Sicily and preformed relatively well. As a consequence of having a low freeboard (the distance between the undercarriage and the water), the Seep couldn't handle more than a light chop and certainly couldn't carry much cargo. The Seep was therefore unable to meet its intended use: to ferry soldiers to and from ships offshore, and to trundle up the beach and continue inland. On land the vehicle was too heavy

---

[192] David Zatz; *The origins of what would become the Bantam;* Published on line by Allpar LLC (2011)

[193] Robert (Bob) Moore and Michael (Mike) Moore: *The 12th Man; Citizen Soldier in Europe 1944-1945:* Unpublished Manuscript (06-10-2010)

[195] Unknown Author; *Jeep History;* Retrieved from Jeepin.com » *Jeep History on 01-01-2012*

and its body too unwieldy to be popular with the soldiers. Adding insult to injury, the Seep frequently got stuck in shallow waters, where the regular Willys MB's water-fording abilities allowed it

Figure 5-13. The 1942 Bantam GPA, an amphibious model.

to plow straight through. Production of the Seep was halted in March 1943 after a run of only 12,778 vehicles.[194]

When the Quartermaster General announced the purchase of "several hundred" jeeps, soldiers assumed the vehicle would replace the motor tricycle in the motorcycle platoons. The 6th Cavalry Regiment (Horse-Mech) received its first eight jeeps in December 1940. With the same zeal displayed by earlier generations of mechanized scouts, the troopers immediately sought to gain familiarity with their new "iron ponies."

The troopers wasted no time in modifying the motorized steeds to meet specific reconnaissance needs. They attached brackets for gas cans and added skid plates to the undercarriage to protect the

---

[194]

drive train and make it easier to slide the vehicle off obstructions. In addition, the troopers fabricated a new trailer hitch to speed the employment of the 37 mm anti-tank gun that the new vehicle was expected to tow into battle. Radio mounts constructed by the men enabled them to install SCR-245 radios, providing the vehicle with the same capability as the scout car.[195]

One of the ongoing criticisms of mechanized reconnaissance units was their inability to swim across water obstacles. Over the years this task had become more difficult for horse cavalry due to its packed weapons and motorized supply systems. Experts wrote articles detailing how to train horses that had never been forced to swim, as well as how to prepare equipment for water crossings.

The arrival of the jeep offered alternatives that were not possible with the heavier scout and armored cars. The troopers at Fort Oglethorpe, Georgia, built makeshift rafts out of 32 empty 10-gallon cans and used the contraptions to float their jeeps.[196]

Figure 5-14. Troopers of the 6th Cavalry Regiment teach their "iron ponies" to swim near Fort Oglethorpe, Georgia.
The Cavalry Journal, March-April 1941

Next, the troopers improvised two different means of propelling the vehicle across the water under its own power. One approach

---

[195] Matthew Darlington Morton; *Men on Iron Ponies (The death and rebirth of the modern U.S. Cavalry):* Published by Northern Illinois University Press-2009 (Page 87-88)
[196] ibid (Page 88)

used paddles attached to the jeep's rear wheels; the other involved the conversion of a vehicle axle into a scaled-down version of a riverboat paddle wheel.

The men of the 9th Reconnaissance Troop stationed at Fort Bragg, Georgia, were no less enamored with the newest addition to their reconnaissance organization. They modified their jeeps using a technique described in training circulars and in the *Infantry Mailing List*. First the troopers wrapped the jeeps with tarps taken from large trucks. Then soldiers floated the jeep—now ensconced in green canvas—across the river, or towed it using the winch on a truck.

Having solved the problem of how to cross water obstacles, the men turned their attention to integrating the jeeps into the tactical operation of their platoons.[197]

The jeep completely captured the attention of the Army in the months leading up to America's entry into World War II. To their credit, horse cavalry advocates were able to exert their influence on the development of a major piece of equipment used for mechanized reconnaissance during World War II.

The Army's 37 mm anti-tank gun wasn't "packable" but the new jeep would be able to tow the weapon. In January 1941, the 1st Cavalry Division began running tests that pitted jeeps against scout cars and motorcycles under a variety of conditions. Major General Innis P. Swift, commander of the Division, was "very enthusiastic over the performance of the Bantam car." He noted, with few exceptions, that the "bantam car" outperformed the other vehicles, and was convinced "that the bantam is a grand car for such purposes as the British use as a Bren gun carrier." Swift assured Major General Herr that "neither food, water, forage nor weather is going to interfere with our cutting loose to ride from

---

197 ibid (Page 88)

hell-to-breakfast on the maneuvers, but I really believe the Jeeps can accompany us anywhere." Swift used his own jeep, equipped with an SCR-245 radio set, to travel 200 miles per day while maintaining contact with his command post. He was convinced

Figure 5-15. SCR-245 radio set, weighing aprox 26.5 pounds and designed primarily for installation in vehicles for the purpose of inter-vehicular communication. *U.S. ARMY*

that the "bantam can supplant the scout car" and looked forward to the day when all of the scout cars "disappeared."[198]

Given the premium value horse soldiers placed on mobility and stealth, it was no surprise that the troopers immediately fell in love with the jeep when the Army procured it in large numbers in 1941. As the jeep entered service, Major General Herr continued to remind everyone who would listen that, in the next war, roads were going to be "mighty unhealthy places" and that the cavalry needed to place more emphasis on cross-country mobility "after

---

198 ibid (Page 87)

the manner of the hordes of Genghis Khan." Herr's office told people who inquired that the "Bantam Car" was not intended to replace the horse but rather, primarily, the motorcycle. The same views were echoed at Fort Knox.

In the end, the jeep did replace the horse, but it certainly did not feature all of the characteristics long advocated by the leaders in mechanized reconnaissance. The horse cavalrymen could take credit for integrating the jeep into mechanized reconnaissance against the objections of officers such as Colonel Charles L. Scott, who had consistently called for more armored protection and firepower for soldiers operating at the forefront of friendly forces.[199]

Figure 5-16. Major General Innis P. Swift, commander of the 1st Cavalry Division. Portrait by *Life* photographer Robert Landry, April 1941.

---

199 ibid (Page 87)

Relying on the jeep's low silhouette and high mobility to avoid casualties, emerging doctrine placed jeep-mounted men on "point" to conduct reconnaissance for their platoon's scout cars. Scouts in jeeps were expected to detect hostile anti-tank weapons and ambushes. A cunning enemy might let the jeep pass by and save their first round for the armored scout car. Innovators in the field of jeep-mounted scouting argued for the liberal use of "reconnaissance by fire"—spraying suspected enemy positions to detect hidden foes.

Meanwhile, horse platoon leaders rode in their own jeeps, accompanying mechanized platoons in order to conduct personal reconnaissance "very rapidly" before returning to the portee detrucking point to commit their platoons. This was yet another slow but sure encroachment on the horse's continued usefulness.[200]

Ironically, the April 1941 *Life* article that featured horse cavalry maneuvers also took a swipe at cavalrymen who joined the Armored Force, calling them "cushion pounders." The article depicted Major General Swift, a rough, crusty cavalryman, saluting as he reviewed the 1st Cavalry Division on Fort Bliss's dusty parade ground. The look on General Swift's face foretold what was coming. The 1st Cavalry Division would no longer hear the squeak of saddle harnesses or see troopers saddle up and lead their horses out of the corrals to formation. By August 1943, horses were long gone from the ranks. General Swift would take the division—consisting of the 5th, 7th, 8th, and 12th Regiments—to the Pacific Theater, where the cavalrymen fought dismounted.[201]

---

200 Captain Bruce Palmer, Jr., "*The Bantam in the Scout Car Platoon*, Published in "*The Cavalry Journal*, vol. XLIV (March-April 1940), pp. 89-92.
201 George F. Hofmann; *Through Mobility We Conquer (The Mechanization of U.S. Cavalry):* Published by The University Press of Kentucky-2006 (Page 277)

CHAPTER VI

1941 LOUISIANA MANEUVERS: "THE BIG ONE"

Shortly after the beginning of the German blitzkrieg against Poland in September 1939 and President Franklin D. Roosevelt's announcement of a limited national emergency, the U.S. Army implemented its Protective Mobilization Plan (PMP). Days earlier, *Newsweek* had reported that the U.S. Army was ranked 17th in effectiveness among the armies of the world. By December 1939, the *Army and Navy Register* reported that a reorganization of the cavalry was planned. The chief of cavalry, General John K. Herr, planned to increase each horse-mounted regiment from 790 to 1,275 horses and boost the number of scout cars in each regiment from 7 to 10. At the time there were 14 regiments (12 horse-mounted and 2 mechanized). It was clear that

Herr was determined to ensure that mechanization would not take over his branch.[202]

With countries across the world switching to a wartime footing, the Army began to grow at a rapid pace due to the mobilization of conscripts, reservists, and the National Guard. On 16 September 1940, President Roosevelt signed the Selective Service Act into law. Unfortunately, the Regular Army and National Guard divisions were ill equipped to absorb the spike in manpower. Poor economic conditions caused by the Great Depression resulted in congressional budget restraints along with a public attitude of isolationism and pacifism. This contributed to the Army's unpreparedness as a new war loomed.[203]

During the fall and winter of 1940-1941 the Army underwent a transformation. The Army War College class for the year was canceled to free up more staff officers for the expanding Army. A General Headquarters for the Army (GHQ) was being organized and occupied the buildings of the War College. New Army headquarters were replacing the corps areas, and Army Corps was being established to assist in the training of the divisions. An intensive training program for all divisions got underway under the direction of GHQ. It was a period of the "Phony War" in Europe. No one could foresee American involvement in the European war, but the nation was preparing for every possibility.[204]

Since staff officers were needed for the newly organized army and corps headquarters, as well as for the divisions and other units, it was not surprising that the excess of field officers in the armored force at Fort Knox was gradually thinned and transferred to organizations in other areas. Even a few months of experience in the armored force brought knowledge of the capabilities and

---

202 George F. Hofmann; *Through Mobility We Conquer (The Mechanization of U.S. Cavalry):* Published by The University Press of Kentucky-2006 (Page 260)
203 ibid (Page 260)
204 Lucian K. Truscott, Jr.; *The Twilight of the U.S. Cavalry (Life in the Old Army, 1917-1942):* Published by the University Press of Kansas-1989 (Page 165)

1941 LOUISIANA MANEUVERS: "THE BIG ONE"

limitations of armor and some concept of the views regarding missions and methods of tactical employment. Fort Knox was truly a cavalry station, even though the horses were made of iron.[205]

The 1st and 13th Cavalry Regiments, both steeped in cavalry tradition, had formed the nucleus of the armored force. The first chief of the force was Brigadier General Adna R. Chaffee; other cavalrymen, such as Bruce Palmer, Charles L. Scott, and George S. Patton, had provided impetus, initiative, and leadership in the drive to form the organization. They and other cavalrymen had long recognized that aviation, motors, and armor would perform many of the missions that mounted men had performed in past wars, and perform those missions effectively. The enthusiasm that these officers shared with all personnel in the armored force during these early months was truly a cavalry spirit, and it made this period of service all the more valuable to those who were fortunate enough to experience it. Sadly, many officers who looked forward to more experience with the Armored Force received unrequested and unexpected assignments for duty with the General Staff or with troops at other stations. The officers of the Armored Force had to leave their "iron horses in the bluegrass" with some measure of regret.[206]

THE BIG ONE

Large-scale maneuvers were held in Louisiana each year from 1940 through 1944. However, the 1941 maneuver, or "The Big One," was the largest of them all.

By mid-1940 the Army stood at 300,000 regulars and 200,000 Guardsmen, but by the time Pearl Harbor was bombed the number of troops was in excess of 1.6 million. In 1941 the Army was capable of maneuvers that went far beyond the scope of the

---
205 ibid (Page 165)
206 ibid (Page 166)

1940 exercises. Louisiana again played host to some 400,000 soldiers and airmen for maneuvers over two, three-week periods in August and September 1941—only this time there were real trucks, tanks and airplanes. Even though some deficiencies remained to be corrected, the soldiers who participated in "The Big One" demonstrated without question that they knew their jobs, and they performed in a highly proficient military manner. Finally the nation possessed an Army that was at least partially capable of going to war.[207]

General Marshall replaced General Embick, who was retiring, with Brigadier General Lesley "Whitey" McNair, commandant of the Army's Command and General Staff School at Fort Leavenworth, Kansas. McNair became chief of staff of GHQ, U.S. Army, from July 1940 through March 1942. During that period McNair was promoted to major general (in September 1940) and temporary lieutenant general (in June 1941). The self-effacing McNair, whom Marshall described as "the brains of the Army," had not only crafted the military's 13-week basic training regimen but had also reoriented and reformed Leavenworth's curriculum, passing on to Marshall the names of his best students.

Too Old to Serve?

To some extent the previous August 1940 maneuvers were designed to test the officers at the higher levels of the National Guard divisions. Few of these officers passed the formal observation and scrutiny of higher command. General Marshall, fearful that overage, physically unfit Army officers hindered preparedness, instituted an age-in-grade policy in mid-1941. The policy established maximum ages for each officer grade. Men exceeding

---

207 Christopher R Gabel; *The U.S. Army GHQ Maneuvers of 1941:* Published by U.S. government Printing Office, Washington, D.C. 1991 (Page 15)

1941 LOUISIANA MANEUVERS: "THE BIG ONE"

the upper-age limit were removed from combat command or honorably retired.[208]

As the Guard was in federal service, the age-in-grade regulation affected state officers and fell most heavily on company grade officers (second lieutenants, first lieutenants and captains). Marshall weeded out, without mercy, officers who failed the standards. In some eyes, Marshall acted heartlessly, for these were men whose weekends and vacations had been loyally sacrificed over two long, dreary decades; and now that they had a chance to serve their country, they were being shoved aside to make room for regular officers. Many of the "victims" were influential and well connected, and Marshall himself was far more politically attuned than is often realized. However, he intended to have the best officer corps possible, and he let the chips fall where they might.

A few examples: Major General Ralph E. Truman of the Missouri National Guard was dropped from command of the 35th (Sandstorm) Division even though his cousin was the influential Senator Harry S. Truman. Major General Edward Martin of the Pennsylvania National Guard was dropped from command of the 28th (Keystone) Division even though he would soon be governor of his state. And Major General Claude Birkenhead of the Texas National Guard lost his command of the 36th (Texas) Division even though he was a prominent San Antonio lawyer with significant political connections.[209]

GENERAL MCNAIR GETS TO WORK

McNair, with Marshall's support, pushed an aggressive anti-tank philosophy that soon gained momentum. McNair and his chief of staff, Lieutenant Colonel Mark W. Clark, now had the authority to deal with the branch chiefs and the new

---
208 ibid (Page 15-16)
209 John B. Wilson; *Maneuver and Firepower-The Evolution of Divisions and Separate Brigades (Army Lineage Series):* Published by the Center of Military History –United States Army-Washington, D. C. 1998 (Page 144)

Figure 6-1. General Lesley McNair. *NATIONAL ARCHIVES*

protobranches—especially the Armored Force and its tanks, which he felt were too expensive. Another issue confronting McNair was how the horse-mechanized cavalry would maintain itself as a combat arm. He had more faith in the importance of infantry backed by artillery.

McNair wanted to increase the flexibility and mobility of infantry divisions by reducing numbers and eliminating the brigade headquarters. He became known for changing the heavy "square" infantry division of four regiments into a light triangular division of three regiments.[210] For example, after the experimental trials of

---

210 George F. Hofmann; *Through Mobility We Conquer (The Mechanization of U.S. Cavalry):* Published by The University Press of Kentucky-2006 (Page 262)

1939, the 3d Infantry Division was reorganized as a "triangular" division with three regiments capable of reforming into three regimental combat teams with supporting artillery, engineers, and service troops.

The military reservation at Fort Lewis, home to the 3d Infantry Division, is a vast area of nearly 100,000 acres of flat, gravelly soil. The terrain is heavily wooded, threaded with small streams, and dotted with small ponds and lakes. It is located east of U.S. Highway 99 between the cities of Tacoma and Olympia, Washington, and east of the southern reaches of Puget Sound.

When the National Guard was called into federal service for training during the expansion of 1939 and 1940, the 41st Infantry Division—composed primarily of troops from Washington and Oregon—was assembled at Fort Lewis and quartered in the cantonment area of temporary construction typical of so many camps of the day. The Guard unit still retained the old "square" organization with two infantry brigades, each of which had two regiments, an artillery brigade, and the usual service elements.[211]

With the organization of General Headquarters under General McNair, the old corps area organization, which had been in effect since 1920, was replaced with four individual armies. Under these armies, corps were established as tactical and training commands. Administration was handled for the most part through a post administrative organization.

The 9th Army Corps, operating under 4th Army Headquarters in San Francisco, was established as a training and tactical command at Fort Lewis. The 3d and 41st Infantry Divisions were the principal combat units of the command, and the 115th Cavalry of the Wyoming National Guard was the 9th Corps' cavalry regiment. Major General Kenyon A. Joyce, who had commanded the 3d Cavalry at Fort Myer, Virginia, in the early thirties, had been promoted to brigadier general in 1936

---

211 Lucian K. Truscott, Jr.; *The Twilight of the U.S. Cavalry (Life in the Old Army, 1917-1942):* Published by the University Press of Kansas-1989 (Page 168-169)

and major general in 1939. He was assigned command of the 9th Army Corps and would supervise its organization and training. Joyce, an able and astute commander, wanted a competent chief of staff to assist him in organizing 9th Corps headquarters and carrying out its training mission. Joyce was thoroughly familiar with many of the graduates of the Command and General Staff School as well as the Army War College. In early spring of 1941 he selected Lieutenant Colonel Dwight D. Eisenhower as his chief of staff. Eisenhower was promoted to colonel on 6 March 1941 prior to assuming his new role at 9th Army Corps.[212]

The GHQ Training Program

Army General Headquarters in Washington, D.C., directed a training program for all the divisions that were then in service. These exercises were to be prepared and conducted by the newly organized corps headquarters. In addition, GHQ would select one exercise during which its inspection teams would examine the state of training of the division and, incidentally, the performance of the corps commander and his staff.

GHQ prescribed five exercises, all repeated within each division in a corps. In general, the exercises involved command post exercises (CPXs) involving command staff and communications personnel. There were also 24-hour field exercises (FEs)—one-sided maneuvers in which umpires represented the enemy and the divisions executed such operations as night marches and organization of positions. The final division exercise was a free maneuver with one division operating against another and for which, in one case, the division would use ball ammunition.[213]

The War Department had recently acquired a large portion of the California ranch owned by newspaper magnate William Randolph Hearst. The new military installation was named

---

212 ibid (page 169)
213 ibid (Page 171)

the Hunter Liggett Military Reservation. For the upcoming maneuvers, the division-against-division and corps field exercises would take place at Hunter Liggett, while the remainder of the exercises would be conducted at Fort Lewis.

After the maneuver of division against division, the training period terminated in the corps field exercise, with the corps—using live ammunition—attacking an enemy position represented by targets. There was the usual horde of visitors and observers from Washington, from 4th Army Headquarters, and from other commands. This required the corps to provide a sizeable visitors' camp at Hunter Liggett Military Reservation, taxing the already overburdened facilities of King City and other communities in northern California's Salinas Valley.

During the maneuvers a large task force of staff officers from General Headquarters came out from Washington to conduct an inspection of the 1st Division. Inspectors were assigned to practically every element of the division and followed them throughout the exercise. Brigadier General Mark W. Clark, McNair's deputy, led the task force. He was one of two officers who had recently been promoted from the rank of lieutenant colonel to brigadier general.

Immediately following the exercise, the officers of the division, the umpires, and members of the corps staff assembled for a critique session. The umpires and GHQ inspectors voiced little criticism of the 1st Division's performance. On the contrary, the GHQ staff officers loudly praised the realistic nature of the exercise and the manner in which it had been conducted. General Joyce, the corps staff, and the officers of the division were pleased with themselves and congratulated each other for a job well done.

Unfortunately the euphoria was short-lived. Despite their praise for the troops, every inspector had compiled a long list of critical comments on the elements of the division he had observed. When the task force returned to Washington, the comments were compiled in a thick document that criticized practically everyone connected with the exercise, from General Joyce on down.[214]

AMERICA'S LARGEST PEACETIME MANEUVERS

Toward the end of the maneuver period at Hunter Liggett, Colonel Eisenhower departed 9th Corps and traveled to San Antonio, Texas, to be chief of staff of Third Army under General Walter Kruger. It was a step up for Colonel Eisenhower and would lead to a promotion in the near future.

Like General Marshall, McNair understood the challenges the United States faced in fighting the Germans and was concerned about his service's preparation. McNair decided to enlarge what General Embick had started, replacing the 70,000-soldier exercise held by First Army in the Carolinas in November 1940 with the largest peacetime exercise in American history. "We didn't know how soon war would come," McNair later observed, "but we knew it was coming, and we had to get together something of an army pretty darn fast." By the summer of 1941 the U.S. Army had grown large enough for McNair to engage it in maneuvers, which would involve Second Army (headquartered in Memphis under General Ben Lear) and Third Army (in San Antonio under General Kruger). The maneuver area would encompass most of the state of Louisiana and much of Arkansas and Eastern Texas.[215]

The 1941 Louisiana and Texas maneuvers were the first large-scale exercises held by the U.S. Army. Approximately 350,000 to 400,000 troops gathered in central Louisiana that rainy September to stage what *Life* magazine described as the "greatest sham battles in history." Fifteen Army divisions participated, including 10 from the National Guard: the 27th (NY), 31st (AL, FL, LA, MS), 32nd (MI, WI), 33rd (IL), 34th (IA, MN, ND, SD), 35th (KS, MO, NE), 36th (TX), 37th (OH), 38th (IN, KY, WV), and the 45th (AZ,

---

214 ibid (Page 173)
215 ibid (Page 174-175)

CO, NM, OK). Also involved were 12 Guard aerial observation squadrons and numerous other non-divisional units.[216]

As conscripted troops reported to their units, Merton Glover of Washington County, Wyoming, reported for his induction physical in December 1940 at Hot Springs, Wyoming. In January 1941 he received orders to report to Fort Meade, South Dakota, for induction into the U.S. Army. He would serve with the 4th Cavalry Regiment.

> I reported with several other local inductees for transport to our point of induction. They placed Ed Iron Cloud, Jr., A. Livermont, Last Horse, Red Eyes and Shot to Pieces on a bus headed to Custer, Wyoming. Once at Custer we met up with the Smith brothers (Henry and Fred), Bill Gould, Verlin Hunt, and Page More. The Army put us up at the Harney Hotel with tickets by rail to Fort Meade, South Dakota. We were inducted into the 4th Cavalry on 26 February 1941, the same day as our arrival. I left for one year's training, and it would be 4 years, 7 months and 25 days before I came home.
>
> Fort Meade, an old frontier cavalry post, still had a squadron of horse cavalry along with the 2d Squadron, which was called "mechanized" because it consisted of several armored scout cars, half tracks, trucks and about 200 motorcycles.
>
> G Troop was considered the first mechanized troop and had nearly all the bikes, which were largely Harleys except for eight new Indians. The troop's commanding

---

[216] George F. Hofmann; *Through Mobility We Conquer (The Mechanization of U.S. Cavalry):* Published by The University Press of Kentucky-2006 (Page 279)

officer kept these eight Indian motorcycles for his scouts, of which I was assigned.

At the induction orientation I claimed not to know anything about horses, and it became the reason I got in a mechanized squadron. In training and while learning to ride bikes (motorcycles), we covered a lot of open gumbo pastureland in Meade County as well as the rather large military reservation. One of the training exercises called for a one-week bivouac northeast of the fort. As it turned out, we had a big two-day rainstorm swoop through the area, resulting in all the bikes' wheels locking up as the thick gumbo rolled up on them. They ended up being hauled back to camp on a 6x6 truck.

About mid-summer of 1941 the whole 4th Cavalry Regiment was ordered to Louisiana for maneuvers. The horses were hauled by semi trucks (horse portees), [with] eight horses and eight men. The men, along with their individual tack and feed, rode over the fifth wheel. Part of the troop rode in big sidecar bikes (motorcycles). Each troop had a kitchen truck (6x6) and supply truck, accompanied by numerous armor-plated scout cars.

We went in a convoy that stretched several miles long, while those of us on bikes were used as traffic control. When our security officer passed a street or busy crossroad, he would motion the first bike to drop off and close the street to cross traffic. The trooper would wait until the whole convoy came by, and then he could go like hell (no four-lane traffic) and pass the whole convoy against traffic and fall in behind and wait to be dropped off again. That was about the only time we could speed up over 30 miles per hour (the Army speed limit).

1941 LOUISIANA MANEUVERS: "THE BIG ONE"

The first day we only made it to Chadron, Nebraska. We had to travel via Custer State Park and Hot Springs, as Highway 79 did not exist then. The only incidents that first day were a biker missed a curve and ran off into Legion Lake, while at Oelrichs a semi truck of horses messed a sharp curve and ran into a lumber yard—no damage except to the fences.

The folks at Chadron held a dance at the fairgrounds, but we always had an early bed check.

As I recall, the next night our convoy was in Oshkosh, Nebraska, down old Highway 30. We made 100 to 150 miles a day. The convoy was around five to six miles long. We stayed near Lincoln and Grand Island one night. I think we may have stopped one night in northern Kansas before getting to Fort Riley.

We laid over three to four days, resting horses and doing maintenance on vehicles. It was not a pleasant stay; we were on a second bench of a riverbank, newly leveled, which was the start of Camp Funstore. There was lots of rain and it was real muddy while we were living in pup tents.

From Fort Riley we traveled southeast cross the corner of Oklahoma into Arkansas. I remember we stayed one night in Pawhuska, Oklahoma, an Indian Reservation headquarters. They put on a war dance in our honor. We had several Pine Ridge Sioux boys at the time; they enjoyed it.

We eventually got into northeast Louisiana. We maneuvered up and down the Sabine River, the border between Louisiana and Texas, for the rest of the summer. I can't remember how long, but do remember it was early November before we got back to Fort Meade, by much the same route we had come.

Louisiana was a terrible country: hot, wet, rain, mud, mosquitoes, ticks, snakes of all kinds. No place to get dry or keep dry. It was very hard on horses, machinery, men and equipment.[217]

Another early Army conscript, Tilford "Pat" Olson, had the notoriety of being the youngest man to register for the draft in his hometown of Cyrus, Minnesota. He joined the 4th Cavalry Regiment at Fort Meade, South Dakota.

> I was inducted into the U.S. Army for a period of one year, to be paid $21 a month for my service. When leaving for boot camp we were to report to the courthouse in Glenwood, Minnesota, where we were escorted to the train depot. Our destination was Fort Snelling, Minnesota. This being my first time away from home, I was not the happiest fellow in this world. Nonetheless, I joined other men on the train from Minnesota, Montana, North Dakota and South Dakota, who were easy to get acquainted with. Two of these men were a part of my circle of friends during our four-and-a-half-year stay in the Army.
>
> Our first stop was Fort Snelling, where we were given a physical examination and were issued our uniforms. In most cases the size didn't seem very important. Then came the shoes. Standing in stocking feet, we were handed a bucket of sand for each hand, and then we stepped to a measuring device that recorded our shoe size. I had been wearing size $7\frac{1}{2}$ for a few years. Now it changed to $8\frac{1}{2}$ and was a much heavier shoe than I had ever worn before. These were regular work shoes with added tops and two buckles, bringing the

---

217 Merton Glover; *86 and counting:* Unpublished personal manuscript of author's life history-2003 (Page 29-31)

shoe top well over the ankle. This style was basic for the next few years.

We were sent from Fort Snelling on the long train ride to Fort Meade, South Dakota, 35 miles from Rapid City and the home of the 4th Cavalry Regiment. Upon arrival we were escorted to the theatre for pep talks, etc. The Sergeant Major began reading our names. We were to stand and give our weight. Anyone who weighed less than 150 pounds was directed to go to one side of the theatre. It was then that we found out that this outfit was half horse troops and half mechanized. Now all I was thinking was "horses." I liked them a lot but only to look at. I didn't know how I was going to handle this! We learned that a horse was assigned to each man, and he alone was responsible to feed, ride, clean and take care of it—which sometimes meant sleeping by it! I was very relieved when they got their quota before getting to my name, as I weighed only 132 pounds.

The remainder of us were assigned to the newly organized mechanized troops, and this made me feel much better. This group was a reconnaissance unit, and our purpose in battle would be to find and report all the information we could gather about the enemy—kind of unit, number, any landmarks, type of equipment, etc.—to our unit commanders.

At this time our quick mobile units were armored cars with large rubber tires (M8 armored cars known as Greyhounds) and driven by all four wheels. It had armor ¼-inch thick and weighed about 3½ tons. It was capable of speeds up to about 50 miles per hour. These armored cars were also equipped with one .50 caliber machine gun and one .30 caliber machine gun.

The U.S. Cavalry: Time of Transition

```
In the summer of 1941 the Little Eagle
tribe on the reservation of McLaughlin,S.D.
requested that their their soldier members
of the 4th Cavalrytake part ina religious
ceremony praying for peace,They also requested
white soldiers and equipment.
We were inthe process of converting from horse
to mechanized Cavalry.(note boots &britches)
The ceremony lasted 3 days. They treated us
very well.
This was my first trip as maintenance man,
whenever that many vehicles were out the
maintenance men went along. We carried tool
box and spare parts. That is my Jeep.
```

Figure 6-2. *Ambrose Zen*

Figure 6-3. *Ambrose Zen*

The machine guns were mounted on a rail around the whole car so they could be used in any direction.

We also had jeeps equipped with a .30 caliber machine gun, while all cars had two-way radios with a range, under good conditions, of about seven miles. We also had motorcycles. All noncommissioned officers had to be tested and licensed to operate all three units (armored cars, jeeps, and motorcycles) as these were used to relay orders and messages.

Figure 6-4. General Krueger (left) and Colonel George S. Patton discuss the maneuvers at Camp Beauregard in 1941. *PATTON MUSEUM*

Our time at Fort Meade was spent on many things. While maintaining our equipment we had inspections of all kinds including clothes, shaves, close order drills (with rifles) and learning how to get the most out of our equipment. Our physical fitness was tested in many ways—long marches with full field pack weighing 30 pounds as an example.

We had field maneuvers in the area of Belle Fourche and Spearfish, South Dakota. This land was primarily used for grazing sheep, so it was open range with very few fences. This made travel open to most any direction crosscountry, solving problems and missions assigned to us. Fort Meade was our home base for about a year and a half, but I did leave it on several occasions. One time I left was a drive with all our equipment to Arkansas,

Louisiana and Tennessee for more maneuvers in other areas with entirely different terrains. All units made this long trip, even the horses, which were transported using semi trucks. There were eight horses and eight men in each. The horses numbered about 250.

We took part in a number of parades en route and, of course, the horse troops stole the show as they were curried clean and washed bright, just shining in the sunlight. I believe some of these horses had been in more parades than most of the G.I.s. They marched nearly always in perfect lines, keeping time to the beat of the drums. The riders, too, in clean, pressed uniforms, shiny boots and trooper hats, made a very impressive parade unit.

Our outings were used in a lot of the war bond drives at that time. I, for one, thought we would never see action because of all the attention to the parades we were asked to do. I was wrong. It was about this time the beautiful horses were sent to Fort Riley, Kansas, and were replaced with light tanks.[218]

General McNair conceived a groundbreaking war game that mobilized 400,000 soldiers in two armies: the Red Army of the nation of "Kotmk," representing Kansas, Oklahoma, Texas, Missouri and Kentucky, with its capital at Houston; and the Blue Army of the nation of "Almat," comprising Arkansas, Louisiana, Mississippi, Alabama and Tennessee, with its capital at Birmingham. These maneuvers would test corps deployments and coordination between air and ground reconnaissance units, while a second set of corps-on-corps exercises would hone combat

---

218 Tilford "Pat" Olsen; *Memories of a Mission Accomplished:* Unpublished manuscript completed in 1997 (Page 2-4)

leadership skills. Headquarters for the maneuvers was the newly built Camp Polk (later Fort Polk) near Leesville, Louisiana.[219]

The scenario: following a war between the two nations in 1919, tensions continued to increase when Kotmk failed to secure navigation rights on the Mississippi River. The two nations squared off to do battle as negotiations between them broke down and their armies prepared to compete for control of the Mississippi River.[220]

Preliminary maneuvers began in late May 1941 as the two "countries" deployed their troops to strategic locations as a "navigation conference" between their "Inland Waterways Commissions" dragged on in Memphis. To acclimate the troops to battle noises, loudspeakers broadcast recordings throughout the Beauregard practice range. The sounds included dive bombers, machine guns, cannons and the wails of gas warning sirens.

The first skirmish of the maneuvers occurred on 17 June 1941, but the scenario did not call for full hostilities to break out until August 1941. As the starting date of the maneuvers neared, Central Louisiana was inundated with people and equipment. During the latter part of July 1941, soldiers began arriving at nearby camps, and as many as 300 to 400 Army vehicles passed through Alexandria each day. On 30 July 1941, 5,000 troops arrived. Ten thousand more came on 31 July 1941, with another 5,000 on 1 August 1941. Things continued this way until the simulated hostilities began.

Unfortunately the weather did not cooperate with General McNair's plans. The maneuvers were scheduled to begin in mid-August and run through September 1941, but a hurricane struck Louisiana just a week before the planned start date. All of the

---

[219] ibid J.R. "Bill" Bailey; *1941 Louisiana Maneuvers: The Big One:* Published by F+W Media Inc.-(2010 Military Vehicle Trader Magazine)]
[220] Jerry Purvis Sanson, PhD.; *Studying War: Central Louisiana and the Training of United States Troops 1939-1945*: Published as part of Sanson's college dissertation by Louisiana National Guard Public Affairs Office, 1994.

Figure 6-5. Army commanders during the 1941 Louisiana maneuvers. Left to right: Lieutenant General Ben Lear, Second Army (Red), and Lieutenant General Walter Krueger, Third Army (Blue). *U.S. ARMY*

rivers swelled; trucks got stuck in the mud and the soldiers suffered many hardships.[221]

As with General Embick's 1940 maneuvers, umpires graded individual supervisors and units on leadership and combat skills. Senior officers were warned to ensure proper supply and preparation of their troops. Communications systems that had plagued Embick the year before were improved with upgraded equipment, including new radios for senior commanders and their subordinates. This time, McNair insisted, senior commanders would stay as close to the front as the situation demanded.

---

221 ibid (Studying War: Central Louisiana and the Training of United States Troops 1939-1945)

RED VS. BLUE, SEPTEMBER 1941

General Marshall had spent considerable time on the 1941 maneuvers, calling them "a combat college for troop leading" and a laboratory to test the "new armored, anti-tank and air forces that had come of age since 1918." He personally observed many of the corps- and division-level maneuvers and, in the autumn, an expanded training exercise in the hills of North and South Carolina.

But Marshall's major focus was on the Red vs. Blue conflict in Louisiana and East Texas. The mock war began on 15 September, just three months before Pearl Harbor. As previously mentioned, the two "adversaries" were Lieutenant General Ben "Yoo-Hoo" Lear's Second Army (Red) and Lieutenant General Walter Krueger's Third Army (Blue).

Lear's Red Army was to act as a foreign army that invaded Louisiana from the coast, with the goal of defeating the Blue Army and occupying Louisiana. A hard-bitten, gruff-talking disciplinarian, Lear was not well liked by his troops, but he had an eye for detail and was surrounded by a cadre of talented and aggressive officers, including veterans of Embick's 1940 exercises. Among them was George S. Patton, whom Lear tasked to lead a lightning combined-arms strike against Krueger's Louisiana defenses.[222]

The first problem of the exercise had the Second Army (Red) V Corps, with 130,000 troops commanded by General Lear, deploying in an egg-shaped area and moving north to seize the Pleasant Hill-Noble-Mansfield oil field in northwest Louisiana near Shreveport. To accomplish this mission, V Corps had the 32d, 34th, 37th and 38th Infantry Divisions, the 1st Cavalry Division, and the 1st Tank Group. The men of the Red Army wore red armbands and "tin hats" (M17A1 helmets).

---

222 ibid [J.R. "Bill" Bailey; *1941 Louisiana Maneuvers: The Big One:* Published by F+W Media Inc.-(2010 Military Vehicle Trader Magazine)]

Playing defense, the Blue Army's VIII Corps had the 2d Armored Division; 2d, 36th and 45th Infantry Divisions; 18th Artillery Brigade and the 56th Cavalry Brigade. The Blue Army's mission was to attack southward, destroying the enemy and pushing the Red forces back into the Gulf of Mexico.[223]

Figure 6-6. **General Dwight D. Eisenhower.** *U.S. ARMY*

Lieutenant General Walter Krueger, commander of Third Army (Blue), had come to the United States from Germany at the age of eight. After serving as an enlisted man in the U.S. Army, Krueger was commissioned in 1901 as a second lieutenant. An aging veteran and competitive taskmaster who too quickly bristled at unintended slights, Krueger desperately wanted to beat Lear. He gathered a staff of brainy if little-known assistants, including Lieutenant Colonel Dwight Eisenhower as his chief of staff.

---

223 ibid J.R. "Bill" Bailey; *1941 Louisiana Maneuvers: The Big One:* Published by F+W Media Inc.-(2010 Military Vehicle Trader Magazine)]

1941 LOUISIANA MANEUVERS: "THE BIG ONE"

Eisenhower was an old friend of Patton's and, in May 1941, began planning Louisiana's defenses against Patton's tanks. Marshall, who had doubts about Eisenhower, accepted Krueger's word that "Ike" was a brilliant planner and tough soldier.

The Blue Army, using Colonel Eisenhower's detailed plans, edged north toward the Red Army. As the two armies converged, the rain made the roads slippery and dangerous. [224]

During the General Headquarters maneuvers the chief of cavalry, General John Herr, attempted to validate his horse portee-mechanized units. By then the mounted cavalry had lost its prestige to a new arm, the Armored Force. Herr was not optimistic.

Nonetheless, there was some satisfaction for the cavalry branch during the maneuvers. To some observers the mixed horse portee-mechanized cavalry regiment functioned best as a corps reconnaissance element. An observer from the Command and General Staff School noted that the cavalry mix functioned best when the horse-portee squadron deployed as a firebase while the mechanized squadron maneuvered.

There were the usual debates over the issue. General Bruce Palmer, Jr., then a cavalry captain, recalled that regimental control of cavalry favored mechanized elements rather than the horse. In spite of mixed feelings over the role of the cavalry, the maneuvers gave Herr some satisfaction, however short-lived. He continued to believe that his branch would not be decimated in favor of armor.

The maneuvers, however, demonstrated that the horse cavalry had lost its mobility. McNair found the cavalry no longer useful. Times were changing, and Herr's attempt to marry the horse with the machine had failed—a point even the Louisiana locals could sense, noting that many of the horses were being turned in for mechanized equipment such as scout cars.[225]

---

224 J.R. "Bill" Bailey; *1941 Louisiana Maneuvers: The Big One:* Published by F+W Media Inc.-(2010 Military Vehicle Trader Magazine)
225 George F. Hofmann; *Through Mobility We Conquer (The Mechanization of U.S. Cavalry):* Published by The University Press of Kentucky-2006 (Page 279-281)

First Phase, Red vs. Blue, August 1941

The first phase of the maneuvers began in the early morning darkness of 17 August 1941 in spite of cloudy skies and torrential rain showers. The Red Army made the first move.

The exercise soon ran into trouble. In Tennessee, the division had specialized in long marches and wide turning movements. However, during its initial activity in the maneuvers, it was forced to operate in narrow corridors between large boggy areas. Poor roads and ridgelines running perpendicular to the attack route made it difficult for the Red Army to advance against enemy anti-tank guns.

The Red Army made initial contact with the enemy along the Anacoco-Kurthwood-Hornbeck line. The reconnaissance battalion was delayed about one-and-a-half hours south of Kurthwood by a destroyed bridge, while the left column was held up for 35 minutes by a scout car south of Anacoco. After these delays, a platoon of tanks was placed in the lead and encountered little resistance until they met the 32d Infantry Division in a defile north of Rosepine.[226]

The exercise ended two days later, on 19 August 1941, with the Red Army's 66th Armored Regiment having advanced over 10 miles. Along the way the regiment captured towns and enemy supply trains and took many "enemy prisoners." The prisoners were turned over to the friendly motorized infantry, who had recently been rescued from a prisoner-of-war camp.

In an enveloping attack, the 45th Infantry surrounded the 1st Cavalry, while the 2d Armored had almost reached DeRidder. The reconnaissance battalion headed south; one of its companies was at Lake Charles.

---

[226] Donald E. Houston; *Hell on Wheels (The 2d Armored Division):* **Published by Presidio Press – 1977 (Page 176-177)**

1941 LOUISIANA MANEUVERS: "THE BIG ONE"

After the infantry set out smoke pots to hide a tank company's attack around the flank—and while the tank company was scaring the artillerymen—a tank platoon from the 3d Battalion, 66th Armored Regiment attacked from the rear and destroyed the artillery. Afterward the regiment began to move into the Lake Charles area.

The exercise ended at 3:00 p.m., with units bivouacked in place and keeping all roads open. During the lull, the men began the necessary maintenance on their iron machines while fighting off chiggers, mosquitoes and snakes. Some troopers found time to swim in the Sabine River. Unfortunately, some men had died in accidents, others from snakebites. Nonetheless, morale was high.[227]

Patton's tankers awaited their next challenge. The last two exercises were to be on a large scale: Second Army vs. Third Army.

The first exercise began at 5:00 a.m. on 15 September 1941 with Krueger's Third Army (Blue) having invaded southern Louisiana. Blue Army's mission was to attack up the Mississippi River Valley, thereby cutting the United States in half.

General Lear's Second Army (Red) was given the mission of repelling the invaders. The 2d Armored Division, part of Lear's 1st Armored Corps, was to move after dark on 14 September, cross the Red River at daylight, and seize the Fort Jesup-Many line that extended to the Sabine River. Once the line was taken, reconnaissance would push southward.

The Red Army's advance guard from the 1st Armored Division slipped across the Red River Bridge at Shreveport with the peep (later called the jeep), motorcycles and scout cars leading the way. The unit turned southward towards bivouac positions around Mansfield and stayed there to await the great armored attack scheduled for two days hence. Farther south, the 2d Armored Division's reconnaissance, artillery, and infantry elements crossed

---

227 ibid (Page 177)

the Clarence-Grand Ecore highway bridge north of Natchitoches and raced west. Before the last units had cleared the bridge, leading reconnaissance elements were already on the division's initial objective, located between the small town of Many and Fort Jesup. The 2d Armored Division's tanks crossed at the Coushatta highway bridge, midway between Shreveport and Natchitoches, and lumbered toward their concealed assembly positions near the town of Many, behind the division's reconnaissance screen.[228]

No sooner had operations begun than Lear's plan for Second Army began to unravel. Pilots of the Blue air force braved cloudy skies to attack columns of the 1st Armored Division on the roads leading south from Shreveport. The first planes appeared at about 8:20 a.m., and thereafter a continuous stream of Blue aircraft harassed the division. Other pilots penetrated the Red fighter umbrellas over Second Army's vital bridges. Overhead armadas of pursuit planes fought great dogfights, while sleek A-20A attack bombers and Navy dive bombers strafed the columns of tanks and trucks moving up to the front. At Coushatta, a Navy dive bomber collided with a defending Red P-40 at an altitude of 800 feet. Although the dive bomber landed safely, the fighter crashed, killing the pilot.[229]

Even more serious than the Blue air activity was the unexpected discovery of Blue reconnaissance along Second Army's initial objective line. At the town of Many, 2d Armored Division's reconnaissance battalion, the 82d, collided with a strong detachment of Blue cavalry from VIII Corps before the division had completely cleared the Red River bridges.

General Krueger's ground and air forces had located both Red armored divisions at the outset of the maneuver. Clearly the Third Army was moving much faster than General Lear had expected.[230]

---

228 Christopher R. Gabel; *The U.S. Army GHQ maneuvers of 1941:* Published by Center of Military History United States Army-Washington, D. C. 1991 (Page 69-70)
229 ibid (Page 70)
230 ibid (page 70)

Figure 6-7. The Douglas A-20A Havoc, an American WWII light attack bomber. *U.S. ARMY*

Beginning at 5:30 a.m. on 15 September 1941, General Krueger's supposedly ponderous square infantry divisions poured across their restraining line and pressed north, utilizing a procedure known as shuttling, in which troops alternately marched and leapfrogged ahead in quartermaster and artillery trucks. Red pilots, peering through the clouds and rain, spotted marching columns up to 36 miles long, with convoys varying from 95 to 400 trucks on the roads leading north.[231]

On Third Army's east flank, the Blue V Corps staged a textbook advance on Alexandria, launching a powerful counteroffensive to the east, with 106th Cavalry Regiment in the lead. V Corps reached the city without encountering serious opposition and started crossing the Red River. The Red Army blew all the bridges, but 37th Division crossed three battalions (1,200 men) to the east by boat. In the center of Third Army's line, IV Corps encountered

---

231 ibid (Page 70)

poor roads but no opposition as it advanced two divisions abreast behind the 6th Cavalry.[232]

Much to General Krueger's surprise, the bulk of the Red Army appeared to be in VIII Corps' zone on the western flank. The 113th Cavalry Regiment—the unit that had countered 2d Armored Division's reconnaissance elements in the small town of Many—fought a steady covering action all day against a growing force of Red tanks, infantry, and cavalry from the First Armored Corps.

By nightfall, Red troops of the 2d Armored Division's 41st Infantry Regiment had pushed the Blue cavalry back through Florien on the Leesville-Many highway and had established an outpost on the highlands to the east. But VIII Corps was nearby, pounding north from Leesville with the 45th and 36th Divisions in the lead.

Once he ascertained that the Red armored force was massed on his west flank, General Krueger attached the 1st Anti-Tank Group to VIII Corps. There was fighting around Peason Ridge, a stump-knobbed sector that had been part of the virgin pitch pine forests.[233]

By nightfall on 15 September 1941, the Red 2d Army had reached the initial objective line at Many-Colfax, although with incomplete and overextended units. In the 2d Armored Division sector, 2d Armored Brigade held approximately 20 miles of front from the Sabine River to Fort Jesup with a reconnaissance battalion, an infantry regiment, and one of the division's three armored regiments. These forces also held an outpost line that covered Mount Carmel and Florien, giving 2d Army a vital toehold on Peason Ridge, the dominating terrain feature of the maneuver area.

The 27th Division front extended from Fort Jesup to the vicinity of Provencal. The inexperienced and underequipped 6th

---
232 ibid (Page 70)
233 ibid (Page 70-71)

Figure 6-8. Men of the 4th Cavalry Regiment during the 1941 maneuvers. Note WWI "tin hat" on the gunner's head. *AMBROSE ZEN*

Figure 6-9. Reds in possession of Mount Carmel guard front of chuch but remain in half-track personnel carriers and bantam car.
DMITRI KESSEL/RALPH MORSE/TIMEPIX

Division held a line of no fewer than 30 miles from the 27th's left to the Red River at Colfax. The greater part of the Red Army was either east of the river or in reserve, awaiting the general offensive that was scheduled for 17 September.[234]

On Tuesday, 16 September 1941, Red 2d Army consolidated its positions and brought up the last elements of 1st Armored Corps and VII Corps. Along most of the front, action was limited to patrolling and skirmishing. The only major Red initiative of the day was a feint by the 1st Armored Division and 4th Cavalry Regiment toward Tenaha, Texas. The demonstration was uncoordinated and poorly executed, and apparently deceived nobody in Third Army except for some civilian journalists.[235]

Merton Glover of the 4th Cavalry Regiment recalled the difficulties that the troops faced during the maneuvers:

> I felt sorry for the horses: rain, mud and mosquitoes, plus being ridden on long marches. I don't think the hay was any good either. There were several horse regiments besides the 4th Cavalry, as well as horse pack artillery.
>
> It was a sight no one will ever see again: long columns of cavalry and artillery on the move, taking hours to pass a given point. I recall one incident I had with horses when riding my bike (motorcycle) one rainy, muddy night, trying to deliver a message to another unit. I had to half-ride and half-walk my Indian cycle through rain and mud six inches deep, until the machine got red-hot and had to lay it down to cool.
>
> I sat with my back to an oak tree and heard a noise ahead that I soon knew to be running horses. They ran by me and over my bike, stampeding. It was a picket

---

234 ibid (Page 71-72)
235 ibid (Page 72)

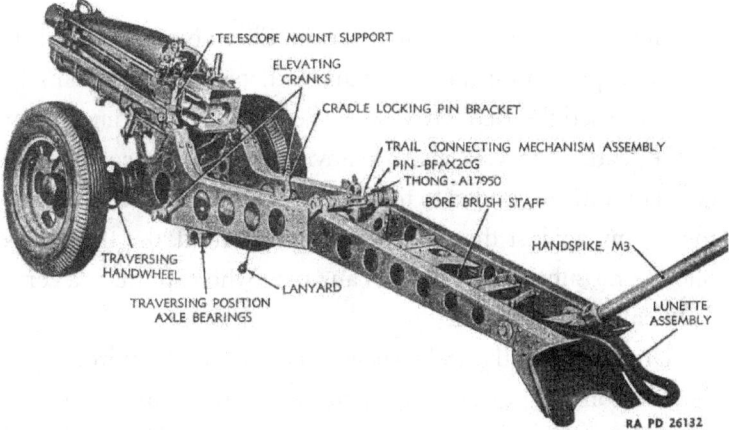

Figure 6-10. The pre-war 75 mm M1 pack howitzer had a "box trail" and wooden wheels and was designed to be pulled by a cavalry horse or artillery crew over friendly ground. The gun could be disassembled and packed onto six mules for movement through rough terrain.

line spooked and running wild, scattering gear and equipment. I heard later it took a couple of days to find all of the scattered equipment.

A picket line was a large rope anchored at each end and held about three feet high. Horses were tied to either side overnight when not in use. That maneuver was very tough on everything.

Every time we bivouacked, cavalry custom was to have a garbage pit—regulations said 6x6x6—dug if only for the night. Every time we broke camp someone was detailed to get in the pit before filling it and throw out the razorback pigs that fell in while looking for a bite to eat. Those woods were full of the half-wild hogs.

It was not uncommon to find a snake in your pup tent or blanket, seeking a warm dry place . . . not to mention lots of flies, ticks and mosquitoes. You had to inspect your body every day to pull ticks off.[236]

General Krueger's confidence in Eisenhower's tactical skill was soon proven on the Louisiana battlefield. When Lear's Red Army crossed the Red River on 15 September with Patton's tanks in the lead, Eisenhower was ready. Three of Krueger's mobile corps rapidly responded to the Red Army threat and moved to pin the enemy against the river. Patton laughed off the threat, even offering his subordinates $50 to any man who captured "a certain SOB called Eisenhower."

Unperturbed, Ike and Krueger ordered their armored units to flank Patton and prevent a breakout. As the two armies converged, the rain made the roads slippery and dangerous. Nonetheless, the umpires deemed the Blue Army's maneuver to be successful.[237]

AIR ACTIVITY

The Blue Army's air arm was stationed at Esler Field, near Camp Beauregard, and at Lake Charles. At Esler Field the Blue troops painted a mock orchard on the runways for camouflage, built false houses and dummy airplanes, and installed machine gun nests as protection against paratroopers. Both the Red and Blue armies began the exercises with more than 400 airplanes each. As the skies cleared, more surveillance airplanes appeared. The bombers found more targets and the fighter aircraft engaged in dogfights. The Blue Army maintained air supremacy by flying more missions and using more airplanes on each mission.[238]

Blue Army positioned itself in front of the Red Army near Provencal, south of Natchitoches. On 17 September 1941, the

---

[236] Merton Glover; *86 and counting:* Unpublished personal manuscript of author's life history-2003 (Page 31-32)
[237] Mark Perry; *The Greatest War Games-Louisiana Maneuvers (1940-41):* Article Published in Military History Magazine- February/March 2009
[238] ibid

Blue Army dropped 127 paratroopers behind Red Army lines, where they fought toward a pontoon bridge across the Red River at Clarence, south of Campti, and disrupted the Red Army's supply and communications. An ingenious squad of Blue troopers captured several trucks and used them to enter Red Army headquarters, where they rolled a smoke bomb into the command post. One paratrooper—a private—entered the command post with his pistol at the ready, drew a bead on the occupants, and ordered everyone to surrender. When a high-ranking officer scolded the paratrooper for being foolish and ordered him to lay down his gun, the paratrooper refused and replied, "Nuts to you, General! This is war."[239]

Phase 1 of the combined Second and Third Army maneuvers opened on 18 September 1941 at Red River, Louisiana. The Red Army attacked the Blue Army southeast of Shreveport.

The battle went poorly for the Red Army, whose tanks were bogged down in swamps or destroyed by anti-tank guns. Within 24 hours, General Patton's 2nd Armored Division lost 20 percent of its tanks. The Red Army retreated in the Horse's Head Maneuver Area near Natchitoches, and eventually the entire Red Army retreated along the hundred-mile front.

During the Red Army retreat, Blue Army aircraft dropped propaganda leaflets that stated, "Your commanders are withholding from you the terrible fact of your impending defeat. . . . Your food stores have been captured. No one is going to bring up any of the steaks that the men of the Army will have tonight. Rout, disaster, hunger, sleepless nights in the forest are ahead of you. Surrender while there is yet time."

General McNair monitored the reports and on Friday, 19 September 1941, ordered a cease-fire. The first part of the war

---

[239] J.R. "Bill" Bailey; *1941 Louisiana Maneuvers: The Big One:* Published by F+W Media Inc.-(2010 Military Vehicle Trader Magazine)

Figure 6-11. Soldier from the 106th Cavalry during the 1941 Louisiana maneuvers.

was over. The Blue Army, and Eisenhower, had won. The second phase was scheduled to begin.[240]

The fight had lasted just five days and ended with the defeat of the Red Army. The Blue forces had turned the Red Army's flank and destroyed its bridges. The terrain proved unsuitable for armor. Instead of keeping its original tank attack moving, the Red Army had halted, waiting for unavailable motorized infantry to move up from the rear. The tankers tried to break through at various points with some success, but they were captured or destroyed by Third (Blue) Army's hunter-killer anti-tank units.

Blue Army had superior manpower (213,000 troops against the Red Army's 123,000) and superior firepower, plus three provisional anti-tank groups. Using these advantages, Blue Army deftly swung its main forces from the vicinity of Alexandria to a

---

[240] Mark Perry; *The Greatest War Games-Louisiana Maneuvers (1940-41):* Article Published in Military History Magazine- February/March 2009

position squarely in front of the Red Army's armored divisions. There, the Blue Army placed great masses of men, artillery and anti-tank guns. Furthermore, the Blue Army's air force, under the command of Major General Herbert A. Dargue, won command of the skies and gave the Red forces a terrific pounding well to the rear of their lines.

The question of whether a smaller unit, using tanks, could hold off a non-armored force three times its size was answered, for the time being, in the negative. In their defense, the tankers pointed out that had the maneuvers occurred elsewhere, the results would have been different. "Wait 'til the next time," grumbled Patton's men. They felt that they had been denied the opportunity to use their speed and power properly, and they were anxious to show what they could do.[241]

Although the Blue Army had outperformed the Red Army in the first phase of the maneuvers, military authorities considered the maneuvers to be a success. General McNair, GHQ chief of staff, said, "The principal weakness was deficiency in small unit training due fundamentally to inadequate leadership." To this weakness Army leadership added another: the lack of enough highly motorized infantry that were trained to work with the armored forces.

In spite of these problems the Army was extremely pleased. Its men were in magnificent physical condition and, even in the rain and darkness, hungry and tired, they had fought continuously and well for days at a time. In the swamps and amongst the chigger-infested fields of Louisiana the troops had achieved higher morale than ever attained during past training camps.

The maneuvers were not without casualties: 17 soldiers died during the first week. Seven men died in motor vehicle accidents,

---

[241] Jerry Purvis Sanson, PhD.; *Studying War: Central Louisiana and the Training of United States Troops 1939-1945*: Published as part of Sanson's college dissertation by Louisiana National Guard Public Affairs Office, 1994.

five were killed in airplane crashes, two drowned, two died from disease, and one committed suicide. However, this number was much lower than the 130 the Army had predicted.[242]

Figure 6-12. "Take Five!" Troops resting on the side of the road. Note the command car and two M3A1 scout cars parked alongside the roadway. ERVIN ADEN

While GHQ approached these maneuvers with the utmost seriousness, there were soldiers—as is normal within the ranks—who perceived the exercises as games to be played. Cecil (Mick) Maguire recalled his experiences during the maneuvers:

> At my age I now realize the seriousness of, and the actual need for, the maneuvers at the time. The U.S. Army was small, inexperienced, and outmoded. The government was in a near panic to try to catch and surpass the foreign powers. But in the early '40s I was

---

242 ibid

1941 LOUISIANA MANEUVERS: "THE BIG ONE"

just a kid, and I thought that the General Staff had invented these war games so that I could have a lot of fun, which I proceeded to do.

On the maneuvers we identified the opposing armies as the Red and the Blue armies. We identified the vehicles with red or blue bunting. Infantry and other dismounted troops wore red or blue armbands. An article about the Louisiana maneuvers mentioned that a couple of generals had done some cheating. I hadn't known that. I *did* know that a lot of lesser ranks cheated a whole bunch. I know I cheated—not often, but big time.

One time quite early, before Pearl Harbor, as a motorcycle messenger I was supposed to deliver a packet of map overlays to a division headquarters via a long circuitous route, but instead I left the maneuver boundaries and took a really short route up a Louisiana state highway. I saved enough time to stop at a small drive-in restaurant to have a nice lunch. I delivered the packet on time.

A couple of years later, as a tank commander, I left the maneuver area legally, just me and my tank driver, to go to an ordnance depot to get a new auxiliary motor installed. (It was a motor/generator unit, mostly to support round-the-clock radio use.)

When I had left the maneuver area, I was in the Blue Army, but we took off the blue bunting when we left. So when we got back we tried to enter the area at the same place we left. The MPs stopped us and asked, "Reds or Blues?" Looking around I could see nothing but red banners everywhere, so I blurted out "Red!" The MP told me to get my markings out and "put 'em on," which I did. (Everybody in the 106th carried both colors.)

Louie (my driver) and I set off northerly to find my headquarters. I didn't want to stop to ask anyone in the Red Army for directions, so we headed for a small town called Robeline, which was right in the middle of the maneuver area and off limits to the military.

We went into Robeline with red bunting wrapped around the turret, stopped in the middle of town, changed to blue ID, and drove out the other side. After about three to four miles of seeing nobody but civilians, we blundered into a Blue roadblock that had an anti-tank gun. They were waving a white flag, signifying that they were shooting at us. The officer in charge quizzed me as to who we were and what we were doing there. I told him what he wanted to know, he told me where he had seen cavalry a few hours before, and we were home free.[243]

Figure 6-13. Trooper from the 106th Cavalry Regiment beside an M3A1 Stuart light tank. *JOHN BECK*

---

243 Cecil (Mick) Maguire; email to Gary Palmer dated 01 September 2005

Maguire also recalled General Herr's infamous horse portees:

> I participated in the Louisiana maneuvers every year, and in between there was a multitude of tactical problems and field exercises to keep us sleeping among the pine trees as often as we slept in camp. The regiment had done the 1940 maneuvers in Camp McCoy, Wisconsin, as a 100-percent horse regiment.
>
> We did the 1941 Louisiana maneuvers as a half-horse and half-mechanized regiment. Are you familiar with "portee" equipment? We had semi-trailer trucks with large stake trailers on them. The trailers had roll-up canvas tops, and the tailgates folded down to make ramps. The trailers held eight horses, eight riders, eight saddles, eight bridles, eight blankets, eight bales of hay, and eight bags of oats. The idea was to get the horses over the highway quickly to the scene of action.[244]

Figure 6-14. Oh well, it was just an idea: horse portee used during the 1941 Louisiana maneuvers. *CAMP BEAUREGARD COLLECTION*

---

244 ibid

Figure 6-15. A 4th Cavalry horse portee making a river crossing during maneuvers. *Ambrose Zen*

Figure 6-16. 2d Lt Robert Moore of the 106th Cavalry. This photo was taken while he was attending Texas A&M University's ROTC program in 1942. Moore was a close friend of Sergeant Raymond Teske. *Michael Moore*

Figure 6-17. Sergeant Raymond Teske of the 106th Cavalry Regiment, mounted in full cavalry gear during the 1941 Louisiana maneuvers. RAYMOND TESKE, JR.

Figure 6-18. Rain—big drops of it—driven by the furious winds of a tropical storm, pelts down on the crew of a topless infantry weapons carrier. The .30 caliber machine gun is better protected than the men, who hunch their backs into wind and try to keep water from rolling down the back of their necks.
Note splashes on pavement.

Figure 6-19. A Troop, 106th Cavalry Regiment, at Camp Livingston.
Ervin Aden

Figure 6-20. (Left to right) Captain Oscar Wilson and Lieutenant Colonel John Homfeld walk the company streets at Camp Livingston. ERVIN ADEN

Figure 6-21. M3 White scout cars—so called because they were manufactured by the White Motor Company—in the 106th Cavalry's parking area. EUGENE JOHNSTON

Figure 6-22. Cavalry regiment with an instructor in background teaching aircraft recognition, 1941 Louisiana maneuvers.
EUGENE JOHNSON

Figure 6-23. Rare photograph of mounted cavalry with an M3 scout car providing defense, 1941 Louisiana maneuvers.
CAMP BEAUREGARD COLLECTION

1941 LOUISIANA MANEUVERS: "THE BIG ONE"

Figure 6-24 Mounted cavalry troop with an M3 scout car during the 1941 Louisiana maneuvers. *U.S. ARMY*

SECOND PHASE, 24 SEPTEMBER 1941

The second phase of the maneuvers began at noon on 24 September 1941 with General Krueger and the Blue Army making the first move. The Blue Army held a large number of tanks in reserve near Lake Charles, including General Patton's 2nd Armored Division, which had been transferred from the Red Army to the Blue Army. The 1st Cavalry Division crossed the Sabine River into Texas and turned north, while the Blue Army in Louisiana advanced along a front between the Sabine and Red Rivers.

Third Army was deployed near Lake Charles and Deridder in southwest Louisiana. The unit was made up of 215,000 men with three anti-tank divisions but fewer tanks than it had during the first stage of the maneuvers. The men wore blue armbands and fatigue hats. The umpires wore white armbands and white bands around their campaign hats.

Figure 6-25. An M2A1 medium tank of the 192nd Tank Battalion charges across an open field during the 1941 Louisiana Maneuvers. Note the sign that reads MEDIUM TANK. The American Army was so unprepared for war in 1941 that it had few real medium tanks, so lighter versions such as this the M2A1 stood in for their heavier counterparts during the maneuvers.

Among the non-divisional National Guard units participating in the 1941 Louisiana maneuvers were the 192nd and 194th Tank Battalions. Each was organized by combining the 16 prewar divisional tank companies, assigned one per division, into separate tank battalions. The 192nd was composed of four tank companies from Wisconsin, Illinois, Ohio and Kentucky. The 194th only had three Guard tank companies, one each from Minnesota, Missouri and California. It never had a fourth line company.

Both of these battalions (minus Company B of the 194th from California, which was reassigned) fought against the Japanese in the Philippines during the opening days of World War II. Both were compelled to surrender and their men were taken into captivity, participating in the infamous Bataan Death March. FORT GEORGE G. MEADE MUSEUM

Some units lacked adequate weaponry and used signs to represent equipment that was unavailable. According to James Bollich of Lafayette in his book, *Bataan Death March: A Soldier's Story*, "Instead of having actual machine guns, anti-aircraft guns, foxholes, etc., there were wooden signs all around to indicate these. If the air raid siren went off we were supposed to run to one of these signs. The one way the maneuvers did apparently help us with down the line was to adapt to hard, rough outdoor living."[245]

Figure 6-26. Simulated .50 caliber machine gun. Lack of adequate weaponry forced the Army to use facsimiles in the field. *CAMP BEAUREGARD COLLECTION*

Following his failure to break out from the Red River "beachhead" while acting as Red Army's armored division commander, Patton was made a commander in Krueger's Blue Army, which was scheduled to take the offensive during the second set of exercises.

---

[245] Jerry Purvis Sanson, PhD.; *Studying War: Central Louisiana and the Training of United States Troops 1939-1945*: Published as part of Sanson's college dissertation by Louisiana National Guard Public Affairs Office, 1994.

The Red Army stiffened its defenses in Louisiana; a battle erupted at Mansfield. The Blue Army's 1st Cavalry crossed the Sabine River at Logansport, Louisiana, and Carthage, Texas, and attacked Shreveport from the south. Simultaneously, Patton's forces crossed into Louisiana and attacked Shreveport from the north. Meanwhile, Patton's 2nd Armored Division crossed the Sabine River into Texas at Orange, and headed to Beaumont before turning north.

In the latter part of September, as McNair watched in amazement, Patton led his armored corps in a massed flanking attack against the Red Army's defenses. The 2nd Armored Division advanced 200 miles through northern Louisiana and East Texas in three days, enveloping Lear's flank. It was a brilliant maneuver. The Red Army was caught in a vise, and the Red Army was surrounded. McNair called a halt to the second and final stage of the maneuvers on 28 September 1941, after only four days of operations.[246]

Results of the 1941 Louisiana Maneuvers

The 1941 Louisiana maneuvers—the largest training exercise held in the United States at that time—were considered a great success. All of the umpires agreed that the Louisiana weather was unpleasant, with soldiers struggling through rain, mud, dust and heat. It was acknowledged that "realistic military training can lead to injuries and death due to safety risks incurred through various factors including lack of sleep, lack of energy, the presence of heavy equipment, traffic accidents, and the presence of firearms. During the Louisiana maneuvers, 26 men died. Most men lost their lives from drowning in the Sabine River and vehicle accidents. One died from getting struck by lightning, and one had a heart attack at age 24."

---

246 ibid (Studying War: Central Louisiana and the Training of United States Troops 1939-1945: etc)

1941 LOUISIANA MANEUVERS: "THE BIG ONE"

Army staff officers from Washington, D.C., led by Lieutenant General Leslie McNair and Chief of Staff General George C. Marshall, monitored the battles throughout Louisiana from their headquarters at Camp Polk. Decisions of all types concerning the maneuvers were made at this location.

Marshall made his intentions clear: "I want the mistakes made in Louisiana, not made in Europe," he said. "If it doesn't work, find out what we need to do to make it work."

Coincidentally, one of the officers who participated in the maneuvers was the same officer who, in 1940, had decided where in the cut-over timberlands Camp Polk would be built. That officer was none other than Colonel Dwight Eisenhower. He was promoted to the rank of general following the completion of the 1941 Louisiana maneuvers.[247]

Other officers involved in the maneuvers would go on to fame during World War II. General George C. Marshall continued to serve as chief of staff of the Army, Dwight D. Eisenhower became Supreme Allied Commander in Europe, and Mark Clark commanded the 5th Army in Italy.

In addition, J. Lawton "Lightning Joe" Collins, who was from New Orleans, commanded the 25th Infantry Division on Guadalcanal before going to England to command VII Corps.[248]

Tilford Olson, who served in the 4th Cavalry Regiment, recalled an interesting story about Collins:

> It was on our maneuvers in the South that the unit I was in was selected to take our commanding general to a new forward position. This was done at night in a complete blackout. We felt it was an honor to be selected. These cars (armored cars) had a crew of

---

[247] Rickey Robertson; *Do You Remember Camp Polk and the Louisiana Maneuvers:* Published in Army Motors Magazine-Number 122 (Page 30)
[248] ibid (Page 30)

five: car commander, driver, radio operator, and two gunners. The armored windshield was down, the side armor up, leaving an opening of about a ½ inch by 6 inches for the driver to look through.

On this occasion the General [Collins] sat beside the driver and had the same amount of vision. The only one standing to improve his vision was the car commander. This was Sergeant Stackhouse from Sioux Falls, South Dakota. The sergeant stood behind the driver, and from this position he could pass signals to the driver without using his voice. For instance, a push on the back meant to go forward. The harder the push, the faster the speed. Pulling back meant to back up or stop. To go right or left required a push on the corresponding shoulder: the harder the push, the sharper the curve. There were many other signals as well.

We were to advance our position through a densely wooded area. Yes, the woods can be very dark at night! Near the end of our ride the road became just a trail, barely visible, running through the woods, which actually helped because the trees brushing on either side of the armored car would guide us up the trail.

When we reached our destination, the Sergeant jumped out of the car to check the area and came back to open the door for the General, telling him it was "all clear." The General spoke to the Sergeant and thanked him "for a job well done." Then the General turned to the driver, shook his hand, and said, "Thanks for the good ride." This recognition was something out of the ordinary.

Years later, back home again in Cyrus, Minnesota, my family and I sat in our living room watching our very first TV. There was a special program on and

1941 LOUISIANA MANEUVERS: "THE BIG ONE"

the guest was being introduced. He was an especially good-looking man and his buttons, pins and medals shone under the bright TV lights. The introduction continued. . . . The four-star general, Lawton Collins, came to the microphone and he waved a greeting. I, in my living room, waved back.

One of my daughters saw me and asked, "Are you cracking up, Dad?" I assured her that I didn't think so, not at the present time anyway.

The wave had been a spontaneous thing. I considered the General on TV to be a friend. I told my family this same story about driving the armored car in blackout conditions, and how I had been the driver of that car as we moved through the woods during the black of night in the countryside of Tennessee.[249]

Before the United States entered World War II, three major maneuvers were conducted in Louisiana. These exercises helped recast the entire U.S. Army: its strategies, equipment, and leadership. Many of the nation's most recognizable and decorated military leaders developed their strategic theories at these maneuvers. General Courtney Hodges, General Robert Hasbrouck, Brigadier General William Hoge and Major General John Devine would go on to long, distinguished careers, forged in battle, using the skills that were developed in Louisiana.[250]

---

[249] Tilford "Pat" Olsen; *Memories of a Mission Accomplished:* Unpublished manuscript completed in 1997 (Page 5-7)
[250] Rickey Robertson; *Do You Remember Camp Polk and the Louisiana Maneuvers:* Published in Army Motors Magazine-Number 122 (Page 30)

CHAPTER VII

THE ARGUMENT OVER MECHANIZATION GOES ON

The Louisiana maneuvers served as a classroom for future leaders and as a vast laboratory for testing strategies and innovations. Army Chief of Staff George Marshall declared central Louisiana the "finest training area" he had ever seen. Dwight D. Eisenhower's career took a dramatic upward turn as a result of his performance during the maneuvers. General Lesley McNair oversaw the 1941 armored maneuvers and was responsible for training the Regular Army and National Guard troops. More than anyone else, McNair was credited with preparing millions of young soldiers to fight in World War II.[251]

General McNair was impressed with the deployment of tank destroyers during the maneuvers. He believed these new

---
251 ibid (Page 30)

mobile, self-propelled weapons would increase the pace of battle. Moreover, he was convinced that "combined arms" meant the employment of the traditional infantry-artillery team.

The tank destroyer doctrine supported a reactive defense-mobile force that could counterattack armored breakthroughs. This anti-tank doctrine benefited from a tactical mistake that occurred during the 1941 Louisiana maneuvers: Lieutenant General Ben Lear, a testy old cavalryman who commanded the Red Army, misemployed his two armored divisions. Consequently, the I Armored Corps commander, General Charles Scott, lacked firm control of the Corps' 1st and 2d Armored Divisions. The tankers were embarrassed, but Patton, who had commanded the 2d Armored Division since November 1940, received compliments from Lieutenant General Walter Kruger, the commander of the Blue Army, for displaying "high morale, technical proficiency, and devotion to duty. . . . Your leadership has produced a fighting organization."[252]

General Krueger's motorized infantry and anti-tank guns outmaneuvered the tankers, who were confined to a main highway and were unable to make flank attacks. General Lear was concerned that the swampy terrain would swallow up his tanks. *Life* magazine reported, "Swamps, airplanes and anti-tank guns stop advances of tanks."

Lear and his armored divisions were not the only ones who were embarrassed. The 1941 maneuvers also saw the temporary decline of large armored units because McNair began to favor independent tank battalions being assigned to infantry divisions.

Colonel Sydney Hind, who commanded an armored infantry regiment during the maneuvers, added that the maneuvers proved "beyond a doubt the necessity for a combined arms team." One issue that bothered Colonel Hind during the maneuvers was a lack of close-in tactical air support. He maintained that there was "no

---

252 George F. Hofmann; *Through Mobility We Conquer (The Mechanization of U.S. Cavalry):* Published by the University Press of Kentucky-2006 (Page 281)

direct communication between the troops on the ground and the supporting pilots in the air." This problem was solved later when tactical air put one of its forward observers—a pilot—inside a tank with an air radio to direct ground assaults. It was interesting to recall, Hinds claimed, "That only one air-ground observer ever volunteered for a second tour. He was determined to win a Silver Star, which he did, along with a Purple Heart."[253]

CONTINUED DEVELOPMENT OF MECHANIZATION

As word of the unfolding European tragedy reached the United States, Army Chief of Staff General George C. Marshall was already working to transform the Army's anti-tank defenses. Although most agreed that the U.S. Army, as it was currently organized, could do little to thwart the same type of German attack shown to be so effective in Europe, few knew how to transform the Army to meet this threat. As early as 14 April 1941, General Marshall directed that immediate consideration be given to the creation of additional highly mobile anti-tank units at corps and army level. On 15 April, Brigadier General H. L. Twaddle, the War Department's assistant chief of staff, G-3, held the first of several conferences that focused on anti-tank operations. All branches present at the conference decided in favor of offensive rather than defensive anti-tank tactics.[254]

Unfortunately, because of an extremely limited budget, the chiefs of infantry, artillery, and cavalry each sought ownership of the development of anti-tank defenses to increase their sphere of influence. Armor branch stood out, however, as not wanting this mission, fearing it would be counter to the offensive character of the fledging armored force.[255]

---

253 ibid (Page 282)
254 Bryan E. Denny, Major, US Army; The Evolution and Demise of U.S. Tank Destroyer Doctrine in the Second World War: Published at Fort Leavenworth, Kansas 2003 (Page 9)
255 ibid (Page 9)

Figure 7-1. General George C. Marshall, the Army Chief of Staff.
U.S. Army

While the conference did create a divisional anti-tank battalion by transferring 37 mm anti-tank guns from the field artillery, its numbers were still relatively small. To the dismay of General McNair, the infantry regiments were able to retain their anti-tank companies, thereby keeping things piecemeal rather than focusing on building anti-tank units. McNair had developed a strong attachment to the belief that you did not need a tank to beat another tank, calling it "poor economy to use a $35,000 medium tank to destroy another tank when the job can be done by a gun costing a fraction as much."[256]

McNair had experimented with anti-tank organizations in 1937 in San Antonio and while serving as commandant of the

---

256 ibid (Page 10)

Command and General Staff School at Fort Leavenworth. His frustration at the Army's inability to adopt or even discuss a solution to the German blitzkrieg is evident in a statement he made on 12 April 1941:[257]

> It is beyond belief that so little could be done on the [anti-tank] question in view of all that has happened and is happening abroad. I for one have missed no opportunity to hammer for something real in the way of anti-tank defense, but so far have gotten nowhere. I have no reason now to feel encouraged but can only hope this apathy will not continue indefinitely.[258]

McNair's belief—that tanks should be confined to infantry support and exploitation operations while utilizing anti-tank guns to destroy enemy armor—contributed greatly to the development of Army anti-tank doctrine.

However, Marshall was not overly enthused about the results of the conference on anti-tank operations. He felt that rivalry between the branches would prevent a quick and effective solution to the problem. In an address on 14 May 1941, Marshall indicated that the defense against armored forces was a problem beyond the capabilities of any one branch. In addition, Marshall said that the issue probably required a special force of combined arms—capable of rapid movement, interception, and active—rather than passive defense tactics. Marshall directed the assistant chief of staff, G-3, to take "immediate action on anti-tank measures to include an offensive weapon and organization to combat armored forces."[259]

---

257 ibid (Page 10)
258 ibid (Page 10)
259 ibid (Page 10)

Figure 7-2. Major General Andrew D. Bruce. *NATIONAL ARCHIVES*

The following day Lieutenant Colonel Andrew D. Bruce was named as the head of the Anti-tank Planning Board. Bruce quickly took over responsibility for the anti-tank conferences and began a campaign to unite all officers assigned to anti-tank units and share the developments in anti-tank organization, weapons, and doctrine.[260]

One of Colonel Bruce's first orders of business was to organize the anti-tank units into elements that could train, deploy, and fight. In August 1941 he issued a directive to the commanding general

---
260 ibid (Page 11)

of the Third Army, instructing him to organize his anti-tank units into groups of three battalions each. The new anti-tank groups would operate under the control of General Headquarters and would be committed as necessary, depending upon the armored threat. Brigadier General McNair's influence here is undeniable as he was the GHQ chief of staff and, as early as August 1940, had "expressed his preference for anti-tank 'groups' of three battalions, in order to afford a better control of large numbers of guns concentrating at a threatened point."[261]

Figure 7-3. M3 tank destroyer. *NATIONAL ARCHIVES*

The planning board also procured the anti-tank branch's first weapons system. With little time before the country would be at war, Bruce made the best use of the weapons systems available. A French ordnance officer told Bruce that the 75 mm gun the Army had on hand was used effectively to combat German armored forces in Europe. The guns mounted on the Army's M3 half-track would provide an intermediate anti-tank weapon to equip provisional units for field testing. This improvisation resulted in the Army's first self-propelled anti-tank gun, known as the M3 or

---

261 Ibid (Page 11)

75 mm gun motor carriage. The weapon made its debut during the Louisiana maneuvers of September 1941. [262]

The Louisiana maneuvers pitted Second Army, in control of 1st Armored Corps (two armored divisions), against Third Army, commanding three General Headquarters anti-tank groups. Leaving nothing to chance, General McNair issued specific directives to the commanding general of Third Army on the organization and tactical employment of the groups. This directive, dated 8 August 1941, laid the foundation for tank destroyer doctrine. Each group was to consist of three anti-tank battalions, with each having its own "headquarters company, ground and air reconnaissance elements, and intelligence, signal, engineer, and infantry units, all fully motorized."

Although both offensive and defensive operations were discussed, General McNair stressed "speedy and aggressive action to search out and attack opposing tanks before they had assumed formation." Although only one group out of the three would participate in major anti-tank action during the two weeks of maneuvers, the end results led to strong opinions among Army officers. The proponents of anti-tank units claimed the groups had performed well "except for a tendency" of higher headquarters "to dissipate their strength and to commit then to positions prematurely."[263]

THE TANK DESTROYER AND FIRING CENTER

Anti-tank units needed their own place to train. Army posts of the time were small and inadequate for the maneuvers envisioned by the tank destroyer planners. On 19 December 1941, Colonel Bruce and his aides traveled in civilian clothes to inspect several possible sites for the new school. On 20 December 1941—just two weeks after the Pearl Harbor attack by the Japanese and the

---

262 ibid (Page 11-12)
263 ibid (Page 12)

The Argument Over Mechanization Goes On

United States' entry into World War II—Bruce toured Killeen, Texas, and decided it was adequate for the Army's needs.

On 10 January 1942, the Army announced that its new Tank Destroyer and Firing Center would be located at and around Killeen.[264] The initial land purchase was 108,000 acres and involved the displacement of many local families. Army land agents opened an office in Gatesville and purchased the land. As families moved out, the communities of Clear Creek, Elijah, Antelope, Sugar Loaf and others ceased to exist. The state highway department began constructing roads that would allow the large numbers of men and equipment to reach the new Army installation. Bruce recommended that the new post be named Camp Hood, after General John Bell Hood, a Texas Civil War hero.[265]

All construction was to be completed by 15 August 1942. Several contractors were hired to build the various facilities on post, including facilities for 4,000 German POWs. Construction of the initial 108,000 acres was completed by 1 September 1942. More land was added to the camp, and the remaining construction was completed a year later on 1 September 1943.

Camp Hood grew to 158,000 acres and boasted 5,630 buildings and 35 ranges. The Tank Destroyer and Firing Center headquarters, commanded by Bruce, moved from temporary quarters in Temple, Texas, to Camp Hood on 21 August 1942; and Camp Hood officially opened for business on 18 September 1942.[266]

Based on guidance from the War Department, Colonel Bruce quickly organized his new department. He had two primary missions: one, to develop the doctrine that tank destroyer forces would train and fight with; and two, to liaise with the Ordnance Branch, the National Defense Research Committee and the Inventors Council in the testing and developing of future weapons.

---
264 ibid (Page 12)
265 ibid (Page 12)
266 ibid (Page 13)

The tank destroyer field manual (FM 18-5), published in June 1942, became the doctrinal basis for tank destroyer training and combat operations. The manual put into print the principles General McNair had emphasized and continued to develop the aggressive offensive spirit already forming in the tank destroyers. The FM stated in its foreword, "There is but one objective of tank destroyer units, this being plainly inferred by their designation. It is the destruction of hostile tanks." The manual further defined tank destroyer units as being "especially designed for offensive action against hostile armored forces."[267]

The FM was very specific about the general nature of tank destroyer deployment. It stated that the minimum number of tank destroyers should be left to cover obstacles, but the maximum number should be held in reserve to increase their effectiveness once they were committed against the bulk of the enemy armor. The FM also characterized tank destroyer action as "rapid movements, sudden changes in the situation, or brief but extremely violent combats separated by sporadic lulls."

The manual admitted that the light armor protection made the crews vulnerable, but offset this issue with the fact that the vehicles were mobile and could move into and out of firing positions rapidly. To meet the massive German armored formations, FM 18-5 also prescribed that tank destroyer battalions should be the basic tactical unit of operation against the enemy, in conjunction with or in support of infantry, cavalry, motorized, or armored divisions. To ensure the battalion remained a decisive yet independent element, it was organized around a headquarters and headquarters company, with three tank destroyer companies and a reconnaissance company.[268]

The FM warned against "slugging matches" with German tanks, but stressed that tank destroyers must rely on mobility and superior observation to carry the day. This would require

---
267 Ibid (Page 14)
268 ibid (Page 15)

"vigorous reconnaissance to locate hostile tanks and movement to advantageous positions from which to attack the enemy." In short, the tank destroyer crewmen would have to know the ground on which they were expected to fight, identify likely firing positions along avenues that German tanks would travel, move rapidly to those firing positions, and identify and strike the German armored column in the flank. Naturally the Germans were expected to be at a disadvantage because tanks were less mobile and the tank crews suffered from limited visibility.

The manual also served as a warning to division commanders that "uncoordinated action and dispersion with consequent loss of effectiveness" might result from the "employment of small tank destroyer units," their "distribution with a view to covering every possible avenue of tank approach," or "affording immediate protection to all echelons of the forces."

The second major task of the Tank Destroyer Tactical Firing Center was the development of the ultimate tank destroyer. With the M3 already in production as an expedient vehicle, serious consideration was given to the procurement of a vehicle designed specifically for the new force. The Tank Destroyer Board's decision to procure an additional vehicle was also intended to correct deficiencies identified in the M3 during the maneuvers in the Carolinas and Louisiana. Colonel Bruce wanted the new weapon to be a "fast-moving vehicle armed with a weapon with a powerful punch, which could be easily and quickly fired," and that it have "enough armor protection against small arms fire, so that the weapon could not be put out by a machine gun."

The new vehicle would have 13 specific characteristics, of which mobility was the most important. The tank destroyer would have greater mobility, under all conditions, than German tanks. Unfortunately, no existing vehicle possessed these characteristics, meaning significant work needed to be done to bring this "super duper" new tank destroyer to life. In the field the M3s and their crews would pay for any lack of proper research and development, unless another solution could be arranged.

An interim vehicle would bridge the gap between the hastily improvised M3 and the vehicle called for by Bruce. The vehicle would feature the characteristics already established by the Tank Destroyer Board, but would have to compromise some of those characteristics to utilize current production vehicle designs and equipment.[269]

This new vehicle utilized the already proven M4A2 Sherman medium-tank chassis. For armor penetration the three-inch (76.2-millimeter) anti-aircraft gun seemed to do the job. The gun had already undergone sufficient testing to be fielded as an anti-aircraft weapon, and little modification was required to mount it on a self-propelled platform. Additionally, the gun fired a high-velocity round that allowed for direct-fire operations and provided the kinetic energy to penetrate German armor.

The vehicle would also have to provide basic armored protection for its crew. The vehicle would be turreted, but the turret armor would provide protection only against small arms and machine guns. The light turret also allowed the gunner to traverse the turret easily since it was entirely manually operated.

In addition, the turret top would be open—a controversial decision that many tank destroyer crewmen would question throughout the war.[270] The board's official reason for keeping the tank destroyer topless was to create the maximum observation area in which to seek out enemy tanks. The topless, lightly armored turret also minimized the weight of the vehicle, increasing its mobility. As tank destroyer crewmen would attest, the topless turret gave the crewmen the feeling of vulnerability and served as a constant reminder that they were not in a tank and that tank tactics would not work.

---

269 ibid (Page 15)
270 ibid (Page 15)

The Argument Over Mechanization Goes On

The resulting combination of equipment and ideas produced the three-inch gun motor carriage M10 and the M10A1 (Wolverine). The only difference between the M10 and the M10A1 was in the engine. A 375-horsepower twin six diesel engine powered the M10, while a 500-horsepower Ford V-8 powered the M10A1. Both vehicles weighed around 32 tons, primarily from their Sherman hulls, and had maximum speeds of 39 miles per hour.[271]

Figure 7-4. M10 tank destroyer.

Camp Hood continued training tank destroyers through the war. In 1944 the installation also began training artillerymen and, on 10 March 1944, became the Infantry Replacement Training Center. Camp Hood processed an average of 55,000 to 60,000 personnel.[272]

As a result of the maneuvers a new quasi arm of the Army was activated on 1 December 1941 and designated the Tank Destroyer Center. In March 1942 it was redesignated as Tank Destroyer Command, and in August 1942 it was renamed the

---
271 ibid (Page 16)
272 ibid (Page 16)

Tank Destroyer Center. Additional quasi arms were added: the Anti-Aircraft Command and Airborne Command were activated in March 1942.

The Army considered the Christie suspension system for a full-tracked, fast-moving tank destroyer. The Buick Division of General Motors, employing the long, helical independent Christie suspension system, built a few models for the Ordnance Department. Eventually this design gave way to a new suspension: torsion bars that ran under the chassis, eliminating the side spaces required for the helical springs.[273]

OFFICERS MOVE UP

A new generation of officers moved to the forefront, including Generals George S. Patton and Dwight D. Eisenhower, and Brigadier Generals Adna R. Chaffee, Jr., and Jonathan Wainwright. Within weeks of the conclusion of the maneuvers, Chaffee received a promotion and orders to form the nation's first armored divisions. He authorized the acquisition of land near Leesville, Louisiana, for the 3rd Armored Division, which would later distinguish itself in the battle to retake Normandy and in other crucial European engagements. The new post that Chaffee helped establish would ultimately become Fort Polk.

Unfortunately, Chaffee's exhaustion and a bout with cancer took their toll. In December 1940 General Marshall received a letter from Dr. Edward D. Churchill of Massachusetts General Hospital. A confidential report about Chaffee's condition stated that it was not reasonable to expect an arrest of his tumor. In fact, the physicians were not optimistic, giving Chaffee not much longer than a year to live. He could no longer carry on his fight for a separate branch, or to deal with the stubborn General Herr. Perhaps Chaffee's growing illness prevented the mechanized

---

[273] George F. Hofmann; *Through Mobility We Conquer (The Mechanization of U.S. Cavalry):* Published by the University Press of Kentucky-2006 (Page 282)

maneuver-oriented principle from being articulated among the Army elite; many of them failed to absorb his revolutionary doctrine before they entered combat. Patton, however, understood this when he commanded the 2d Armored Division during the 1941 maneuvers, as did many other cavalrymen who moved over to armor.[274]

Chaffee's delivered to Congress his last message on the issue of mechanization in May 1941. He blamed the prewar situation that created considerable uncertainty about an independent armor doctrine on the combat branch chiefs' competition over funding. This resulted in many differences of opinion and a lack of responsiveness to the needs of modern warfare.

General Chaffee also took issue with the country's pacifist tendencies, which led to unpreparedness for war. This was the same observation that General Van Voorhis had made when he took over command of the 7th Cavalry Brigade in 1936. Van Voorhis and many senior cavalrymen at Fort Knox believed that branch-specific doctrine and tactics drove separate developmental policies when it came to organization and equipment. This made the funding for new weapons and armored fighting vehicles much too competitive for Depression-squeezed defense dollars.

Chaffee added that the U.S. military "failed to evaluate properly the importance of combined arms in armored units." This was a reiteration of General Parker's argument from the late 1920s.

Shortly after Chaffee's message to Congress, he died on 22 August 1941. Ernest Harmon later wrote, "There can be no tangible record of Chaffee's brilliance, but there were to be times in Africa, Italy, and Germany when the Allied Command could have well used his judgment and shrewd intelligence.[275]

After General Chaffee's death, General Marshall began looking for a replacement who was an expert in firepower.

---

274 ibid (Page 282)
275 ibid (Page 283)

Marshall chose a prominent polo player, Major General Jacob L. Devers—an artilleryman and classmate of General Patton—to take command of the Armored Force. What was missing from the force was a balanced, self-contained, combined arms organization of mechanized cavalry, armor, armored infantry, and armored self-propelled artillery. In addition, there were unresolved equipment issues regarding armored cars, half-tracks, self-propelled artillery vs. towed artillery, and light tanks vs. medium tanks.[276]

Devers had been chief of staff to General Daniel Van Voorhis in V Corps, and as such had the opportunity to discuss the role of mechanized warfare and analyze the successful execution of the German blitzkrieg before Van Voorhis was assigned to the Panama Canal Department. Though Devers was not convinced of the utility of an armored force, he did digest Van Voorhis' ideas and subsequently introduced new organizational changes and operations far beyond those suggested by Chaffee.

When Devers arrived at Fort Knox he immediately began crushing whatever jealousies remained between the mechanized cavalry and the infantry-tank branch. Devers shifted the Armored Force from a light to a heavy combined arms ground force. In addition, Devers expanded the firepower of the Armored Force.

Chaffee had tried but failed to emphasize the importance of self-propelled field artillery. Part of Chaffee's dilemma was a lack of support from the chief of field artillery, who saw no need to develop self-propelled artillery for the mechanized cavalry. Devers, however, changed this approach by adding self-propelled artillery to increase firepower, thus enhancing the operational mobility of the tank-dominated Armored Force. Devers—along with his chief of staff, Lieutenant Colonel Edward H. Brooks, a future armored division commander during World War II—played a major role in acquiring the M7 105 mm self-propelled howitzer and the M8

---

276 Ibid (page 283)

75 mm self-propelled howitzer assault gun so critical for mobile armored and mechanized cavalry tactics.

Another one of Devers' innovations was adding light spotter aircraft and ground forward observers for battalions. Also, earlier semi-tracked vehicles called half-tracks had gone through a series of developments; now they became standard for armored infantry regiments and battalions.[277]

Chaffee's cavalryman ideas dominated early Armored Force doctrine, and now Devers moved to set new doctrine corresponding with his reorganization of the Force. However, General McNair responded caustically. He believed the Armored Force was trying to become an autonomous branch and suggested that it "should join the Army." Meanwhile, McNair's tank destroyer idea moved forward under the command of an infantryman, Colonel Andrew D. Bruce. Consequently, the autonomy and status of the Armored Force began to decline. McNair's doctrine was clear: "The counterattack long has been termed the soul of defense." However, McNair did accept the possibility of a tank-vs.-tank counterattack; however, he felt "the procedure would be too costly."

While Devers was taking command of the Armored Force and beginning to implement changes, General Herr's negative influence continued to plague Marshall's attempts at reorganization. With the Armored Force splitting from the cavalry branch and creating its own identity, a question arose: how would mechanized and horse-mechanized cavalry units fit in during this period of organizational turbulence and McNair's attempts to centralize control?[278]

Herr's response was explained in the Army's 1941 Cavalry Field Manual 2-15. The traditional combat mission of cavalry was outlined under his direction. It reiterated the call for greater mobility and firepower in both the horse and mechanized elements. At the regimental level, the mission was reconnaissance and security for

---

277 ibid (Page 285)
278 ibid (Page 285)

army corps. At squadron level, the emphasis was on "sneak and peek" reconnaissance, and how to avoid combat when necessary. The mechanized cavalry squadron was also assigned security or delaying missions. The manual added that horse portee units from cavalry regiments could, if necessary, reinforce the mechanized squadron. Furthermore, FM 2-15 emphasized Herr's belief that various combinations of mechanized elements and horses allowed for greater flexibility.

The manual further defined the role of mechanized reconnaissance troops assigned to infantry divisions: to engage in pursuit and exploitation after a breakthrough. In addition to reconnaissance, the mechanized cavalry troop was to perform operations such as gap filling, providing a mobile reserve, and liaising between larger units. Mechanized cavalry elements, the manual stated, "were to be equipped with armored and self-propelled motor vehicles designed for combat purposes and in which weapons are mounted."[279]

Figure 7-5. The M7 105 mm self-propelled gun, also known as the Priest, running through a French town. *U.S. ARMY*

---

279 ibid (Page 286)

The War Powers Acts of 1941 and 1942 gave President Franklin D. Roosevelt, as wartime commander-in-chief, the legal right to exert authority over war agencies, including the War Department. This authority was passed down to General Marshall, giving him the legal power to reshuffle the antiquated branch system. In March 1942, Herr and the other branch chiefs' influence finally ended when Marshall eliminated the offices of the chief of cavalry, infantry, field artillery, and coast artillery.

While these events were unfolding, General Marshall made reference to the branch chiefs, believing them to be bitterly opposed to the reorganization. He was referring to General John K. Herr and Major General Robert M. Danford, the chief of field artillery. (General Lynch had stepped down the year before and was succeeded by Major General Courtney H. Hodges, whom Marshall considered a supporter.)

The old-order chiefs were not perceived as loyal members of the Army's new team. General Herr was gone, as were his horses. After the elimination of the line branch chief offices, the Army Ground Forces began to mechanize the remaining Regular Army and National Guard horse-mechanized and horse-motor units.[280]

THE NEW TEAM

With the last impediment to wholesale mechanization removed, the process went forward rapidly. The Army's two cavalry divisions, the 1st and the 2d, did not ship a single horse overseas during World War II. The 1st Cavalry Division dismounted before shipping to Australia. It retained its "square" organization to compensate for its smaller numbers. Members of the division fought with distinction under General Douglas MacArthur throughout the remainder of World War II, but they fought as infantrymen. The next time the old horse division remounted, it

---

280 ibid (Page 287)

would see the sons of these men in helicopters in another Asian theater, Vietnam.[281]

The 2d Cavalry Division, with its African-American brigade composed of the 9th and 10th Cavalry Regiments, was broken up to create other units—primarily service troop units in North Africa. The 2d and 14th Cavalry Regiments that made up the other brigade of the 2d Cavalry Division, along with the other Army non-divisional regiments, supplied a large number of personnel to form the newly created 2d, 3rd, 11th and 14th Armored Regiments of the newly created 9th and 10th Armored Divisions.

None of the National Guard's horse cavalry divisions were federalized, and many of the division's members saw service in field artillery, coastal artillery, and tank destroyer units. Only later, after personnel had been distributed to new units, did the Army Ground Forces resurrect the regimental headquarters of the 2d, 3d, 6th, and 11th Cavalry Regiments, around which they formed mechanized cavalry regiments.[282]

Once the chief of staff "decided to mechanize all . . . corps cavalry regiments on the advice of General McNair and his G-3"—and "without any consultation with General Herr" —the process moved swiftly. This led to the full mechanization of the 4th and 6th Cavalry Regiments of the Regular Army as well as the National Guard regiments operating in the horse-mechanized configuration. The result was an all-mechanized regiment consisting of a regimental headquarters and two mechanized cavalry squadrons. Each squadron consisted of two reconnaissance troops and a support troop that included light tanks and assault guns.[283]

---

281 Matthew Darlington Morton; *Men on Iron Ponies (The Death and Rebirth of the Modern U.S. Cavalry):* Published by Northern Illinois University Press-2009 (Page 93)
282 ibid (Page 93)
283 ibid (Page 93-94)

The Argument Over Mechanization Goes On

Wartime events in Europe taught valuable lessons as mechanized equipment proved more useful than the horse for reconnaissance missions. In the summer of 1940 the British became convinced that light tanks were good only for reconnaissance. The British also abandoned all of their open scout cars and simple armored cars, finding them insufficient. Believing that "the need for an overhead armor is absolutely imperative," the British sought improvement in the form of wheeled reconnaissance vehicles with tank-like bodies, or light tanks.

The Cavalry School at Fort Riley was not oblivious to what was happening in North Africa and Europe. "The scout car is not considered a suitable ... vehicle for mechanized reconnaissance"— but it had to serve as a substitute until something better was available. A replacement for the scout car was not expected to be available until September 1942, so American scouts went to North Africa in open scout cars and jeeps. (The new scout car didn't appear until 1943.)

Motorcycles also remained in all the reconnaissance organizations, but they were also viewed as having limited utility for carrying messages and performing traffic control, and they continued to be replaced by jeeps.[284]

The largest weapon found in any reconnaissance organization was the 75 mm howitzer. The weapon was organic to the platoons of the armored reconnaissance battalions and was also part of the support troop of the 1942 mechanized cavalry squadron. This particular weapon system was not controversial.

The 37 mm cannon, on the other hand, gained more attention. Army doctrine in 1942 viewed the 37 mm cannon—installed on light tanks of the mechanized cavalry squadrons and armored reconnaissance battalions—as an effective anti-mechanized weapon system. Also considered effective were the .50 and .30 caliber machine guns, which fired armor-piercing bullets at close

---

284 ibid (Page 94)

Figure 7-6. Howitzer motor M8 carriage showing stubby 75 mm in front of open turret.

range against light armored vehicles. However, reports from abroad changed this view and led to the modification of existing doctrine in staff studies conducted at the Cavalry School at Fort Riley.[285]

The Army published its premier how-to-fight manual, FM 100-5, *Operations*, in May 1941—the first official update of doctrine since 1923. This extremely important publication established the foundation that guided the efforts of a rapidly expanding army of citizen-soldiers. To accomplish the tasks that soldiers had performed in the past, the 1941 edition of FM 100-5 anticipated that the cavalry would continue to have a mission. The Army defined cavalry as a force composed of "highly mobile ground units, horse, motor, and mechanized," characterized "by a high degree of battlefield mobility" that allowed it to rapidly and easily move firepower from "one position or locality to another."

---

285 ibid (Page 94-95)

The Argument Over Mechanization Goes On

> Cavalry is capable of offensive combat; exploitation and pursuit; seizing and holding important terrain until the arrival of the main forces; ground reconnaissance; ground counter-reconnaissance (screening), both moving and stationary; security for the front, flank, and rear of other forces on the march, at the halt, and in battle; delaying actions; covering the retrograde movements of other forces; combat liaison between large units; acting as a mobile reserve for other forces; harassing action; and surprise action against designated objectives deep in hostile rear areas.

The Cavalry Branch retained all of its former missions, including combat.[286]

Because the Armored Force was not recognized as a branch unto itself, it was not described in the chapter detailing the basic characteristics of the arms and services. Rather, FM 100-5, *Operations*, placed the description of the armored division in the same chapter as the description of the horse cavalry division. There, the armored division was described as a "powerfully armed and armored, highly mobile force chiefly characterized as possessing a high degree of 'protective fire power' and battlefield mobility." These characteristics allowed the armored division to operate at extended distances with its self-contained logistical support assets, and were remarkably similar to the characterists assigned to the cavalry. Unlike the cavalry, with its horses, the doctrine still described the armored division as being sensitive to "obstacles, unfavorable terrain, darkness and weather."

Unlike the cavalry, the armored division's list of possible missions did not include reconnaissance. The armored division was considered to be "capable of engaging in all forms of combat, but its primary role is in offensive operations against hostile rear

---

286 ibid (page 95)

areas." One could argue that by 1942 the Armored Force had usurped the prized missions of the horse cavalry, leaving the Cavalry Branch with reconnaissance as its primary responsibility.[287]

The cavalry field manual, FM 2-15, *Employment of Cavalry*, was also published in 1941. This document superseded the Cavalry Field Manual, Volume 3, which was dated 3 January 1938. The new manual echoed FM 100-5, *Operations*, in regard to the branch's identity as a combat arm organized primarily to perform missions requiring great mobility and firepower.

More emphatically, the doctrine stated that "the primary mission of Cavalry is combat." A key limitation, however, was the inescapable fact that animals and machines required care and maintenance. The "effectiveness of cavalry over extended periods" depended on "the efficiency of the supply and maintenance system." Even so, horses still only needed food, water, and rest to "renew their strength wherever they happened to be," while vehicles were "dependent upon supplies, such as fuel, oil, and spare parts."[288]

In regard to organization, the 1941 version of the FM 2-15 manual was out of date by the time the United States entered World War II, as it reflected General Herr's greatest vision: a cavalry corps composed of "two or more cavalry divisions" and assorted "supporting or reinforcing units." Description of horse divisions, brigades, regiments, and horse-mechanized units were now irrelevant, but the manual used the same definitions of reconnaissance as the 1941 edition of FM 100-5, *Operations*. The "mobility of its mechanized elements on roads and of its horses on practically any type of terrain" made cavalry "well-suited to perform reconnaissance missions using horse elements, mechanized reconnaissance elements, or a combination of the two."

---

287 ibid (Page 97)
288 ibid (Page 96)

The Argument Over Mechanization Goes On

Cavalry doctrine in 1941 called for the reconnaissance detachments to operate "from 1 hour to 2 days" in advance of the main body of forces, with the normal distance being "one day's march." This allowed enough time for the supported commander to make decisions using information gained by the reconnaissance detachments.

While the doctrine clearly recognized the large disparity between the distance and speed at which mechanized units could travel, it still bound these units to the march rate of the main body. The doctrine dealt with the disparity by addressing the organization of reconnaissance detachments. Squadrons of horse cavalry could expect the attachment of scout cars, heavy machine guns, anti-tank guns, pack radios, motorcycles, and "transportation facilities." Mechanized elements could expect few attachments because they already had the necessary heavy weapons and communications equipment to forge ahead on their own. In addition, mechanized units could expect the striking power of horse cavalry to follow rapidly in portee trailers. In either case, horsemen or mechanized scouts could also expect to be attached to engineers, and possibly artillery, to help them in their mission.[289]

The Department of Tactics wasted little time examining the doctrinal implications of the War Department's decision to remove the horse from the horse-mechanized regiment. In its *Report on the Organization of a Mechanized Reconnaissance Regiment as the Cavalry Component of an Army Corps*, published at the Cavalry School on 14 February 1942, the Department of Tactics signaled a shift in Cavalry Branch doctrine in regard to mechanization and its capabilities.

In regard to depth, the report stated that mechanized regiments in support of corps could be expected to move as far as 125 miles in advance of the corps they supported. As they moved forward,

---

289 ibid (Page 98)

mechanized reconnaissance units were still to use "stealth," but there was now a greater emphasis that they be "provided with strength to penetrate the opposing screen" rather than seeking gaps or finding flanks. Having gained contact with the enemy at extended range, it was now recognized that contact had to be maintained.

Subsequent review of tactical doctrine also called for a force with the strength to "pierce the enemy screen" and continue until the "enemy contour" could be discerned. This action was meant to prevent the enemy from gaining the same kind of information.

The changes for what was expected of a mechanized cavalry regiment were subtle, but represented the first acknowledgment that Cavalry Branch had to find a way to perform its long-standing doctrinal mission of reconnaissance—without the horse.[290]

The tactical doctrine reviews also captured the essence of what had taken place with the removal of the horse from the horse-mechanized regiment. The 530 riflemen who rode on horses to assist the mechanized men were no longer needed. These riflemen were replaced with thirty-four light tanks and twelve 75 mm howitzers in the support troops of the newly organized regiment. The reorganization earned the remark that "the traditional cavalry shock element is in the support troops." The regiment gained a substantial amount of firepower at the expense of small arms capability, but it also lost the troops doctrinally deemed essential to support the light tanks offered in lieu of rifle troops.

At the same time, *un*official doctrine recognized that without the horses and the men who rode them, mechanized elements had to act alone in some cases to fight for the information the corps needed. Unlike their brothers in the armored reconnaissance battalions, soldiers in the mechanized elements couldn't necessarily depend on the swift arrival of supporting arms directly under the

---

290 ibid (Page 100)

control of a division commander. Only time would tell if the new organization would support the increasing burden being shifted to mechanized reconnaissance units.[291]

What was the fallout from General Herr's reluctance to totally mechanize the cavalry?" Many cavalrymen saw the inevitability of change and rejected the horse cavalry and Herr's attitude. They believed that changes would provide new opportunities to integrate doctrine and technology. These cavalry officers left their branch and grew to be dominant leaders in the new Armored Force and influential in molding a new doctrine of combined arms. They made their own doctrine as the war went on.

THE CAVALRYMEN RIDE ON

By 31 December 1941, cavalry strength stood at only 59,804 personnel within an Army of 1,686,403 troops. Virtually all who joined the Armored Force were influenced by what Van Voorhis and Chaffee had accomplished during the 1930s at Fort Knox. Certainly, General Patton's name is at the top of the list of opportunists; he was constantly aware of events that affected the mechanization of the Army. This is confirmed in histories of Patton including Martin Blumenson's *Patton Papers*, Carlo D'Este's *Patton: A Genius for War*, and Roger H. Nye's *The Patton Mind: Professional Development of an Extraordinary Leader*.[292]

Major Ernest N. Harmon was one of a number of distinguished cavalrymen who moved over to armor. Harmon, who eventually commanded armored divisions and a corps during World War II, recalled a painful meeting with General John K. Herr, the chief of cavalry: Herr told Harmon that if the latter moved over to tanks, their friendship was over. It was evident to Harmon that Herr was angry and distressed over the events that would replace his beloved

---

291 ibid (Page 111)
292 George F. Hofmann; *Through Mobility We Conquer (The Mechanization of U.S. Cavalry):* Published by the University Press of Kentucky-2006 (Page 292)

horse cavalry. In the end, Harmon did go to tanks. He wanted to learn more about a new method of war fighting. Harmon was assigned to the 1st Cavalry (Mechanized) and became acquainted with General Chaffee. This launched Harmon's legendary career in armor, where he gained the reputation of being hot-tempered and acquired the nickname "Old Gravel Voice."[293]

Another one of Eisenhower's renowned cavalrymen who eventually commanded an army during the war was Lucian K. Truscott, Jr. Truscott came into the army from civilian life and spent most of his long military career in the cavalry, which he dearly valued because of its historical tradition. He recalled that Herr possessed great charm and welcomed him as an honest and forthright chief of cavalry. Yet Truscott noted Herr was impatient with cavalrymen who held contrary views. As he had with Harmon, Herr made his opinions known to Truscott.[294]

After what he called his "gorgeous years" at Fort Riley, James Polk was assigned to the famed 3d Cavalry, which had provided the escort for the burial of the Unknown Soldier at Arlington National Cemetery in Washington, D.C., on 11 November 1921. (Until 1941 members of the regiment stood guard at the Tomb of the Unknown Soldier.)

Polk later noted that the "old horse cavalry" opposed armor. The disturbing part of this attitude, said Polk, was that it affected a cavalryman's efficiency rating in his branch if he went over to armor. Herr—whom Polk felt was too horse-bound—let it be known that if cavalrymen went to Fort Knox, their standing in the cavalry branch was in jeopardy. Polk would later say that "dedicated horse people were stupid in not going to the mountains and the tough terrain where cavalry could hold its own against any enemy." He supported the use of horse cavalry under certain conditions. Polk believed that what killed the cavalry as the traditional mounted

---

293 ibid (Page 293)
294 ibid (Page 293)

arm were the tank activities during the western desert maneuvers that took place before the United States entered World War II.[295]

General Robert W. Grow, who served in the office of the chief of cavalry during Herr's tour, also began to "think armor." In 1940 he joined the 2d Armored Division and began a long, admirable association with Patton. However, Grow and Patton had markedly different personalities: whereas Patton was flamboyant and theatrical, Grow was methodical and businesslike. Yet they got along because of their common belief that armor was the new form of mounted warfare. Later, when Grow commanded the 6th Armored Division under Patton's Third Army in Europe, the colorful general referred to Grow as one of his top armored division commanders. Grow felt that Patton exemplified the principles of leadership with his actions, "but most were good and some were not so good."[296]

Herr had no use for Grow's opinions on using new mounts for exploitation and pursuit. After World War II ended, Herr let his displeasure be known again. He openly criticized Grow, especially for Grow's support of a separate armored branch. In a short article in the *Cavalry Journal* at the end of 1945, Herr wrote that the bulk of armored divisions in Europe executed the mission of cavalry, thus establishing the fact that a separate arm had to be defined by law. Herr still believed—even after the successful deployment of armored divisions and mechanized cavalry elements during the war—that his position on the value of horse cavalry element was correct. Herr failed to understand the significance of mechanization as the future of cavalry, and that mechanization caused the loss of many cavalrymen to armor.

It was Grow's belief that if Herr had taken a strong position for complete mechanization of the cavalry, there would have been no Armored Force. Instead, said Grow, the Army would have had

---

295 ibid (Page 293)
296 ibid (Page 293-294)

mechanized cavalry divisions. Grow's well known comment about Herr was, "He lost it all."[297]

Back in 1937 those who sought the most from mechanization in all aspects of cavalry missions, including reconnaissance, were doing their best to advance their ideas. The appointment of General Herr as the new chief of cavalry could be viewed as a sign of resistance to the thoughts of those at Fort Knox.

The two previous chiefs, Henry and Kromer, held balanced views on mechanization. Herr's arrival signaled the end of that approach. Now there was no question that the horse would be supreme and that the voice of Brigadier General Hawkins, Herr's former division commander, would be more influential than it had in the past.

Herr visited Fort Knox as he traveled to Washington in March 1938 to assume his new command, but until his position as branch chief was eliminated in 1942, his actions and words unquestionably championed the horse. He did not deny the importance of reconnaissance, but he did not want to see his beloved horse cavalry relegated to this task alone.[298]

EXERCISE ON THE EAST COAST

During an exercise that suggested hostile forces had landed on the Atlantic seaboard, the 7th Cavalry Brigade (Mech) marched south to respond to the intrusion. As it entered Chattanooga, Tennessee, the 7th Cavalry was met by the scout car platoon of the 6th Cavalry Regiment. The mechanized men may have lost the polo matches that ensued after their arrival, but they had once again demonstrated their ability to conduct mechanized reconnaissance across a broad front.

---

297 ibid (Page 294)
298 Matthew Darlington Morton; *Men on Iron Ponies (The death and rebirth of the Modern U. S. Cavalry)*:Published by Northern Illinois University Press, DeKalb, Illinois 2009 (Page 54)

The Argument Over Mechanization Goes On

In this exercise the armored car troops of each regiment covered a 200-mile front. Brigadier General Van Voorhis experimented with the use of light aircraft to command and control the vastly dispersed force. Colonel George S. Patton, the Cavalry School's observer, noted that this approach was "the obvious answer" for "maintenance of liaison between the several columns of the mechanized cavalry command." Patton also saw the usefulness of aircraft in directing the ground reconnaissance troops to new routes and bridges. The link between ground and air observation was recognized but remained unresolved.[299]

Figure 7-7. Lieutenant General Daniel Van Voorhis. *U.S. Army*

---

299 ibid (Page 54)

After a brief visit to Fort Oglethorpe, Van Voorhis turned his iron steeds to the north. This time the opposing force took the form of a hostile infantry brigade that penetrated south of the Ohio River. Aviation provided the mechanized brigade commander with some early and detailed reports about the enemy's disposition, but it was up to the ground reconnaissance units to examine the situation in greater detail.

Once the entire force reached Nashville, the armored car troops moved forward of the brigade. The next morning, the brigade went on the attack in what they must have considered their own backyard by now, prompting one observer's surprise that such a feat would be attempted without preliminary reconnaissance. The observer was unaware of the 20 radio messages and motorcycle courier messages that had been delivered to the brigade commander as his unit marched north through the night. Even if the infantry brigade that opposed them was operating on the cavalrymen's "stomping grounds"—which certainly facilitated the collection of reconnaissance information from both the air and ground—it was a considerable accomplishment. An entire body of mechanized warriors had marched through the night and into the attack without pause. No horse unit could have carried off any aspect of the operation in this way—not even the reconnaissance troops.[300]

The conclusion of the exercises reinforced Van Voorhis' desire to see his reconnaissance units augmented with additional air support. He exchanged letters with Lieutenant Colonel Willis D. Crittenberger, a mechanization-friendly staff officer assigned to the chief of cavalry's office. In a letter to Crittenberger about how future mechanized divisions should be organized, Van Voorhis expressed hope that General Herr would "sacrifice the necessary amount of horse cavalry to meet the War Department's wishes in expanding to a division."

---

300 ibid (Page 55)

The Argument Over Mechanization Goes On

Van Voorhis wanted to add a reconnaissance and support squadron so that he could "at once work them into the combat team." Just like Robert W. Grow had warned, an expanded division, especially as other branches contributed large units to fill out the structure of the new unit.

With Van Voorhis' letter in mind, Crittenberger drafted a document that he presented to Herr. Specific to reconnaissance, the document suggested that there should be no reduction in the number of soldiers in the existing armored car troops and that, in fact, the number of troops should be increased. The need for an entire squadron of reconnaissance and support personnel was justified by the inability of existing reconnaissance troops to "function efficiently for more than 24 hours' straight run."[301]

Additional debate within the cavalry community focused on what types of vehicles to procure for mechanized reconnaissance. Inside the chief of cavalry's office, Colonel Crittenberger prepared a memorandum entitled "Improvised Mechanized Reconnaissance," which repeated many of the same points that others associated with the mechanization process had previously stated. Crittenberger started softly with the horse-minded chief but finished strong. If a war occurred on the morrow, said Crittenberger, Cavalry Branch would have to maximize the availability of commercial vehicles, especially for reconnaissance. This would be problematic, for there was an expectation that the scouts would make contact with the enemy and then need some means of fighting—at minimum, machine gun mounts.

Crittenberger urged Herr not to allow cost to drive the decision, since the less expensive alternatives lacked the combat strength for offensive or defensive action. Crittenberger emphasized the following statement: "*No other country in the world with any kind of mechanization program is going solely with a light commercial car for mechanized reconnaissance missions.*"

---

301 ibid (Page 55)

After he reviewed the "Improvised Mechanized Reconnaissance" memorandum, Van Voorhis sent a letter to Crittenberger in which Van Voorhis agreed that "improvisation" would be a mistake. By contrast, members of the horse-minded community were less interested in developing better-designed reconnaissance vehicles, because they felt that the ultimate vehicle was already in their inventory: the horse.[302]

The stress of maintaining a single-branch identity continued to grow in late 1938 as a new round of cavalry maneuvers entered the final stages of planning. Crittenberger recommended that Herr consider integrating aviation assets as a way to show the mounted arm's willingness to be progressive. Crittenberger also urged Herr to maximize the publicity for the exercise and get many of the War Department General Staff officers to attend: "Unless an early and determined effort is made to publicize these maneuvers," said Crittenberger, "they will be shoved into the background by the anti-aircraft GHQ Air Force maneuvers now scheduled to be held at Fort Bragg during the first two weeks of October."

A successful showing at Fort Riley would demonstrate that the horse cavalry could not be reduced any more than it already had, and that none of the remaining horse units should be converted into air defense units.

Crittenberger left nothing to chance. He asked his fellow mechanized cavalryman Colonel Charles L. Scott to make sure that 1st Lieutenant Henry Cabot Lodge received "a good look at the mechanized cavalry." (Senator Lodge had requested that he be brought into active duty status for the Fort Riley exercise and be attached to the staff of the chief of cavalry.)[303]

A 1938 memorandum from General Herr to the Army chief of staff reflected the views of those most closely associated with the process of the development of mechanized cavalry. Mechanization

---

302 ibid (Page 56)
303 ibid (Page 57)

The Argument Over Mechanization Goes On

advocates—and the cavalry branch as a whole—felt that the American force was the equal of any similar organization in the world.

Even so, the official Army position held that the mechanized men were in no position to replace the traditional horse cavalry. Horse advocates envisioned that mounted units would draw the enemy's fire, thus "enabling the horse cavalry in close support to seize the objective without great loss."

While the chief of cavalry agreed to the expansion of the 7th Cavalry Brigade (Mech) into a division with at least a troop-size reconnaissance organization, he also wanted a mechanized unit stationed at Fort Riley. In addition, Herr wanted to station a new horse cavalry unit in Panama. He also wanted the Army to consider creating a cavalry unit at the Infantry School. Herr's bottom line was clear: "No further horse units should be converted to mechanized units. Horse units are already at the irreducible minimum."[304]

Even with the future of some form of mechanized reconnaissance secured, there were still many unresolved issues. The notion that armored cars would operate in excess of 100 miles to the front of the main body seemed to be diminishing, and this type of mission was absent from any of the exercises carried out in the first half of the 1930s. While commanders grew more reliant on the command and control capability provided by scout and armored cars, others questioned the combat and survival capabilities of these specialized units.

With these questions came debate over what could and should be expected from the mechanized forces. And how would these forces be equipped to perform their missions, even as troopers continued to practice shooting at targets from the backs of galloping horses?[305]

---

304 ibid (Page 59)
305 ibid (Page 61-62)

The U.S. Cavalry: Time of Transition

"Flowing Horses," an interesting article in the 23 December 1940 issue of *Time* magazine, supported General Herr's view of mounted cavalry.

A line of Army scout cars rolled out of Fort Bliss, down a rutty road, and out on the Texas plain. Beyond the stubby noses of the cars stretched wave on wave of "boondocks" (sand hummocks, topped by sage and greasewood) and deep arroyos. Behind the scout cars, a mile across the twisted land, stood file after file of horsemen, half-hidden in the brush. The U.S. Cavalry was about to have some fun.

An officer's voice crackled in the scout-car radios. The four-wheel drives hit the sand, and the cars lunged side by side over the plain. Where the boondocks were low, the light-armed cars, carrying three-man crews and two machine guns could do 10 mph. Where the hummocks were four and five feet high, 4 mph was the top. The cars were slow, but the boondocks did not stop them.

Back where the cavalry waited, the right hand of an officer rose, swung forward. Horses and horsemen spurted from the brush. In the scout cars, above the pattering exhaust, the men heard the crying breath of horses on the run. Mounted riflemen, machine-gun squads, four horse drawn howitzers overtook, enveloped, rushed past the cars at 20 mph. The horsemen vanished ahead into a shallow arroyo, arched over the far side, rode on. The artillerymen pulled up, dismounted, within a few minutes had their horses hidden, their guns barking blanks.

Where the desert abruptly broke and dropped down a pitted, 40-foot slope to a lower plain, the scout cars had to stop. But the horses did not. Over the brow of the slope, down the sandy ridge they leaped and slid. All along the ridge poured a river of men and horses, breaking the edge, spilling downward and riding on. Half a mile beyond, they clustered again. Riflemen dismounted—jerked guns from holsters. Machine-gunners ripped at their packs, vanishing into the brush with the guns. Within five minutes the squadron was deployed for battle, the horses had disappeared among the sand hills.

"Now gentlemen, you see what I meant," said horse-proud Major General Robert Charlwood Richardson, Jr., commander of the First Cavalry Division at Fort Bliss. What he meant was that horses could "flow" over terrain where no truck, scout car or tank could go. He spent an evening last month expounding his doctrine of flowing horses and horsemen to visiting newspapermen, then put on his show next day. He had indeed demonstrated that modern cavalry could flow off roads, through brush and sand, over ridges and through gullies which would slow or balk any mechanized force. And horsed units, within the limits of a rough battlefield, could speedily transport an impressive array of fire power: a modern U.S. Cavalry division's 6,476 horses and 10,100 officers and men should carry, among other things, 9,764 pistols, 942 light and heavy machine-guns, 117 artillery pieces, 4,863 Garand rifles.[306]

German Cavalry Units

In 1935 Adolf Hitler restored conscription in Germany. Among other plans, he was bent on creating three Panzer tank

---

306 Unknown Times Magazine writer; Flowing Horses::Published by Time Inc 23 December 1940

divisions before the end of the year. Despite highly ballyhooed emphasis on the employment of mechanized forces and on rapid movement, the bulk of the German combat divisions were horse-drawn throughout World War II. Early in the war the American public believed that the Hitler's blitzkrieg rode forth to battle in swift tanks and motor vehicles. But that notion of the mechanized might of the German Wehrmacht was largely a myth born in the fertile brains of newspapermen. Actually, the lowly horse played a most important part in enabling the German Army to move about Europe.[307]

The Blitzkrieg was so dependent upon the horse that the German Army maintained an average of 1,100,000 of the animals during the war. Of the 322 German Army and SS divisions extant in November 1943, only 52 were armored or motorized. Of the 264 combat divisions on duty in November 1944, only 42 were armored or motorized. The great bulk of the German combat strength—the old-type infantry divisions—marched into battle on foot, with their weapons and supply trains propelled almost entirely by four-legged horsepower. The light and mountain divisions had an even greater proportion of animals, and the cavalry divisions were naturally mainly dependent on the horse.[308]

The old-type German infantry division had approximately 5,300 horses, 1,100 horse-drawn vehicles, 950 motor vehicles, and 430 motorcycles. In 1943, due to the great difficulties in supply and upkeep of motor vehicles in the wide stretches of the Eastern Front, the allotment to divisions in that theater was reduced to approximately 400 motor vehicles and 400 motorcycles, and the number of horses was increased to some 6,300. In 1944 the divisions had about 4,600 horses, 1,400 horse-drawn vehicles, 600 motor vehicles, and 150 motorcycles.[309]

---

307 Unknown Author from Lone Sentry Press; "German Horse Cavalry and Transport" from Intelligence Bulletin-March 1946 (Page 1)
308 ibid (Page 1)
309 ibid (Page 1)

The Argument Over Mechanization Goes On

The only fully motorized unit in the old-type infantry division was the anti-tank battalion. Most of the divisional supply trains were horse-drawn. Motor vehicles were used chiefly to transport fuel and for the workshop company.

A far greater degree of motorization existed among German GHQ troops, the supply units of which were mostly motorized. Motorization of GHQ troops was to a large degree a necessity since these units included such types of outfits as heavy artillery, for which horses would have been a practical impossibility. These motorized GHQ units were assigned to armies, corps, and divisions as required.[310]

The use of independent horse cavalry units varied inversely with German fortunes during the war. During the first three years of the war, when Germany was ascendant, such units were nearly abandoned; they never exceeded one division. From 1943 on, new cavalry units were formed; and by early 1945 there were six cavalry divisions and two cavalry corps.[311]

The marked growth of the independent cavalry toward the end of the war did not signify a basic change in German military theory. Instead, the new units were required primarily to protect communication lines in the Balkans, where they operated in small independent groups, or to cover the flanks of armies during large-scale withdrawals from the Eastern Front. In both cases, the use of cavalry was largely dictated by lack of motor transport.

In late 1943 and early 1944 German military requirements began seriously to exceed production capacity. This was also the period in which the Allies' strategic aerial bombardment began to cripple the ability of German factories to meet established production targets. Meanwhile, the great East Prussian horse breeding farms were unaffected by B-17 and Lancaster bombing missions, so the availability of horseflesh continued undiminished.[312]

---

310 ibid (Page 1)
311 Unknown Author from Lone Sentry Press; "German Horse Cavalry and Transport" from Intelligence Bulletin-March 1946 (Page 2)
312 Ibid (Page 2-3)

Figure 7-8. Photograph from German Horse Cavalry and Transport. COURTESY OF LONE SENTRY PRESS

The later use of cavalry units was also necessary from a military standpoint. Balkan and Russian terrain conditions favored the use of mounted units. The Balkans were mountainous, while the trackless wastes of Russia had few roads and many swamps and forests. The steppes, which could be flat and smooth for cross-country motor travel in summer, became morasses after heavy rains. Most roads had nearly bottomless ruts in spring and fall. But the Germans had numbers of light (*Jäger*) and mountain (*Gebirgsjäger*) divisions to cope with such conditions, so cavalry units were not the only element of the German Army that was useful in mud and difficult terrain.[313]

The employment of horse cavalry in an old-fashioned offensive role was confined to the early campaigns of the war, when Germany enjoyed overwhelming air superiority. Even then, cavalry operations were on a small scale. Indications are that the German high command had no intention of reviving the offensive use of large numbers of mounted units in normal terrain, but that it did intend, in the event of victory, to organize such units on a considerable scale for screening and reconnaissance activities in Eastern Europe and the Near East. Questions of expense and materials involved in the provision of motorized and armored equipment probably played a part in this decision, as did the ability of cavalry to live off the country, especially in agricultural areas.[314]

---

313 Ibid (Page 3)
314 ibid (Page 3)

CHAPTER VIII

PEARL HARBOR, PANAMA, AND BEYOND

Not long after the August 1941 maneuvers came to a conclusion, the world changed forever.

It began on a quiet Sunday morning at a border cavalry station. Warm sunshine had dispelled the early morning chill. Officers, soldiers, and families pursued the activities normal for Sunday mornings on cavalry posts. Families were returning from Sunday school and church. Children were playing on the parade ground and among the lawns. Casual riders, on the "postman's holiday" usual in cavalry stations, were returning to the stables. The troop horses frisked about corrals, where they had been loosed after Sunday morning stables.

In troop kitchens and those of private quarters, preparations for the midday meal were nearing completion. Off across the mesa, a flash of color, the sound of the huntsman's horn, the baying of hounds and a trail of dust marked the course of the Sunday-morning drag hunt to its final check. On the parade ground a few soldiers idly tossed footballs back and forth. In day rooms of troop barracks, radios were blaring, and radios echoed along the line of officers' quarters.

Suddenly the music stopped. An excited announcer interrupted the scheduled programming and, in a voice charged with emotion, said: "The Japanese are attacking Pearl Harbor!" No further details were available, only the repetition of the original announcement.

So it was that war came to Fort Bliss, Texas and the 1st Cavalry Division. [315]

The 4th Cavalry regiment, another Regular Cavalry outfit, left Louisiana following the conclusion of the maneuvers, retracing their original route of travel back to Fort Meade. Merton Glover noted that by this time many bikes (motorcycles) were not running, so they were loaded on trucks and the troopers rode in the back with them.

> My Indian (motorcycle) was using a lot of oil and should have been loaded, but I bought a quart a day myself all the way home. (This was a no-no, by the way.) It was late October or early November—I can't recall which—when we got back to (South) Dakota. I do well remember it was quite chilly as we started through Hot Springs and the Hills. Highway 79 did not exist then.
>
> Every morning at breakfast, [when we were] breaking camp we were given a cheese and baloney sandwich in a big brown paper bag for lunch on the go. It was common practice to put our raincoats on backwards to turn more wind. As I recall, we went

---

315 Lucian K. Truscott, Jr.: *The Twilight of the U.S. Cavalry (Life in the Old Army, 1917-1942):* Published by University Press of Kansas-1989 (Page 181)

through the Hills to or by Newcastle and Deadwood to Sturgis and Fort Meade to avoid Custer State Park.

There were no furloughs upon return from 4th Cavalry maneuvers as expected, for at that time we were only to serve for a year's training and go home. That all changed come 7 December 1941.

I was in the day room of the barracks on Sunday, looking at a newspaper and listening to the radio when the Pearl Harbor news broke. Next day, Monday, 8 December 1941, we were all assembled and told to get rid of civilian clothes (allowed until then), and to read all the Articles of War, for wartime was much tougher than peacetime. Training got tougher and meaner from that date.[316]

As for those units still participating in the Louisiana maneuvers in late November 1941, 2d Squadron, D Troop, 106th Cavalry was somewhat unique. Staff Sergeant Ervin Aden remembered that they served mainly as transportation for the engineers from Camp Claiborne.

After checking all bridges' capacity in preparation for the maneuvers, we trained in various areas of simulated combat and were graded by our performance. D Troop used scout cars, but there were other groups that had trucks with canvas over them. Printed on the canvas was [the word] TANK, as we had no (or very few) tanks there as yet.

Maneuvers in the humid Louisiana weather were awful. Red bugs, coral snakes, other snakes and abundant rain made life miserable, but we were being trained for any unpleasant situation in war.

---

316 Merton Glover; *86 and counting:* Unpublished personal manuscript of author's life history-2003 (Page 33)

Following additional time at Camp Livingston I was sent with my group of four troopers in my scout car to participate in the Carolina maneuvers. We were the only ones who went there.

Let me mention an interesting experience we had on 4 December 1941 as we listened to our radio. This was on the night before the Carolina maneuvers ended and we were scheduled to return to Livingston. The news was being broadcast and we learned that our intelligence sources had reported that a large Japanese task force was steaming south out of Japan, and intelligence had lost contact with them. Of course you know shortly thereafter Pearl Harbor was attacked.

The Carolina maneuvers were over on 5 December 1941, and my group drove back down to Camp Livingston. On 7 December 1941, I had a pass, so I went into Alexandria, Louisiana.

Shortly I arrived in Alexandria the MPs came around with a foghorn and told all of us in D Troop of the 106th Cavalry to return to Livingston immediately. Once back at Livingston we were told to pack our gear and be ready to move out. By then it was late evening and we drove all night to get to Slidell, Louisiana.

We were the first soldiers there to guard all the bridges surrounding New Orleans, as there was the fear that the Japanese would blow them up. Three days later an infantry group relieved us.

In the first week of January 1942, D Troop, 106th Cavalry, packed up to go to New Orleans in preparation for shipping out. We were encamped out on Lake Pontchtrain along the beach front in tents in an area called Tent City, which was used to keep those who were being sent overseas. These tents on the lakefront were just Regular Army tents, not perennial.

There were four cots to a tent with a potbelly stove in the center. This stove did little good that particular year, as New Orleans experienced its coldest spell about the time we arrived: seven degrees! Ice was forming on the edge of the lake and fish were frozen on the beach.

Two days after our arrival—a Sunday—three of us walked from the lakefront to the closest church, about three miles or more inland towards the Mississippi River. We found it an extremely friendly church.

We met a young lady who was preparing to enter the choir loft, as she was the soloist. Following the church service she approached me and asked if I would like to have dinner with her family in their home. Her mother told her family to invite servicemen home to dinner every Sunday, as most were lonely and some had never left home before. And we, of course, were extremely homesick. This was a family with five children—three girls and two boys. The eldest was this young lady who invited me.

With several Army camps, Navy bases, Coast Guard Stations, etc., New Orleans was a city overrun with servicemen from all branches. And being a port of embarkation and debarkation only added to the numbers.

This family was very hospitable to me, giving me a sightseeing tour of the city. Before leaving that evening I asked this young lady if I could see her the following night, and she agreed to it. Being confined to the base I sneaked out, and we went to the famous old St. Charles Hotel to dance, which we both enjoyed since we liked dancing.

She agreed to see me again the next night, and again I had to sneak off base to keep our date. We had had so much fun at the St. Charles that we decided to go there again. During our dancing on both nights we learned so much about each other. Neither of us drank or smoked and we were from Christian homes. She sang with the USO and went to dances for the military every week.

Although she had been dating a Navy cadet for the past two years, at the time, we both felt that we were meant for each other. When I said my last goodnight, as we were shipping out the following day—our destination unknown—I asked her to wait for me. To my surprise she agreed to. Our romance for the next seven months was through the mail.[317]

The troopers from D Troop, 106th Cavalry Reconnaissance Regiment (Mech), were absorbed by the 32d Cavalry Reconnaissance Squadron (Mech), which was redesignated on 14 March 1942 as the 27th Cavalry Regiment. On 1 April 1942, the 27th Cavalry Reconnaissance Regiment absorbed more troopers from the 1st Cavalry Reconnaissance Squadron to complete its ranks.)

Frank (Lindy) Fancher faced similar confusion when Pearl Harbor was attacked:

> On Saturday, 6 December 1941, I went into Alexandria, Louisiana, with Sergeant Graivet and Tommy Depue to work on Graivet's 1933 Plymouth in order to get it ready for the return trip to Springfield, Illinois. This was the day we had completed our year of service. All our discharge papers were on the captain's desk waiting to be signed on Monday, 8 December 1941.

---

[317] Ervin Aden; e-mail sent to Gary Palmer regarding World War II service; 26 September 2006

We had a lot of trouble finding parts for the car, so we decided to stay in town. The next day, we finished with the car and went out to get something to eat. While we were in town the news came over the radio that Pearl Harbor had been attacked by the Japanese. We were all to report back to camp for assignment, as a state of war existed between the United States and Japan—soon to include Germany. We finished eating and headed back to camp.

When we got back to camp we were surprised to find that our outfit was already gone. They had left a guard at the supply tent. He issued us each a .45 caliber revolver and a Thompson submachine gun with 250 rounds of ammo and a boot for the Thompson.

We were instructed to report to the motor pool. There we were issued three Harley Davidson motorcycles and told to head for New Orleans without delay and meet the rest of our unit at the Huey P. Long Bridge. After a 223-mile run we arrived at the bridge and reported to Captain Greenup. He ordered us to do dock patrol. After that they assigned dock, bridge, beach and government building patrols.

We took over an Army camp by an amusement park near Lake Pontchartrain. This was where we spent our time when we weren't on patrol. That night it snowed about an inch and a half and the temperature dropped down to about 29 to 33 degrees. Those four-man tents had no heat. I don't think I have ever been so cold in my life. In the middle of the tents was a 50-gallon oil drum for garbage. Within 24 hours there wasn't a wooden fence or tree within a half a mile of this camp.

The drum made a good stove and the smoke went out the vent in the top of the tent."[318]

Merle Roughton, another member of the 106th Cavalry Regiment, 2d Squadron, D Troop, recalled the events of 7 December 1941:

> I joined the National Guard in November 1940 and remember being issued blue fatigues which would turn your skin blue if you were caught out in the rain. On 6 December 1941 I had gone to a movie. I woke up early the next morning to learn that the Japanese had bombed Pearl Harbor.
> We were ordered to New Orleans in order to protect all bridges and roads between Alexandria and New Orleans. I subsequently went to Lake Pontchtrain Beach where, along with five other guys, I lived in a six-man tent. I recall it was extremely cold, even with the roaring fire we had going in the small potbelly stove sitting on the floor in the middle of the tent.
> On 3 January 1942, we marched some seven miles to the port area, where we were loaded onto a troop ship that eventually took us to Panama."[319]

After the initial shock of the Pearl Harbor attack, life for those attached to the 1st Cavalry Division settled back down to normal—modified by the realization that they were at war, by the security measures that became necessary, by the intense training activity, and by everyone's thirst for news from the war front.

Family life continued its normal pattern. Children attended primary schools on military posts and high schools in the city.

---

[318] Frank 'Lindy' Fancher; *WWII: Through These Eyes:* Published by Author House, 1663 Liberty Drive, Suite 200, Bloomington, Indiana 47403 – 04-26-2005 (Page 9-10)
[319] Merle Roughton: Interview given to Gary Palmer (Interviewed in June 2008 during the106th Cavalry Groups annual reunion in Urbana, Illinois)

There were the usual dances for enlisted personnel. For the 1st Cavalry Division stationed at Fort Bliss, Texas, officers, ladies, and children continued their riding for pleasure, as did many men. Everyone pursued and enjoyed his or her favorite sports. There was somewhat less hunting and fishing, perhaps, but the officers and men who enjoyed the sport found time to treat themselves.

There were only two limiting factors on social life and activities. One, everyone knew the country was at war; and two, the location of every officer and enlisted man had to be known at all times—a requirement that was somewhat restrictive in nature.[320]

There was a great desire on the part of everyone to be of service—a fact evidenced by the vast increase in registration for Red Cross courses such as first aid, canteen management, nursing, and other services designed to support the war effort. This was especially obvious at Fort Bliss, where nearly every woman registered and worked with one or more of this type of activity.

There was never a week without some parade, review, or inspection by regiment or brigade, but the truly thrilling spectacles were the mounted reviews and inspections of the entire 1st Cavalry Division. These were held on occasions when General Krueger made an inspection and for other important dignitaries or visitors. General Swift was always willing to show off the division to VIPs, for his pride in the division and its state of training was boundless.[321]

Following the attack on Pearl Harbor, the "great laboratory" phase for developing and testing organizations—about which Marshall wrote in the summer of 1941—closed, but the War Department still had not developed ideal infantry, cavalry, armored, and motorized divisions. In 1942 the War Department again revised the division structure based on experience gained during the great GHQ maneuvers of the previous year. General

---

320 Lucian K. Truscott, Jr.; *The Twilight of the U.S. Cavalry (Life in the Old Army, 1917-1942):* Published by University Press of Kansas-1989 (Page 185)
321 ibid (Page 185)

McNair, appointed chief of Army Ground Forces (AGF) in March 1942 and responsible for organizing and training all ground combat units, advised General Marshall that the infantry division should have a maximum of 15,000 men with the arms being fixed accordingly, and that it should not be increased in size at the insistence of arm-conscious chiefs. McNair's view did not prevail. General Hodges won the armament battle, and a cannon company became a part of each infantry regiment. [322]

The GHQ maneuvers of 1941 had also revealed a need for more trucks in each division. McNair, however, believed that the suggested number of trucks was excessive, requiring too much space on ships when sent overseas. Although the number of trucks was cut at his insistence, the division still had 315 more vehicles under the 1942 tables than those of 1940.

Finally, the new tables split the division headquarters and military police company into two separate units, a headquarters company and a military police platoon. Together these changes added about 270 men to the division.[323]

Modifications continued even after publication of the new tables of organization that directly affected the cavalry divisions. After the 1941 maneuvers the cavalry retained its square configuration, but with modifications. The division lost its anti-tank troop, the brigades their weapons troops, and the regiments their machine gun and special weapons troops. These changes brought no decrease in divisional firepower, but placed most weapons within the hands of the individual cavalry troops. The number of .50 caliber machine guns was increased almost threefold. In the reconnaissance squadron, the motorcycle and armored car troop were eliminated, leaving the squadron with one support troop and three reconnaissance troops equipped with light

---

322 John B Wilson; *Maneuver and Firepower (The Evolution of Divisions and Separate Brigades):* Published by Center of Military History, United States Army, Washington, D.C.-1998 (Page 161)
323 ibid (Page 161)

tanks. These changes increased the division from 11,676 to 12,112 officers and enlisted men.[324]

A Brief Interlude in Panama

The Panama and Caribbean defenses felt the initial impact of war chiefly in the shape of repercussions from Washington. At least two fields of activity were affected, namely, the problem of command and the matter of reinforcing the garrisons. The entry of the United States into the war radically and immediately altered the situation in each of these fields.

As a result of the attack on Pearl Harbor, the vexing problem of who should command when the forces of two or more services were involved was, as far as the North Atlantic bases were concerned, unsolved. However, in the Caribbean-Panama area, the problem was taken care of immediately. The only difficulty that remained was to make the solution work. Secretary of War Henry Stimson's biographer observed that

> The attack at Pearl Harbor emphasized again the importance of unity of command; all the armed forces in any area must have a single commander. Stimson was ashamed that the lesson had to be so painfully learned; for months he had read it in the experience of the British in North Africa, Crete, and Greece. Incautiously he had assumed that it was equally well learned by others. . . ."

As late as 5 December 1941 the Army-Navy Joint Planning Committee was struggling with the task of formulating a statement of general policy governing the application of unity of command.

---

324 ibid (Page 161)

No agreement had been reached by the time the attack on Pearl Harbor occurred.

Then, out of the flood of rumors and alarms that followed the Japanese onslaught, came a report that two hostile aircraft carriers had been sighted off the west coast of Mexico.[325]

On Friday, 12 December 1941, five days after the attack on Pearl Harbor, Secretary Stimson was amazed to find that no scheme for establishing unity of command in Panama had been worked out. Assuming that the canal would probably be one of the next objectives of the Japanese, General Marshall (at the request by Secretary Stimson) drew up a proposed directive placing all Army and Navy forces in the Panama Coastal Frontier, except fleet units, under Army command. Later in the day Stimson laid the proposal before the Cabinet. The President approved the idea by taking a map, writing ARMY over the area of the Panama Coastal Frontier, but at the same time writing NAVY over the Caribbean Coastal Frontier, and then adding his O.K.—F.D.R.

The draft proposal said nothing about the command of the Caribbean area except that "the Commanding General, Caribbean Defense Command, within his means and other responsibilities, will support the Naval Commander of the Caribbean Coastal Frontier."[326]

At the same time that Stimson presented the draft proposal to Roosevelt and the Cabinet, GHQ noted that two infantry regiments, two barrage balloon units, one field artillery battalion, and two hospital units were to be sent to Panama in addition to some 1,800 coast artillery filler replacements. A few days later, arrangements were made to send the 53d Pursuit Group to reinforce the air garrison. Negotiations were begun to acquire seventy-two 40 mm antiaircraft guns from the British and to dispatch one

---

325 Stetson Conn, Rose C. Engelman and Byron Fairchild; *Guarding the United States and its Outpost (Chapter XVI):* Published by U.S. Government Printing Office, Washington D.C. 20402-1964 (Page 408)
326 ibid (page 409)

heavy bomber squadron and one flight of pursuit planes to Talara in northwestern Peru. The December 1941 reinforcements—both ground and air—were more than double the number that were deployed during the first 11 months of the year. By the end of December the Panama garrison had increased to about 39,000 men; at the end of January it had reached 47,600.[327]

But who would command the ground and air units in the Caribbean? The Navy War Plans Division prepared a written statement on the subject, which Admiral Stark forwarded to General Marshall on Monday, 15 December 1941. The Navy's position was that the President's notation on the map of the Caribbean Coastal Frontier indicated that he intended unity of command to be established under the Navy in that area, while the Army oversaw Panama. This was what the Navy had proposed almost a year before. The Army countered with the same argument that had brought on the previous stalemate: that it was impossible to consider the Army defenses of the Panama-Caribbean area except as a unit—and that if unity of command was necessary in the Caribbean it should, as in Panama, be under the Army.

When the question came up for discussion at another meeting of the Joint Board on 17 December, still no agreement was reached. But the same consideration that helped solve the Panama question no doubt played a similar part with respect to the Caribbean. In any event, on the morning of 18 December, General Marshall instructed the War Plans Division that in the Caribbean the Navy would exercise unity of command. Thus, within a week after Secretary Stimson became aware of the serious situation, the question of who should command was solved.[328]

Several days after that, all the details of the directives to be issued were likewise settled. In order to allay any uneasiness on the part of the naval commander at Panama, General Marshall proposed a list of special restrictions and exceptions that limited

---

327 ibid (Page 411)
328 ibid (Page 410)

the Army's exercise of command. However these were soon laid aside, at Admiral Stark's suggestion, in favor of a simpler directive modeled on the one that had been adopted for Hawaii. All forces "assigned for operations" in the respective coastal frontiers came within the scope of the orders, which were limited only by the provisions of joint action of the Army and the Navy.

The urgency of the situation had prevented the War Department from consulting General Frank Andrews, commander of the Caribbean Defense Command. Now the success of the decision rested on Andrews' good judgment. The decision presented Andrews with a difficult problem of organization, but barring an immediate interruption in the shape of a serious threat to the Caribbean, Andrews believed the plan could be made to work.[329]

While the War Plans Division, General Marshall, and Secretary Stimson had been occupied chiefly with the question of command, GHQ and General Andrews were more concerned with reinforcing and strengthening the Caribbean garrisons. By directing the various commanders to put the RAINBOW 5 war plan into effect, the War Department triggered a barrage of requests for reinforcements, since the deployment of forces required for RAINBOW 5 was incomplete. Because the Panama Canal seemed to be one of the objectives of the Japanese, General Andrews' requests for additional troops fared better than most.[330]

The naval forces available for local defense were, like the Army garrison, concentrated in the Panama area, where Rear Adm. F. H. Sadler, commander of the Panama Naval Coastal Frontier, had at his disposal a small and motley force of patrol planes, submarines, and sub-chasers. In his "heavy" units Admiral Sadler had two old destroyers and a gunboat. The rest of his command consisted of

---

329 ibid (Page 411)
330 ibid (Page 411)

six submarines, three converted yachts, five sub-chasers, one mine sweeper, and twelve patrol planes with their tender.

Even before General Andrews assumed overall command in the area, his superior responsibility had been informally acknowledged by Admiral Sadler, who considered himself a task force commander of sorts under General Andrews, as well as a task group commander under the commander-in-chief of the U. S. Atlantic Fleet.

In the Caribbean, Rear Admiral J. H. Hoover's naval forces were divided between a patrol force consisting of two old destroyers, three small submarines, two sub-chasers of World War I vintage, and twelve patrol planes, and smaller local surface forces at Guantanamo and Trinidad. The latter two locations were virtually undefended; at Trinidad on 7 December 1941 there were only two converted yachts, two "Yippies" (district patrol craft, YP-63 and YP-64), and four of Admiral Hoover's patrol planes.

As in the case of the Army, the Navy's first action was to strengthen the defenses at the Pacific end of the Canal. On 14 December 1941, the Navy sent two submarine divisions (eight to twelve vessels) and a patrol squadron of twelve planes to Panama with orders to establish advanced patrol bases in the Galapagos Islands and Gulf of Fonseca.[331]

In October 1941 a group of General Andrews' staff officers, headed by Brigadier General Harry C. Ingles, G-3 of the Caribbean Defense Command, arrived in Washington to prepare an operations plan for the Caribbean theater. GHQ had prepared a draft modeled on its plan for Iceland that had been written a few months earlier. When General Ingles and his group returned to Panama on 31 October 1941, GHQ's plans had been brought into agreement with the views of the Caribbean Defense Command. The rest of the work would be done in Panama and submitted to GHQ for approval. By the date of the Pearl Harbor attack, the

---

331 ibid (Page 412)

basic part of the operations plan was finished, but some of the 17 annexes were incomplete.[332]

Based as it was on the RAINBOW 5 war plan, the Caribbean operations plan placed its military strength facing the Atlantic, as it anticipated a war in which Germany and Italy would be the major opponents, the Atlantic and Europe the principal battleground, and the Caribbean relatively immune to attack. The plan contemplated a garrison of a little more than 112,000 men for the Caribbean theater.

Given this, the practicality of the operations plan could be called into question. The actual deployment of forces in November 1941 was based on the possibility of a carrier raid against the canal from the Pacific. The total garrison of the Caribbean Defense Command had fewer than 60,000 men at the end of November, and the establishment of separate unified commands in Panama and the Caribbean created a different scheme of organization from that envisioned by GHQ.

As it turned out, the canal itself was never seriously threatened from either side; nor were the outposts, except for Aruba and Curacao, ever fired upon. Nevertheless, by December 1942 the Caribbean Defense Command garrison was built up to a peak of 119,000 men. More than half of them were in Panama, guarding the canal from attack or sabotage.[333]

In early December 1941, the Army Air Corps was involved in a little-known response to the attack on Pearl Harbor. This event corresponded to the immediate military buildup in Panama. Charles E. Jerman—who went on to become the deputy commander at Edwards Air Force Base, California, in his later career—was an enlisted airman at the time.

---

332 ibid (Page 413)
333 ibid (Page 413)

In early 1941 I was assigned to General Andrews' command as a result of a stunt I had engineered during one of the Army's Louisiana maneuvers. The stunt originated from an incident that occurred during the first days of the maneuvers.

The G.I.s participating in the maneuvers wore white bands on their hats and sleeves to identify themselves as "targets." I was to drop small flour bags as bombs from my plane onto them and their trucks. On our first day of flight operations we reported that we had hit their trucks, but they cleaned the flour off before the umpire could get there to see it, so we were made to look bad.

Figure 8-1. The Northrop A-17A was a single-engine attack aircraft of 1936 vintage. Its armament consisted of four fixed .30-cal machine guns and one flexible mount .30-cal machine gun. The aircraft could carry up to 1,100 pounds of bombs.

There was an A-17 assigned to the squadron as a hack (When the improved A-17A was delivered, the A-17 was taken out of first line service and used for secondary duties like staff transport and training.). Subsequently, a friend of mine and I cooked up an idea that would allow us to get back at the infantry for their less than honest tactics.

Behind the hangar were a couple of chemical tanks for spraying. We filled the tanks with water and a couple of gallons of syrup from the mess hall. The next day, I flew low over the trucks and sprayed the troops with the syrup and water mixture. My buddy then flew over with his flight and hit them with the flour, which they could not "wipe off."

Of course the infantry was pissed to say the least! After that I don't think it was safe for an Air Corpsman to be seen in town. For that escapade I received an Article 104 Court Martial and was fined three months' flight pay.

While grounded I was given an assignment that took me to a place called Rio Hato in Panama. I was told that I would be assigned a sergeant of the Corps of Engineers and a detail of workers. General Andrews' chief of staff informed me that my job would be to clear brush and make a runway there. I would be given the men and tools necessary, and go by barge.

I met the men from the Corps of Engineers as they were busy loading the barge. I was informed that the rest of the men would arrive in the morning. The next morning 50 "prisoners" were escorted to the dock, roll was called and I signed for them. The Army had emptied the guardhouses in the Canal Zone! I was given a short-barreled shotgun and a .45 pistol, along with the dubious warning to "watch my back."

I was surprised that I was able to handle the mob, and they actually settled down and went to work. In 27 days we were ready to receive our first planes. I almost hated to lose my crew, but they all were returned to their brigs with shorter sentences. The base became "gunnery camp" for the Canal squadrons that would go there for a week at a time to train. As for my part, I was promoted to technical sergeant and reassigned to Rio Hato to help build the base.

My squadron, which was stationed at Albrook Field in Panama, was upgraded with the P-36 pursuit plane, and I wanted back. I was overdue, so when I went back I was met by the line chief (the supervisor in charge of maintenance), who informed me that I was up for promotion to master sergeant. I could not believe it!

The P-36 was an improvement, and I will never forget the engine was started with a large shotgun shell. The chamber was situated between your legs. I was so afraid of it that I squatted on the seat every time I started the engine. While the P-36 was a great airplane it didn't match up to what other countries like Germany and Japan had in their inventory. It was later upgraded with the in-line Allison engine and became the P-40 Warhawk, which was around through the war years.

Figure 8-2. The Curtiss P-36A Hawk was the predecessor to the Curtiss P-40. The single-pilot aircraft had one .50 caliber machine gun and three .30 cal machine guns.

Due to another fiasco perpetrated by yours truly I was assigned as the co-pilot on General Andrews' C-33 aircraft. The pilot was Sonny Williams, a technical sergeant who later married the General's daughter. General Andrews was in charge of all military American personnel south of Texas, including those assigned throughout South America. Subsequently, we made many trips visiting other countries' military organizations.

After getting to see most of the large cities in South America, I was worn out. Therefore I asked to be sent back to the pursuit squadron at Albrook. However, Sonny Williams, who had become a good friend, told me to hold off—something was coming up. He was promoted to captain and, as a wedding present, the General told him he was to command a new attack squadron with Douglas A-20 "Havoc" airplanes. To my surprise Sonny called me and welcomed me to the 59th Attack Squadron. To celebrate, he handed me master sergeant chevrons and said we would start getting personnel shortly.

So back to Rio Hato I went, to start forming the new outfit. To my surprise we received a bunch of castoffs. I am certain that when other outfits were told they had to give five or ten men, you can rest assured we got what they were glad to get rid of—their deadwood.

The Air Corps was building up fast. They were constructing a large new field across the Canal from Albrook, and we were scheduled to be the first outfit there. I found out that new quarters were about to be available, so I stopped by to see the base Sergeant Major. To my surprise they gave me the first set of quarters on Howard Air Base. However, shortly after that, Pearl Harbor was bombed, and we were involved in World War II.

Figure 8-3. The Douglas A-20 Havoc, a light attack bomber, was one of the most extensively built of the light bombers of WWII. Its armament consisted of seven .50 caliber machine guns, and the aircraft could carry up to 4000 pounds of bombs. *NATIONAL ARCHIVES*

Jerman continued, recalling what happened in the Panama Canal Zone after the outbreak of hostilities:

> About 10:00 a.m. local time on Sunday, 7 December 1941, I got a call to report to the flight line, which was only two blocks away from my quarters. We were told about the war starting and given one hour to pack, as we had received orders. We were the first to receive orders issued from the War Department that day. So, leaving home again, I packed my bags and said goodbye. We immediately left for Aguadulce, which is located about 150 miles north of the Panama Canal Zone. We had no ammunition or bombs, and the planning was the worst ever. There was not one bomb in the whole Canal Zone.

We gassed up the next day and landed at Albrook Field to get our .30 caliber machine gun ammunition. For lack of anything else available, we loaded 100 pounds of blue, sand-filled practice bombs aboard our planes. Then, off to Bogotá, Colombia, for fuel, and on to Curaçao, with half the squadron going to Aruba.

The Dutch Islands were about 90 miles off the coast of Venezuela. They had a refinery for making gasoline and were supplied by very small tankers located on the mainland. Our job was submarine patrol and to escort convoys of small tankers to the refiners. If we had encountered a submarine, the enemy would have thought we had been drinking, because about all we could have done was to drop sand bombs on them.

About a month later we did receive real bombs and ammo, but still there was no enemy in sight. In the meantime, the East Coast from New York to Florida was becoming a battlefield with ships being sunk at a high rate every day.

Figure 8-4. The Douglas B-18A "Bolo," with its crew of six, was regulated to a patrol role during WWII. The Bolo was credited with sinking the U-654 on 22 August 1942. U-654 was the first German U-boat sunk in Caribbean waters. *U.S. ARMY AIR CORPS*

The schedule was really tough, as the missions were short and we were flying four-and-a-quarter hours each mission. We landed and got out of the airplane. The crew chief gave us some bread and meat with a canteen of water, and we took off in another plane, flying dawn to dusk. If you didn't get 150 to 175 hours per month you were grounded for some reason.

Later, during January 1942, the Army assigned two B-18s with radar for night missions, which I considered a waste of time. The trouble was these old bombers had new radars that hardly worked, and they both crashed into the ocean while flying too low looking for a ship.

In late February 1942 I received word that my brother and best friend had been killed on 22 February of the coast of Fort Prince, Florida. My brother Bill's ship, the *City Service Empire*, was en route from Texas to Boston and was right in "Killing Alley." I'm sure—as the submarine had been tracking the *Empire* for some time—that it was not a complete surprise that they were hit. As the captain of the ship, my brother made sure all hands were clear and in the lifeboat before he abandoned ship. In the process of departing the ship he fell and was crushed between the ship and the very large life raft.

What a terrible night! Until that time I had accepted it as a duty for which I was trained. Now it became personal and I wanted to inflict as much damage on the enemy as possible. I wanted to fight back! I have never had anything as overpowering hit me. I lost my religion instantly and wanted to disobey God's will and kill all that were connected with the enemy. Up until that time I really had not given it much thought.

THE U.S. CAVALRY: TIME OF TRANSITION

Figure 8-5. La Quira, the sea-level airport in Caracas, Venezuela, in early 2000.

We had a good record in our area and did not lose any ships that were under our protection, although we knew they were around. The KLM Royal Dutch Airlines were flying an old 1930 Junker tri-motor to Venezuela and on to Trinidad. They frequently flew right over a sub on the surface, with the crew standing on deck, waving. It was so hard to believe that we put one of our people aboard who took pictures to prove it.

We knew their submarines were getting fuel from Spanish oil tankers but couldn't catch them in the act. The Spanish were supposedly neutral, and the one and only time a sub was sighted was alongside a three-masted sailing ship that operated between Curacao and Caracas carrying produce. But the submarine submerged and got away.

On one of our routes it was necessary for us to land at La Quira, the sea-level airport for Caracas. The city was actually over 3,000 feet high in the mountains. The airport was a "way stop" for Pan American Airways, from whom we purchased our fuel. The only building at the airport was the small Pan American station, and there was a small lunch area composed of a U-shaped counter as there was no room for tables.

Upon landing one day I taxied up and parked next to a German tri-motor Ju 52 transport, complete with a swastika printed on the wings and tail. I can assure you that my hair stood on end! When I entered the lunch room, there sat two German Luftwaffe officers drinking coffee. We sat across the counter and just glared at each other.

Figure 8-6. A 1930 German Junkers Ju 52 tri-motor. DONALD PITTENGER

I found out from the Pan American employees that the plane was being used by the German embassy for travel around South America and that the German officers and crew came in about once a month. For a change I didn't report it, but I did tell a couple of my close friends. Through them and Pan American we found out when the Germans were coming in again and going to stay overnight. My good friend, Lieutenant Hiram Conant, landed there for a fuel stop and saw that the Germans had returned. He told me, "They're back!" I had a bad cold and said I needed a day to save my ears.

The next day I was in the back of Conant's plane and we landed late in the afternoon at La Quira. Conant delayed takeoff almost until dusk. My crew chief, Sergeant Bill Milano, and I were left behind—on purpose. Sergeant Milano was a natural-born mechanic who figured out the German tri-motor engine controls.

As soon as it was dark, I took off in the German airplane for Curaçao (a small Caribbean island off the coast of Venezuela). Upon landing, not one person noticed our arrival. I told Sergeant Milano to get some paint to cover the swastikas and told my CO to come outside; I had a "present" for him. When he saw the plane he was speechless for a short time. Then he called me every name in the book he could think of!

After a couple of days we came up with a plan. The CO was to take off at dawn, land at Bogotá for fuel, and go on to Panama. I would fly the German plane straight through with a seven-hour delay. I waited over Rio Hato for two P-40s to escort me so that the anti-aircraft gunners would not shoot me down—a precaution I found unnecessary as the gunners appeared rather lax, in my opinion.

To my astonishment, upon landing at Albrook Field I was treated like a prisoner and immediately taken to Quarry Heights, the Army headquarters. After getting chewed out, my friend Sonny Williams, now a major, came out and returned me to Albrook. It seems the headquarters staff didn't care about the situation. I'm sure they had too much on their minds with the war.

Shortly thereafter I was told I was being transferred to the States and would leave on the next plane. Leaving all my gear in Curaçao, I was sent via Ramey Field, Puerto Rico, to Tampa, Florida, and a new field called Drew Army Airfield. From there I was sent to a replacement depot in town, which was quartered in the city stadium. I was denied leave and told to wait.[334]

THE BATTLE OF THE CARIBBEAN

The battle of the Caribbean, heralded by the attack at Aruba, was a sustained and damaging U-boat assault against shipping. Its first victims were five tankers—four British and one Venezuelan—that were torpedoed and sunk during the early morning hours of 16 January 1942. Two of the ships were sent down while lying at anchor in Aruba's San Nicolas Harbor.

After the German submarine U-156 entered the anchorage and sank the two tankers, it came boldly to the surface and lobbed a few shells at the Lago oil refinery. Shortly thereafter, on 26 January 1942, a naval intelligence report reached Caribbean Defense Command headquarters at Quarry Heights in the Panama Canal Zone. The report stated that a large number of German submarines had entered the Caribbean Sea, destination unknown. The radioed report warned that "attacks on tankers from Venezuela, Curaçao and [the] vicinity [of] Trinidad [are] possible."

The German raiders, reinforced during the next by the arrival of two more U-boats, sank 21 ships totaling about 103,000 tons in the space of two weeks. Losses to the shallow-draft Maracaibo tanker fleet seriously cut the oil production of the huge refineries on Aruba and Curaçao.

---

[334] Charles E. Jerman; *The Early Years (The Glass is half full):* Unpublished Manuscript-1992

The enemy onslaught reached a new peak in May 1942, when 8 U-boats sank 35 ships totaling more than 145,000 tons in the Caribbean Sea Frontier west of the shipping control line. In June there were 14 undersea raiders operating in the Caribbean Sea Frontier and the adjacent waters of the Gulf and Panama Sea Frontiers. By the middle of June 1942, 22 percent of the bauxite fleet had been destroyed, and 20 percent of the ships in the Puerto Rican run had been lost. Of 74 vessels allocated to the U.S. Army for the month of July, 17 had already been sunk. By the end of 1942 the enemy had sunk a total of 270 vessels in the Caribbean, in the Atlantic sector of the Panama Sea Frontier, and in the nearby fringes of the Gulf Sea Frontier. These losses comprised more than 1,200,000 tons of shipping.[335]

There were deficiencies in the Caribbean defense network that were not entirely the result of a shortage of equipment and trained men. Tests in Panama repeatedly disclosed that the radar system failed to detect low-flying planes approaching directly over the Bay of Panama. Visiting British experts had noted this problem in American radar sets and attributed it to a basic defect of the equipment. However, the Army Signal Corps insisted that—properly placed and operated by competent crews—the American equipment was just as good as, if not better than, the British radar. Whatever the cause, the blind spot remained. Furthermore, neither the SCR-270 nor the SCR-271 radar was designed to show the elevation of approaching planes, and neither gave a continuous tracking plot. These capabilities were indispensable for successful ground-controlled interception (GCI), which British experience had demonstrated to be the most successful method for conducting an air defense.[336]

---

335 Stetson Conn, Rose C. Engelman and Byron Fairchild; *Guarding the United States and its Outpost (Chapter XVI):* Published by U.S. Government Printing Office, Washington D.C. 20402-1964 (Page 423)
336 ibid (Page 425)

Much of the construction activity in Panama during the early months of 1942 was devoted to the preparation of sites for additional radar equipment, to the building of access roads, and the preparation of landing strips at some of the sites. A number of SCR-268 radar sets were converted for use against low-flying planes, and a proposal was studied to place picket patrol boats off the coast for visual sighting.

Meanwhile, at the suggestion of Mr. Watson-Watt of the British Air Commission, Secretary Stimson took steps to obtain special low-angle equipment (British CHL or Chain Home Low radar) from Canada, and had personally requested the Canadian minister of defense to give first priority to four sets for the defense of the Canal. The Canadian government promised to do an evaluation on these sets, which were scheduled for delivery to Panama during March and early April 1942.

At Secretary Stimson's request, Mr. Watson-Watt, after completing his inspection of the radar defenses of the west coast, undertook a survey of the situation in Panama. Watson-Watt's report on Panama was as critical as the one he had made a few weeks earlier on the west coast situation, and it aroused much the same reaction. Compared to British radar sets, Watson-Watt found the American SCR-271 and SCR-270 radar systems to be very poor instruments, operated by untrained and apathetic crews. He recommended that both models be replaced as soon as possible with Canadian CHL sets. [337]

The beginning of American contraction and retrenchment in Panama and the Caribbean coincided with the end of the U-boat threat, but this connection was only fortuitous. As early as February 1942 the War Plans Division had been concerned about the demands for reinforcements that were coming in from all directions. Major General Leonard Townsend Gerow, in rejecting

---

337 ibid (Page 426)

a Navy suggestion that the problem of command in Bermuda could be solved by relieving the British garrison, said, "I believe we should make every effort to limit further dispersion of our forces. Unless we call a halt somewhere, we will never have forces for an offensive."

A number of factors needed to be weighted: the desire to provide the fullest possible defense for the Canal, the need to complete and defend the air route to Brazil, and the fact that the Army garrisons were below their authorized strength. In February, about 3,500 troops went to Panama and the Caribbean (some arriving as early as the middle of January 1942). During March 1942, over 9,500 reinforcements and replacements arrived from the United States.

By October, however, the wind had begun to blow in a different direction. Brazil had entered the war against the Axis in August. Preparations for the North African landings were in the final stages. In the Pacific the growing Allied offensive rendered a Japanese sneak attack against the Panama Canal highly improbable. Accordingly, the possibility of a reduction in troops for the Caribbean Defense Command was discussed with General Andrews in October, and a decision was reached to place the ceiling tentatively at 110,000 men. This was approximately the actual strength at that time; however, in the three-month interval before the decision took effect, nearly 10,000 additional troops arrived in Panama and the Caribbean. The peak strength of more than 119,000 men was reached at the end of December 1942. The buildup had taken 13 months to complete.[338]

THE CAVALRY RIDES INTO PANAMA

Playing a small role in the initial Caribbean buildup, the 106th Cavalry Regiment (Horse-Mechanized), 2d Squadron, D

---

338 ibid (Page 437)

Troop—also known as "the downstate squadron" because it came from Urbana, Illinois—received orders to prepare to move on 18 December 1941. The orders were signed by then-General Mark Clark, who would later lead the 5th Army into Rome in 1944. The 106th Cavalry's 2d Squadron was one of the first Army units to be deployed from the United States and sent to the Panama Canal Zone to reinforce the 14th Infantry Division garrison there. The 2d Squadron contained 21 officers and 389 enlisted men.

The 2d Squadron, without its motorcycle troop, was to proceed to the embarkation center at New Orleans and join Force 1202, headed to Fort Clayton in the Canal Zone. At this time, Panama was listed under the code name of Mercury, and Force 1202 was a mixed organization that included hospital units, field artillery, and engineers. Force 1202 left New Orleans on 8 January 1942, en route to Panama aboard the U.S. Army transport *Algonquin*. During the ocean voyage D Troop shared the *Algonquin* with elements of the 32d CavReconSqd.

Frank (Lindy) Fancher of the 106th Cavalry Regiment recalled his voyage to Panama aboard the *Algonquin*:

> We were informed that we would be replaced by an infantry unit as soon as possible and that we would be leaving the United States. We started getting shots, etc. I don't remember how many days we were there. In addition to our patrols we repaired and serviced our vehicles and equipment.
>
> We were told our ship, the *Algonquin*, had been a coastal cattle boat, and would soon be ready. They had washed it all down and installed bunks, but it still smelled like cattle. We boarded early one morning and headed out into the Gulf of Mexico. Every time the propeller shaft turned over, our heads bounced about

Figure 8-7. The *Algonquin* was an ocean liner built in 1926 for the Clyde Mallory Line. The ship caught fire and sank in 1940 while docked at New York. It was salvaged and repaired, then transferred to the Puerto Rico Line and returned to service in 1941. In January 1942, the *Algonquin* was requisitioned and put into service as a troop ship. Her port of registry was changed to Charleston, South Carolina. In July 1943 she was acquired by the United States Army for conversion to a hospital ship operated by the Army Transport Service (ATS).

an inch off our bunks. This was a real "rust bucket." I think you could have kicked a hole through the side with your foot.

We traveled four days and three nights going from New Orleans to Panama.[339]

Force 1202 disembarked at Fort Clayton, which was located at the southern end of the Canal Zone. Since its construction in 1919 Fort Clayton had been a cornerstone of the Panama Canal Defense Forces. The installation was built upon fill provided by the digging of the Miraflores lock and dam.

---

339 Frank 'Lindy' Fancher; *WWII: Through These Eyes:* Published by Author House, 1663 Liberty Drive, Suite 200, Bloomington, Indiana 47403 – 04-26-2005 (Page 10)

The 2d Squadron was at Fort Clayton for only a few days when they began patrol duties to places they would come to know quite well, including cities such as Aguadulce and Nueva Gorgona.[340]

By the end of December 1941 the Panama garrison had increased to about 39,000 men; at the end of January 1942 it had reached 47,600.

Figure 8-8. Fort Clayton in Panama, 1941.

According to Ervin Aden, the 106th Cavalry's arrival at Fort Clayton was an interesting experience:

> Rumors spread that we (D Troop) were headed for the Philippines, but those islands fell to the Japanese. Our ship docked in Panama on the Pacific side, which is Fort Clayton; and we were immediately sent to the Colombian border, where we assembled our own tents.
> Our first duty was to comb the beaches in search of any Japanese. It turned out that was to become

---
340 William H. Collier; *The 106th Cavalry Story:* Published by Trafford Publishing-March 2012 (Page 18-19)

our regular duty. The friendly natives in our area told us that five miles into the interior of the jungle was inhabited by "head-hunters." However, they were extremely frightened by the fact we were armed with Thompson submachine guns; therefore, we had no problem with them.

We washed our clothes against the rocks in streams just like the natives, and hung them on the branches of the trees to dry. The area was populated with boa constrictors and the largest poisonous snake in the Americas, the bushmaster."[341]

Figure 8-9. Troops arriving in Panama. *VICENTE PASCUAL*

---

341 Ervin Aden; e-mail sent to Gary Palmer regarding World War II service; 26 September 2006

Having a camp near the beach had its advantages and disadvantages, according to Frank Fancher:

> After arriving in the Canal Zone, we spent a short time at Fort Clayton, and then moved to the Gorgona Beach area, located west of the Canal entrance on the Pacific side. There we set up a field encampment with tents a short distance from the beach.
>
> Off-duty time in this area may not have been paradise, but it was pretty close. The water was warm and the beaches were all white sand, so swimming just came naturally.
>
> In order to set up the camp we had to dig latrines and a large hole for the kitchen iceboxes. The ground was rock hard after you got down about 12 inches, so I, as demolitions sergeant, had to blast out the holes for the latrines and kitchen iceboxes at several different locations.
>
> The latrines were located about a block from our tents, across a little ice-cold rocky stream that came down from the mountains. Due to the difficulty of digging new holes, we poured them about one-third full of creosote to keep down the odor and covered them with a wooden two-hole seat.

On 4 February 1942 the War Department sent a directive to Panama that activated the 27th CavReconSqd. Elements of this unit would form the nucleus of the fledgling command. On 1 April the 27th absorbed elements of the 1st Cavalry Troop; and on 14 April, added the 106th Cavalry Regiment, 2d Squadron, D Troop.

The Defense Sites Agreement, signed on 18 May 1942, gave the United States the right to use the 134 bases and other sites throughout the Republic of Panama for the duration of the war. The Panamanian government would be compensated for the use of these sites, which ranged from the air base at Rio Hato to temporary camps for troops, aircraft warning stations, searchlight and anti-aircraft gun positions, and miscellaneous tactical and logistical installations.[342]

Figure 8-10. The Chepo River in Panama, April 2007. *RAY VON LUCIFFER*

The 106th Cavalry in Panama did not remain at its original campsite, according to Frank Fancher:

> Our next move was to a new camp called Camp Pacora. It was on the Pacific side of the canal at the Panama City entrance, or on the Colombian side close to the Chepo River and Darien Indian (headhunter) country. The troop outposted Juan Diaz, Chepo, and patrolled the shoreline from one to the other.
> While patrolling this stretch of beach, my number-two combat team spotted a Japanese sub that evidently got stuck when the tide went out. We opened up with

---

[342] William H. Collier; *The 106th Cavalry Story:* Unpublished Manuscript-July 2006 (Page 15-16)

our .50 and .30 caliber machine guns, but they were having little effect, so I called the Coco Solo Navy base for air support. We, in the meantime, kept up our machine gun fire. While this did little damage, it kept the Japanese away from their deck gun. While waiting for Navy dive-bombers I called for another combat team because we were running low on ammunition. The two Navy planes got there first and made short work of the sub.

This is the only time I know of that a Japanese sub was spotted along the Central America or Panama coast. On 23 February 1942, a Japanese sub shelled an oil refinery at Goleta, California. I later learned that on 22 June 1942, a Japanese sub shelled Fort Stevens, Oregon, and in September an aircraft from a sub dropped incendiary bombs on Brooking, Oregon.[343]

The Japanese submarine attack of 23 February 1942 was the first enemy attack on U.S. soil since the War of 1812, when the British assaulted Fort Bowyer in Alabama. The 1942 incident occurred when Japanese submarine I-17, captained by Commander Nishino Kozo, surfaced a mile offshore, west of Goleta, California, and 12 miles west of Santa Barbara. At 7:18 p.m. the submarine's two 5.5-inch guns started firing. The target was the Ellwood Oil Field facility onshore. For the next 20 minutes about 25 shells were fired at the refinery and pump house buildings as workers dropped what they were doing and fled the area. Very little damage was done before the I-17 left the scene and moved south.

After serving only seven months in the Canal Zone, Ervin Aden received an unexpected set of orders:

---

[343] Frank 'Lindy' Fancher; *WWII: Through These Eyes:* Published by Author House, 1663 Liberty Drive, Suite 200, Bloomington, Indiana 47403 – 04-26-2005 (Page 10)

During the second week of July 1942, early in the morning, our CO was summoned to a meeting in Fort Clayton. Upon his return that evening we were assembled, and he read a list of names, including mine. We were told to have our gear ready for departure early the following morning.

Figure 8-11. **Eleventh Officer Candidate Class (Mechanized), 27 July 1942 to 17 October 1942, Third Platoon.** ERVIN ADEN

None of us had any idea where we were headed. We took a train to Cologne, where we boarded a troop ship, the *Florida*, a former passenger cruise ship. We found that it was completely occupied by noncoms of all branches of the Army from that entire area. We still did not know where we were headed. As we sailed out across the Gulf of Mexico, our ship was escorted by three destroyers and, during the day, by a Navy PBY plane.

Scuttlebutt had it that we were going to Officers Candidate School. When we approached closer to the mouth of the Mississippi River, radar picked up a German U-boat in the area, and our alarm alerted us to put on our Mae West (life jacket). One destroyer went out ahead while the other two stayed with us.

Approaching slowly, we entered the mouth of the river, and arrived safely in New Orleans. Everyone on the ship stayed at the Domino Sugar Plant on the Mississippi River for about three or four days before we continued our journey.[344]

I looked forward to going to Officers Candidate School at Fort Riley, Kansas, and found it was not as difficult as I had been told. In fact, I finished in the top 10 percent out of 126 men. Interestingly enough, instruction at Fort Riley was still being given on horseback. About 25 men did not graduate with us and had to repeat courses for the next three weeks. Whether all graduated I do not know. The men on our ship who were with other branches of the Army were sent to various other schools.

We had no choice as to what regiment we would be assigned. About 10 or 12 of us were assigned to the 4th Cavalry Regiment. The others were split up to other cavalry units. Before reporting to Fort Meade we got a 15-day leave. It was at this time I became engaged to my future wife, Iona Mae.[345]

---

344 Ervin Aden; e-mail sent to Gary Palmer regarding World War II service; 26 September 2006
345 ibid

The U.S. Cavalry: Time of Transition

According to Frank Fancher, guerrilla warfare, and dealing with enemy spies, were everyday experiences in Panama:

> At this time Panama was the spy crossroads of the world. People from all over the world lived in Panama at this time, so it was quite a problem—but that was not our worry. Our problem was with the small undercover German radio stations that operated in Panama.
>
> We had directional finders, so it wasn't difficult to locate German radios that were operating from a permanent location. On the other hand, enemy mule-pack radios, which were always on the move in the jungle or mountains, proved much more difficult to locate.
>
> One of our more interesting jobs was locating a station hidden only a short distance from our camp. We kept getting a reading from our direction finder that this radio was located nearby in a cantina or tavern called the Sunny California. Though it was just a short distance from our camp, they would hear us coming every time and shut off the radio before we could locate it. We finally parked our jeep about a half-mile away and walked to the cantina. We found the radio concealed in the piano and traced the antenna outside to a hollowed-out palm tree. We destroyed both. Higher headquarters decided we should check this tavern several times a day, the last check being between 10 and 12 at night. I took duty several times a week.
>
> While we were stationed in Panama we spent every other six weeks living in the jungle, training in guerrilla warfare. The other six weeks we ran our beach, dock and road checkpoints and lived at one of our outposts

or at Fort Clayton or Fort Davis. These were mostly fun times when we were off duty, but as I said, Panama was the spy crossroads of the world at that time. One reconnaissance operation was to check along the International Highway (it was still unfinished then) from Panama City to a small town just inside Costa Rica in Central America. This check was to see if it would be possible to move a large army of troops and vehicles along this road to meet an invasion of Japanese forces, if such should occur. This trip was between 360 and 400 miles one way. Aside from a few muddy spots, the road was pretty good until we were about 60 miles from Costa Rica. There we had to lay down some corduroy roads (logs laid across the road to create a firm road bed) for several yards in a few locations.

We had some problems with gas due to having to operate our vehicles in low gear most of the time. The problem was not too great, as we were able to send some vehicles ahead to our next stop and return with enough gas to get the others through.

Figure 8-12. Jungle warfare training in Panama, July 1942. *U.S. ARMY*

The U.S. Cavalry: Time of Transition

These were just a few of the things that took up our time, besides the constant beach checks and roadblocks, manning check points, guarding trains, and doing our guerrilla warfare training, during which we had to carry 75-pound jungle packs in addition to our gun and ammo.

In spite of all that, this was one place (besides the United States) that I think I could have lived happily ever after. The time spent in the Canal Zone was not all work. Spare time was spent exploring the jungle and visiting the Indian villages. Most still practiced their art, but our troops were on good terms with them and stayed out of their hunting areas.

While in Panama, A Troop was sent up to La Chorrera to act as security for a fighter plane base. My 3d platoon of A Troop was sent to another air base, located at Aguadulce, to provide security there.

We served as guard for installations on both the Atlantic and the Pacific sides of the Canal Zone, including the Gatun Locks, those lakes formed behind the locks, and the Madden Dam.

While in Panama and stationed at Fort Davis, I was assigned to a detached service unit—I still don't know what kind—that was headed by the FBI, who were in charge of most security problems at that time. This was before the CIA was formed. German submarines were sinking many ships in the Gulf of Mexico—even one in the mouth of the Mississippi River. This got so bad that something had to be done about it. To keep these subs on station, they had to be refueled and supplied. They used German supply ships in the remote inlets along the Central and South American coast to do this. Big German radio stations in Colombia and Ecuador (both of whom were supposed to be neutral) coordinated these efforts.

Since I was a pioneer and demolition sergeant, trained in working with explosives and in guerrilla warfare, I was chosen by the FBI to take a fire and demolition team into these countries, through the jungle, and destroy these stations. We had to remove the serial numbers from our weapons and had to wear civilian clothes. The unit was headed by the FBI.

The United Fruit Company supplied a large ship because they had lost so many ships to the subs. We landed on the coast and went in through the jungle. Most of the stations were in Colombia, so it was much easier that way. Our orders were to destroy these stations without killing, if possible.

Once we were on the beach we were on our own. We were informed that if we were caught, no one would help us. To make a long story short, we got the job done without any casualties, but I'm afraid the enemy was miserable for a few days.

We then returned to our regular duty, but were told not to talk about this operation to anyone. We must have been effective because sinkings by German subs in the Gulf dropped greatly. Of course there were still some sinkings, but with most of their supplies cut off the Germans were unable to do the job they were doing before.

After more of these same types of missions, our tour of duty in the Canal Zone, Central America and South America came to an end in November 1943. We sailed from Balboa, Canal Zone, and spent a pleasant, uneventful 10 days on the Pacific before docking in San Francisco, California. An overnight trip by ferry put us at Camp Stoneman, California, and another week by rail put us at Camp Maxey, Texas."[346]

Merle Roughton was also part of the Panama contingent of the 106th:

> Besides D Troop, the War Department sent part of the 106th Cavalry Regiment's 2d Squadron, service troop (supply and transportation), and part of its headquarters troop to Panama. Shortly after our arrival in Panama we began patrolling the interior, scouting for enemy agents and portable radio stations. It was mountainous and, as you would expect, covered in a heavy tropical forest or jungle.
>
> We discovered a road on the western side of Panama that ran from north to south. Known as the International Highway, it was incomplete and presented a hazard to travelers over certain sections. In January 1942 the government had just started building a third set of locks in the Canal that were designed to take larger ships. It was part of our duty to provide security for its construction as well as other airfields and campsites scattered throughout the Panama area.[347]

---

[346] Frank 'Lindy' Fancher; *WWII: Through These Eyes:* Published by Author House, 1663 Liberty Drive, Suite 200, Bloomington, Indiana 47403 – 04-26-2005 (Page 18-24)
[347] Merle Roughton: Interview given to Gary Palmer (Interviewed in June 2008 during the 106th Cavalry Groups annual reunion in Urbana, Illinois)

CHAPTER IX

LIFE STATESIDE DURING 1942

With the Axis powers on the move, War Department plans for mobilization of the Army began to affect the First Cavalry Division stationed at Fort Bliss and the rest of the Regular Army. However, the Army could stand up divisions only as fast as camps could be constructed and cadres formed to receive and train the men assigned to the new units.

The Cavalry Division was directed to constitute a cadre for the organization of the 91st Infantry Division. Each subordinate unit in the division was likewise directed to build a cadre of its own. This resulted in units such as the 106th Cavalry Regiment, which would remain stationed at Camp Livingston to train newly arriving draftees to replace personnel from D Troop who had been sent to Panama.[348]

No old-line unit could be expected to place its best men on such cadres, and oftentimes such units disliked parting with even their second best troops. The need for cadre personnel provided an opportunity for first sergeants and inexperienced company commanders to remove some of their less desirable personnel by transferring them. Supervisors were anxious to keep good personnel in their units. To overcome this natural reluctance, the 5th Cavalry, for example, directed the creation of two separate cadres. One cadre was dispatched to form the new unit when the time came; the other remained with the parent 5th Cavalry. The cadre to be dispatched, however, was to be selected by the regimental commander by lot. It was an excellent method and proved to be a great morale builder.[349]

Shortly after the Pearl Harbor attack, the 106th Cavalry Regiment was reorganized and became fully mechanized. Cecil R. (Mick) Maguire noted the following:

> In short order in 1942, several big events took place:
>
> 1. On 3 January 1942 we cut the regiment in two parts and shipped half of the guys to guard the Panama Canal. (I never heard anything about those people again!)
>
> 2. We were formed ("we" being the remainders) into cadres, received a contingent of draftees, and gave them basic training ourselves.

---

348 Lucian K. Truscott, Jr.; *The Twilight of the U.S. Cavalry (Life in the Old Army, 1917-1942):* Published by University Press of Kansas-1989 (Page 184)
349 ibid (Page 184)

3. Sometime around 8 April 1942 we rode the horses down to the railhead and loaded and shipped them all to Fort Riley, Kansas.[350]

Following the departure of the 106th Cavalry Regiment, 2d Squadron, D Troop (Mechanized), the regiment's commanding officer, Lieutenant Colonel Charles Radcliffe Johnson, Jr., was promoted to Colonel on 1 February 1942. Johnson was then assigned as military attaché to Morocco and Algeria. From 2 March 1942 until 8 April 1942, Colonel Kenneth Buchanan returned temporarily to command the regiment while it was still stationed at Camp Livingston.[351]

During this period the regiment continued to experience personnel upheavals. Many men left for Officers Candidate School (OCS), and numerous cadres were formed to start new units such as airbase security battalions. Fortunately, not many officers left the regiment. To fill the resulting personnel gaps a training squadron was organized to train new draftees. This lasted a couple of months. Training during this period emphasized vehicle maintenance and vehicle road marches, which stressed road spacing, driver maintenance halts, and vehicle maintenance as well as vehicle maintenance before, during, and after operations. In the tradition of the horse cavalry days, "motor stables" (the washing and minor daily maintenance of the new mechanical horse) were conducted daily. In addition to the road marches, marksmanship training with individual and crew served weapons was conducted on regular basis, and physical fitness training was scheduled daily.[352]

---

350 Cecil R. (Mick) Maguire; Orange Socks and Saddle Shoes: Unpublished manuscript as of 06-10-2010
351 William H. Collier; *The 106th Cavalry Story:* Unpublished Manuscript-July 2006 (Page 16)
352 ibid (Page 18)

Cecil (Mick) Maguire participated in training of new draftees for the 106th Cavalry Regiment.

> When the 106th was split into two parts and one group was sent to Panama, almost 100 percent of the remaining men were promoted one or two grades and formed into a cadre. We went down to the railhead and welcomed enough draftees into the 106th to bring us back up to strength.
> The cadre gave these draftees basic training, advanced training, and specialized training. When it was over, very few of the new men were anything but privates. During our draftee training period I taught classes in aircraft identification, the .30 caliber machine gun, Tommy gun, .45 caliber pistol, motorcycle riding, tank driving, and an assortment of others.
> Through many subsequent reorganizations and changes, the one-time National Guardsmen still held on to most of the ranks above PFC (private first class).
> Of course there were a few who were so good they couldn't be ignored. One thing helping the newcomers was that the Army developed a new set of "technician" ratings. These ratings were for radio operators, motor mechanics, machine gunners, medics, various drivers, etc. The new ratings allowed these specialists to earn paychecks equal to various sergeants and corporals.[353]

Next, the 106th Cavalry Regiment rolled through a quick succession of organizational changes. On 12 January 1942 the 106th was assigned to Third Army. Soon the 106th was relieved from assignment to Third Army and reassigned, on 1 May 1942, to the IV Army Corps. Subsequently, the 106th Cavalry Regiment

---

353 Cecil (Mick) Maguire; e-mail sent to Gary Palmer on 08 September 2005

LIFE STATESIDE DURING 1942

(Horse-Mechanized) was assigned to the XV Corps and received orders for reorganization on 30 March 1942 as the 106th Cavalry Regiment (Mechanized), per Army Ground Force Order 320.2 (3-25-1942) MR-M-GN. The changeover was completed on 8 April 1942.

The 106th was now a mechanized cavalry regiment under TO&E 2-71. The headquarters, band, headquarters troop, service troop, and medical detachment remained essentially the same. The 1st Squadron (Horse) lost its horses and became fully mechanized. Each squadron now consisted of a headquarters and two reconnaissance troops with armored cars, jeeps, and motorcycles; a support troop of three light tank platoons, each equipped with five light tanks; and an assault gun platoon with three vehicles mounting 75 mm howitzers.

At full authorization the regiment was allotted 79 officers, 5 warrant officers, 1,558 enlisted men, 53 armored cars, 34 light tanks, 6 assault guns, 55 motorcycles, 183 jeeps, and fifty-five 2½-ton trucks. While it was stationed at Camp Livingston the regiment retained its scout cars (in place of the M8 armored cars) and was issued M3A1 light tanks. Likewise, scout cars were substituted for the assault guns, which were not seen until the regiment's arrival at Camp Hood in August 1943.

On 15 May 1942 Major Octave M. Smith assumed command. This lasted until 27 May 1942, when Smith was relieved by Major Max Flewelling. Finally, on 22 June 1942, Colonel Thomas Wade Herren took command.[354]

Elbert Julius Gebhardt, Jr., was a tank commander with the 106th Cavalry Regiment's F Company.

I enlisted in F Troop (a motorcycle troop) in the Illinois National Guard in 1939 at Camp Lincoln in

---

[354] Raymond Mucha: Posting of the 106th Cavalry 1940-1945 (Formerly Illinois National Guard): Reproduced from the National Archives, Washington, D. C.

Figure 9-1. The 106th Cavalry marching band at Camp Livingston, 1941. *Eugene Johnson*

Springfield, Illinois. I was housed and trained at the Illinois State Fairgrounds and on 25 November 1940 inducted into federal service.

On 4 January 1941, I traveled by rail to Camp Livingston, Louisiana, where we lived in the mud while the gas-heated tents at the camp were still being built. There we trained on motorcycles, learning motorcycle combat and riding traffic guard for the 1st Squadron horse portees (horse trailers) on road marches and field exercises.

On 8 April 1942, the unit was reorganized and F Troop changed from motorcycles to a tank troop, redesignated as F Company, and equipped with the M5 tanks armed with a 37 mm cannon. From 15 September 1942 to 10 November 1942, we participated in large-scale maneuvers in Louisiana.[355]

---

355 Gebhardt, Elbert Julius Jr.; *World War II Illinois Veterans Memorial » Blog Archive » Gebhardt* ... Interview by the WWII Illinois Veteran's Society-Unknown Date of Interview.

LIFE STATESIDE DURING 1942

Training in the field became progressively more realistic as the units took part in maneuvers with thousands of men participating in the swamps and bayous of Louisiana, the sand and clay of the Carolinas, the mountains and mesas of Texas, the woods and hills of Tennessee, and the desert Training Center near the West Coast. In those areas the cavalry and soldiers of other arms learned to play the game as they would experience it on the battlefield.

Trained soldiers were still scarce in the late summer and early fall of 1942 as the Allies prepared Task Force A to participate in Operation TORCH, the invasion of North Africa. To fill the task force, the War Department deferred the reorganizing and filling of the 7th Infantry Division, the last of the Reserve divisions to enter active military service, and reduced three partially-trained divisions to less than 50 percent of their authorized strengths. To avoid stripping divisions again and disturbing their training, the War Department designated the 76th and 78th Infantry Divisions as replacement units to receive, train, and hold men until needed. Those divisions served in that capacity from October 1942 to March 1943, when replacement depots took over.[356]

Besides the shortage of trained manpower, the nation also faced a severe shortage of ships large enough to transport divisions to the combat theaters. For this reason and other military and political reasons, plans for an early invasion of Europe across the English Channel were postponed. Also, the expansion and deployment of Army Service Forces and Army Air Force units placed heavy demands on available shipping, while the success of German submarines off the Eastern Seaboard of the United States made the shortage of tonnage even more acute. Finally, the demands of the hard-pressed Pacific theaters put an unprecedented strain on shipping facilities. Therefore, from October 1942 to March

---

356 John B Wilson; *Maneuver and Firepower (The Evolution of Divisions and Separate Brigades):* Published by Center of Military History, United States Army, Washington, D.C.-1998 (Page 179-180)

1943 no division departed the United States, and from March to November 1943 only 11 divisions went overseas.[357]

Meanwhile, on 24 July 1942, the 7th Cavalry Regiment was attached to the 56th Cavalry Brigade, and on 25 September 1942 the 7th was released and reverted to the Division. On the same date the commanding general of the 1st Cavalry Division was relieved of command of Southern Land Frontier by the commanding general of the 56th Cavalry Brigade. It is assumed by military historians that on this date 1st Cavalry Division was relieved from attachment to Southern Defense Command and remained assigned to Third Army. It is further assumed that upon return from maneuvers in September 1942, the commanding general of the 1st Cavalry Division reassumed command of Southern Land Frontier. At that point the 1st Cavalry Division was reattached to Southern Defense Command until February 1943, when the 1st Division was again relieved by the 56th Cavalry Brigade.

Merton Glover remembered several changes that affected the 4th Cavalry Regiment early in 1942:

> Sometime toward spring and a bit warmer weather, I was part of a detail transported in the back of a 6x6 truck to Omaha, Nebraska, to drive back 16 prototype jeeps. As I recall there were four each of Fords, Bantams, General Motors and Willys-Overland jeeps. These were experimental models for approval by the War Department. They all had similar bodies, were four-wheel drive, but they steered on all four wheels and each company had their own engine they hoped to sell. Some steered the rear wheels a few degrees after the front. Two other models steered rear the same time

---

357 ibid (Page 180)

as the front; they were impossible to straighten out of a whip if you turned too much, too fast.

Several of these experimental models were wrecked on good roads. As a result, the War Department settled on what became the standard Jeep. Most had Ford motors and Bantam (Ford) or Willys-Overland-made bodies.[358]

Figure 9-2. Experimental Ford GP four-wheel-drive vehicle.
CLINTON ALEXANDER

In April 1942 the 4th Cavalry Regiment was ordered to Omaha, Nebraska, to participate in a parade known as "Army Day," [which was scheduled for] 6 April 1942. We formed up in a convoy, hauling horses, equipment, and armored cars. We set up a model camp in Ak-Sar-Ben Field complete with picket lines,

---

358 Merton Glover; *86 and counting:* Unpublished personal manuscript of author's life history-2003 (Page 34)

pup tents, trucks, and an armored car park. The city of Omaha was invited to visit us on Sunday; hundreds of people came.

On the way back to Fort Meade we came west on Highway 30 (later known as I-80) and cut north at Bridgeport to Fort Robinson. We camped in open area and held a last formal review for the horse cavalry troops. At the end of the review the troopers unsaddled their mounts and handed the halters to the quartermaster personnel at Fort Robinson. Some of the old saddle bumpers were said to have cried. It was a moving experience for us all, to have witnessed the passing of an era as well as some American history.[359]

Figure 9-3. The 4th Cavalry Regiment participating in the Army Day parade. Omaha, Nebraska, 6 April 1942.
FORT ROBINSON MUSEUM, FORT ROBINSON, NEBRASKA

---

359 ibid (Page 35)

Life Stateside During 1942

As stated, the 4th Cavalry turned all horses of A and B Troops back to remount service at Fort Robinson, Nebraska, with one exception: C Troop kept their mounts and was later transferred to the 10th Mountain Division near Colorado Springs.

Years later, after the war, I met with some of these fellows—Ed Iron Cloud and Livermont—from near home. Some of the horses were used for pack trains (mules) over the Burma hump to supply Chiang Kai-shek food and ammo as the Japanese were overrunning China. Another part went to Italy and did something over some snowy mountains there.

The 1st Squadron—formerly horses—went to tanks and retrained, making the whole 4th Cavalry a mechanized reconnaissance regiment. On 4 July 1942 the 4th Regiment was ordered to Gregory, South Dakota, for a Fourth of July parade.[360]

Figure 9-4. 4th Cavalry Regiment encampment outside of Fort Robinson, Nebraska, prior to dismount.
FORT ROBINSON MUSEUM, FORT ROBINSON, NEBRASKA

---

360 ibid (Page 36)

Figure 9-5. End of an era: 4th Cavalry, A Troop, on parade. Date unknown, but prior to April 1942.
FORT ROBINSON MUSEUM, FORT ROBINSON, NEBRASKA

Cecil (Mick) Maguire of the 106th Cavalry Regiment, F Company, recalled a chance meeting with then-Colonel George S. Patton during the 1942 summer maneuvers in the Kisatchie National Forest:

> One day we had a 12-hour rest period to clean weapons, vehicles, and ourselves. We also got a couple of meals out of the kitchen truck as a relief from canned C-rations. I had dispersed my platoon of five tanks along a ridge, below the crest in what is known as "hull defilade" position. In this position an enemy force approaching from the opposite side of the hill couldn't see the whole tank, only the upper part of the turret and the cannon barrel. This view of a tank is very hard to see from a couple hundred yards away and, when spotted, makes a very small target or almost none, when artfully camouflaged with leaves and branches.

CAVALRY UNITS ARE CHANGED

Fort Meade Fourth Cavalry To Be Wholly Mechanized Modern Unit

Complete mechanization of the army's ten combination horse-mechanized cavalry regiments was announced today by the War Department. In their new form, the regiments become highly mobile units of great fire power capable of carrying out the mission of cavalry in modern vehicles at modern battle speeds.

Three of the regiments are regular army units, the 4th, 6th and 15th cavalry regiments. The latter has been reorganized after a lapse in active service since 1922. The other seven are Federalized National Guard, the 101st cavalry of New York; 102nd, New Jersey; 104th, Pennsylvania; 106th, Illinois; 107th, Ohio; 113th, Iowa, and 115th, Wyoming.

With their reorganization, there passes from the army the picturesque "Portee" cavalry. This was part of the horse-mechanized regiment in which one squadron was mounted on horses while the other operated in scout cars and motorcycles.

The horses, men and equipment of the Horse Squadrons Portee were carried from place to place in motor-drawn vans, unloaded at the scene of action and rushed directly into combat, fresh and ready. In this manner, it was hoped they could equal the road speeds of completely mechanized troops and yet be available for action in swampy, sandy or otherwise difficult country where the horse was more mobile than the motor. As horse-mechanized cavalry, these regiments contained about 5,000 horses which now are made available to other army units.

Experience gained in the maneuvers of the fall of 1941, however, dictated that they may be entirely mechanized to better fulfill their function of Army Corps reconnaissance units, flank guards and powerful, fast-moving assault forces. While the use of the horse vans has speeded transportation, it had not completely solved this vital problem.

In their new form, the number of officers and enlisted men in these regiments will remain approximately the same, about 1,500. But they will be mounted in speedy armored cars with greater fire power and better protection than the scout cars provided, and capable of much higher road speeds and far greater mobility than the cumbersome horse vans.

Mechanization of these regiments leaves the army with two divisions and one brigade of horse cavalry, the 1st and 2nd cavalry divisions and the 56th cavalry brigade. The 1st and 2nd cavalry divisions are regular army troops while the 56th brigade is composed of the 112th and 124th cavalry regiments, both of the Texas National Guard.

Included in the 101st cavalry is the famous "Squadron A" of New York City, its units now designated as Troops E, F and G. The 102nd cavalry includes another famous National Guard mounted unit, the Essex Troop, of Newark, New Jersey, now designated as Troop A.

NORTHWEST NEBRASKA NEWS
April 16, 1942   p.1 c.5

Horse-Mechanized Cavalry Motorized

Washington, D. C. April 9 (INS) —Complete streamlining of the 10 combination horse-mechanized cavalry regiments was announced today by the war department.

Under the new setup all the regiments will be mechanized fully to increase their mobility and striking power.

Three of the regiments are regular army units, the 4th, 6th and 15th Cavalry regiments. The other seven are federalized national guard units, including the 106th of Illinois; 113th, Iowa, and 115th, Wyoming.

Figure 9-6. A Nebraska newspaper article from the period described which Regular Army and National Guard cavalry regiments were to be mechanized. *Northwest Nebraska News*, **16 April 1942.** CLINTON ALEXANDER

Figure 9-7. The 4th Cavalry Regiment following dismount at Fort Robinson, Nebraska, on 6 April 1942. *Fort Robinson Museum, Fort Robinson, Nebraska*

(Officers like to see stuff like that on maneuvers; it seems to reflect well on their "leadership qualities.")

So there we were: guns and tanks cleaned, faces shaved, a number of men having just returned from lunch at the kitchen truck, minding our own business and eating watermelon. Several of us were wearing clean coveralls, orange socks, and brown-and-white saddle shoes. I had sent my only pair of G.I. boots to the quartermaster three days before to be half-soled and re-heeled. Due to the fact that Army size 5½E was difficult to find, I had only one pair instead of the required two. During the previous three days, the only time I was seen by anyone of importance, I was probably seen standing in the turret, so my feet were concealed. No sweat!

We continued eating watermelon, trying to spit all the seeds into a canvas bucket and failing miserably. Into this idyllic scene blew a fierce summer storm!

What well-known, high-ranking Army officer was known to demand that his troops be "tough, efficient, and extremely aggressive" and, at the same time, well-dressed, bathed, shaved, boots shined, and tie tied and tucked in between the second and third buttons? Colonel George S. Patton, Jr., that's who!

I saw a cloud of dust boiling up behind a jeep that was flying down the dirt road parallel to the ridge where we were. As I watched I saw that the officer was looking up at the tanks as he passed. When he saw my position, he reached over and hit the driver on the steel helmet with his hand. The driver slid the jeep to a stop, jammed the vehicle into reverse, and backed up to a position even with ours. The officer jumped out and came stomping up the hill, growing taller with each stride. I saw his rank and jumped off the tank, bringing myself and the crew to rigid attention.

Colonel Patton stood there, $8\frac{1}{2}$ feet tall, his face a brilliant crimson, and proceeded to torture me for a good 15 minutes at about 180 decibels. The dust arose around us like the muzzle blast from a 155 mm cannon. I was really scared, but I discovered that Colonel Patton had a rather high-pitched voice. I stood there at attention, all muscles tight, struggling to not wet my pants and trying not to laugh or even smile at the sound of that voice.

The Colonel proceeded to enumerate my transgressions and sins against the Army, the government, God, and himself. I wish I could remember the exact dialogue that followed, but I was under immense pressure.

The Colonel roared, "Who's in charge here?"

I reported—not in the proper manner— "I am, sir."

He increased the volume somewhat, asking me, "And who in the hell are you? Are you in my Army? Are you a soldier?"

I stammered a bit and reported properly: name, rank and organization, commanded by Regimental CO and Troop CO.

Colonel Patton then demanded that I explain my shoes and socks.

I told him my sad story, starting each sentence with "SIR!"

By this time a crowd was forming (it was the Colonel's entourage); and Patton, detecting a movement on his left, turned and told a lieutenant colonel to go and make a "quick inspection of the rest of the platoon and be back in five minutes—clean guns and vehicles only!" (From this point on, he looked at his watch three or four times.)

Returning to me, he inspected our cannon and machine guns carefully, and I gained a few points. (I had checked all five tanks just before I bit into the watermelon.)

Patton then wanted to check our personal weapons (sidearms).

Oh crap, I thought, *everybody else (sergeants and corporals only) is wearing Colt .45 automatics, Model 1911, and I'm carrying a civilian model Colt .45 revolver—loaded!* I thought, *Oh-oh! Fort Leavenworth for five years minimum.*

I fished the gun and holster out from behind the tank radio and, with a quick glance, discovered that I hadn't reloaded it after our big gun cleaning session after breakfast. The revolver was new, blue, and had handle grips made of stag horn. Patton hefted it, aimed it somewhere in the distance, hefted it again, and handed it back to me.

Life Stateside During 1942

He said, "Chambered for .45 automatic." It was more of a statement than a question. Then he said, "Ammo?"

I replied, "I'm all out, Sir. I used it all up target practicing last January."

He paused, and then told me either to borrow some G.I. shoes from the supply sergeant or go barefoot and report my treasons to the CO. He said he would be in contact with the 106th headquarters to set my punishment.

As he turned to go, he said, "I'm going to make soldiers out of you goddamned college boys or else!"

The whole bunch of brass hats and flunkies found its way down the hill to their vehicle. Patton found a rag in the back of the jeep and knocked the dust and grime off his boots, standing on one foot and resting the other in the door cutaway of the jeep.

George was apparently talking to his driver and telling him how he scared the expletive out of me. At one point the driver threw back his head and laughed. I was relieved to see that. It made me think that maybe the Colonel wasn't quite so steamed after all.

I've talked about the "good ol' boys club" elsewhere in this epic, and it came to my assistance here. Our Regimental CO and my captain, the Troop CO, both had to explain away in writing—in many letters—why I had no respect for the uniform and why our supply sergeant couldn't get shoes to fit me. I suffered the really severe punishment of being "confined to quarters" for the rest of the maneuvers—about 20 days. When one's "quarters" are loosely limited to the entire maneuver area, which contains countless small towns and several larger towns—well, you can see the severity of the punishment.

During the next three months I had numerous "interviews" with my CO. He told me of the "thousand ways" I had inconvenienced him and how I had endangered his good record. I remember at one point he said, "Your ass belongs to me now; I want you to only do things that will make *me* happy. If not, I will personally break your nose before I drag you to the stockade!"[361]

Merton Glover of the 4th Cavalry also participated in the Tennessee maneuvers:

> Sometime later, maybe August 1942, the mechanized part of the regiment loaded on the train in Rapid City, South Dakota, for the Tennessee maneuvers. We had to wire and block every vehicle down on flat cars, in accordance to Army specs. As I recall, four jeeps and two armored scout cars to a flat car. Our other equipment was loaded in baggage cars. The cooks' field stoves and other related items were loaded onto a separate car. They had to cook on the go. We did get Pullman beds—two beds down and one over, or three per compartment. It turned out to be the best travel we had while in the Army.
>
> As I recall, we were two nights and most of two days on the road. I don't think our troop train had any priority given it on the way to maneuvers. I recall our train switched through Chicago railyards, which consisted of hundreds of acres of tracks. I think we

---

[361] Cecil (Mick) Maguire; e-mail sent to Gary Palmer on 24 September 2005.

went southeast from Chicago through Indiana and Kentucky into Tennessee to Gallatin to de-train.

I will always remember how the engineer laid on the train whistle through the hill country. I can still almost hear that mournful old steam engine whistle every mile or so. I wondered if it was to clear the tracks of livestock and animals.

That summer and fall were hot, humid and rainy. It was not pleasant camping out full-time. Tennessee has its share of mosquitoes, bugs and snakes. The maneuver was probably in the poorer hill area the Army no doubt leased—no doubt the best money those hillbillies ever made. The hills were rocky, thin soil, terraces maybe six to eight feet wide, corn two feet apart and some eight feet tall, some tobacco and truck gardens (local produce farms). This was in the Cumberland River area— a mighty river, and deep. There was a high rock bluff running down one side with a little narrow road at the river's edge that ran under a bluff on the other.

Some Army brain decided our troop could cross the river on a raft and outflank the enemy. The Army had some small pontoon boats to lash together to make a larger boat, meant to hold a scout car and jeep. An engineer company had some stakes and rope to tie the raft to the bank on the bluff side. They took a big rope across the river and anchored it to keep our raft from going downriver, as there was a strong current.

I was an armored car driver. I would drive down a real steep incline onto this makeshift raft to go to the far side to a very low bank, not much higher than the river itself. I did not have to be warned not to step on the gas until all four wheels were on ground, for fear of kicking the poorly anchored raft out from under the car and falling backward into the river. It was very tempting to not gun the engine until the rear wheels were clear. We learned later that some tank outfit dumped a big Sherman tank off some similar deal and drowned the whole crew.

That Tennessee maneuver wound down around 1 November 1942. We loaded our vehicles again on rail flat cars, the kitchen in a baggage car, and ourselves in nice clean berths with sheets. That was a real treat after three months in mud, bugs and rain.[362]

On 18 December 1942 the War Department reactivated two regiments of cavalry, the 2d and 29th, as mechanized units. A TWX (telegram) from the War Department through Army Ground Forces, Birmingham, Alabama, reached then-Lieutenant Colonel Charles H. Reed at the 42d Armored Regiment of the 11th Armored Division, where he was assigned as executive officer. The TWX designated Reed as regimental commander of the 2d Cavalry Regiment (Mechanized), which was being reactivated at Fort Jackson, South Carolina. At the same time, orders were received at Headquarters, Fort Riley, Kansas, directing that headquarters to furnish the regimental staff.[363]

The original staff as selected by headquarters at Fort Riley carried Major S.W. Benkosky as regimental executive and included Captain T.B. Hargis, Jr., formerly of the 15th Cavalry Regiment, as regimental adjutant; Captain Shelby Greene, formerly of the 4th Cavalry Regiment, as intelligence officer; Major Benjamin Stahl, of the Fort Riley motors department, as operations officer; Captain James H. Pitman, formerly of the 15th Cavalry Regiment, as supply officer; and Captain Allan C. Peck of the Fort Riley motors department as regimental motors officer. First Lieutenant John S. Higgins was appointed communications officer,

---

[362] Merton Glover; *86 and counting:* Unpublished personal manuscript of author's life history-2003 (Page 36-38)
[363] Isaac Golding on behalf of the Second Cavalry Assn.; *2d Dragoons (Second Cavalry Association Regimental History Center):* Word Press-2011

and Captain Lowry as regimental surgeon. Major W.J. Easton and Major W.A. Hill, from the Cavalry Replacement Training Center, were later designated as squadron commanders.[364]

Major Benkosky, on 2 January 1943, was the first of the new staff to arrive at Fort Jackson, the new station of the 2d Cavalry Regiment (Mechanized). Colonel Reed arrived on the following day, and arrangements were made with the station commander for the assignment of a portion of "North Camp," an area with temporary wood barracks, to house the regiment. A temporary regimental headquarters was set up in one of the barracks for the reception of the incoming staff officers, and arrangements for mess were made with a nearby unit of the station complement, since the cooks were in the enlisted cadre, which had not yet reported for duty.[365]

By 14 January 1943 the enlisted cadre—experienced men from the 15th Cavalry Regiment at Fort Riley—had arrived at the new station, and with the already functioning staff formed the trained nucleus of a regiment that was to gain the praise of the Germans as well as of its own higher command.

It was at that time, in the second week of January, that the regiment really began to take form. Now a mechanized cavalry regiment, in the spring of 1943 it had a table of organization that listed a regimental headquarters troop, a service troop, four reconnaissance troops and two support troops. The regimental headquarters included two squadron commanders and staffs as tactical headquarters only, thereby giving the regimental commander great flexibility in the formation of his squadrons for any tactical situation. This practice is still followed in armored divisions with their use of combat commands.[366]

---

364 ibid(Isaac Golding on behalf of the Second Cavalry Assn.; *2d Dragoons (Second Cavalry Association Regimental History Center):* Word Press-2011)
365 ibid
366 ibid

The U.S. Cavalry: Time of Transition

New Troops, New Regiments, and Newly Trained Officers

During 1942 and 1943, officer selectees were sent to Fort Riley for Officers Candidate School (OCS). Ironically, the trainees still received training for mounted cavalry while the Army as a whole was making the move towards mechanization. Perhaps Ervin Aden stated it best: "I looked forward to going to Officers Candidate School at Fort Riley, Kansas, and found it was not as difficult as I had been told. In fact, I finished in the top 10 percent. Interestingly enough, instruction at Fort Riley was still being given on horseback."

Faris "Jake" Hess served at Fort Riley during 1942 as a junior officer and instructor.

> Leta Mae Phillips and I were married on 18 April 1942. I was graduated from Texas A&M in May of 1942. I immediately entered the service on 17 May 1942 as a 2d Lieutenant. I was first stationed at Fort Riley, Kansas. The temperature was so hot you could fry an egg on the sidewalk.
>
> Since I was an officer, Leta Mae and I could live off base. We shared our first home with three other couples. We lived in an upstairs bedroom. Kitchen privileges entailed one hour to get in and out, and all families shared one bathroom.
>
> Understandably, Leta Mae found us a different apartment, over a movie theater. There we shared a kitchen and bath with only one other couple. At night we would open our door and get air conditioning from the movie theater.

LIFE STATESIDE DURING 1942

Officer Candidates gain experience with the aid of their classmates . . .

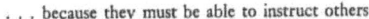

. . . because they must be able to instruct others.

With the aid of this chart, students quickly learn the names of an automatic's different parts.

These trainees are learning the nomenclature and functioning of the rifle.

Life Stateside During 1942

Every man knows the name and function of every part of a machine gun.

Daily calisthenics are a "must" for condition.

Trainees scramble over a 12-foot log obstacle.

From the sandbag obstacle, the students leap 10 feet to the ground.

Life Stateside During 1942

Group instruction in hand-to-hand, or "dirty," fighting.

A 16-foot rope climb builds muscle.

Phases of first aid in the field: the one- and two-man carry and the use of the first-aid kit.

Keep that head down. Instruction in creeping and individual protective measures.

Life Stateside During 1942

A small reconnaissance patrol advances through a difficult ravine.

An instructor (right foreground) explains the preparation and use of a standing-type fox hole (left).

Scaling a cliff is part of the obstacle course.

Under cover of a friendly machine gun, trainees take the next objective in village fighting.

Life Stateside During 1942

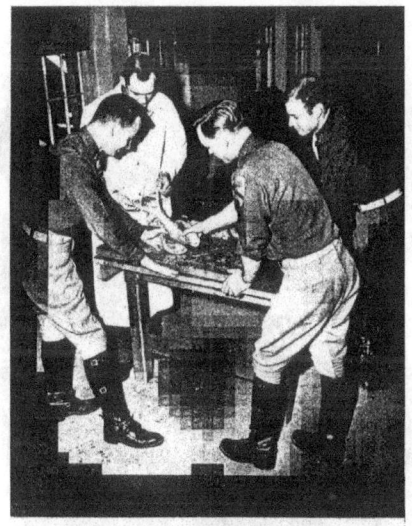

Student officers must learn the anatomy of the horse for a better understanding of animal care.

Students in the Saddlers' School learn by doing.

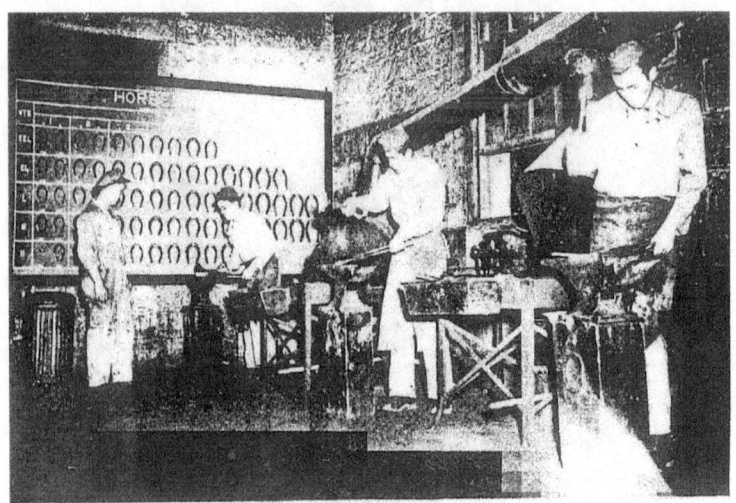

Horseshoers' School.

Horse and mechanized Cavalry co-operate as a reconnaissance team.

LIFE STATESIDE DURING 1942

Light tank "Vinegar Joe" maneuvers over the famous Fort Riley rimrock.

A maintenance check is made on every vehicle after each 1,000 miles of service.

An electrical trouble-shooting class in the Motor Mechanics School.

Successful Officer Candidates march to graduation.

Life Stateside During 1942

I loved my first assignment. My main job was to teach horseback riding. We had show horses and I trained them to jump obstacles.

The older officers' wives would invite the younger wives to social activities. One of these activities was horseback riding, "English" style. One day Leta Mae was riding and did not realize that her horse was a jumper. When they came to the first log her horse jumped. Leta Mae was thrown forward in the jump. She lost her stirrups and grabbed the horse around the neck and held on for dear life until the horse finally stopped.

We had a lot of fun in Kansas. On Sunday mornings there were several couples of friends who would go horseback riding.

In the fall of 1942 our unit was transferred to Camp Livingston, Louisiana. It is located near Alexandra, Louisiana. It was exciting for us because about 14 couples were transferred to Camp Livingston. When we got to Louisiana we got the bad news that the cavalry had been mechanized. This was a completely different situation because we had to do away with the horses and learn how to drive jeeps and armored cars.[367]

---

[367] Captain Faris 'Jake' Hess and Nancy 'Hess' Blackburn; *My Story-106th Cavalry Group in Europe 1942-1945:* Personal Manuscript written for the Hess' family in 2004 (Page 5)

CHAPTER X

CAMP COXCOMB, CAMP HOOD, CAMP MAXEY

While Patton directed maneuvers, Major General Charles L. Scott traveled to North Africa to observe how the British army conducted desert warfare. Scott was preparing to take command of the Armored Force Replacement Training Center at Fort Knox. When he returned he published an indictment of the current American approach to mechanized reconnaissance.

Scott, a long-time advocate of armored reconnaissance vehicles, had suggested in the early 1930s that in the future tanks would accompany the leading elements of the reconnaissance effort. He saw his reasoning validated in North Africa. Field Marshall Erwin Rommel changed the nature of the reconnaissance game by raising the stakes on the desert battlefield. Units organized to conduct "pure reconnaissance"—going, seeing, and reporting—

were unable to survive long enough to complete their missions. In some cases the units couldn't pause to send a warning message.

Scott warned that mechanized reconnaissance units had to do more than passively observe the enemy; they had to act offensively to fulfill their assigned tasks of long-range reconnaissance and security for the flanks and rear. Scott concluded, "We'll never win the war by observation—but by [employing] fighting units that can both observe and do some killing."[368]

Early in 1942 the War Plans Division of the War Department General Staff concluded that in order to prepare American troops for fighting in the desert of North Africa, the Army needed an area to train and equip troops for this type of combat. In addition,, the American armored fighting unit was in its infancy, and new equipment was being added to this new type of service.

General HQ assigned General George S. Patton, Jr., as the commanding general of the 1st Armored Corps and asked him to locate a place in the southwestern desert of the U.S. that would be suitable for a training site. Patton flew over California and Arizona and chose a location that could be supported by rail and had access to water. He made arrangements with the Metropolitan Water District and set up advance parties to prepare the facilities.

On that ground, training for the 1st Armored Corps began on 20 April 1942 and ended six weeks later.[369]

Patton—no stranger to the subject of mechanization—believed that the Desert Training Center served to teach Army soldiers the finer points of living and fighting in the desert. In the first two paragraphs of his instructions on tactics and techniques, Patton pointed out that the desert, with its lack of "terrestrial cover," challenged the ability of friendly forces to remain hidden. The natural conditions also lent themselves to "inevitable air attack" and opposition by enemy armored forces.

---

368 ibid (Page 112)
369 custermen.com/AtTheFront/DesertCamps.htm (Accessed on 02-27-2012)

Patton concluded that the only way to properly secure friendly forces from ground attack was through "distant reconnaissance, both by ground units and by air observation units." Air units had to "have a radio which is capable of covering two ways with the reconnaissance on the ground" if they were to effectively synchronize their efforts with the ground forces. Unfortunately, even though this reflected every level of army doctrine pertaining to mechanized ground reconnaissance and mechanized operations, it was a notion that remained unsupportable for lack of proper radios.[370]

Patton anticipated the use of armored reconnaissance battalions or the occasional "corps reconnaissance battalion" preceding the main body of friendly forces by "three to five hours." Once in contact with the enemy; the battalion "must maintain contact and work around the hostile flanks to discover what is in the rear." Departing from the teachings of the Armored Force School at Fort Knox, Patton explained that at this point in battle the reconnaissance battalion's "primary mission is information, not fighting."

Later in the document, in his characteristic clipped prose, Patton remarked on how best to arm the men performing the reconnaissance mission. Aside from supporting the seemingly difficult task of maintaining contact with the enemy without fighting them, Patton distorted his message when he stated the following: "They should have a 37 mm gun with a co-axially mounted .30 caliber machine gun." This, he allowed, would permit troops performing reconnaissance to fight. Patton's vagueness on the proper employment of mechanized reconnaissance elements mirrored the U.S. Army's ongoing confusion about how things would really work on the battlefield.[371]

---

370 Matthew Darlington Morton; *Men on Iron Ponies (The Death and Rebirth of Modern U.S. Cavalry):* Published by the Northern Illinois University Press-2009 (Page 111)
371 ibid (Page 112)

The Desert Training Center

The Desert Training Center, California-Arizona Maneuver Area (DTC-CAMA), was created in 1942. This simulated theater of operation was the largest military training ground in the history of military maneuvers, consisting of some 18,000 square miles of land. Its mission was to train United States Army and Army Air Corps units and personnel to live and fight in the desert, to test and develop suitable equipment, and to develop tactical doctrines, techniques and training methods.

A site near Shavers Summit (now known as Chiriaco Summit) between Indio and Desert Center was selected as the headquarters of the Desert Training Center (DTC). This site, called Camp Young, was the world's largest army post. Patton came to Camp Young as the first commanding general of the Desert Training Center. His first orders were to select other areas within the desert that would be suitable for the large-scale maneuvers necessary to prepare American soldiers for combat against the German Afrika Korps in the North African desert.

Ten other camps were established in an area stretching from Boulder City, Nevada, to the Mexican border; and from Phoenix, Arizona, to Pomona, California.

After General Patton was sent to North Africa, the name of the training center was changed to the California-Arizona Maneuver Area (CAMA). Twenty separate divisions consisting of more than one million men trained there. When the direction of the war shifted to the Allies' favor in 1944, the camps, plagued by shortage of supplies and equipment, were closed, thus ending the largest simulated theater of operations in the history of military maneuvers.[372]

---

[372] U.S. Department of the Interior – Bureau of Land Management:www.blm.gov/ca/st/en/fo/needles/patton.html (Accessed on 17 January 2012)

A total of 13 infantry divisions and 7 armored divisions, plus numerous smaller units, were trained in this harsh environment. The Training Center was in operation for almost two years and was closed early in 1944 when the last units were shipped overseas. During its brief period of operation over one million American soldiers were trained for combat.

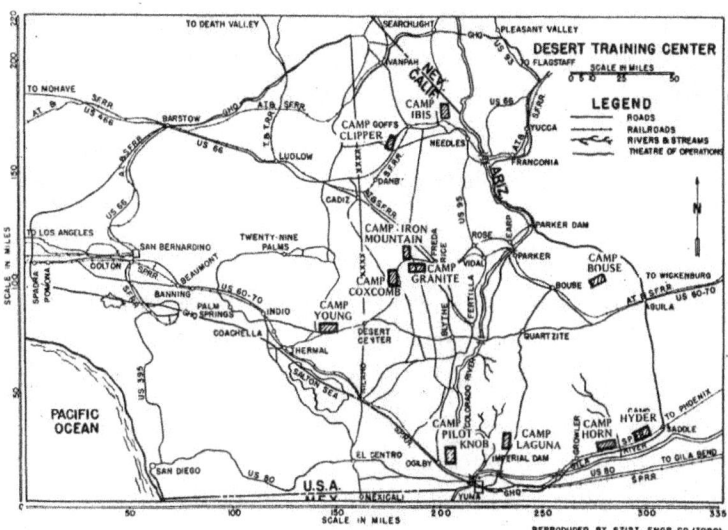

Figure 10-1. *U.S. Army via United States Bureau of Land Management*

Ervin Aden completed Officers Candidate School (OCS) at Fort Riley 17 October 1942. He and 10 other classmates were assigned to Fort Meade, South Dakota. The rest of his graduating class was split up and assigned to various other cavalry Units. Upon his arrival at Fort Meade, Aden reported to the 4th Cavalry Regiment (Mechanized) and was assigned to the service troop. His first task was to train new recruits who had reported to the unit within days of his arrival.[373]

Meanwhile, the 4th Cavalry Regiment prepared to vacate old Fort Meade in anticipation for a move to the deserts of sunny

---

373 Ervin Aden; e-mail addressed to Gary Palmer on 16 October 2006

California. The regiment followed a prescribed ritual when a unit was transferred to a new station, including the servicing and cleaning of all weapons and vehicles, most of which were badly in need of such a cleaning following the 1942 maneuvers in Tennessee.

In January 1943, the regiment left Fort Meade for the last time, en route to the Mojave Desert to train for the North African campaign. The troopers had just received their winter clothing, but shortly after their arrival at their new station in California in early January 1943, they were reissued tanker suits.

Ervin Aden recalled the 4th Cavalry's move to California:

> The 4th Cavalry Regiment was transferred from its home post in Fort Meade, South Dakota, in January 1943, to Camp Young and Camp Coxcomb. Mobile transportation was by jeeps, motorcycles and scout cars in a convoy. Some other regimental equipment was shipped by train.
>
> After a couple of days we arrived at this desolate spot in the Mojave Desert that was to be Camp Young. There was actually nothing there. Our first duty was to make the area safe. This consisted of killing the numerous sidewinders (rattlesnakes) that inhabited the campsite before we pitched our tents. (Let me interject here that, during our entire stay in the desert, there were men who reported that when they shook out their sleeping bags in the morning after a night's sleep, out came a rattler, who had spent the entire night with them to keep warm.)
>
> Although days were extremely hot, nights were cold. Once the campsite was established, we spent the first four or five months scouting around the desert in

preparation for upcoming maneuvers in mid-June and July 1943.

It was during this time that I received a 15-day leave to go to New Orleans, Louisiana, to marry my fiancée, Iona Mae Heuer. She returned with me to the desert by train. It was quite an experience, taking almost five days, as there were many stops. The coaches were old, dusty and crowded. Some men slept on the floor at night.

Upon arriving in Indio, California, we were met by my buddy and his wife, who invited us to stay in the small rented house that they shared with another officer and his wife. This house was one of a group of only 10 that were directly across the paved road from Camp Young. The community was called Palm Village. Officers with families stayed in this village, the only place for miles and miles.

After a few months we all moved to Palm Springs, where we rented apartments. Officers with families joined other families and rented homes of famous movie actors who vacated for the summer. Some of the houses were lavish. There was, of course, no air conditioning, but a window fan with water dripping outside of it would cool the air somewhat. That happened to be the year a record was broken: it was 130 degrees. All public buses and some grocery stores closed for the summer, so living there was most inconvenient.

Our training at Camp Young ended on 28 July 1943. We left for Camp Maxey, which is located seven miles outside of Paris, Texas. I received a promotion to 1st Lieutenant, and then in November 1943 we were transferred to Europe.

These desert camps were planned for use by

Figure 10-2. 1st Lieutenant Ervin Aden at Camp Young. *Ervin Aden*

General Patton as a training area in preparation for the African campaign; however, I don't recall ever running into him. I believe he spent most of his time at Camp Coxcomb while I—as a new 2d Lieutenant—was stationed at Camp Young and attached to the service troop. Our troop was responsible for delivery of supplies for the units. There was a restriction during maneuvers that we were not allowed to travel on the paved roads that bordered the camp while performing our duties.

Camp Coxcomb, Camp Hood, Camp Maxey

We could, however, travel in the sand adjacent to the paved road. All of this was at night under blackout conditions.

Once the maneuvers began, my young wife left to visit her brother, who was temporarily stationed with the Navy in San Diego. She traveled by bus. An interesting thing about travel during the war was that military came first. On her way from the desert to San Diego she had to change buses in Los Angeles. It was rather late at night, and an announcement was made in the station that the buses were to be occupied first by the servicemen, and if any room was left over, private citizens could board.

Knowing the overflow of military my wife knew she would be stranded in the station until available space became available. She became frightened and began tearing up. A young soldier noticed her plight and offered to say she was his wife. He told her as soon as they boarded the bus she could sit somewhere else, and there would be no need to feel bound to sit with him. His offer was accepted—she was allowed on the bus—and she never spoke to him again She said that her thanks to him was given before boarding. Those were some of the inconveniences experienced during the war.[374]

Merton Glover, an enlisted man at the time, was one of many 4th Cavalry soldiers who traveled by train to California.

The Army loaded the 4th Cavalry Regiment onto two trains, each consisting of a series of flatcars for vehicles, baggage cars (the old passenger train type) for

---

374 Ervin Aden; e-mail addressed to Gary Palmer on 26 September 2006

the kitchen stoves, as well as other smaller equipment, duffel bags and small arms. The troops rode in Pullmans and enjoyed good beds and two meals a day prepared by their regimental cooks.

The train passed through Tucson, Arizona, early on the morning of the third day, arriving in Yuma late that afternoon. The train continued through Blythe, California, to Indio, where the regiment detrained. Indio was a huge training area for all services.

After unloading their old well-traveled equipment, we convoyed back to eastern California, turning north from Blythe onto Route 177 and heading to Camp Coxcomb, a huge tent city located within the Coxcomb Mountains that today are part of Joshua Tree National Park.

The main street was bladed off for miles, leaving room for a whole division plus numerous other unattached units. The eastern boundary of the camp ran north along Route 177 towards Needles, California, and parallel to the aqueduct that carried water to Los Angeles and San Diego.

The maneuver area ran from Bakersfield, California, to Yuma, Arizona. Red Army would start at some northern location and go until meeting the Blue Army.

The next week Red Army started in the south and moved off in a northerly direction to meet the Blue Army.

At this point in time we were getting ready for the war in North Africa. The training was tough and as realistic as possible: heat and dust by day, and real cool at night. There was a minimum amount of water allowed per day, even while digging holes (hull defilade positions) for the armored cars to hide in. The first foot or so was easy digging, but below that it was rocky, hard and required a bar and pick axe.

We got to shower once a week. Dust picked up by moving armor could be seen for untold miles.

We arrived there in the desert about mid-January 1943 and did not leave until mid-July or August 1943. Except for not being shot at, this was the worst physical endurance we encountered in all the years of our training.[375]

During this extensive desert training, Tilford Olson stayed at Camp Young, California.

The day we left Fort Meade, South Dakota, and loaded our equipment on flat railroad cars at Rapid City, 35 miles away, the temperature was 38 degrees below zero. It was one of the coldest days on record in this area. A large number of our men were hospitalized with frostbite and joined us later in California.

And so we were off to Camp Young and the Desert Training Center at Indio, California. We arrived there in mid-January 1943. I don't remember ever seeing a thermometer out there. It was reported that a heat wave would soon begin, and it was predicted to reach 120 degrees. Sunglasses, suntans, and less clothing were par, but on duty we were required to wear our regular issue clothing. At this time, mid-January, we were able to pull up our shirtsleeves by noon each day. By nightfall we put on more and more clothing, so that by bedtime we had put on all we had to wear to keep warm through the night. This was winter in the desert.

---

375 Merton Glover; *86 and counting:* Unpublished personal manuscript of author's life history-2003 (Page 40-41)

We spent the next few months in the desert, and by mid-February the air was getting warmer. We were confronted by new companions such as rattlesnakes and tarantulas. We kept a watchful eye for them since they both are poisonous. They were a common enemy in the hills and mountains of the area.

When we were going out on maneuvers by day and night, our noon meal was prepared the night before and stored in a paper bag. Inside we would find a peanut butter and jelly sandwich—which, after lying around for several hours, was found to consist of toasted dry bread that was soggy from the jelly. To this day I do not like peanut butter and jelly sandwiches.

Drinking water and salt pills were rationed. We all had our canteens full each day, but it didn't last very long and none of it was wasted. We could purchase a canvas bag to put our drinking water in; they were a common sight. When the bags became moist, the process of evaporation took place and the water in the bag would stay kind of cool. We all had a water bag hanging from our cars.

Some nights after maneuvers we would come back to camp and the ice cream vendor would show up about every other day. He did a land-office business while we were at our home station. These treats were consumed in a hurry, by the pints and quarts! He usually ran out of supplies before leaving. This, of course, was quite a treat for all of us.

While there we were bunked in six-man tents—big enough so we could stand up in them. We were able to roll up the sides for better circulation. We used our footlockers for our personal goods and clothing. We slept many nights on a good old canvas cot.

Camp Coxcomb, Camp Hood, Camp Maxey

> In the desert we got a lot of sunshine and blowing sand. Most of us thought we would be sent to North Africa. This, we thought, would not meet with our approval, as not many of us liked the California desert.[376]

Meanwhile, Merton Glover spent his time during the desert maneuvers at Camp Coxcomb.

> While at Camp Coxcomb we did get two long weekend passes to Los Angeles. I rode in the rear of a 6x6 truck to a Red Cross-run hotel. Got to hear two big-time orchestras, I think—Lawrence Welk and maybe Harry James. This was the time of the Zoot Suiter gangs in Los Angeles, and we were warned not to go out alone. When G.I.s fresh from the desert got to town they made Zoot Suiters pretty scarce.
>
> At the wind-down of the desert operations, about half of us were offered a 30-day leave and the other half were transferred along with the 4th Regiment to Camp Maxey. I think someone in the family met me on the train in Alliance, Nebraska. This may have been about August 1943. I went to the family ranch and helped a little, but mostly visited with neighbors and family saying goodbye, for we knew we were headed to England. No one spoke of it directly, but we all knew the invasion lay ahead and the likelihood was that I might not come back.
>
> When we left Camp Coxcomb we also left all of our old vehicles behind. Once we arrived and reported in at Camp Maxey we were issued new clothes and

---

376 Tilford "Pat" Olson; *Memories of a Mission Accomplished:* Unpublished manuscript completed in 1997 (Page 14-15)

uniforms. Everyone underwent a complete medical checkup and got new shots or had old ones renewed.

Sometime in late November 1943 we shipped out to Camp Shanks, New York. It was while there a week or two that they started to check our teeth for the first time. Think I had four wisdom teeth, all decayed at that time, plus some others they filled in on an assembly-line basis. Had a couple of good passes to New York City—Times Square—which some buddies and I went together, looking at the sights. [377]

After seven months in the desert, the 4th Cavalry Regiment received orders for England to serve as the reconnaissance regiment for VII Corps. Arriving in England on 15 December 1943, the 4th was encamped in the town of Singleton, West Sussex, near the English southern coast.

Immediately upon their arrival the 4th Cavalry Regiment was redesignated and reorganized as the 4th Cavalry Group, Mechanized. The 1st Squadron was reorganized and redesignated as the 4th Cavalry Reconnaissance Squadron, Mechanized; and the 2nd Squadron was reorganized and redesignated as the 24th Cavalry Reconnaissance Squadron, Mechanized.[378]

Allen Halloway was part of the 4th Cavalry. His grandson Kyle related the following story:

> My grandfather (Halloway) worked for a neighbor, Mr. Brunnemeyer, who owned a farm in Rock Lake, North Dakota. He paid my grandfather $7.50 a month, with room and board. Halloway had every other Sunday off, but he never took it because Sunday work

---

377 Merton Glover; *86 and counting:* Unpublished personal manuscript of author's life history-2003 (Page 41-42)
378 Ervin Aden; e-mail addressed to Gary Palmer on 02 October 2006

CAMP COXCOMB, CAMP HOOD, CAMP MAXEY

was just chores. The first hourly wage he received was during thrashing time, when he ran bundles through the thrasher at 25 cents an hour.

Halloway worked for Mr. Brunnemeyer until 3 January 1941, when he enlisted in the U.S. Army shortly before his 22d birthday.[379]

President Franklin Roosevelt had instituted the Selective Service to train young men in case the United States entered the war in Europe. Halloway went to Fort Meade, South Dakota, for basic training. He received $21 a month from the U.S. Army, the same pay as he received on the farm. He spent six months there doing close-ordered drills and keeping in shape. "I gained 12 or 14 pounds because I was getting three good meals a day and didn't have anything to do," he recalled. "I got used to working half a day and then eating."[380]

That year at Fort Meade, Halloway learned that his girlfriend at the time, Naomi Gall, had married his best friend, Howard "Bud" Hunt. "She didn't tell me, but I found out," Halloway said. "In the back of my mind, after I got out of the service, I thought I would ask her to marry me. Obviously that didn't happen."

While on furlough, Halloway returned to Rock Lake and went into Bellocks Tavern. Bud Hunt was standing at the bar. "I walked up to the bar and stood next to him," said Halloway. "We started talking and he said, 'I'll bet you feel like killing me.' I don't remember what I said. We were still friends, though."[381]

Over the years, Halloway had lost contact with Emma Sampson, who had a twin sister, Donna. The Sampsons moved to Bisbee, North Dakota, about

---

[379] Kyle Halloway (15 years old); Biography of Allen Halloway (An Ordinary Hero): Written as a term paper for Kyle's United States History Class (Page 7)
[380] ibid (Page 7)
[381] ibid (Page 7)

11 miles away from the Halloway's. Then Halloway heard that the Sampsons had moved to Kansas City, Missouri. He met up with Emma again in Rapid City, South Dakota. The match was made in the summer of 1941, thanks to one of his Army buddies and a jukebox-playing dance hall named the Sunken Barrel.

As Halloway recalled:

> Jon Victor in our outfit came back and said he met someone at the Sunken Barrel who knew me. He said she had a twin sister, but he didn't know her name. The next Saturday night I went to the Sunken Barrel and it was Emma, Donna and a woman named Fern DeNoma. I went there and danced with all three of them. Then I started going to Rapid City every other weekend.[382]

Emma and Donna Sampson were living with their older sister, Ida Ehlers, and her husband Otto. Halloway continued: "I would hitchhike to Rapid City, walk to Otto's house, and then Emma and I would walk to the Sunken Barrel. I would walk home with Emma and then go to Bacon Park; that's where all the G.I.s would spend the night. We'd just sleep on the lawn. In the morning I'd go to church with Otto and the girls."[383]

Allen Halloway married Emma on 12 July 1942 in Rapid City, South Dakota. Halloway was originally supposed to be discharged in January 1942, but following the bombing of Pearl Harbor,

---

382 ibid (Page 7)
383 ibid (Page 7-8)

President Roosevelt declared war and Halloway was given another four years of enlistment.

"Wartime rules went into effect," remembered Halloway. "Up until that time, we had two lockers—one for Army clothes, one for civilian. When that happened, civilian clothes were sent home."[384]

CAMP HOOD, TEXAS

On 31 May 1943, the 2d Cav Sqd Headquarters, C and D Troop of the 106th Cavalry Regiment, received orders from Headquarters XV Corps, Camp Beauregard, transferring them from Camp Livingston, Louisiana, to Camp Shelby, Mississippi, for a temporary change of station. Their orders read:

> *Army Ground Forces (AGF) 370.5–GNMOC dated 12 May 1943.* Upon completion of temporary duty unit will return to Camp Livingston per same orders on 12 June 1943. Following the Mississippi maneuvers, and per Army Ground Forces (AGF) orders 370.5–GNMOC, Headquarters XV Corps, Camp Beauregard, Louisiana dated 7 June 1943, the 106th Cavalry Regiment was directed to transfer from Camp Livingston to Camp Polk, Louisiana, for temporary change of station. Furthermore, per AGF orders 370.5–GNMOC, Headquarters XV Corps, Camp Beauregard, dated 7 June 1943, the unit would not return to home station after maneuvers.[385]

---

384 ibid (Page 8)
385 Raymond Mucha: Posting of the 106th Cavalry 1940-1945 (Formerly Illinois National Guard): Reproduced from the National Archives, Washington, D. C.

While stationed at Camp Polk, Louisiana, the regiment turned in its M3A1 tanks and scout cars. As part of the turn-in procedures the "on vehicle equipment" (OVM) inventory for each vehicle was laid out on canvas tarpaulins alongside the parked vehicles. This area happened to be outside of and adjacent to the wire fence surrounding a prisoner of war camp where German prisoners from the Africa Korps were imprisoned. Much to the troopers' discomfort, many of the prisoners took great delight in watching the troopers laying out their OVM.

Upon completing the turn-in of equipment, and per an amendment to the above set of orders dated 21 June 1943, the unit transferred on 25 June 1943 to Burkeville, Texas. However, their stay at Burkeville was brief, as they received orders (Ltr Hqs AGF 370.5/26 Cav) dated 14 July 1943 for a permanent station change that relieved them from assignment to XV Corps on 24 August 1943 and assigned them to the Tank Destroyer Center at Camp Hood, Texas. Upon the regiment's arrival at Camp Hood they relieved the 101st Cavalry Regiment and assumed their duties as a unit assigned to the Tank Destroyer School.[386]

To comply with AGF 320.2 (21 July 1943) PE-A-M-C, dated 20 August 1943, the 106th Cavalry regiment began making the necessary administrative changes to reform as a cavalry group with two separate but identical squadrons. Therefore in accordance with the above order which directed that the Regimental Headquarters, Headquarters Service Troop and Headquarters Medical Detachment, 106th Cavalry Regiment (Mechanized), to be redesignated as Headquarters and Headquarters Troop, Medical Detachment, 106th Cavalry Group (Mechanized), the regiment began its transformation, subsequently revamping Headquarters, Headquarters & Service Troop, with A and B Troop, along with F Company (Tanks), as the newly designated 106th Reconnaissance

---

386 ibid [Raymond Mucha: *Posting of the 106th Cavalry 1940-1945 (Formerly Illinois National Guard)*: Reproduced from the National Archives, Washington, D. C.]

Squadron (Mechanized) organized in accordance with T/O & E 2-22 (13 October 1943).

What had been previously designated as Headquarters 1st Squadron, A, B, and E Troops, 1st Section Medical Detachment, 106th Cavalry Regiment (Mechanized) were redesignated Headquarters, Headquarters Service Troop, A and B Troop, and F Company, 106th Cavalry Reconnaissance Squadron/ respectively, and would be organized in accordance with T/O & E 2-25 effective 15 September 1943. In addition, C and E (Assault Gun Troop) Troops would be activated when unit is reorganized.

Headquarters 2d Squadron, C, D Troops, and F Company and 2d Section Medical Detachment, 106th Cavalry Regiment (Mechanized), were redesignated Headquarters, Headquarters Service Troop; and Medical Detachment C, B Troops and F Company, 121st Cavalry Reconnaissance Squadron, (Mechanized), reorganized in accordance with T/O & E 2-25 effective 15 September 1943.

The 106th Cavalry Regiment was relieved from its assignment to the Tank Destroyer Center on 23 October 1943 and transferred to VIII Corps, Third Army, per AGF 321/221 (Cav).

On 29 October 1943 the unit was relieved from its assignment to VIII Corps, per AGF 322/7 (XVIII Corps) (C), effective 8 November 1943, and assigned to XVIII Corps. A and E Troops were to be constituted and activated when the unit was reorganized per AGF 322 (2 December 1943) OB-I-GNGCT-M, dated 8 December 1943.[387]

Camp Hood, named for the Confederate General John Bell Hood, was located adjacent to Killeen, Texas, in Bell County. The camp was about halfway between Waco and Austin. It occupied the site of old Fort Gates, which was erected in 1849 as an Indian defense post and comprised some 217,337 acres. The installation

---
[387] Reproduced from the National Archives, Washington, D.C.; Posting of the 106th Cavalry-1940-1945 (formerly Illinois National Guard)-Historical Data

was reopened on 18 September 1942 and served as the Tank Destroyer Center during World War II. It was there that the regiment first received its complement of vehicles as assigned by the TO&E. The vehicles included the M5A1 Stewart light tank, M8 assault gun, and M8 (Greyhound) armored car. Since these would be the same types of vehicles they were to later use in combat overseas, the regiment concentrated on familiarizing and training its crews with assigned vehicles and completing Preparation for Overseas Movement (POM) training.[388]

Bluford (Buddy) Smith came into the Army from the hills of Kentucky. His initial enlistment was with the Army Signal Corps, where he received his training in radios. He was attached to the 106th Cavalry Regiment in 1943 as a communications specialist.

> The allies were having a difficult time in North Africa against the German Afrika Korps. It seems every time there was a major sandstorm the Allies lost all means of effective radio communications. To make matters worse, the Germans would choose these times to launch a major attack. The effective coordination of the German attack made it obvious to the Allied command that the Germans were able to successfully communicate with one another.
> The order came down through higher channels that an all-out effort was to be made to capture a German vehicle with a radio intact. Once a radio was captured it was removed from the enemy vehicle and sent stateside for examination by Bell Labs in New Jersey. The Bell Labs people, upon seeing the German radio set, stated, "This is nothing but an FM radio. We invented this in the 1920s."

---

[388] William H. Collier, *The 106th Cavalry's Story:* Published by Trafford Publishing March 2012 (Page 21-22)

It seems the Germans picked up on the benefits of FM transmission and used it within their military. The Allies, on the other hand, were still communicating on AM. Bell Labs was asked to replicate the German radio. They sent two units to the Army for testing.

I was attending school while participating in the ROTC program and was subsequently sent to the Signal Corps, where I received instructions on the use and care of FM radios. Due to this unique opportunity I earned the distinction of receiving the first FM operator certificate issued in the United States.

I got married on 31 October 1942. Under the program I was supposed to be inducted into the Army as a warrant officer, but I requested leave to visit my family in Kentucky. I was informed at the time it would change my status and most likely I would not receive a commission as a warrant officer at the completion of my training. The commanding officer of the school told me that if I left the school he would give my name to the draft board, and that it would be less than two weeks before I would be inducted into the Army. I decided it was more important to spend some time with my family and risk losing his commission, especially with a war in Europe going on.

I expected to be home on leave for maybe three to four weeks before being recalled to school, but almost three months passed before I heard anything further from the military. Finally, in late 1943 I received orders for induction into the Army. I was given verbal orders to report to the 106th Cavalry Regiment, which was then stationed at Camp Livingston, Louisiana, for basic training. My orders were to precede me via the U.S. mail.

The U.S. Cavalry: Time of Transition

I reported into the regiment and was assigned to a training cadre based strictly on my verbal orders. I had completed about three weeks of basic training when the "new" FM radios started to appear. However, no one knew how to install the new sets or tune them properly.

One day while undergoing basic training I noticed a communications sergeant sitting in front of a radio set, listening to field units but not responding to their calls. I asked the sergeant why he wasn't answering the units calling on the radio, and was he said that he could not make the radio work. I offered my assistance, but the sergeant doubted my ability to make the "new FM radio" work properly.

I asked for the small service bag that accompanied each of the radios. The sergeant got the kit for his radio and was surprised that it contained the meter and tuning equipment as I had described. I took a few minutes to tune the radio so that the sergeant could transmit on it, and then the sergeant surprised the field units by answering up.

I returned to basic training without further thought about the radio situation. However, after about more two weeks of training I was met at the end of the day by two very large MPs who escorted me to the commanding officer's office. He said the Colonel had heard of my ability to repair the new FM radios, and began questioning me about several pieces of mail he had received from Washington.

Basically, the Colonel wanted to know if I was an FBI agent sent to spy on the troops or working for some other governmental agency, as he had no orders assigning me to the regiment. I tried to explain as best I could the circumstance that brought me to the 106th

Cavalry, but I could see by the look on the Colonel's face that he wasn't buying the story.

The Colonel asked me that if my story was true, then why was I receiving mail from Washington? I said I wasn't receiving any mail from Washington. The Colonel responded that was correct, as he had intercepted the mail and was holding it there in his office.

Finally, the Colonel presented me with several pieces of mail from Washington, D.C., that were addressed to me. He instructed me to open the letters in while still in his presence. Upon doing so I discovered my long-awaited orders, which were accompanied with an explanation of my previous training on the new FM radios.

The Colonel sent me back to complete basic training during the day, but assigned me the additional task of repairing the regiment's radios at the end of each day's training.

Upon completing basic training I was assigned to Headquarters and Service Troop. I stayed there even after the regiment transferred to Camp Hood.[389]

Second Lieutenant Robert Moore of the 106th Cavalry Regiment was another soldier who underwent training at Camp Hood.

> Later it would become Fort Hood and a major Army base. There was no more "playing around." The instructors there were very serious about their jobs and ran the camp like an army camp training men for a war. The only problem was they took it personally

---

[389] Personal interview conducted by Gary Palmer on 29 June 2010 with Bluford Smith during the 106th Cavalry Groups Reunion at Rantoul, Illinois.

and let their egos get in the way of proper training. When General Herren asked about the heavy-duty transmission in the half-tracks, Lieutenant George H. Earing tried to explain it to the older horse cavalryman. When it was obvious that the General didn't have a clue, George said, "I'm sorry I can't explain it properly, sir. I know that you are still confused."

General Herren said, "Generals do not get confused," and walked off in a huff. He didn't have a clue how they work, but he was responsible for training men to risk their lives in them.

At this time, we were assigned to Tank Destroyer School, probably because all our equipment hadn't arrived yet. The school would set up field scenarios for attack and defense but we would always lose. It was not like a teaching environment—more like an ego trip for them. When we got fed up with it, Captain Ed Cavanaugh happened upon an unattended Bantam of theirs parked outside the mess hall. In the seat was their code book.

During the next exercise, we sent false radio messages for them to assemble at a certain spot where we had already set up an ambush. The referee decided in our favor—we finally won one. We really paid for that in extra physical training and early morning assemblies, etc. They were going to get even with us for winning one of the war games, but I thought that was what we were supposed to do.

When the rest of our new equipment arrived, it was brand new and thick with cosmoline (rust preventative). The really good news was that a training staff that actually knew how to use the new equipment, and to train us on its use, came along with it. We really learned how to use the very good quality material that we had been issued, as well as the tactics that would make them effective in combat. By the time we left Camp Hood we were very close to being ready.[390]

Second Lieutenant Faris "Jake" Hess also recalled his stay at Camp Hood:

> On 25 August 1943 we moved to Camp Hood, Texas. It is located near Temple, Texas. I drove our car to Temple, and Leta Mae, my wife, followed on the train since she was pregnant. There was no place to live so we stayed with friends from McLean, Texas. After six weeks we moved on base.
>
> Our daughter Nancy was born on 30 November 1944 in Temple, Texas. As first-time parents we were nervous and unsure of things. Car trouble delayed us in getting to the hospital; however, we made it in plenty of time. They took Leta Mae into the delivery room, and shortly the doctor announced that I was a father of a little girl and that everything was fine. He said they would be out soon.
>
> I waited 45 minutes and no one came. I went back to the delivery room area and found them alone. The transport personnel had gone on strike and no one wanted to cross the picket line, so I wheeled them out myself.
>
> Major Joseph (Buzz) McCarthy came to the hospital to visit. He had been a friend of ours since Fort Riley. He told Leta Mae, "I came to see her eat"—referring to our little baby girl being breast-fed. This embarrassed Leta Mae.

---

390 Robert (Bob) Moore and Michael (Mike) Moore: *The 12th Man; Citizen Soldier in Europe 1944-1945:* Unpublished Manuscript (06-10-2010)

On 20 February 1944 I left Camp Hood for New York and, ultimately, overseas. We had been getting prepared ever since we left Louisiana. We were told to pack only a bare minimum of personal items. The boxes were marked To FOLLOW ME OVERSEAS. Leta Mae broke down and cried when she saw the wording.

Leta Mae took Nancy, our six-week-old, to McLean, Texas, where they could be near our families. They lived with Leta Mae's parents, Rish and Effie Phillips, during my absence. I traveled by passenger train to New York.

On 27 February 1944 we shipped out of New York. Leta Mae and another wife were planning on flying to New York to see us off. I wanted to let her know when we were leaving. I was unable to call her because we were loaded on the ship as soon as we got there.[391]

On 17 January 1944, about one month before leaving Camp Hood, the 106th Cavalry Regiment lost its band. Per General Order #2, the unit was renamed as the 217th Army Band on 19 January. The order was signed by Captain Prentiss C. Mabry, the regimental adjutant. This was in anticipation of the regiment's reorganization, which did not authorize a regimental band. It was another sorrowful loss. Simultaneously, the 106th Cavalry Regiment received orders WD 370.5, dated 15 January 1944, OB_S_E_M, dated 18 January 1944, advising them of their upcoming transfer from Camp Hood, Texas, to New York or Boston point of embarkation for further movement to overseas destination by way of ship 9542-B.

An advanced detachment, 106th Cavalry Regiment, was instructed to move to Fort Hamilton, New York, to arrive on

---

391 Captain Francis "Jake" Hess and Nancy Hess Blackburn; *My Story-106th Cavalry Group in Europe 1942-1945:* Personal Manuscript written for the Hess' family in 2004 (Page 6)

13 February 1944 per SPTAA_P (CB) 370.5. A month later, 11 February 1944, the regiment was ordered per AGF 370.5, Headquarters XXIII Corps, Brownwood, Texas, to turn in its vehicles in preparation of departing for Camp Shanks, New York, no later than 20 February 1944 by train. Subsequently, the 106th Cavalry Regiment departed Camp Hood, Texas, on 17 February 1944, and arrived at Camp Shanks on 20 February 1944.[392]

CAMP MAXEY, TEXAS

The men of the 4th Cavalry Regiment found themselves in the Mojave Desert in southern California during the early months of 1943. This was about the time that the fighting was going on in North Africa and names like Mussolini and Rommel (The Desert Fox) crept into the minds of the men training at Camp Young. Most of the men thought they would be sent to North Africa to join the ongoing battle, although most did not relish the idea as they found their experience in the Mojave Desert less than agreeable.

Fortunately, by late 1943 the North African Campaign was going well and it became readily apparent that the 4th Cavalry Regiment would not be going to the desert after all. Instead, the regiment was moved to Camp Maxey, Texas, where they heard rumors that they might be going to England.[393]

By the end of 1943 the security threat to the Panama Canal had been greatly reduced, and many of the units in that area were reassigned elsewhere to help with the war effort. This included the 27th Cavalry Reconnaissance Squadron, which left Panama beginning 15 June 1943 with the majority of troops en route to Camp Maxey, Texas. The 27th Cavalry Regiment was disbanded and the men were divided amongst other newly formed or

---

[392] Gary Palmer-Raymond Teske Jr., Copied from 106th Cavalry Group Documents at the National Archives, Baltimore, Maryland-2009
[393] Tilford "Pat" Olson; *Memories of a Mission Accomplished:* Unpublished manuscript written in 1997 for Olson's immediate family (Page 16)

reorganized units such as the 14th Cavalry Regiment, the 4th Cavalry Regiment, and the 3d Cavalry Regiment.

Frank Fancher recounted the rapid changes that the cavalry troops experienced:

> At the end of November 1943 we sailed from Balboa, Canal Zone (Panama), en route to California. After 10 uneventful days on the Pacific we arrived in San Francisco Harbor. An overnight trip by ferry put us in Stoneman, California; and another week by rail put us at Camp Maxey, Texas. The last part of the year and the first part of 1944 were spent reorganizing and training for the invasion of Europe.[394]

It was in Texas, at Camp Maxey, that the men got their new M8 armored cars. These were 6x6 vehicles with rubber tires and 3/8-inch armor. Each car had one .30 caliber machine gun and one .50 caliber machine gun. The .50 caliber machine gun was mounted on a steel track located on the turret of the car so it could be moved in any direction. The car was also equipped with a 37 mm gun that also could be rotated in a 360-degree circle. These cars had good six-cylinder engines, some made by Hercules Manufacturing Company and some made by the White Motor Company.

Each car weighed about 6½ tons and was driven by all six wheels, with speeds upward of 55 miles per hour. Each car had a crew of four men: a radio operator, who was able to transmit signals for about seven miles depending on the terrain; a gunner who would take charge of the 37 mm gun and coaxially-mounted .30 caliber machine gun; a driver; and a car commander, who

---

[394] Frank 'Lindy' Fancher; *WWII: Through These Eyes:* Published by Author House, 1663 Liberty Drive, Suite 200, Bloomington, Indiana 47403 – 04-26-2005 (Page 24)

could also act as a gunner by operating the .50 caliber ring-mounted machine gun.³⁹⁵

Figure 10-3. First Sergeant Lloyd L. Alexander of F Troop, 4th CavReconSqdn (Mech.), at Camp Maxey, 1943. *CLINTON ALEXANDER*

The 4th Cavalry Regiment stayed at Camp Maxey, near Paris, Texas, for a few months while getting acquainted with their new armored cars. Tilford "Pat" Olson recalled his time at Camp Maxey:

> Rachel and Terry [wife and daughter] endured a long train ride down there to stay with me for a few months. I don't believe they enjoyed the train ride or the transfer, but I sure was happy to see them! We rented a small apartment

---

395 ibid (Page 17)

in the back part of one of the older houses, with a minimum of furniture.

The first night after we got settled we left to go to the movies, as I remember it, and we returned home in the dark. As we turned on the lights it seemed like the whole place moved! It was full of cockroaches, as most of the rental houses were. We kept all food well covered, and washed everything before use. Those cockroaches sure gave us a creepy feeling.

The next night we left all of our lights on, and that helped considerably. We looked for another apartment but didn't find any that were in our price range. We discovered we were not the only ones with a cockroach problem.

We soon learned that we would be on the move again—this time to Camp Shanks, New York, for preparation to go to England as we had expected. Rachel and Terry left on the long train ride home. These were ordinary cars, so Rachel and Terry were required to eat and sleep in their own seats with all kinds, nationalities, and ages of passengers. It was certainly a "no-frills" trip.

Rachel and I had purchased a pair of white majorette boots for Terry when she was here in Texas. They were white leather boots with white tassels of which she was very proud. (She still has them.) I was told that upon their return to Cyrus, Minnesota, Terry was asked where she had been. "Paris!" was her quick reply. She did not tell anyone that we lived with the roaches while there, and that this "Paris" was in the very northern part of Texas.[396]

Shortly after the 4th Cavalry Regiment departed Camp Maxey for Camp Shanks, New York, and points further east, the elements of the Panama contingent arrived at Camp Maxey on 1 December 1943. They were redesignated as the 32d Cavalry Reconnaissance

---

396 ibid (Page 17-18)

Squadron and attached to the 14th Cavalry Group (Mechanized) under the command of a spit-and-polish West Pointer, Colonel Mark Devine.

The 14th Cavalry Group had been activated on 12 July 1943 at Fort Lewis, Washington. However, it was not until 20 April 1944 that the 14th Cavalry Group (with the 18th Cavalry Reconnaissance Squadron) completed its move to Camp Maxey and joined the 32d Cavalry Reconnaissance Squadron. Each squadron was composed of a headquarters troop, three reconnaissance troops (lettered A, B, and C), an assault gun troop (lettered E), and a light tank company (designated as F Company).[397]

Each reconnaissance troop had a headquarters platoon and three reconnaissance platoons. Each reconnaissance platoon was divided into three combat teams. Each team consisted of an armored car, a machine gun Bantam, and a mortar Bantam.

The armored cars (M8 Greyhounds) mounted a 37 mm gun and a coaxial-mounted .30 caliber machine gun in a movable turret. Each car was equipped with two powerful radios. The machine-gun Bantam was armed with a .30 caliber machine gun mounted on a pedestal or mounted on the right side of the vehicle and level with the dash so as to be operated by the right front passenger. In addition, the Bantam carried a voice radio of limited range.

The assault gun troop had six self-propelled 75 mm howitzers mounted on light tank carriages and capable of direct or indirect fire. These six guns (M8 assault guns) were divided into three platoons of two assault guns each.

The light tank company was equipped with M5A1 Stewart tanks, each of which carried a 37 mm cannon, two .30 caliber machine guns, and a .50 caliber machine gun. The light tank company was considered the "heavy fist" of the squadron. It had

---

[397] Frank "Lundy" Fancher; *WWII: Through these Eyes:* Published by Author House 1663 Liberty Drive, Ste 200, Bloomington, Indiana-2005 (Page 24)

17 tanks divided into a headquarters platoon with two tanks and three combat platoons with five tanks each.

A typical reconnaissance troop consisted of three reconnaissance platoons, two assault guns, and five M5A1 tanks, all working together as a team.

At times, especially in static situations, all six assault guns would be used as a field battery unit. Most of the time the group was assigned a Piper Cub airplane from corps artillery for observation missions.[398]

Frank Fancher, 32d Cavalry Reconnaissance Squadron, was involved in the reorganization that took place at Camp Maxey:

> The 14th Cavalry Group experienced several Table of Organization changes while stationed at Camp Maxey. This included the replacement of the standard Smith & Wesson revolvers with the M1 carbine.
>
> It was also at Camp Maxey that the 14th Cavalry Group first received the new M8 armored cars. Besides being equipped with a 37 mm anti-tank gun and a coaxial-mounted .30 caliber machine gun in a movable turret, it came standard with a ring-mounted .50 caliber machine gun.
>
> The M8 armored car was designed to hold 80 rounds of 37 mm ammunition for the main mount, with additional storage room for 400 rounds of carbine, 1,500 rounds of .30-06 ammunition for the machine gun, 750 rounds of .50 caliber ammo, 16 hand grenades, 4 smoke pots, and 6 anti-tank mines.
>
> The M8 armored car was very fast and could travel at approximately 60 miles per hour on a paved surface . . . but it had one major problem. If you had to rise

---

398 ibid (Page 24-25)

Figure 10-4. Basic M8 Armored Car (Greyhound) as equipped prior to Normandy landings. *Army Signal Corps Archives*

up out of the movable turret, you couldn't get your M1 carbine up at the same time.

The Army told us we could have a sidearm if we wanted to buy one, so on my way to New York from Camp Maxey I stopped by home and bought a gun from Coonhound Johnny's Gun Shop. Since I was in uniform the owner looked at me and said, "Son, doesn't the Army trust you with a gun?" I explained the problem.

He said, "My son is in the Army. I'd give the gun to you, but that's bad luck. You give me $4.35 for this Colt .45 and I'll throw in a shoulder holster and 50 rounds ammo."

I carried this gun with me in European campaigns, to the hospital in England, and back to Paris with the criminal investigation division.[399]

---

399 ibid (Page 26)

The 14th Cavalry Group sailed from New York in May 1944 aboard the *Queen Elizabeth* for England. While the 14th Cavalry Group crossed paths with the 106th Cavalry Group on several occasions, members of the original 2d Squadron, D Troop, 106th Cavalry Regiment, did not have time to reunite with old friends in the 106th Cavalry Group.

Nevertheless, a few members of the original 2d Squadron (Mechanized) honored themselves while serving with the 14th Cavalry Group, 32d CavReconSqd, during the Battle of the Bulge. Some of these men were Captain Stanley F. Palmer, Captain Joseph R. Oline, Captain Samuel E. Woods, Lieutenant Will Madigan, Lieutenant Frank Fancher, and Warrant Officer Harrison L. Grigsby.

Others former members of the 2d Squadron (Mechanized), such as Ervin Aden, served with honor while attached to the 4th Cavalry Reconnaissance Squadron during the landings at Normandy.[400]

---

[400] William H. Collier, *The 106th Cavalry's Story:* Paper Published by William Collier, Charlottesville, Virginia-2006 (Page 15-16)

CHAPTER XI

DEPARTURE FROM THE U.S.A., EN ROUTE TO JOLLY OLD ENGLAND

The 4th Cavalry Regiment arrived at Camp Shanks, New York, in the fall of 1943. It was Thanksgiving, so it was important that the troops receive a holiday feast prior to sailing for England. However, as usual, there wasn't enough white meat to go around. Nevertheless, the troops did enjoy the extras, such as cranberries, dressing, yams, potatoes, gravy and pumpkin pie. Overall the meal was quite a treat.[401]

Tilford Olson recalled the occasion:

> We were all given a pass to New York City, and about 95 percent of the G.I.s called home. Most telephones in the immediate area were busy, so we waited in line

---
401 ibid (Page 16)

to use them. It seemed like it took longer because some [telephones] were coin-operated and other [troopers] had to make special arrangements when calling out. We were able to tell the folks at home that we were going to England, but nothing else about the trip.

In a few days we left the States aboard the Liberty Ship *Highland Chieftain*. We were pulled out of the harbor by a couple of tugboats and then joined other ships, making about twenty in our convoy. The convoy included troop ships, cargo ships, submarines and destroyers. We traveled some distance apart, but on a clear day we were able to see two or three ships in the distance. The reason for this was that if we were attacked by aircraft or submarines, each ship would be a target for the enemy and we would not be a group target. We could not all be attacked at one time.

We were continually changing course to confuse the enemy. We left the United States shortly after Thanksgiving in 1943, and arrived in England just before Christmas.

Most of the men spent the time below deck in their hammocks, sleeping, reading and thinking. Hundreds of hammocks hung from the overhead, continuously swaying with the ship's movement in the high waves, which—a lot of the time—reached the deck of our ship. I thought that the hammocks would cut down on the seasickness, but that was not the case.

Being seasick was no joke. Some made it to the head (the Navy term for the bathroom); others didn't. They would be sitting or lying on the floor, vomiting for days at a time. Men turned pale and sometimes green with an unforgettable odor. Keeping the ship clean was almost impossible. The seasickness lasted quite a number of days.

Departure from the U.S.A., en route to Jolly Old England

The unit I was in was assigned guard duty on the ship. This meant we were on deck for two hours of every six, day and night. Being on deck was a good thing under these conditions, so I volunteered for the duration of the trip. Others were not allowed on deck for any length of time.

One of our duties included seeing that the blackout rules were enforced at all times. This meant no smoking or light of any kind at night. Being able to be on deck more than others helped me from becoming seasick, but I must admit I had a "full up" feeling all the time and ate very little.[402]

Figure 11-1. World War II troop transport ship *The Highland Chieftain.*

Merton Glover of the 4th Cavalry Group recalled his his departure from the United States and arrival in England:

> At some point in early December 1943 we were hustled out one night, with everything we had in a duffle bag which must have weighed 80 pounds or

---
[402] Tilford "Pat" Olson; *Memories of a Mission Accomplished:* Unpublished manuscript written in 1997 (Page 19-20)

more, and poured rapidly down to the second hold of an old English freighter named the *Highland Chieftain*. It was a refrigerator ship; small pipes ran up and down the sides and over the top of the ceiling.

There wasn't room for everyone's bedroll on the floor, so some slept on tables, some under, and some in hammocks that were swung from the ceiling. Absolute blackout, heavy double screens over each door, poor ventilation. We were 13 days in convoy and were told it consisted of a hundred ships. They could travel no faster than the slowest ship, and every ship stayed in same relative position constantly.

In these old type freighters, the hold covers (also known as hatch covers) were not much above the water line. The superstructure in approximate center was where the crew lived and where the galley or kitchen was located.

The North Atlantic in winter was rough, and waves washed across the boat over the hold area, which was covered with ice inches thick. There was a large rope two inches or so in diameter tied from the galley to our end of the ship. At mealtime—twice a day—a detail (small group of soldiers) wore a harness with a big ring that snapped onto this rope to prevent washing men overboard while they were en route to the galley for food served to us in our tin pots from the big kettles.

Food was boiled, so being very cold, any oil or grease would be sticking to the side of the kettle by the time the detail returned to our little area. This, of course, did not help those who were either seasick or close to being so. I think the ship was loaded with fresh pork for that is what they served every meal, along with breakfast tea and sweet bread. We would have starved, except the Limey crew seemingly stocked up on candy bars and doled them out so many per day at a healthy profit.[403]

The hold area (a cabin or room) would get so hot, stuffy and smelly you would carefully go out through the heavy draped curtains and stay out on the rails, watching the ships and waves till you started to freeze and were forced back inside. The huge waves were very scary to one raised in South Dakota. One minute our ship would be down in sort of a valley, waves or swells on either side so high you could not see over them, and in the next minute or so we would be on top of a wave and you could see other ships of convoy in every direction.

Sometimes ships would be crosswise in a wave with both ends out of the water. Then you could feel and hear the propeller spin in the air, somewhat like a tire on ice. As the ship descended or sank back into the water and the giant propeller took hold, a terrible noise and vibration took place. As we were almost in the tail or stern of the ship, it seemed as if the whole tail would fly off or break apart. This went on day and night.

I always heard and read of blue oceans. These big waves of the North Atlantic looked very green to me, like a huge monster ready to swallow the ship. On clearer and milder days it was reassuring to see the battleship *Nevada* to our left front, always in the same position. A couple different days a fast cutter-type ship flew (so to speak) down a lane or two from us, dropping depth charges, and we could see tall columns of water like you see in the movies.

We heard years later that the German subs did get a ship from our convoy. All convoys took the long

---

[403] Merton Glover; *86 and counting:* Unpublished personal manuscript of author's life history-2003 (Page 43-44)

or north route to make it harder and farther for the German U-boats to watch for targets. It was above the Arctic Circle, so it was always cold. At night, while looking down the side of the hull of the ship as it passed through water, you could always see a yellowish light—some sort of static electricity. It was rather fascinating.

On the thirteenth day—a few days before Christmas—we docked at Bristol in western England. Several G.I.s were so sick for so long they had to be carried off on stretchers. I never got "urpy," but felt like I might all the way.

We loaded on an old English train to Chichester, maybe central England, only on the southern side, not far from the English Channel. England was one big campground, so to speak. Troops and armaments parked and stored everywhere, mostly in the open. Row after row of tanks, trucks, jeeps, guns of all kinds and sizes, bombs, shell and ammo stacked everyplace.[404]

Ervin Aden was a young 1st Lieutenant attached to the 4th Cavalry Group, 4th Cavalry Reconnaissance Squadron, C Troop. He arrived in England in 1944.

I was given the order by Colonel Tully to personally supervise the camouflaging of the entire camping area of Goodwood Estates shortly after our arrival. I was to request of each troop commander the required number of men to work with me in accomplishing this task. Although the area was heavily wooded, there were, however, many trees on knolls that had to be

---

404 ibid (Page 44-45)

Figure 11-2. Goodwood Estate in 1930.

leveled so that our vehicles, etc., could be parked and camouflaged by the branches overhead. Mission was shortly accomplished.

Shortly thereafter, I was completely surprised when Colonel Tully told me I was being sent to London to be trained by Scotland Yard to decipher enemy documents and to interrogate German prisoners. During the period of a few months while training, I also experienced several bombings of London and spent time in bomb shelters with the British. To keep us calm, we had entertainment such as sing-alongs, radio music, quiz shows, etc., while we were served fish and chips. There was lots of dart playing, of course—anything to keep our minds off of the bombing. Our and their favorite song was "There'll be Bluebirds over the White Cliffs of Dover." In my limited time off, I did some sightseeing, visited pubs to pitch darts, etc.

On returning to Goodwood Estate, I began training representatives from each troop of the 4th CavReconSqd on how to waterproof their vehicles in preparation for the invasion. They in turn trained the rest of the men in each troop. We used an asbestos compound on the spark plugs and all the electrical wires, etc. Preparing them ahead of time, I warned the men that if they did not do a good job, the vehicles would drown out, stall, and end up like sitting ducks before making the beach.

Because our ship took us to Omaha Beach by mistake, and we had to maneuver through the heavy ship traffic to reach Utah Beach, we landed late that evening. However, the sergeant in charge on the beach all day handed out praise, informing us we were the only ones to land without one single vehicle drowning out. I, in turn, praised my men for a job well done.[405]

Aden was selected to be trained by Scotland Yard because he spoke and understood German to some degree. As he noted, this knowledge was to be used by the entire squadron of 750 men when they reached the European continent and entered combat.

In addition, Lieutenant Aden instructed the men of C Troop in unarmed defense. This was "combat judo"—to be used by the men to maim or kill an enemy, and then only in self-defense.

As if this wasn't enough, Aden also became the sole squadron instructor to teach all drivers and assistant drivers how to waterproof every type of vehicle the troop used. The group used the beach at Southampton for testing, as it was similar to the beaches of Normandy.[406]

Aden said that while in Wales, the staging area for the upcoming invasion, he and Captain McCauley were the only two men of their troop of 150 men to be briefed on the overall plan for the upcoming D-Day invasion. Aden was aware that a backup (alternate) plan existed, but as he would soon experience firsthand,

---

[405] 1st Lieutenant Ervin Aden; *personal account of his arrival and duties while in England:* Received via email on 5 September 2011 to Gary Palmer
[406] Ervin Aden; *Ervin Aden and the Fighting Fourth – WWII;* Unpublished manuscript given to Gary Palmer – 2009 (Page 1)

the Troop always functioned on a "swinging gate" principle all the way to Berlin.[407]

Aden recalled the 4th Cavalry Group's camp on the Goodwood Estates as

> ... a large area near Dover which would look to the Germans like an encampment or staging area that was getting ready to go into battle. There were fake tanks, armored scout cars, etc., all made of plywood (very realistic). The purpose was to give the enemy the impression we were about to evacuate that area and make a landing across the channel from that vicinity. The purpose was to make the enemy spread their troops out farther along the Normandy beach and weaken their strength.[408]

Merton Glover described his arrival in England and 4th Cavalry's living accommodations:

> Our camp was in a part of some large English estate. Small Quonsets, half-round, sheet-metal-covered, like half a big culvert. We were scattered under and around huge oak tree; could hardly see sun even on days when it was out. As I recall, maybe little wooden framed bunks, no springs and thin straw pad for mattress.
>
> Through previous years used by Limey troops, during the Battle of Britain bombing, they had dug elongated foxholes all around and beside these huts for protection. Crooked trails or paths went from one to

---

407 ibid [Ervin Aden; *Ervin Aden and the Fighting Fourth – WWII;* Unpublished manuscript given to Gary Palmer – 2009 (Page 1)]
408 1st Lieutenant Ervin Aden; *personal account of his arrival and duties while in England:* Received via email on 5 September 2011 to Gary Palmer

another. It was hazardous to go out at night and not fall in a ditch.

It was almost a court martial offense to expose a light at night. Each hut had one small light and it was only on a couple hours before bedtime. They knew how to conserve energy. Each area camp had strategically located washrooms and latrines. Rows of washbasins located inside with overhead water pipes and shower stalls. As I recall, cold water to wash and shower in, except on Saturday when they took the chill off water for showers. Each toilet, 10 in a row, similar to our old outhouses, only under the hole in seat was a tin 12-gallon pail shaped somewhat like an overgrown coal scuttle, with a heavy bail so it could be picked up and poured out in a tank that Limeys drove by every other day. When the tank was full it went to a nearby field where they emptied the tank on a field for fertilizer. You could always see the toilet paper fluttering in the wind when it dried. The G.I. universal name for these containers was "honey buckets."

I want to point out that the whole country is not far from the Arctic Circle, so nights are much longer than here and more intensely dark. In the camp under huge oak trees you could not see any light in the sky when you looked up.

We were free to go to Chichester evenings, usually a dance Saturday nights. Pubs were quite common (warm English beer). Little tea and crumpet shops (sweet breads). Other shops and stores have very meager stocks of anything because of war. Everything closed up early, say 10 p.m., I think to save energy and costs also. All buildings had heavy shutters and drapes so no light showed whatever. Bikes and cars had very dim yellow lights, shaded downward. All British footwear

Departure from the U.S.A., en route to Jolly Old England

had leather hobnail heels, and most with metal caps to wear longer, as nearly everybody walked, men and women. Few cars and little gas or petrol.

When the town closed up maybe a hundred hit the cobblestone streets and roads home or camps. Very dark; can still hear the clatter and clicks of people walking. You knew they were English for we G.I.s had softer soles and rubber heels. As I recall it was at least a two-mile walk, maybe three to town, a good hike anyway.

As I mentioned before our camp was in a large old English estate known as Goodwood. A short walk up an open ridge was called the Shell House. Maybe 12 feet square, high ceiling, completely covered with seashells of every size and shape and color you can imagine, inside and out. There could have been several thousand. Had window for light; very attractive.

The American Red Cross leased some old hotels in London for G.I.s. Each unit could by lottery send limited few each trip. As I recall, two days and a night; it took part of each day traveling. Got to see Big Ben, Trafalgar Square (London's version of Times Square), Windsor Castle, Number 10 Downing Street, many famous statues and cathedrals.

Probably the most memorable sight I recall was the countless number of searchlights, almost every night, as Germany flew bombing runs over London area. These lights all pointing up, weaving and criss-crossing the sky. Once in a while, many seemed to come to the same point as many locked onto a plane.

And of course, we were close enough to hear some of the big bombs and AA (anti-aircraft) fire in the distance. If it looked or sounded too close, people still out, ran for shelters; not many out very late.

I mentioned that we lived in huts among the big trees. We heard the air raid sirens and saw the searchlights nearly every night, off towards London and Channel coast. Became used to ignoring them. Then one night, heard a plane that was close and sounded different; local ack-ack and lights came on. He dropped a large bomb up on hill not too far, maybe three hundred yards. A lot of our guys, spooked, ran out and fell into trenches. Supposition was that German jettisoned his load as no cities or targets were near. We all had to go up the hill next day to view the big deep hole. That was our cheap initiation to live bombardment. All of which became all too familiar in next 12 months.

After Christmas or from January 1944 on, we had lots more training and much more hiking or marching through the English countryside. In part, physical conditioning, but I always thought to keep boredom down.

April and May 1944 the hikes got longer, 20 miles a day common, and last of all worked up to 30 miles full-pack. We did it and back at camp by mid-afternoon. As I recall marched army gait 40 minutes, or double-time 10 minutes and rested 10 minutes every hour. In our hiking around English countryside we saw whole pastures covered solid. One was full of tanks, next with trucks, next jeeps, next self-propelled guns and large guns of all sizes and types. Am sure every warehouse in England full of clothing and food and things needing shelter from rains. It was sort of a standing joke: U.S. was going to sink the British Isles.

As we left all our equipment in the States, if I recall, maybe March or April, we got all-new jeeps, armored cars, trucks (kitchen and supply) and small arms as called for in T.O. (Table of Operations). This occupied a lot of time, cleaning up as all metal surfaces were covered with cosmoline, a thick, very sticky tough greaser, before being shipped overseas.

Jeeps and trucks were similar to what we used and trained with, but armored cars much improved: six-wheel drive, a revolving turret armed with 37 mm gun. Three type shells armored piercing; H.E. (high explosive) and a canister in tin case, maybe a hundred rounds of steel balls, maybe 3/8-inch big shot. Also had a .30 cal machine gun beside the 37 mm gun and a .50 cal on rail on top of turret.[409]

THE 106TH CAVALRY GROUP DEPARTS FOR ENGLAND

Figure 11-3. The *Colombie* was in Casablanca when Operation TORCH began and was taken by the Americans to be converted into a troop ship. After conversion in New York, the ship was renamed the USAT (U.S. Army Troopship) *Colombie* and remained in that capacity until January 1945. She was converted into a hospital ship and work was completed in April 1945. At that point the ship was renamed the *Adela E. Lutz* and remained in that capacity until after the war, when she was returned to France.

---

409 Merton Glover; *86 and counting:* Unpublished personal manuscript of author's life history-2003 (Page 45-49)

The 106th Cavalry Group arrived at Camp Shanks, New York, on 20 February 1944. The camp was located on the west side of the Hudson River at Orangeburg, some 30 miles north of New York City. The men were oriented on embarkation procedures and received personal records checks.

After seven days at Camp Shanks, the 106th Cavalry Regiment left the Port of Embarkation on 27 February 1944 aboard the USAT *Colombie*. As was typical of most troop ships, the officers were assigned cabins and ate excellent French cuisine in the main dining room while the enlisted men ate standing up at metal tables and were housed in the ship's holds in four-tiered bunks. The holds smelled terrible as a result of soldiers getting seasick during the voyage. The enlisted men's latrines provided no privacy and the urinals were metal troughs.[410]

Figure 11-4. Picture of typical sleeping arrangements for troops in transit to England. *NATIONAL ARCHIVES*

---

410 William H. Collier, *The 106th Cavalry's Story:* Published by Trafford Publishing- March 2012 (Page 23-24)

DEPARTURE FROM THE U.S.A., EN ROUTE TO JOLLY OLD ENGLAND

On 9 March 1944, following a sea voyage of ten days, the *Colombie* arrived at Glasgow, Scotland. An all-night train ride followed, during which the men first experienced eating K-rations, combat meals packaged in small waxed cartons about six by ten inches in size. The regiment arrived in the early morning hours at its assigned camp at Doddington Park in the English midlands near the city of Stoke-on-Trent. Everyone was promptly served breakfast, at which time they ate powdered eggs and spam (potted meat) for the first time, with dehydrated milk to drink or to use in their coffee.[411]

The buildings of the camp were a type of Quonset hut with straight walls and small windows along the sides. The heat was provided by two small iron coal-burning stoves which were difficult to ignite and put out only minimal heat. The soldiers' mattresses were straw-filled and came with cover. Called "ticks" by the British, the mattresses took some getting used to!

The wash huts (called ablutionaries, meaning "a ritual washing of the hands or body") and latrines were in separate buildings. All of this must have been considered part of the hardening process for the troops.[412]

Almost immediately after arriving in England the regiment was reorganized under TO&E 2-22 into a cavalry group, with a small headquarters and headquarters troop and two CavReconSqd (Mech). Each squadron consisted of a headquarters, headquarters and service troop, three reconnaissance troops, an assault gun troop, and a light tank company.

The total strength of the group remained essentially the same, as did its equipment. The Group's designation remained the 106th Cavalry Group, but the 1st Squadron became the 106th CavReconSqd and the 2d Squadron became the 121st CavReconSqd.

---

411 ibid (Page 24)
412 ibid (Page 24)

The U.S. Cavalry: Time of Transition

At approximately the same time as the reorganization was taking place, all vehicle drivers were taken to a vehicle storage area where they picked out and drove their new vehicles back to Doddington Park. This was no easy job for the drivers of these large military vehicles, as they had to navigate through the narrow and twisty roads of the local towns and villages in England.[413]

The regiment was reorganized and redesigned as a cavalry group effective 14 March 1944 per radio instructions received from London. (CM-IN-10307 dated 15 March 1944)

1st Lieutenant Faris "Jake" Hess recalled the unit's reorganization:

> The original plan called for me to be part of headquarters staff. I was unhappy with this plan. I told the commanding officer that I wanted to go to battle with the troops. I was assigned to A Troop, 121st Cavalry Reconnaissance Squadron, as the assistant troop commander. I was promoted to 1st Lieutenant at this time. The A Troop commander was Captain Jay Clinton.[414]
>
> Most of the training in England was conducted in platoons. Usually the platoons road-marched to separately assigned areas about an hour's hike from Doddington Park. Platoon leaders supervised the training.
>
> Daily, before the retreat ceremony, every man was required to run one mile around the camp with his individual weapon as well as his cartridge belts and gas

---

413 ibid (Page 25)
414 Captain Faris 'Jake' Hess and Nancy 'Hess' Blackburn; *My Story-106th Cavalry Group in Europe 1942-1945:* Personal Manuscript written for the Hess' family in 2004 (Page 7)

Departure from the U.S.A., en route to Jolly Old England

mask. After this run, the officers quickly returned to their Quonset and changed clothes for dinner.

Most evenings after supper, each squadron used 6x6 trucks—one for officers and at least one for enlisted men—to take men some 20 miles away to Stoke-on-Trent for the evening. The trucks returned to camp promptly at 2300 hours (11 p.m. civilian time). Missing the truck meant a 20-mile hike back to Doddington Park.[415]

On two occasions all platoons took their vehicles on a 70-mile road march driving through the city of Manchester to a firing range on the moors near the city of Leeds. There, everyone fired his individual and vehicular weapons. It was quite a task to drive tanks through Manchester with people walking in the middle of the street. Fortunately there were no accidents or injuries.

At one point the assault gun troops went about 175 miles south to the coast near Portsmouth, where the 4th Cavalry Group was stationed for training. To assist the assault gun troops, an artillery officer who had served in an armored artillery battalion in North Africa visited Doddington Park and provided helpful hints on how to operate in combat. These hints were most useful and simplified assault gun use when the troops arrived on the battlefield.[416]

Samuel "Scotty" Pegues of the 106th Cavalry Group was given the task of coordinating these live-fire exercises. He made certain that each man qualified with his personal weapon and was able to perform the duties required of him during live firing of crew-operated weapons. In order to fulfill his duties, Pegues stockpiled large amounts of ammunition. At one point he was summoned to headquarters and questioned about the amount of ammunition

---

415 William H. Collier, *The 106th Cavalry's Story:* Published by Trafford Publishing-March 2012 (Page 25-26)
416 ibid (Page 26)

he was ordering. After he explained that it was in compliance with the TO&E for each weapon, he was given the go-ahead.[417]

Robert Moore (106th Cavalry Group) recalled England and his training:

> What a lovely country with lots of friendly people. A few aren't, but a very few. If I could just understand them when they speak English? It sure does rain a lot here and I suppose that's why everybody carries an umbrella.
>
> There were lots of maneuvers, war games, weapons training, bomb and mine disposal schools, and strategy sessions. Finally we are taught about the German method of conducting a war and not General Custer's. Everybody is anxious to go and get started, but we are living the army axiom of "hurry up and wait."
>
> During a training exercise, I lost some respect for Lieutenant Colonel Polk. The men of B Troop were performing our daily one-mile sprint. Herb and a few young athletes finished noticeably ahead of my platoon as well as the rest of his platoon. The rest of Herb's platoon managed to finish in the required time but we could not keep up with the trailblazers. My assignment was to bring up the rear, and everybody knew that I had two semi-cripples in my platoon. In trying to look good for Lieutenant Colonel Polk, Herb made me look very bad.
>
> Polk signaled me over and told me my job was to keep the men closed-up with the rest of the platoon. That my platoon was dressed very poorly and that the long winter coats looked very unkempt. All I could do

---

417 Statement given to Gary Palmer by Samuel (Scotty) Pegues during the 106th Cavalry Group's Reunion in 2007

Departure from the U.S.A., en route to Jolly Old England

is say, "Yes, Sir." I was not going to win any sprint races against anybody since I was to bring up the rear, and all those who couldn't keep up with the sprinters fell back with mine. One of my men, Private Hall, was 52 and couldn't lift an M1 Garand over his head with both hands.

The same thing happened with Colonel Wilson, commander of 106th Group. He was furious about the appearance and long formations that we "back markers" were in. The others that had already finished were very young tankers who were not in full combat gear. Wilson told me about the appearance we were making with the English civilians and the un-military manner we were presenting. He told me to call them to attention.

We were strung out about 300 yards at this time, and the ones in the rear couldn't even hear me. I tried, but when it was taking too long, he turned to me and said, "You can lose those bars, you know." I implored the men to come to close-order formation and to come to attention, which they eventually did. He pointed over to Herb and the well-dressed tankers and compared our appearance to theirs. All you can say is "Yes, Sir," even when you know he is wrong.

Later that day I went over to troop headquarters and started to go get the two Colonels and drag them over to read the Orders of the Day, which I had read but obviously they hadn't.

Orders of the Day
1. Extended Order Road March
2. Uniform: full combat gear with wool overcoats
   By order of Capt. Fran Weller

Figure 11-5. (Left to right) Cpt. Edward Krebs (E Troop, 121st CavReconSqd), 1st Lt. Faris "Jake" Hess and Maj. Roy J. Clinton (Group Headquarters Troop), and 1st Lt. Robert Moore (B Troop, 121st CavReconSqd) playing a friendly game of pool at Doddington, England.

Their actions were not the professional quality of Lieutenant Colonel Homfeld's query about the staggered formation in Louisiana.

Finally we are given our tactical orders. We will not go in on D-Day. We would go as soon as the lines were established, and then do the job we were trained for. We all wanted to go on D-Day, but orders are orders.

We were in Doddington, several miles to the west of Newcastle-under-Lyme as well as the town of Stoke-on-Trent. Sometimes on the weekends we would go to the Lion's Head Pub at the Newcastle Hotel where there was a very good band and young English girls to dance with. The 6x6 trucks got us there at 6:00 p.m.

and left to come back at 10:00 p.m. I never wanted to miss that 10:00 p.m. truck because it was a 26-mile hike to get back to base and you did not want to be AWOL.

At night we would be serenaded to sleep by hundreds of British bombers taking off to give Adolf his nighttime lullaby. In the morning we would awaken to the American planes taking off. Glad they're all on our side.[418]

THIRD ARMY COMES TO ENGLAND

On 31 December 1943, Third Army was transformed from a training unit to a combat army. On New Year's Eve the unit was alerted for overseas movement to the United Kingdom with all indications it would participate in the invasion of Europe. For the men of Third Army, this was joyous news. Like General Krueger, the staff had come to feel it was fated to remain a training unit— to continue sweating and freezing it out in Louisiana, conducting endless inspections, tests, and maneuvers while watching outfits and men they had trained depart for foreign shores. At long last, Third Army was going to war instead of to another maneuver.[419]

Shortly thereafter, an advance echelon departed for England to set up a command post. Strangely, General Hodges was not summoned to the War Department for conferences, as was the standard procedure. Even more strangely, he remained behind when the main body pulled out in February 1944. He came to the entraining point to see the staff off, but that was the last time they saw him as the commanding general of Third Army. Afterward, Hodges reported to Washington. There some sharp and critical

---

[418] Robert (Bob) Moore and Michael (Mike) Moore: *The 12th Man; Citizen Soldier in Europe 1944-1945:* Unpublished Manuscript (06-10-2010)
[419] Colonel Robert S. Allen; *Lucky Forward (The History of General George Patton's Third U.S. Army):* Published by MacFadden-Bartell Books-1965 (Page 19)

comments were tossed at him about the chief of staff and the way he had utilized him during the maneuvers in Louisiana.[420]

While Hodges' absence caused some comment at Headquarters Third Army, there was no suspicion of a change in command. The staff traveled to Camp Shanks, New York, by train, and was to cross the ocean aboard the transport *Il de France*. It was taken for granted Hodges would be flown over to meet them upon their arrival in England. This belief was strengthened by two factors: the presence of the unpopular chief of staff with the main body, and the members who comprised the General's staff. This last fact in particular served to lull suspicions.

Nevertheless, a week later the headquarters commandant experienced a startling jolt. In a bundle of mail he found a letter addressed to "Lieutenant General George S. Patton, Jr., CG Third Army, APO 403, Postmaster, New York, N.Y." The return address was that of Mrs. George S. Patton, Jr.[421]

Excited, the headquarters commandant ran to the chief of staff with the news. Whatever the chief of staff thought, he kept to himself. But it was obvious that if Patton was the new commanding general, Hodges was out—and if Hodges was out, so was his chief of staff. Patton had the reputation of handpicking his own senior staff officers.

The chief of staff enjoined the strictest secrecy on the headquarters commandant, and the secret was fairly well kept. When Headquarters Third Army arrived in the United Kingdom, fewer than half of the officers knew that Patton was their new commanding general. The remainder learned it from members of the advance echelon a few minutes after debarking in the Firth of Clyde from the jam-packed *Il de France*.

The advance echelon related an interesting story of how Patton had broken the news to them. When their ship docked at Glasgow, they were assembled in a mess hall. They assumed this

---

420 ibid (Page 19)
421 ibid (Page 20)

DEPARTURE FROM THE U.S.A., EN ROUTE TO JOLLY OLD ENGLAND

was to hear a welcoming speech, as was the practice. Even when Patton entered, aglitter in gleaming brass and boots, they still suspected nothing. They thought he would do the spieling. Patton did—but it was not what they expected.

Patton said, "I am your new commander. I'm glad to see you. I hope it's mutual. There's a lot of work to be done and there's little time to do it. There's a special train waiting on the dock to take you to our CP (command post). We will leave in an hour."

That was it. Once they were on the train, the advance echelon was ordered not to say or write anything about the new commanding general.[422]

Patton did not meet the main body when advance echelon arrived. New orders relieved the chief of staff and, with one exception, all of the senior officers on the general staff, who were dismissed before they got off the transport. They were replaced by Patton men who had served under him in the African and Sicilian campaign. Later, a number of the special staff chiefs also gave way to Patton veterans.

The purge did not affect subordinate officers. Subsequent combat operations wrought many changes in their ranks, but Patton confined his head-lopping to the upper ranks.

Almost all of Patton's section chiefs were cavalrymen. A number were also veterans of the 2d Armored Division, his first divisional command. With the exception of MacDonald, Hodges' senior officers had been doughboys (infantry troops).

Under Patton, Headquarters Third Army became predominantly cavalry—the only such headquarters in the European Theater of Operations (ETO). It was the only headquarters where riding breeches and boots were common articles of attire. It was also the only headquarters where every officer always wore a necktie. Hot or cold, rain, snow, or sunshine, in the lines or in the command post—every officer on Patton's

---

422 ibid (Page 20-21)

staff always wore a necktie and shaved every day. Additionally, Headquarters Third Army area always was instantly recognizable by the unfailing and snappy saluting.[423]

The day after they were billeted, all officers and enlisted men of Third Army staff were assembled on the large terrace in front of Peover, an ancient manor house a few miles from Knutsford. It was a raw, gloomy, early spring day. Patton stood on the wide stone steps and faced the staff. To his left was his chief of staff, Brigadier General "Hap" Gay; and to his right was Willie, Patton's pugnacious-looking white bull terrier. On the portal above Patton's head was a weather-beaten stone shield bearing the date 1536.

There was nothing medieval about Patton himself. He was attired in a superbly tailored, form-fitting, brass-buttoned battle jacket that was studded with four rows of campaign ribbons and decorations. He had a pink whipcord, riding breeches, and gleaming, high-topped cavalry boots with spurs. Around his waist was a hand-tooled wide leather belt with a large, embossed, shiny brass buckle. In his hand was a long riding crop; on each of his shoulders, shirt collars, and helmet, rows of three large stars.

Characteristically, Patton didn't talk long. Also characteristically, what he said was pungent and to the point:[424]

> I have been given command of Third Army for reasons which will become clear later on. You made an outstanding record as an able and hard-working staff under my predecessor. I have no doubt you will do the same for me. We now have two staffs merging into one, each with its own procedures. By working harmoniously and intelligently together, a third staff will be developed with a third procedure, which should be better than either of the other two.

---

423 ibid (Page 21)
424 ibid (Page 22)

Departure from the U.S.A., en route to Jolly Old England

I am here because of the confidence of two men: the President of the United States and the theater commander. They have confidence in me because they don't believe a lot of goddamned lies that have been printed about me and also because they know I mean business when I fight. I don't fight for fun and I won't tolerate anyone on my staff who does.

You are here to fight. This is an active theater of war. Ahead of you lies battle. That means just one thing. You can't afford to be a goddamned fool, because in battle, fools mean dead men. It is inevitable for men to be killed and wounded in battle. But there is no reason why such losses should be increased because of the incompetence and carelessness of some stupid son-of-a-bitch. I don't tolerate such men on my staff.

There are three reasons why we are fighting this war. The first is because we are determined to preserve our traditional liberties. Some crazy German bastards decided they were supermen and that it was their holy mission to rule the world. They've been pushing people around all over the world, looting, killing, and abusing millions of innocent men, women, and children. They were getting set to do the same thing to us. We had to fight to prevent being subjugated.

The second reason we are fighting is to defeat and wipe out the Nazis who started all this goddamned son-of-bitchery. They didn't think we could or would fight, and they weren't the only ones who thought that either. There are certain people back home that had the same idea. Both were wrong.

The third reason we are fighting is because men like to fight. They always have and they always will. Some sophists and other crackpots deny that. They don't know what they're talking about. They are either goddamned fools or cowards, or both. Men like to fight, and if they don't, they're not real men.

If you don't like to fight, I don't want you around. You'd better get out before I kick you out. But there is one thing to remember. In war, it takes more than the desire to fight to win. You've got to have more than guts to lick the enemy. You must also have brains. It takes brains and guts to win wars. A man with guts but no brains is only half a soldier. We licked the Germans in Africa and Sicily because we had brains as well as guts. We're going to lick them in Europe for the same reason. That's all, and good luck.[425]

2D CAVALRY GROUP REFORMS AND JOINS THE PARTY

In January 1943 the regiment was reformed as the 2d Cavalry Regiment (Mechanized) at Fort Jackson, South Carolina, under the command of Colonel Charles H. Reed. The regiment consisted of cadre with a small group of regular cavalry non-commissioned officers (NCOs) and officers from throughout the cavalry force. The unit received an influx of draftees and new officers from both West Point and the Cavalry Officer Candidate School (OCS) at Fort Riley.[426] In late 1943 the regiment was reorganized and designated as the 2d Cavalry Group, with attached 2d and 42d Cavalry Reconnaissance Squadrons.

On 9 March 1944, while Patton was organizing his new command, a letter from the War Department arrived. It stated that the entire 2d Cavalry Group (Mecz) was to prepare for foreign duty and was to move to New York or Boston port of embarkation, at a time to be determined by the appropriate port commander,

---

[425] ibid (Page 22-24)
[426] This article is extracted from a supplemental student text (undated) written for the US Army Armor School by LTC (Ret) James W. Cooke

for further movement by water transportation. Preparations, requirements, the date to be ready, and the shipment number for the advance and main parties were specified in this same letter. From that day on the entire effort of the Group was devoted to preparing for overseas movement. Officers, warrant officers, and enlisted men were transferred and acquired until the Group reached its T/O strength on 31 March 1944.[427]

During this time of preparation, each man not previously qualified on his own personal weapon was afforded an opportunity to fire once again. All personnel were required to fire for familiarization the supporting weapons of the rest of their troop. Dental repair work was accorded a high priority. Personal clothing and equipment were checked and rechecked to meet specified requirements. Training was necessarily cut to a minimum except in the field of physical conditioning. Each week all officers and men were required to participate in two nine-mile hikes and two four-mile fast road marches.[428]

Advance detachments from Group Headquarters, Headquarters 2d Cavalry Reconnaissance Squadron, and Headquarters 42d Cavalry Reconnaissance Squadron were organized and prepared to move to the designated port of embarkation on the call of the port commander by 11 March 1944 or any date thereafter. The advance detachments would act as the coordinating agencies at the overseas destination for supply and personnel matters prior to the arrival of their respective units.

The readiness date for movement to the port of embarkation was established as 1 April 1944 for personnel and company equipment.[429]

---

[427] David.Gettman; H&S Troop, 42d Squadron, 2d Cavalry Group (Mecz); *2d Dragoons arrival in England-1944:*
2d Dragoons © 2011 Built by Isaac Golding on behalf of the Second Cavalry Assn. WordPress Themes based on a design by NodeThirtyThree
[428] ibid [David.Gettman; H&S Troop, 42d Squadron, 2d Cavalry Group (Mecz); *2d Dragoons arrival in England-1944:* **2d Dragoons** © 2011 Built by Isaac Golding on behalf of the Second Cavalry Assn. WordPress Themes based on a design by NodeThirtyThree]
[429] ibid

The U.S. Cavalry: Time of Transition

The 2d Cavalry Group left Fort Jackson, South Carolina, by rail for a permanent change of station on 1 April 1944. The unit arrived at Camp Kilmer, New Jersey, on 2 April 1944, completing the first step on its journey to the war zone. Spirits were high as the train rumbled to a stop at Kilmer, and everyone was anxious to learn just when the ship was to leave.[430]

If the soldiers thought they had made all the necessary checks and inspections at Fort Jackson, they were in for a surprise. Barracks were assigned all the troops, and all personnel of the Group were physically screened again, while the personnel records as well as all clothing and equipment were rechecked.

After the first flurry of inspections and showdowns, everyone settled down to a routine of supervised athletics and road marches, with the addition of boat drills and the use of cargo nets in evacuating the wooden ship mockups that abounded at Camp Kilmer. In addition to their outdoor work the troops watched many training films, often repeaters, required for the orientation of men going overseas. Classes in the recognition of enemy planes and combat vehicles were held again, and the whole command felt that it was fit and ready for the big task.[431]

The two squadrons were not scheduled for immediate departure, so the soldiers were issued liberty passes good for 12- to 40-hour periods. This enabled some of the men who lived in New York and New Jersey to spend a few hours at home. For the others there was the glitter of nearby Broadway, with its Astor Bar, and the Empire State Building for those inclined to sightseeing.

Unfortunately, Group Headquarters personnel were unable to take advantage of the passes. The staff was alerted to standby on 8 April 44 for embarkation. Day passes remained in effective for rest of those troopers who held them. However, headquarters staff and members of the advance party had to sweat out the train and ferry ride to New York in order to board the ocean liner RMS

---

430 ibid
431 ibid

Queen Mary. Many of the men knew their wives were watching from shore—so near and yet so far.

On 17 April 1944, Group Headquarters, along with the rest of the advance party, arrived at Greenock, Scotland. Upon disembarking from the *Queen Mary* they proceeded by rail to their new station at Camp Bewdley in Worcestershire, England, a site which Headquarters Third Army had selected for them.[432]

Finally, on 20 April 1944, the 2d Squadron, to be followed on 21 April by the 42d Squadron, boarded the transport liner RMS *Mauretania* bound for overseas. Time aboard ship was spent attending short classes on identification of enemy equipment and orientation on the British Isles, in doing calisthenics, attending boat drill, and carrying out the necessary details of guard and mess attendant. The 2d Cavalry Reconnaissance Squadron operated the message center aboard ship, and radio operators were provided to assist the normal radio crew during the voyage.[433]

3D CAVALRY GROUP REFORMS AND JOINS UP

During the 1920s and 1930s the Regiment underwent a series of organizational changes. 2d Squadron, plus troops C and D of 1st Squadron, were deactivated. 3d Squadron was redesignated as 2nd Squadron and stationed at Fort Myer, Virginia.

Because of its proximity to Washington, D.C., and Arlington National Cemetery, 2d Squadron was frequently called upon to furnish honor guards and escorts for distinguished visitors, and funeral escorts for distinguished civilian officials and military personnel. The squadron became known as "The President's Own" because of these duties. On 11 November 1921, the 3d Cavalry furnished the cavalry escort for the interment of the Unknown Soldier from World War I in Arlington National Cemetery. Until

---

432 ibid
433 ibid

1941, the regiment provided the guard detail at the Tomb of the Unknown Soldier.

This period in the regiment's history also saw the beginnings of mechanization in the cavalry. Early armored cars and motor transport trucks began to appear at Forts Ethan Allen and Myer. The troopers had to develop the first tactics for employment of these vehicles, while also learning how to maintain them.

In February 1942 the 3d Cavalry Regiment (Horse-Mechanized) was moved to Fort Oglethorpe, Georgia, and then to Fort Benning, Georgia. At Fort Benning, the regiment was reorganized and redesignated as the 3d Armored Regiment and assigned to the 10th Armored Division. In January 1943, the regiment was reconstituted as the 3d Cavalry Group (Mechanized). The 1st and 2nd Squadrons were redesignated as the 3rd and 43rd Cavalry Reconnaissance Squadrons, respectively. The 3d Cavalry Group moved to Camp Gordon, Georgia, and began training in mechanized operations.

Allen Halloway, originally a member of the 4th Cavalry Regiment, recalled that period:

> In January 1943, I and the other members of the 4th Cavalry mechanized Regiment were sent to California for training because we thought we were going to fight in North Africa.
>
> In April, about 150 men were taken from the outfit and sent to Camp Gordon, Georgia, near the South Carolina border, at about the same time as the 3d Cavalry Regiment was reactivated. By 1 May 1943, there were about 40,000 soldiers in the camp.
>
> I had learned Morse code in South Dakota, and had been taught voice operation too. Subsequently, I taught radio use to the new soldiers who were sent to Fort Gordon and attached to the 3d Cavalry Group.

Departure from the U.S.A., en route to Jolly Old England

We had a guy, James Dean from Cando, North Dakota, who could talk to you and type Morse code at the same time, and that was without the headphones. He said that you don't count the dots and dashes, you hear the tones and it burns into your mind.

While [I was] stationed at Fort Gordon, a daughter, Sheila, was born on my 25th birthday, 30 January 1944. The fee for the birth was $1, which was to register my daughter.[434]

After extensive field maneuvers in the southeastern United States, which lasted from November 1943 to March 1944, the 3d Cavalry Group arrived in England in June 1944. The 3d Cavalry Group (Mecz), "Brave Rifles," under command of Colonel F.W. Drury, Cavalry, and later replaced by Colonel James H. Polk, Cavalry, with its 3d and 43d Cavalry Squadrons, came over the beach at Omaha on 10 of August 1944. They raced to join XX Corps, part of General Patton's Third U.S. Army, and became XX Corps' covering force in the Le Mans area where they were immediately committed to action.[435]

Allen Halloway related his experiences during his sea voyage and arrival in England:

> I shipped out to Europe in May 1944 aboard the RMS *Aquitania*. The bunk I slept on was one of many poorly constructed cots within the ocean liner's swimming pool. Two pipes ran from ceiling to floor for each set of bunks.

---

[434] Kyle Halloway (15 years old); Biography of Allen Halloway (An Ordinary Hero): Written as a term paper for Kyle's United States History Class (Page 8)
[435] Blood and Steel the History, Customs, and Traditions of the 3d Cavalry, Published by the Third Cavalry Museum Fort Hood, Texas 2008 Edition

Figure 11-6. 21 February 1942, the end of an era: The 3d Cavalry gives up its horses. Headquartered at Fort Myer for over 20 years, the regiment takes its mounts to a train before leaving for Georgia to begin training for World War II.
THIRD CAVALRY MUSEUM, FORT HOOD, TEXAS

The bunks hooked into holes on the pipe with a chain and numbered about four or five high.

Upon landing in Glasgow, Scotland, we went from ship to shore on barges. Once ashore, we found the weather to be damp and foggy. We got on a train that transported us into the country.

We followed Lieutenant Ratliff out into this big meadow to a big pile of five-man tents. You had four guys with you and put up your tent in the middle of the night. Once the tent went up, we got folding cots; we then took a canvas bag, went to a pile of straw, filled the bag with straw, put it on the cot and went to sleep.

Departure from the U.S.A., en route to Jolly Old England

Figure 11-7. Allen Halloway during training at Fort Gordon, Georgia. *Allen Halloway*

The first meal the next day didn't happen until mid-afternoon, because it took forever for the kitchen crew to set up the kitchen. The next day, the truck with the soldiers' duffel bags came and dropped them out in the field.

We spent ten days to two weeks in that field. We couldn't pee or take a crap on their land. They had these pots that you went in, and you put the toilet paper in another container. We called them the honey wagons. These English people came around and emptied them.

We were sent to another area where they got all their vehicles and the radios and other equipment were installed. Lieutenant Lemare was in my platoon and he had a list of all these vehicles. We went to the staging area and got a half-track, two Jeeps and two light tanks. We told the guy there that we were supposed to have a f our-wheel-drive Dodge weapons carrier, so we got an extra car.

Four tanks, six half-tracks, a maintenance truck, a kitchen truck, Jeeps and soldiers were loaded on an LST (Landing Ship Tank), and there they sat for a day and a half. We went up the English Channel aways and then docked. Then we went to the beach at Normandy. We went in on low tide, full-bore, slid up, dropped the door and went out.[436]

PRE-INVASION TRAINING CATASTROPHE

Disaster struck in the midst of Exercise TIGER, a 30,000-man, 300-vessel dress rehearsal for the upcoming Normandy landings of June 1944. For the eight-day exercise, commanders chose Slapton Sands, a three-mile stretch of shingle on the south Devon coast between Torbay and Plymouth, because of its resemblance to what would become Utah beach, on the east coast of the Cotentin peninsula, during the actual D-Day operation.[437]

Earlier in the day, LSTs had landed more than 20,000 infantrymen and amphibious tanks of the U.S. 4th Infantry Division at Slapton. The nighttime rehearsal was for the back-up teams that would be needed on Utah. That second wave consisted of army engineers and heavy equipment that could not be put ashore during the vicious initial stage of the invasion.

For security, the hard-pressed Royal Navy relied mostly on the picket of vessels strung out along the outer edge of Lyme Bay. The World War I destroyer HMS *Scimitar* and a corvette named *Azalea* were assigned to protect the convoy, but *Scimitar* was damaged in a collision the day before and had to put in to port.

---

[436] Kyle Halloway (15 years old); Biography of Allen Halloway (An Ordinary Hero): Written as a term paper for Kyle's United States History Class (Page 8-9)
[437] Ben Fenton; 2004 Newspaper Article entitled "749 US lives were lost when Germans brought chaos to invasion rehearsal: Stanley B. Doyle of Massapequa, N.Y. provided a copy of the article.

A communications failure meant that no replacement for *Scimitar* was sent to help the convoy.[438]

At four minutes past two on the morning of 28 April 1944, eight Allied LSTs (Landing Ship, Tank) were at sea as the moon dropped beneath the horizon. Until that moment, all was going well with Exercise TIGER.

Then, in the darkness, nine German motor torpedo boats (E-boats) sailed undetected through the Royal Navy's protective screen.

Suddenly the landing ship USS LST-507, approaching Slapton Sands, was hit by a torpedo. The ship—packed to the gunwales with men and armored equipment—erupted and was soon aflame from stem to stern. The initial explosion was the first sign for the commanders of Exercise TIGER that things had gone wrong.[439]

During the next 10 minutes the USS LST-531 was torpedoed and sunk, and USS LST-289 was hit and crippled, its stern blown off. By the end of the night, 198 U.S. Navy personnel and 551 U.S. Army soldiers—including hundreds of irreplaceable specialist engineers and 10 senior officers—were dead or missing.

The loss of three LSTs meant that there would be no reserve vessels of any kind for the actual landings that were due to start

Figure 11-8. German E-boat of the type used in the 1944 raid during Exercise TIGER. *NATIONAL ARCHIVES*

---

438 ibid (Same Newspaper Article)
439 ibid (Same Newspaper Article)

38 days later. But the gigantic scale of Operation OVERLORD—the name given to the D-Day landings—and the unstoppable momentum of its build-up meant that the great tragedy of Slapton Sands threatened the success of the overall plans.

Even though the losses were awful, there was an even greater concern to General Dwight D. Eisenhower and his team of D-Day planners. The 10 senior officers lost that night were all "bigoted," meaning that they were cleared to see information in the Bigot category, a classification higher than Top Secret, which was used for all OVERLORD material. If any of the 10 men had been taken prisoner by the E-boats—something that the confusion of the night had made eminently possible—they might be persuaded to part with vital information, including the location of Utah beach.

The whole success of OVERLORD lay in convincing the Germans that the Normandy landings were a diversionary attack, with the real assault to come opposite the Kent coast in the Pas de Calais. While those 10 senior officers missing, Eisenhower might have to work on the assumption that his landings would be met with the full force of the German Army, with disastrous consequences.

Huge efforts were made to recover bodies from Lyme Bay; and against all odds, the 10 officers were found. The U.S. Army did not acknowledge the disaster of Slapton until well after D-Day.[440]

---

440 ibid (Same Newspaper Article)

CHAPTER XII

2D CAVALRY ARRIVES IN ENGLAND AND MEETS GENERAL PATTON

On 30 April 1944, the *Mauretania* put in to Liverpool, where the troopers were met by a band and by Red Cross girls offering coffee and donuts. Anyone who carried a barracks bag from Liverpool to the train station would testify that coffee was a welcome treat.

The train left as soon as loading was completed and rumbled the 145 miles south to Kidderminster by midnight of the same day. The soldiers who stood in the blacked-out isles of the little British coaches eagerly caught their first glimpse of England by moonlight. Truck convoys provided by Group headquarters picked the troopers up at the station, and both squadrons were shortly in their assigned quarters in a recently constructed hospital plant at Bewdley.[441]

Earlier that month, Lieutenant General George S. Patton, Jr., sent a Letter of Instruction to what would become his Third Army. Patton addressed his letter to Third Army Corps, all divisions, and individual unit commanders. He specified that infantry reconnaissance be stressed both day and night and required that junior officers be inquisitive when seeking precise information. Furthermore, Patton instructed reconnaissance elements to maintain continuous contact with the enemy.

During the following month the 6th Cavalry Group, under the command of Colonel Edward M. (Joe) Fickett, received a special mission directive from Patton that deviated from his Letter of Instruction.[442] Patton had the Group switch from its prescribed mission of reconnaissance and security to serve as a unique Army Information Service (AIS) channel for him. The AIS was referred to as Patton's "Household Cavalry."

Joe Fickett was a hard-bitten, mustached cavalryman of the frontier breed and had come up through the ranks beginning as a cavalry private in the Illinois National Guard. In May 1944, Patton gave Fickett a special mission to establish a channel, both physical and technical, directly to the army advance command post. This arrangement bypassed normal communications for monitoring friendly frontline intelligence and operations when the Third Army became operational on 1 August 1944 in France.

According to Patton's G-2 (the staff officer in charge of intelligence), cavalryman Colonel Oscar W. Koch, the "Household Cavalry" was designed to keep the Third Army commander

---

[441] David.Gettman; H&S Troop, 42d Squadron, 2d Cavalry Group (Mecz); *2d Dragoons arrival in England-1944:*
2d Dragoons © 2011 Built by Isaac Golding on behalf of the Second Cavalry Assn. WordPress Themes based on a design by NodeThirtyThree
[442] George F. Hofmann; *Through Mobility We Conquer (The Mechanization of U.S. Cavalry):* Published by the University Press of Kentucky-2006 (Page 343)

apprised of the location of friendly units and their enemy contacts in a timely fashion. The "Household Cavalry" also allowed Patton to gather intelligence on the enemy's intentions.

Koch was fluent in German and during the interwar period had translated German military manuals into English. During August, as Third Army drove south to the Loire and then east to the Seine, the cavalry group kept Patton informed of the location and disposition of his frontline elements and provided flank liaison and security between friendly combat units.[443]

At Bewdley, where the Headquarters of XII Corps was also established, the 2d Cavalry Group entered another short training phase from 1 May to 18 May 1944. During that period the commanders stressed conditioning, road marches, and classes on tactics prior to the arrival of motorized equipment.[444]

On 17 May 1944, the big Camp at Bewdley buzzed with tension. For the hundreds of eager ETO rookies newly arrived from the States, that day marked their first taste of "the real thing." They were no longer puppets in olive drab, going through the motions of soldiering, with 3,000 miles of water between them and English soil. Now they stood in the heart of Britain itself, awaiting the coming of that legendary figure, Lieutenant General George S. Patton, Jr.—"Old Blood and Guts" himself.

Patton—of the brisk, purposeful stride; the harsh, compelling voice; the lurid vocabulary; the grim, indomitable spirit that carried him and his Army to glory in Africa and Sicily. "America's fightin'est General," they called him. He was not a desk commando but a man who was sent for when the going got rough and a fighter was needed. He was the most hated and feared American on the part of the German Army.

---

443 ibid (Page 344)
444 David.Gettman; H&S Troop, 42d Squadron, 2d Cavalry Group (Mecz); *2d Dragoons arrival in England-1944:*
2d Dragoons © 2011 Built by Isaac Golding on behalf of the Second Cavalry Assn. WordPress Themes based on a design by NodeThirtyThree

Patton was coming, and the stage was being set. He would address XII Corps of his own Third Army, of which he had only recently been assigned command—a move that was to have a far-reaching effect on the war.[445]

The soldiers at Bewdley turned out en masse for the first time in full uniform. Today their marching was not lackadaisical. It was serious and the men felt the difference. In long columns they marched down the hill from the barracks, counting cadence, turned left up the rise and into the roped-off field where the General was to speak. Brass and stripes were everywhere. Soon, by company and troop, the hillside was a solid mass of olive drab. The men settled themselves and lit cigarettes.

It was a fresh, beautiful English morning. Soft white clouds floated lazily overhead, and tall trees lining the road swayed gently in the breeze. Across the field a farmer calmly tilled his soil. High upon a nearby hill, a group of Englishmen huddled together awaiting the coming of the General. Military policemen in white leggings, belts and helmets were everywhere.[446]

The twittering of birds could be heard above the dull murmur of the crowd. On the special platform near the speaker's stand, colonels and majors were a dime a dozen. General Patton's specially chosen Guard of Honor stood behind the platform. To their right was the band, playing rousing marches while the crowd waited; and on the platform a nervous sergeant repeatedly tested the loudspeaker.

The moment drew nearer, and everyone craned their necks to watch the tiny winding road that led to Stourport-on-Severn. A

---

445 Sgt. Tom M. Griffin, H&S Troop, 42d Squadron; A General Talks to His Army: **2d Dragoons** © 2011 Built by Isaac Golding on behalf of the Second Cavalry Assn. WordPress Themes based on a design by NodeThirtyThree
446 ibid (Sgt. Tom M. Griffin, H&S Troop, 42d Squadron; A General Talks to His Army: **2d Dragoons** © 2011 Built by Isaac Golding on behalf of the Second Cavalry Assn. WordPress Themes based on a design by NodeThirtyThree)

2D Cavalry Arrives in England and Meets General Patton

captain stepped to the microphone.

"When the General arrives," he said, "the band will play the General's March and you will stand at attention."[447]

By now the rumor had gotten around that Lieutenant General Simpson, commander of Fourth Army, was accompanying General Patton. The men stirred expectantly: two of the big boys in one day!

At last a long black car, shining resplendently in the bright sun, roared up the road, preceded by a jeep full of MPs. A captain near the road turned and waved frantically, and the men rose as one. A dead hush fell over the hillside.

There he was. Impeccably dressed, with high cavalry boots and gleaming helmet, Patton strode down the incline and straight to the stiff-backed Guard of Honor. He looked them up and down, peered intently into their faces, and surveyed their backs. He moved through the ranks of the band and mounted the platform, with General Simpson and Major General Cook, XII Corps Commander, at his side.[448]

The Corps chaplain gave the invocation. The men stood with heads bowed, asking divine guidance for the great Third Army, that they might help speed victory to an enslaved Europe. General Cook then introduced General Simpson, whose Army was still in America preparing for their part in the war.

"We are here," said General Simpson, "to listen to the words of a great man. A man who will lead you all into whatever you may face with heroism, ability and foresight. A man who has proven himself amid both shot and shell. My greatest hope is that someday soon I will have my own great Army fighting with him side by side."[449]

General Patton arose and strode swiftly to the microphone. Patton surveyed the men grimly.

---

447 ibid
448 ibid
449 ibid

"Be seated!" The words were not a request but a command.

The General's voice rose, high and clear. Characteristically, Patton didn't talk long. Also characteristically, what he said was pungent and to the point.

Sergeant Tom M. Griffin, Headquarters & Service Troop, 42d Squadron, 2d Cavalry Group, recorded Patton's remarks:

> Men, this stuff we hear about America wanting to stay out of the War, not wanting to fight, is a lot of crap! Americans love to fight—traditionally. All real Americans love the sting and clash of battle. When you were kids you all admired the champion marble player, the fastest runner, the big league ball players, the toughest boxers. Americans love a winner and will not tolerate a loser. Americans despise cowards. Americans play to win—all the time. I wouldn't give a hoot in hell for a man who lost and laughed. That's why Americans have never lost, nor ever will lose a War, for the very thought of losing is hateful to an American.

Patton paused and looked over the silent crowd.

> You are not all going to die. Only two percent of you here, in a major battle, would die. Death must not be feared. Every man is frightened at first in battle. If he says he isn't, he's a goddamned liar. Some men are cowards, yes. But they fight just the same, or get the hell shamed out of them watching men who do fight who are just as scared.
>
> The real hero is the man who fights even though he is scared. Some get over their fright in a minute under fire, some take an hour. For some it takes days.

2D CAVALRY ARRIVES IN ENGLAND AND MEETS GENERAL PATTON

Figure 12-1. George S. Patton.

But the real man never lets fear of death overpower his honor, his sense of duty to his country, and his innate manhood.

All through your Army career you men have bitched about what you call "this chickenshit drilling." That is all for a purpose. Drilling and discipline must be maintained in an Army, if only for one reason: Instant obedience to orders and to create constant alertness. I don't give a damn for a man who is not always on his toes. You men are veterans, or you wouldn't be here. You are ready. A man, to continue breathing, must be alert at all times. If not, sometime a German son-of-a-bitch will sneak up behind him and beat him to death with a sock full of shit!

The men roared. Patton's grim expression did not change.

There are 400 neatly marked graves somewhere in Sicily, all because one man went to sleep on his job.

He paused, then continued in a soft voice:

But they are German graves, for we caught the fathead asleep before they did!

The General clenched the microphone tightly, his jaw thrust forward.

An Army is a team. Lives, sleeps, eat and fight as a team. This individual heroic stuff is a lot of crap. The bilious fatheads who write that kind of stuff for the Saturday Evening Post don't know any more about real battle than they do about swearing.

The men slapped their legs and rolled their eyes in glee. This was the old boy as they imagined him, and in rare form. He had it.

We have the best food, the finest equipment, the best spirit, and the best men in the world!

He lowered his head and shook it pensively. Suddenly he snapped his head up, facing the men belligerently, and thundered,

2D Cavalry Arrives in England and Meets General Patton

Why, By God! I actually pity those poor sons-of bitches we're going up against. By God, I do!

The men clapped and howled. There would be many a barracks tale about the old man's choice phrases. This would become part and parcel of Third Army history. Patton continued:

My men don't surrender. I don't want to hear of any soldier under my command being captured unless he is hit. Even if you are hit you can still fight. That's not just baloney either. The kind of a man I want under me is the lieutenant in Libya, who, with one Luger against his chest, jerked off his helmet, swept the gun aside with one hand, and busted hell out of the *Boche* with the helmet. Then he jumped on the gun and went out and killed another German! All that time this man has a bullet through a lung! That's a man for you!

He halted and the crowd waited. He went on:

All the real heroes are not storybook combat fighters, either. Every single man in the Army plays a vital part. Every little job is essential to the whole scheme. What if every truck driver suddenly decided that he didn't like the whine of those shells and turned yellow and jumped headlong into the ditch? He could say to himself they won't miss me—just one guy in thousands! What if every man said that? Where in hell would we be now?

No, thank God, Americans don't say that. Every man does his job. Every man serves the whole. Every department, every unit is important in the vast scheme of things. The Ordnance men are needed to supply the guns, the Quartermaster to bring up the food and clothe us—for where we're going there isn't a hell of a lot to steal!

Every damn last man in the mess hall—even the one who heats the water to keep us from getting diarrhea—has a job to do. Even the chaplain is important, for if we got killed and he was not there to bury us, we'd all go to hell! We don't want yellow cowards in the Army. They should be killed off like flies. If not, they will go back home after the War and breed more cowards. The brave man will breed more brave men. Kill off the goddamned cowards and we'll have a nation of brave men.

I saw on top of a telegraph pole in the midst of furious fire while we were in the Africa Campaign one of the bravest men whose courage was outstanding.

I stopped and asked him what the hell he was doing up there at that time. He answered, "Fixing the wire, Sir."

"Isn't it a little unhealthy right now?" I asked.

"Yes, Sir, but this damn wire's gotta be fixed!"

There was a man who devoted his all to his duty, no matter how great the odds, no matter how seemingly insignificant his duty may have seemed at the time. You should have seen those trucks on the road to Gabes. The drivers were magnificent! All day they crawled along those roads under fire, never deviating from their course, with shells bursting all round them. We got through on good old American guts. Many of the men drove over 40 consecutive hours.

The General paused, staring over the silent sea of faces. You could have heard a pin drop anywhere on that vast hillside.

2D CAVALRY ARRIVES IN ENGLAND AND MEETS GENERAL PATTON

The only sound was of leaves stirring in the breeze and the animated chirping of birds in the branches to the General's left.

Don't forget: You don't know I'm here at all. No word of that fact is to be mentioned in any letters. The world is not supposed to know what the hell they did with me. I'm not supposed to be commanding this goddamned Army. I'm not even supposed to be in England. Let the first boneheads to find out be the goddamned Germans! Some day I want them to rise up on their hind legs and howl—Judas Priest; it's the goddamned Third Army and that son-of-a-bitch Patton again!

The men roared and cheered. This statement had real significance behind it—much more than met the eye. The men instinctively sensed it, and they understood the role they would play in world history because of it. Deep sincerity and seriousness lay behind the General's colorful words. The men knew it, and they loved the way he put it, in the way only he could.

We want to get the hell over there. We want to get over there and clean the damn thing up. And then we'll have to take a little jaunt against the purple-pussed Japanese and clean their nest out too, before the Marines get all the damn credit.

The crowd laughed, and Patton continued quietly:

Sure we all want to go home. We want this thing over with. But you can't win a War lying down. The quickest way to get it over with is to go get the boneheads. The quicker they are whipped the quicker we go home. The shortest way home is through Berlin! When a man is lying in a shell hole, if he just stays there all day the *Boche* will get him eventually, and probably get him first. The hell with taking it! Give it to him first! There is no such thing as a "Foxhole War" any more. Foxholes only slow up an offensive. Keep moving! We'll win this War, but we'll win it only by fighting and by showing our guts!

He paused and his eagle-like eyes swept over the hillside.

There's one great thing you men will be able to say when you go home. You may all thank God for it. Thank God that at least, thirty years from now when you are sitting around the fireside with your grandson on your knee and he asks you what you did in the great World War II, you won't say, I shoveled shit in Louisiana![450]

Cecil (Mick) Maguire, 106th Cavalry Group, recalled Patton's involvement in the Louisiana maneuvers:

I encountered Georgie two other times after the incident during the Louisiana Maneuvers, once in Cheshire, England, at the 106th Group barracks at Doddington Park. On this occasion he was chewing out the guard on the main gates because [the guard] was chewing tobacco while on duty and the juice was running out of the corners of his mouth down around his chin. And guards are supposed to be the best dressed of all soldiers!

---

450 *Sgt. Tom M. Griffin, H&S Troop, 42d Squadron; A General Talks to His Army:* **2d Dragoons** © *2011 Built by Isaac Golding on behalf of the Second Cavalry Assn. WordPress Themes based on a design by NodeThirtyThree*

2D CAVALRY ARRIVES IN ENGLAND AND MEETS GENERAL PATTON

The next time I saw General Patton was at a staging area near Southampton, England, where he addressed the whole Group. He told us that we were to always attack and to use all weapons to the utmost. He stressed the fact that a German with his nose in the dirt couldn't get off a shot at you and that a German retreating couldn't dig in or build fortifications. He said to keep our gun barrels hot and not worry about running out of ammo because the taxpayers were sending shiploads every day.

I'm going to rent the movie *Patton,* with George C. Scott, so I can check again on the speech he made that ended, ". . . and we're going to go through them like shit through a goose!" I think he had given that same speech all over England—I can't even guess how many times.[451]

On 31 May 1944, General Patton was scheduled to address the 106th Cavalry Group while they were in Southampton preparing for the D-Day invasion. Colonel Wilson wanted to know the minute Patton arrived. 1st Lieutenant Faris "Jake" Hess was ordered to stay at the main gate and watch for Patton. Hess had heard a lot of stories about Patton and was really excited.

What a sight! Patton pulled up in a long black car that was really shined up. The General was impeccably dressed in full uniform with knee high brown boots and a shiny helmet. He had his pearl-handled Colt .45 pistol swinging from the holster on his hip.[452]

---

[451] Cecil (Mick) Maguire; e-mail sent to Gary Palmer on 24 September 2005
[452] Captain Faris 'Jake' Hess and Nancy 'Hess' Blackburn; *My Story-106th Cavalry Group in Europe 1942-1945:* Personal Manuscript written for the Hess' family in 2004 (Page 7)

General Patton liked to give speeches. He always took the time to speak to whatever group could be assembled. These speeches were later made famous by the 1970 movie *Patton*. The language in these speeches was very colorful, and in fact the scriptwriters for the movie had to tone down some of the General's words. Hess continued:

Patton gave a couple of speeches to the 106th Cavalry Group that I will never forget. His first speech was to the entire Group—the enlisted men and officers. He told us, "You are the luckiest men ever born. You are going to be part of the greatest show ever seen. Instead of whores on the walls, people will have your pictures, because you will be the heroes."

He then dismissed the enlisted troops and asked the officers to remain behind. Once he was certain the enlisted men had left the area, Patton made the following statement:

> Throw away your manuals! Once we land in France put the enlisted men up front and drive down the road at 45 miles an hour. I know that in doing so some of your troopers are going to get killed, but hell—that is what the son-of-a-bitches are getting paid for. If you come upon a French town and are uncertain if it is occupied by the enemy, fire a few rounds into it. If the Germans are there, they will fire back. However, if it is not occupied by the Germans, then the worst you will have done is killed a few Frenchmen. Hell!! If the

son-of-a-bitches would have fought harder we wouldn't be here in the first place.[453]

Merton Glover, 4th Cavalry, recalled that

> As the spring of 1944 came, everyone knew the invasion was near. We had to waterproof our vehicles, which meant covering all electric wiring such as starters, generators, plugs with a gooey asbestos sticky substance. Even the carburetor was covered.
>
> Also, there was a flexible hose placed over the air intake running to the highest part of the vehicle—the purpose being so we could jump off the landing ships into the water and drive ashore for the invasion.
>
> Having carefully done this we drove to the bay near Southampton, drove out in six feet of water, and turned around and came out to test our work. The driver was sealed in lowest part of the car, guided by the car CO who tapped him on the left or right shoulder to signify what direction to go. It was nerve-wracking. We were, in effect, blind and underwater. But no vehicle failed or drowned out.
>
> Sometime about mid-May 1944 our troop (Troop B, 24th Cavalry Reconnaissance Squadron) was assigned a mission for the coming invasion. It was top secret, of course. It involved putting all the troops—except drivers, cooks and maintenance—along with a couple radiomen and executive officers through special training on climbing ropes, throwing grappling hooks and commando-type exercises. As an armored car driver I missed out on this.

---

453 ibid (Page 7-8)

Towards the end of May 1944 our command section moved closer to the channel or Torquay area. We drivers and cooks service-loaded our vehicles—armored cars, Jeeps, and trucks—as our command traveled very light.

We, at the camp, waited as patiently as possible for D-Day. Of course we had no idea when it would be. We learned later our men were dry-running loading in assault boats in Torquay bay.

I learned a stray German plane sneaked in through all the ack-ack (anti-aircraft fire) with a load of bombs. Our fellows were running to bomb shelters as one bomb hit a building, knocking some big stones to the sidewalk. One caught Pat Sheldon on the foot and ankle, so he was the first casualty of the 4th Cavalry before D-Day.[454]

During World War II, Torquay was regarded as safer than the towns of southeastern England, and played host to evacuees from the London area. Torquay suffered minor bomb damage during the war, mainly from planes dumping excess loads after participating in the Plymouth Blitz.

The last air raid on Torquay took place on 29 May 1944, shortly before the D-Day landings in June. In the months leading up to D-Day, thousands of U.S. Army personnel arrived in Torquay, with the 3204th Quartermaster Service Company being billeted in Chelston and Cockington. During Operation OVERLORD more than 23,000 men of the American 4th Infantry Division would depart Torquay for Utah Beach.)

---

[454] Merton Glover; *86 and counting:* Unpublished personal manuscript of author's life history-2003 (Page 49)

2D Cavalry Arrives in England and Meets General Patton

Englishman Charles Prynne was a boy during World War II and saw the American preparations for Operation OVERLORD.

> When I was eight years old, we had many American soldiers here in St. Ives, in the County of Cornwall, England, training for the D-Day invasion. I believe they were from the 99th Division of the U.S. Army. During the months they were with us, they were the kindest, most generous young people that one could meet. To us children, they gave parties, candy and cookies.
> One night, in 1944, they disappeared, and our town became a much sadder place.
> Recently, upon going through some newspapers of the time, I came across this anonymous poem in the 5 January 1945 issue of *The St. Ives Times*. It sums up the local people's feelings about the men who sacrificed for our freedom.
>
> *For Our Freedom*
>
> > They came one day, from far away,
> > Those American friends of ours,
> > And they changed our lives
> > from a wintry grey
> > To a garden bright with flowers.
> > To a merry lilting score,
> > With never a thought of a fight to be fought
> > Or a nation going to war
> > They came that day for a short sweet stay
> > From the land of the fair and free,
> > And they stole our English hearts away
> > and took them across the sea.

The U.S. Cavalry: Time of Transition

They laughed at life,
with no thought of strife,
How they loved to shout and cheer!
They liked to dance
and they whispered romance
Into many a maiden's ear
Our hearts were light
and our days were bright
Though we wondered how long they'd stay.
And then one night,
In the moon's soft light,
They silently slipped away.
When, the next day dawned,
their going was mourned,
And dead was that garden of flowers.
For we miss them still and we always will,
Those American friends of ours.

Figure 12-2. Departing G.I.s headed for Normandy, June 1944. *Associated Press*

GLOSSARY

AEF
World War I - American Expeditionary Forces

Ammo
Ammunition

Army
An Army consists of 50,000+ soldiers. Typically commanded by a lieutenant general or higher, an army combines two or more corps.

A *theater army* is the ranking Army component in a unified command, and it has operational and support responsibilities that are assigned by the theater commander-in-chief. The *commander-in-chief* and *theater army commander* may order formation of a field army to direct operations of assigned corps and divisions.

An *army group* plans and directs campaigns in a theater, and is composed of two or more field armies under a designated commander. Army groups have not been employed by the Army since World War II.

AT
Anti-tank

BAR
Browning Automatic Rifle. In 1917, prior to America's entry to the war, John Browning personally brought to Washington, D.C., two types of automatic weapons for the purposes of demonstration: a water-cooled machine gun (later adopted as the M1917 Browning machine gun) and a shoulder-fired automatic rifle known then as the Browning Machine Rifle or BMR. Both weapons were chambered for the standard U.S. .30-06 Springfield cartridge.

In order to avoid confusion with the belt-fed M1917 machine gun, the BAR came to be known as the M1918 or "Rifle, Caliber .30, Automatic, Browning, M1918," according to official nomenclature. The first major attempt at improving the M1918 resulted in the M1922 light machine gun, adopted in 1922 by the United States Cavalry. The hand guard was changed; and in 1926, the BAR's sights were redesigned to accommodate the heavy-bullet 172-grain M1 .30-06 ball ammunition then coming into service for machine gun use.

Bn
Battalion

Battalion
A battalion consists of 300 to 1,000 soldiers. Four to six companies make up a battalion, which is normally commanded by a lieutenant colonel with a command sergeant major as principal NCO assistant. A battalion is capable of independent operations of limited duration and scope. An armored or air cavalry unit of equivalent size is called a squadron.

Glossary

Brigade
A brigade consists of 3,000 to 5,000 solders. A brigade headquarters commands the tactical operation of two to five organic or attached combat battalions. Normally commanded by a colonel with a command sergeant major as senior NCO, brigades are employed on independent or semi-independent operations. Armored cavalry, ranger and Special Forces units this size are categorized as regiments or groups.

BG
Brigadier General (0-7)

Capt
Captain (0-3)

Cavalry Group
Cavalry groups were usually assigned to corps, but were occasionally attached—by squadron—to divisions. The cavalry group consisted of a group headquarters and headquarters troop but no other assigned units. Two cavalry reconnaissance squadrons were attached to each group. Depending on the mission and situation, the corps or army commander could tailor the group organization by adding additional squadrons, other combat units, and additional combat support and service units as required. Within a month of the June 6, 1944, landings, two cavalry groups arrived to support the operations of the First U.S. Army, the 4th and the 106th Cavalry Groups. With the activation of the Third Army in August 1944, the 3d, 2d and the 6th Cavalry Groups were committed to combat. By May 1945 a total of 13 cavalry groups were in combat in Europe.

Cavalry (Horse-Mechanized) Regiment

During the New York Maneuvers of 1939, a completely new type of mechanized cavalry regiment was first tested when the mechanized squadrons of two horse-mechanized regiments were combined to form one totally mechanized regiment consisting only of armored cars. This unit was very successful, but significantly, its role was limited to reconnaissance.

Subsequently, in April 1941, Field Manual FM 2-15, *Employment of Cavalry*, was issued. This manual represented the cavalry's changed self-image. The most important characteristic of that image was the central position of the horse. FM 2-15 reflected the view of Major General Herr, chief of cavalry, as a predominately horse organization supported by a limited number of mechanized elements. The manual addresses mechanized units throughout, but the theme is consistently horse cavalry supported by mechanized cavalry, usually in a reconnaissance role.

In 1941 the Army also issued the last mechanized cavalry doctrine it would publish prior to the start of World War II: FM 2-10, *Mechanized Cavalry*, dated April 1941. This manual recognized the changes that had occurred since 1938, the lessons learned in the Army maneuvers, and established the standard cavalry doctrine employed at the start of World War II. Horse cavalry retained its traditional missions, however. Unrecognized by either FM 2-15 or FM 2-10 was that, as of 1940, horse cavalry was not a significant player in the minds of the General Staff.

Cavalry (Horse Mounted) Regiment

In 1921 regiments were reconstructed to consist of a headquarters, a headquarters troop, a service troop (redesignated from the former supply troop), and only six lettered troops. The troops, designated as A through F, were grouped into two squadrons of three troops each. The regimental machine gun troop was eliminated, since its pack animals were believed to reduce the regiment's mobility.

Machine gun troops and other surplus elements of the regiment were either moved to newly organized units or disbanded.

Among those newly organized units were machine gun squadrons, separate machine gun troops, training center squadrons, and the headquarters troops of two cavalry divisions and four cavalry brigades.

Cavalry (Mech) Regiment
The organizational structure planned for the new mechanized cavalry regiment in 1932 was similar to the horse regiment. With an authorized strength of 42 officers and 610 enlisted men, the mechanized regiment was divided into a covering squadron, a combat car squadron, a machine gun troop, and a headquarters troop. Like the horse regiment, it had four lettered troops but was equipped with combat vehicles instead of horses. Its covering squadron was divided into an armored car troop and a scout troop, while the combat car squadron had two combat car troops. The mechanized regiment had 35 combat cars (light, fast tanks), which were about equally divided among the troops of the combat car squadron and the scout troop of the covering squadron.

Cavalry (Mech) Squadron
The mechanized cavalry squadrons were organized with three cavalry troops, lettered A to C, each equipped with 13 M8 armored cars (Greyhounds) and jeeps (Bantams); an Assault Gun Troop, E, with six 75 mm Howitzer Motor Carriages (HMC) M8, a self-propelled howitzer vehicle sometimes known as the M8 Scott; a light tank company, F, with 17 M5 (later M24) Stuart tanks; a service company; and a Headquarters & Headquarters Service company. The armored division's reconnaissance squadron was identical except that it had a fourth cavalry troop, D; and the assault gun troop had eight M8 HMC Scott self-propelled howitzer vehicles. Infantry divisions each had a single cavalry reconnaissance troop.

Cavalry (Mech) Troop

Each troop (A through C) was usually equipped with a mix of the three vehicles. The first was the Bantam jeep with a bracket-mounted .30 caliber machine gun, manned by a soldier sitting in the front passenger seat. A second Bantam jeep was mounted with a 60 mm mortar manned by two soldiers. Sometimes the Bantam was mounted with a .50 caliber machine gun. To maximize speed and maneuverability on the battlefield, the Bantams were not given extra armor protection.

The cavalry (mech) troop also deployed in the six-wheeled, lightweight M8 Greyhound armored car, mounted with a 37 mm gun in a movable turret that could swing a full 360 degrees. The vehicle also featured a .30 caliber coaxial machine gun that could move independently of the turret. The M8 was equipped with powerful FM radios to enable battlefield communications.

The troop also utilized two half-tracks to carry their headquarters unit and an ammunition section.

Cavalry E Troop (Mech)

Troop provided with 15 short-barreled 75-mm self-propelled (3.0-inch) howitzers mounted on an M8 chassis with an open turret.

Cavalry F Troop (Mech)

Troop provided with 17 each light tanks consisting of 37mm M5A1 Stuart light tanks. The M5 Stuart light tank was capable of speeds up to 36 mph (58 km/h) on the road. While fast and maneuverable, the Stuart's armor plating and its cannon were soon found to be no match against the German tanks.

CavReconSqd

Cavalry Reconnaissance Squadron

Glossary

Chain of Command
The usual structure is battalion - brigade - division, with battalions organized into regiments as the exception. An example of this exception would be cavalry regiments. Cavalry is unique in that battalions are called "squadrons" and companies are called "troops."

CMTC
Citizen Military Training Corps

C-ration
One-man ration for three meals. Each meal included two 12 oz cans, one with a meat-vegetable combination (different for each of the three meals), the other with biscuits, hard candy, cigarettes, and instant coffee or lemon powder or cocoa.

CO
Commanding Officer

Col
Colonel (0-6)

Company
A company is typically the smallest Army element to be given a designation and affiliation with higher headquarters at battalion and brigade level. This alphanumeric and branch designation causes an "element" to become a "unit." A company consists of 62 to 190 soldiers. Three to five platoons form a company, which is commanded by a captain with a first sergeant as the commander's principal NCO assistant.
An artillery unit of equivalent size is called a battery, and a comparable armored or air cavalry unit is called a troop.

Corps
A corps consists of 20,000 to 45,000 soldiers. Two to five divisions constitute a corps, which is typically commanded by a lieutenant general. As the deployable level of command required to synchronize and sustain combat operations, the corps provides the framework for multinational operations.

Cpl
Corporal (E-4)

Division
A division consists of 10,000 to 15,000 soldiers. Usually consisting of three brigade-sized elements and commanded by a major general, divisions are numbered and assigned missions based on their structures. The division performs major tactical operations for the corps and can conduct sustained battles and engagements.

D-Problem
Divisional Problem, where the major components of the division (battalions and regiments) operate together for training.

D-rations
Emergency concentrated energy chocolate bar

ETO
European Theater of Operations

FUBAR
Fouled Up Beyond All Recognition

Gen
General (0-10)

GHQ
General Headquarters

G.I.
U.S. soldier (stems from "Government Issue")

Hq, hq
Headquarters

ITP
Individual Training Period, where a soldier learned to use his weapon

K-rations
A pocket-sized, waterproof cardboard box containing either a breakfast, dinner, or supper ration for one person. Breakfast consisted of a small tin of meat and egg product, instant coffee, and a fruit bar. Dinner was a small tin of cheese product, lemon powder, and candy. Supper rations contained a small tin of meat product, bouillon powder, and a small D-ration chocolate bar.
Also included in each ration were biscuits, sugar tablets, chewing gum, toilet paper, and cigarettes (usually three). One type of cigarettes furnished was the worthless Chelsea brand, which even the French refused to smoke.

LCT
Landing craft-tank

LD
Line of Departure

Louisiana Maneuvers
A series of military exercises held all over north and west-central Louisiana, including Fort Polk, Camp Claiborne and Camp Livingston, in August and September 1941. The exercise was designed to test U.S. troop training, logistics, doctrine, and commanders.

1st LT
First Lieutenant (0-2)

2d LT
Second Lieutenant (0-1)

LTC (LtCol)
Lieutenant Colonel (0-5)

LTG
Lieutenant General (0-9)

Maj
Major (0-4)

MG
Major General (0-8)

MP
Military Police

M8 HMC
The 75 mm Howitzer Motor Carriage (HMC) M8, sometimes known as the M8 Scott, was a self-propelled vehicle that carried 46 rounds of 75 mm ammunition. Types of ammunition carried were Smoke M89 and HE (High Explosive) M48.

The M8 did not feature coaxial or hull-mounted Browning

GLOSSARY

M1919A4 .30-06 machine guns as featured on standard M5 Stuart light tanks. The only other armament was a Browning M2HB .50-caliber machine gun for local area and anti-aircraft defense. Four hundred rounds of .50-caliber ammunition were stowed onboard for the M2HB machine gun.

MTP
Mobilization Training Program

Plt
Platoon

Platoon
A platoon consists of 16 to 44 soldiers. A platoon is led by a lieutenant with an NCO as second in command, and consists of two to four squads or sections.

Pfc
Private First Class (E-3)

PMP
Protective Mobilization Plan

Pvt
Private (E-2)

Lt
Lieutenant

Recon
Reconnaissance

Reg
Regiment

Regiment

Most battalions that are actually part of brigades still have a regimental affiliation, such as 1/34 IN Rgt, the 1st Battalion of the 34th. This affiliation is pretty much just historical and symbolic these days. It has no real significance as far as the chain of command goes. For example, the infantry battalions of the 3d Brigade of the 2d Infantry Division are 1st Bn 23rd Infantry, 2d Bn 3d Infantry, and 5th Bn 20th Infantry. Each battalion is affiliated with a different regiment but is part of the same brigade.

ROTC

Reserve Officer Training Corps

S-1

Personnel Section of a regiment or battalion. The officer in charge is referred to as "S-1."

S-2

Intelligence section of a regiment or battalion. The officer in charge referred to as "S-2."

S-3

Plans and operations section of a regiment or battalion. The officer in charge referred to as "S-3."

S-4

Supply section of a regiment or battalion. The officer in charge referred to as "S-4."

Sgt

Sergeant (E-5)

SSG

Staff Sergeant (E-6)

Glossary

SNAFU
Situation Normal—All Fouled Up

Squad
A small group of soldiers organized to maneuver and fire is called a squad. A squad consists of 9 to 10 soldiers. Typically commanded by a sergeant or staff sergeant, a squad or section is the smallest element in the Army structure, and its size is dependent on its function.

Square Divisions
This goes back to the old days when the structure was battalion -> regiment -> brigade -> division. Up through the first part of the 20th century a division was made up of two brigades, each of which had two regiments. This was called a "square" division. During World War II the U.S. Army transitioned to "triangular" divisions of three brigades each. (Most other armies had gone triangular during WWI). They did this by cutting out the regiment level; but since the regiment traditionally was thought of as a soldier's "home," battalions kept their regimental designations even though the regiments, as functional units, were no more.

TD
Tank Destroyer—self-propelled

TE&O
Training and Evaluation Outline

10-in-1
Ten in one food packs. A ten-man ration in one pack.

Time of Day
Military Time: 2400 = midnight; 0100 = 1 am; 1200 = noon; 1300 = 1 pm; etc.

489

Triangular Division

This goes back to the old days when the structure was battalion -> regiment -> brigade -> division. Up through the first part of the 20th century a division was made up of two brigades, each of which had two regiments. This was called a "square" division. During World War II the U.S. Army transitioned to "triangular" divisions of three brigades each. (Most other armies had gone triangular during WWI). They did this by cutting out the regiment level; but since the regiment traditionally was thought of as a soldier's "home," battalions kept their regimental designations even though the regiments, as functional units, were no more.

UTP

Unit Training Period. stressing company-level training.

XO

Executive Officer

ABOUT THE AUTHOR

Gary Palmer at the National Archives.

Gary Palmer was an aviator in the U.S. Navy for ten years. He flew the E-2A Hawkeye, a tactical early warning aircraft, during the Vietnam War. Following his military service, Palmer joined the San Diego Sheriff's Department while simultaneously serving as a tank commander in the Army National Guard. Palmer retired from the San Diego Sheriff's Department in 2007 after 33 years of service.

Palmer became interested in his father's World War II service with the 106th Cavalry Group. Palmer became a member of the 106th Cavalry Association and spent ten years researching the development of the U.S. Cavalry. This book is the first in a series.

www.ingramcontent.com/pod-product-compliance
Lightning Source LLC
Chambersburg PA
CBHW071308150426
43191CB00007B/551